尾田栄一郎

You can't see your own face in profile
with one mirror. Is that really true?
What if I whip around really quickly like
this...wip!! And wip!! If I look toward
the mirror like that...! Wouldn't I be able
to see an afterimage or something!?
Wip!! Wip!! Krak!! ...!!

-Eiichiro Oda, 1998

Eiichiro Oda began his manga career at the age of
17, when his one-shot cowboy manga **Wanted!**
won second place in the coveted Tezuka manga
awards. Oda went on to work as an assistant to
some of the biggest manga artists in the industry,
including Nobuhiro Watsuki, before winning the
Hop Step Award for new artists. His pirate adven-
ture **One Piece**, which debuted in **Weekly
Shonen Jump** in 1997, quickly became one of the
most popular manga in Japan.

ONE PIECE VOL. 7
EAST BLUE PART 7

SHONEN JUMP Manga Edition

This graphic novel contains material that was originally published in English in **SHONEN JUMP** #26–29.

STORY AND ART BY EIICHIRO ODA

English Adaptation/Lance Caselman
Translation/Naoko Amemiya
Touch-up Art & Lettering/Mark McMurray
Additional Touch-up/Josh Simpson and Walden Wong
Design/Sean Lee
Editor/Megan Bates

Published by VIZ Media, LLC
P.O. Box 77010
San Francisco, CA 94107

10 9 8
First printing, June 2005
Eighth printing, June 2011

www.viz.com

THE WORLD'S
MOST POPULAR MANGA
www.shonenjump.com

SHONEN JUMP MANGA

Vol. 7
THE CRAP-GEEZER

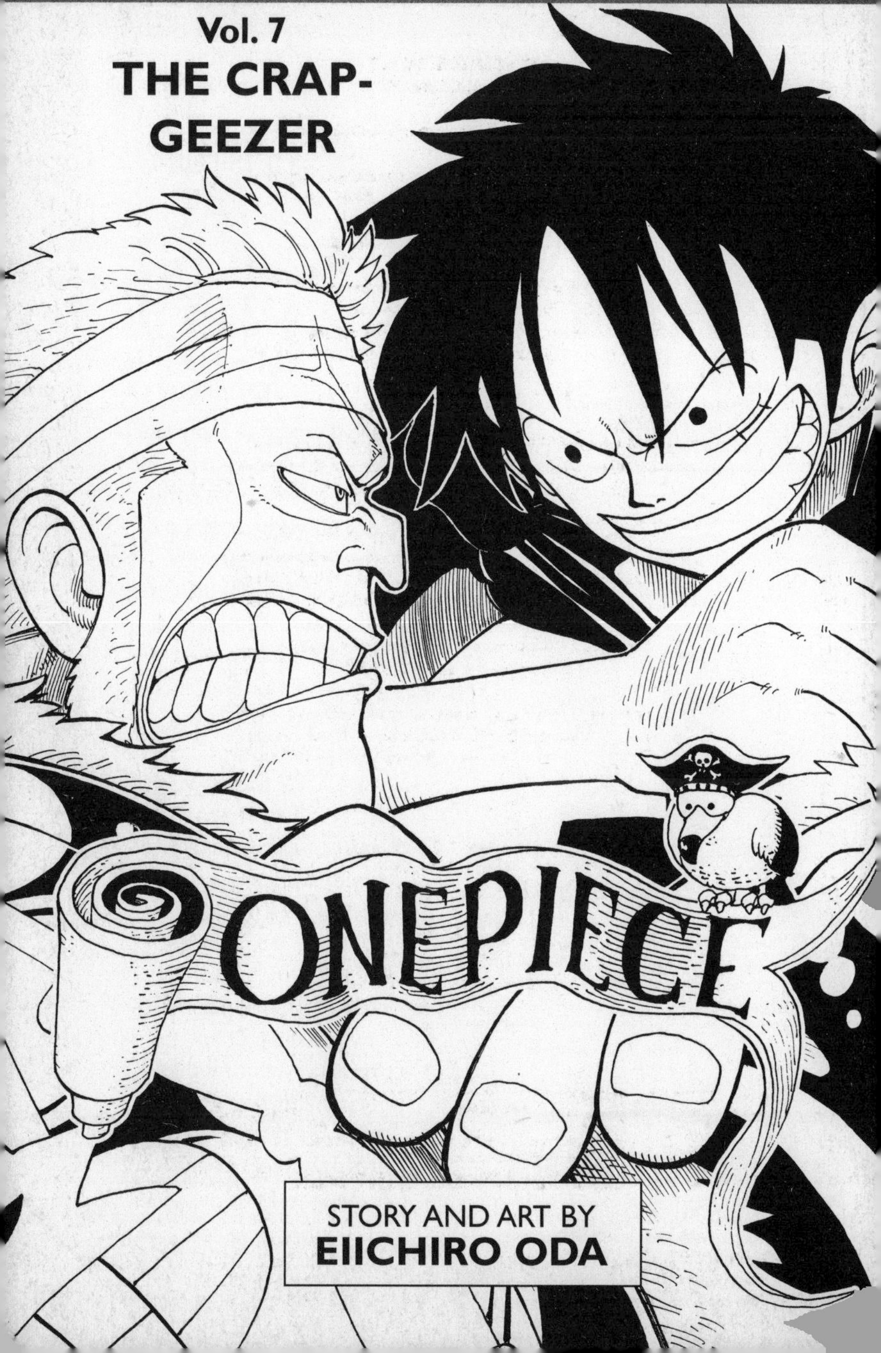
ONE PIECE

STORY AND ART BY
EIICHIRO ODA

Monkey D. Luffy
Boundlessly optimistic and able to stretch like rubber, he is determined to become King of the Pirates.

Sanji
The merciful sous-chef and maitre d' on the oceangoing restaurant Baratie. He's a ladies' man with a keen sense of taste.

"Red-Haired" Shanks
A pirate captain who saved the young Luffy's life and inspired him to be a pirate.

THE STORY OF ONE PIECE

Volume 7

Monkey D. Luffy started out as just a kid with a dream—and that dream was to become the greatest pirate in history! Stirred by the tales of pirate "Red-Haired" Shanks, Luffy vowed to become a pirate himself. That was before the enchanted Devil Fruit gave Luffy the power to stretch like rubber, at the cost of being unable to swim—a serious handicap for an aspiring sea dog. Undeterred, Luffy set out to sea and recruited some crewmates: master swordsman Zolo, treasure-hunting thief Nami and lying sharp-shooter Usopp.

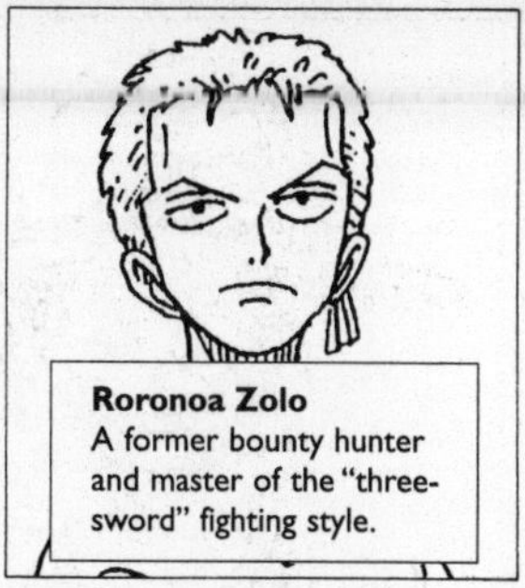

Roronoa Zolo
A former bounty hunter and master of the "three-sword" fighting style.

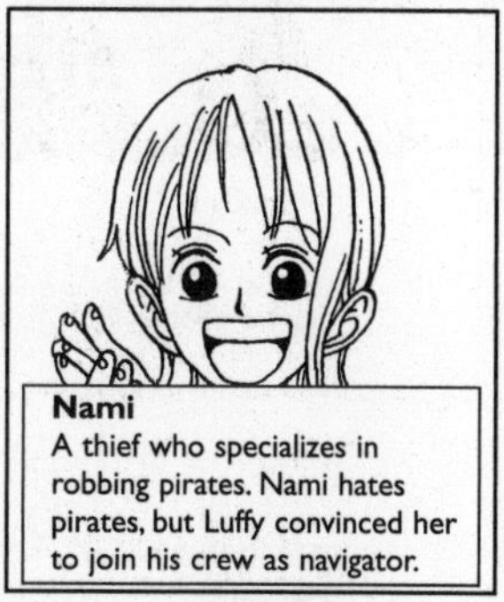

Nami
A thief who specializes in robbing pirates. Nami hates pirates, but Luffy convinced her to join his crew as navigator.

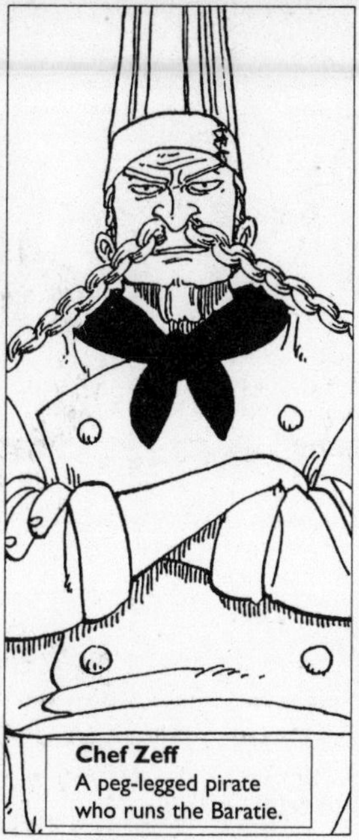

Chef Zeff
A peg-legged pirate who runs the Baratie.

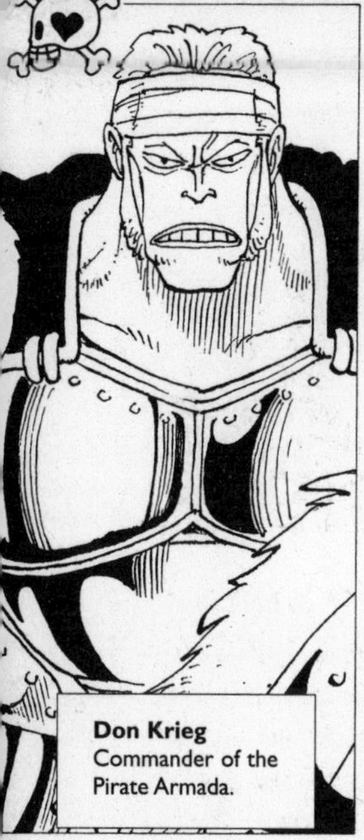

Don Krieg
Commander of the Pirate Armada.

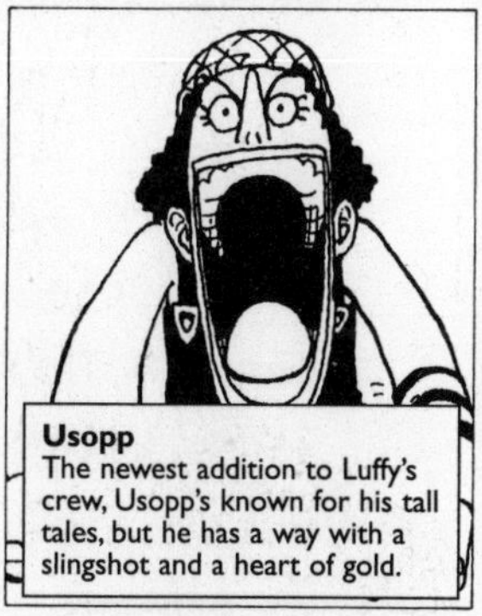

Usopp
The newest addition to Luffy's crew, Usopp's known for his tall tales, but he has a way with a slingshot and a heart of gold.

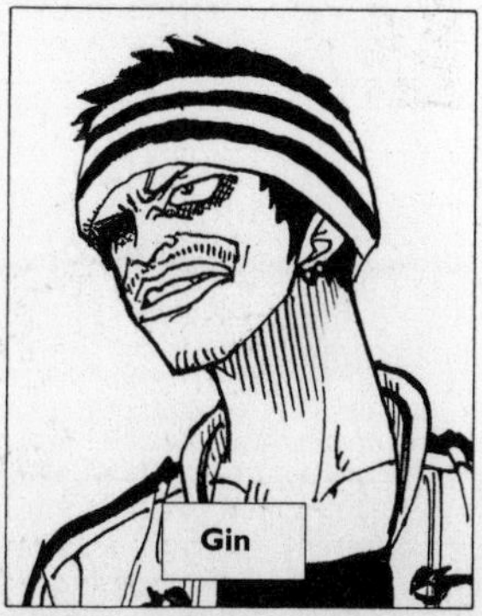

Gin

Luffy and his crew sail to Baratie, the oceangoing restaurant, to find themselves a ship's cook. There Luffy takes a liking to the arrogant-but-merciful Sanji and asks him to join the crew. Unfortunately, before he can be recruited, Don Krieg and his 5,000 pirates arrive on the scene. After Sanji takes pity on the starving Krieg and gives him food, Krieg is completely revitalized. But the pirate repays good with evil by trying to take over the ship! So the battle for the Baratie begins. Then suddenly the sea rumbles and "Hawk-Eye" Mihawk, reputed to be the world's greatest swordsman, appears. Zolo, who aspires to win that title for himself, challenges Mihawk. Zolo is defeated, but vows never to lose again. Mihawk departs and the deadly battle with Krieg's pirates resumes…

Vol. 7
THE CRAP-GEEZER

CONTENTS

Chapter 54:
PEARL

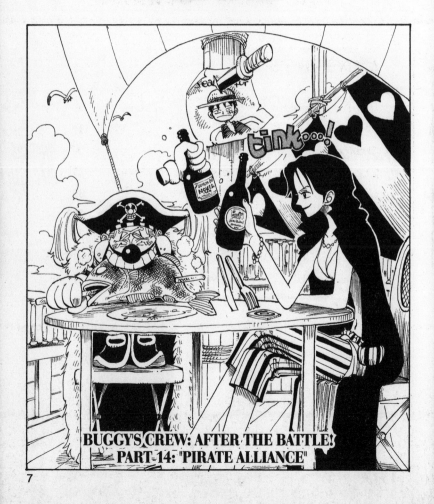

BUGGY'S CREW: AFTER THE BATTLE!
PART-14: "PIRATE ALLIANCE"

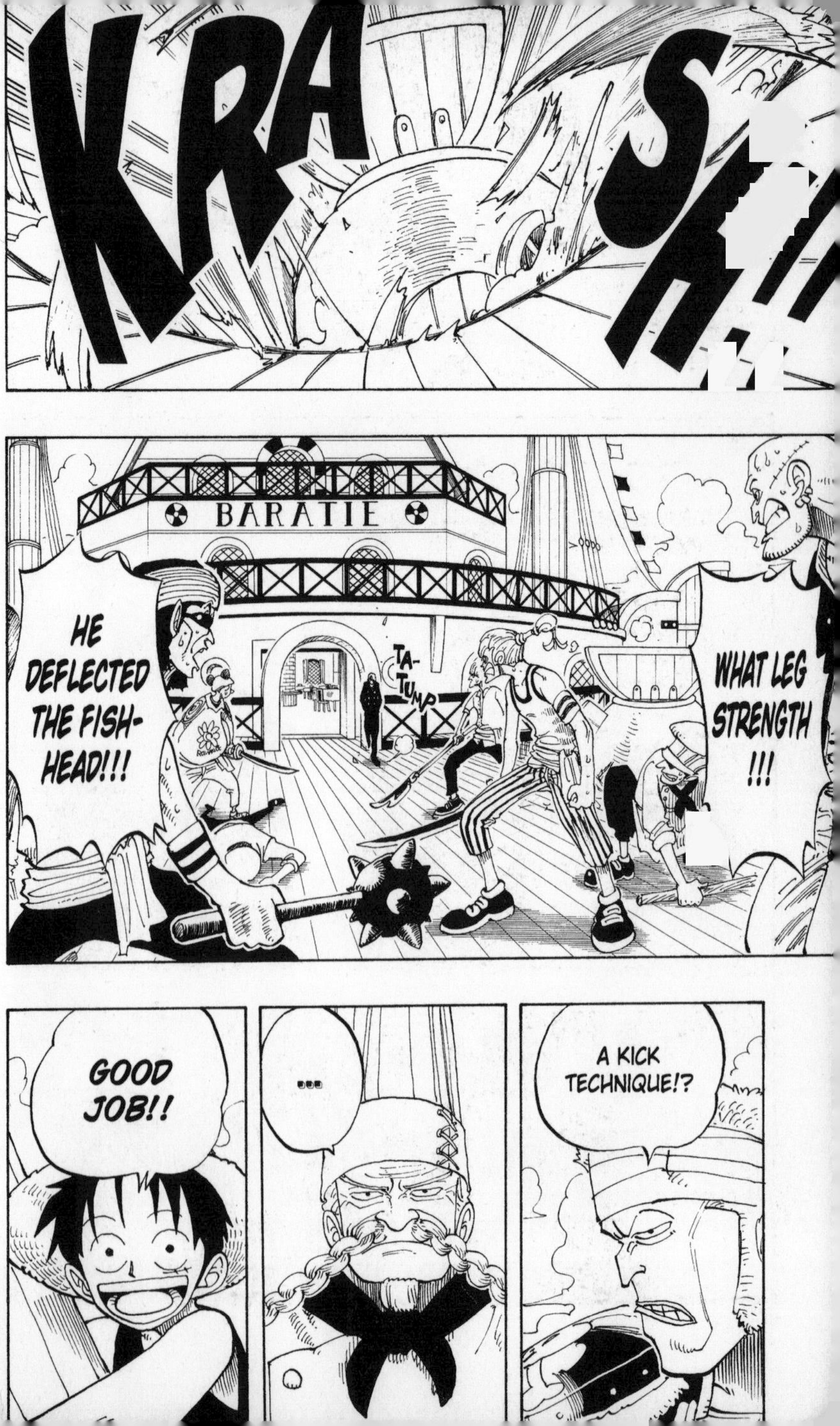
KRASH!!
WHAT LEG STRENGTH!!!
TA-TUMP
HE DEFLECTED THE FISH-HEAD!!!
A KICK TECHNIQUE!?
...
GOOD JOB!!

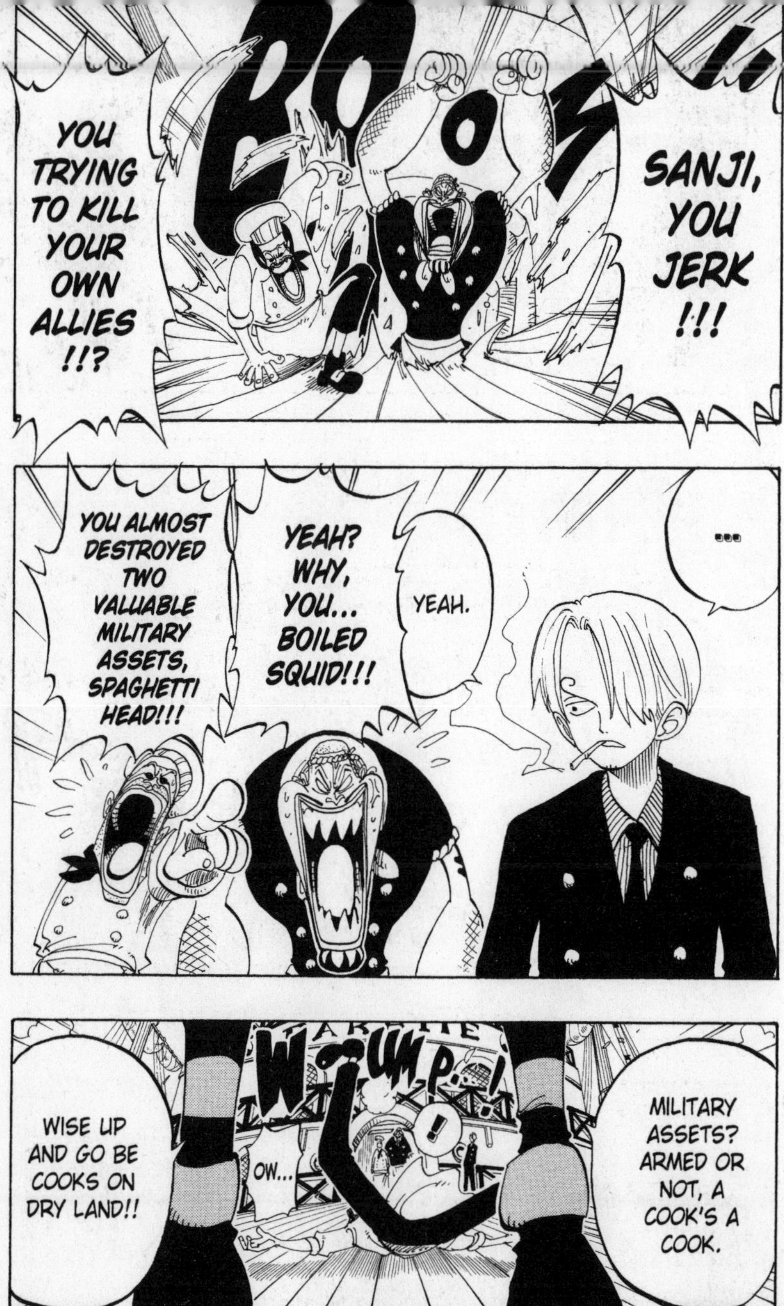
SANJI, YOU JERK!!!
BOOM!!
YOU TRYING TO KILL YOUR OWN ALLIES!!?
...
YEAH.
YEAH? WHY, YOU... BOILED SQUID!!!
YOU ALMOST DESTROYED TWO VALUABLE MILITARY ASSETS, SPAGHETTI HEAD!!!
MILITARY ASSETS? ARMED OR NOT, A COOK'S A COOK.
WHUMP..!
!
OW...
WISE UP AND GO BE COOKS ON DRY LAND!!

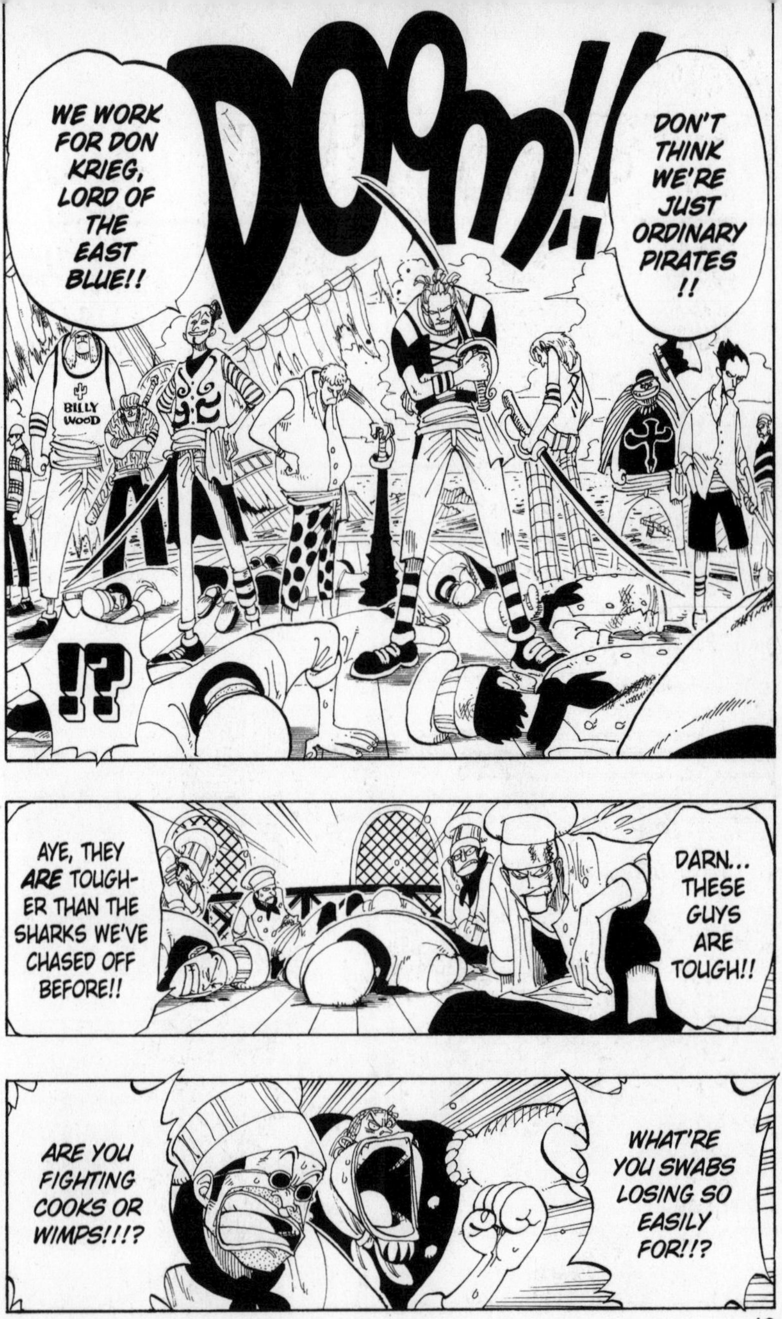
DON'T THINK WE'RE JUST ORDINARY PIRATES !!
DOOM!!
WE WORK FOR DON KRIEG, LORD OF THE EAST BLUE!!
!?
BILLY WOOD
DARN... THESE GUYS ARE TOUGH!!
AYE, THEY ARE TOUGHER THAN THE SHARKS WE'VE CHASED OFF BEFORE!!
WHAT'RE YOU SWABS LOSING SO EASILY FOR!!?
ARE YOU FIGHTING COOKS OR WIMPS!!!?

READ THIS WAY

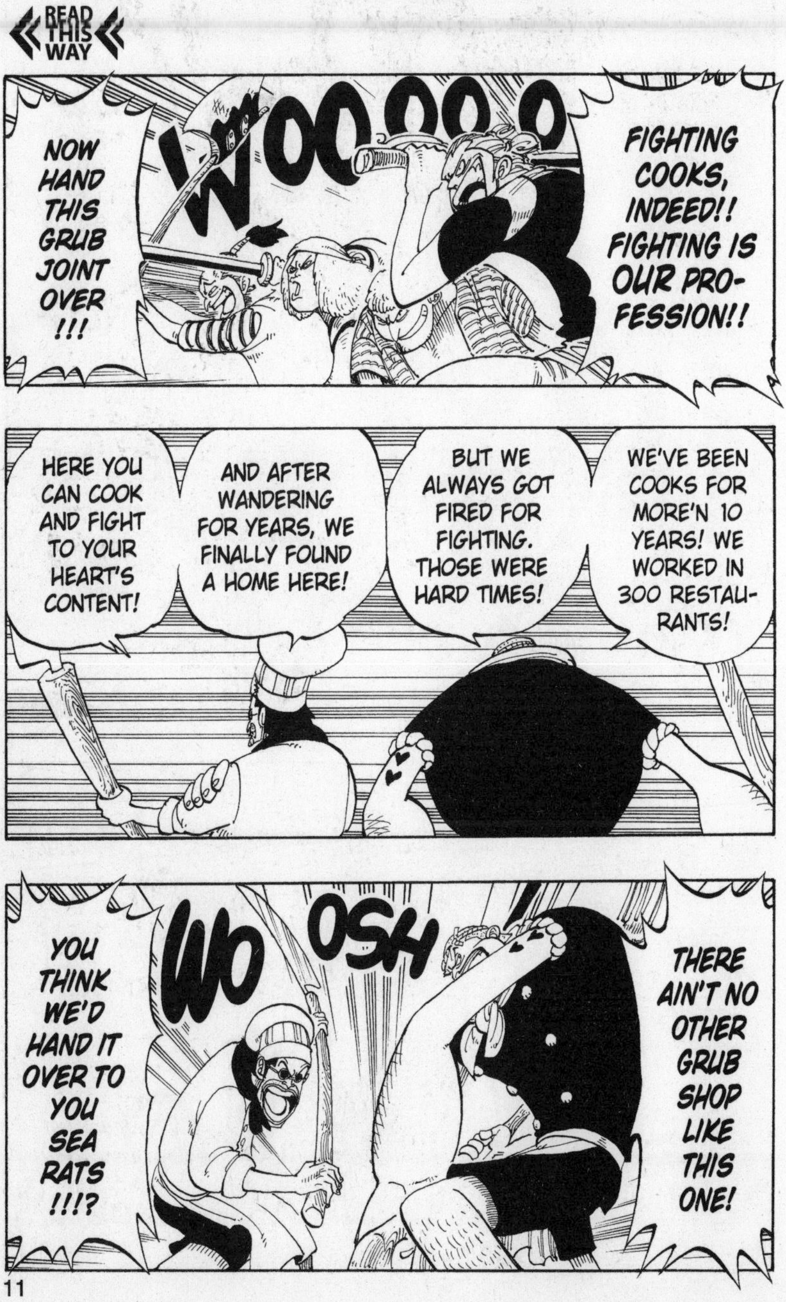
FIGHTING COOKS, INDEED!! FIGHTING IS OUR PRO-FESSION!!
WOOOOOO
NOW HAND THIS GRUB JOINT OVER!!!
WE'VE BEEN COOKS FOR MORE'N 10 YEARS! WE WORKED IN 300 RESTAU-RANTS!
BUT WE ALWAYS GOT FIRED FOR FIGHTING. THOSE WERE HARD TIMES!
AND AFTER WANDERING FOR YEARS, WE FINALLY FOUND A HOME HERE!
HERE YOU CAN COOK AND FIGHT TO YOUR HEART'S CONTENT!
THERE AIN'T NO OTHER GRUB SHOP LIKE THIS ONE!
WOOSH
YOU THINK WE'D HAND IT OVER TO YOU SEA RATS!!!?

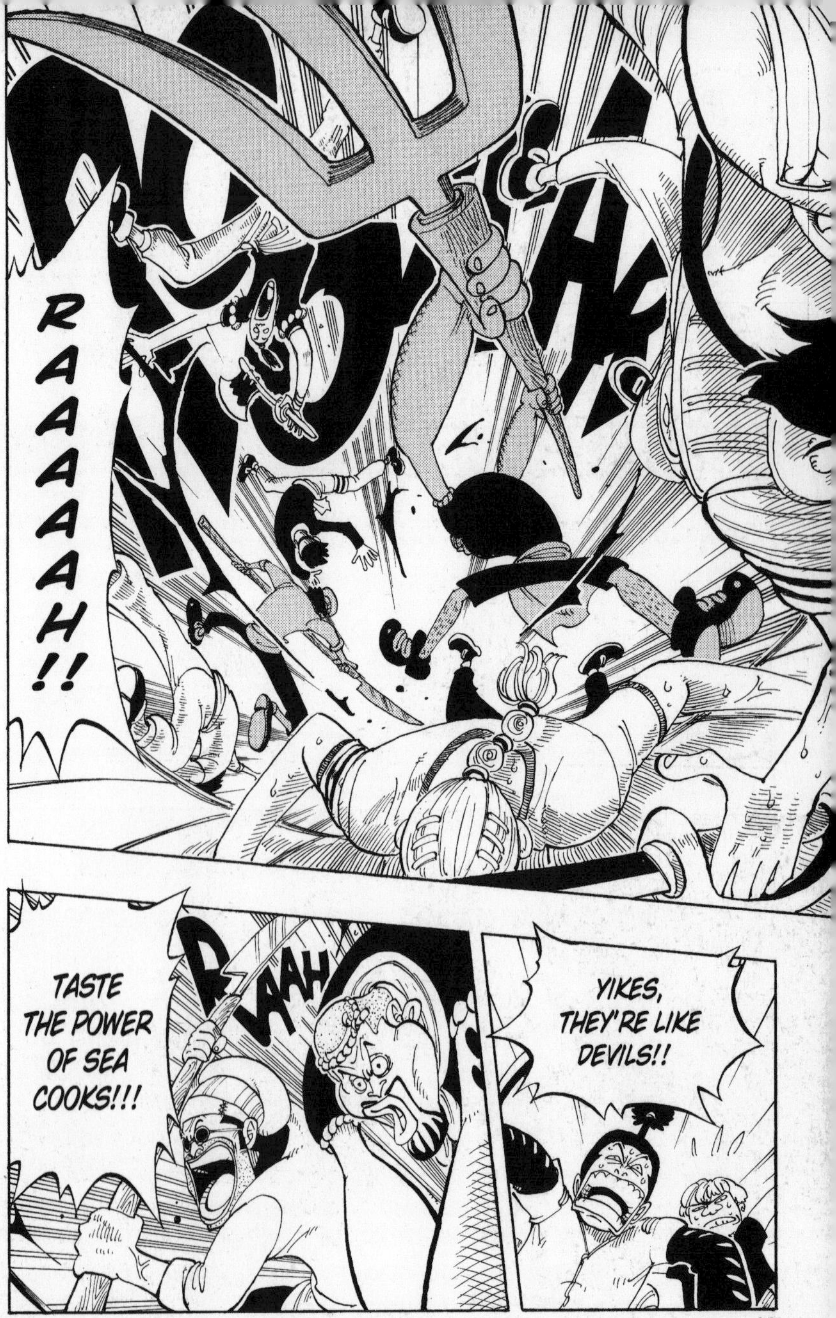
RAAAAAAAH!!
RAAAH
YIKES, THEY'RE LIKE DEVILS!!
TASTE THE POWER OF SEA COOKS!!!

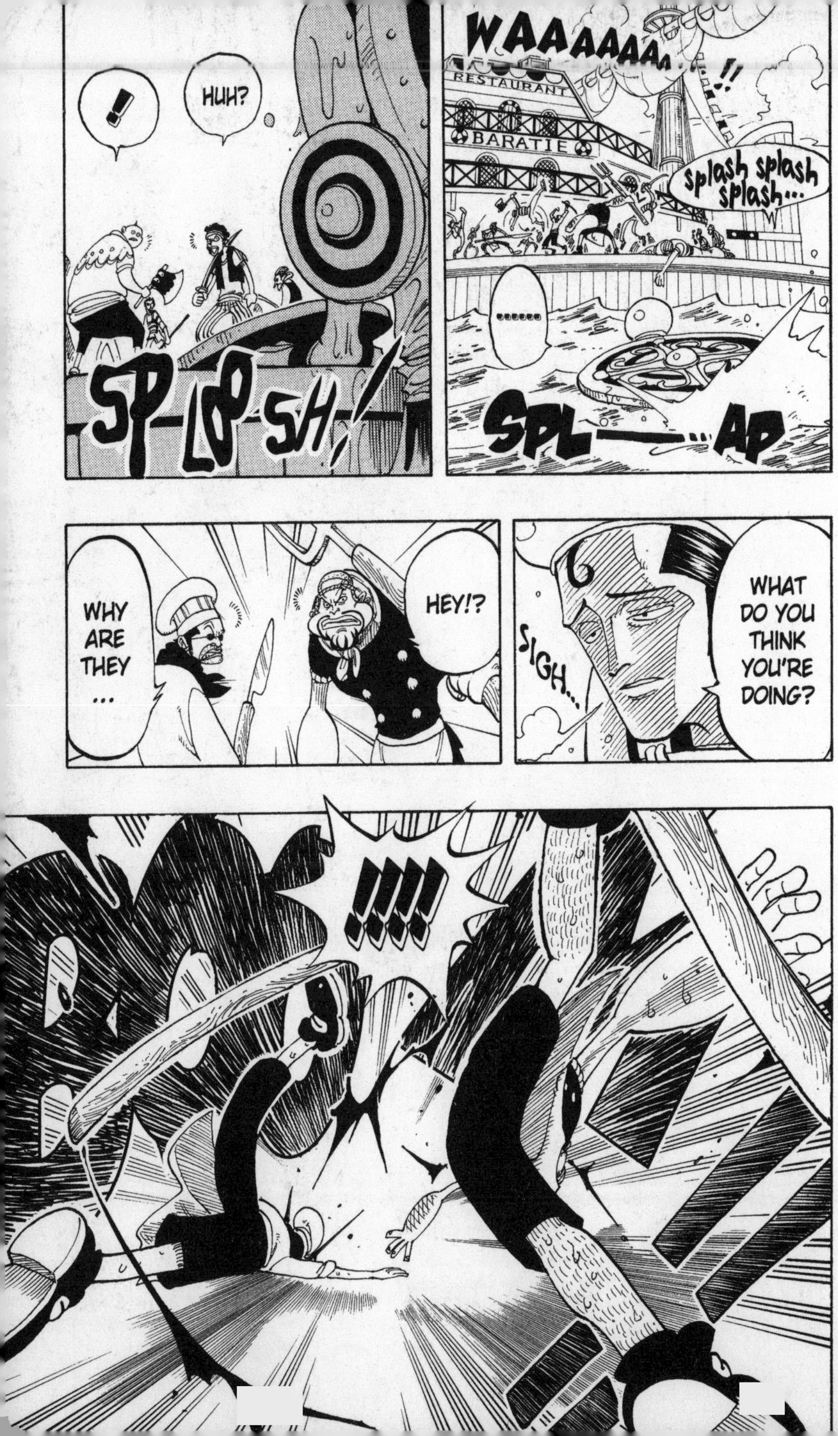
WAAAAAA...!!
RESTAURANT
BARATIE
splash splash splash...
......
SPL——...AP
!
HUH?
SPLOSH!
WHAT DO YOU THINK YOU'RE DOING?
SIGH...
HEY!?
WHY ARE THEY ...
!!!!

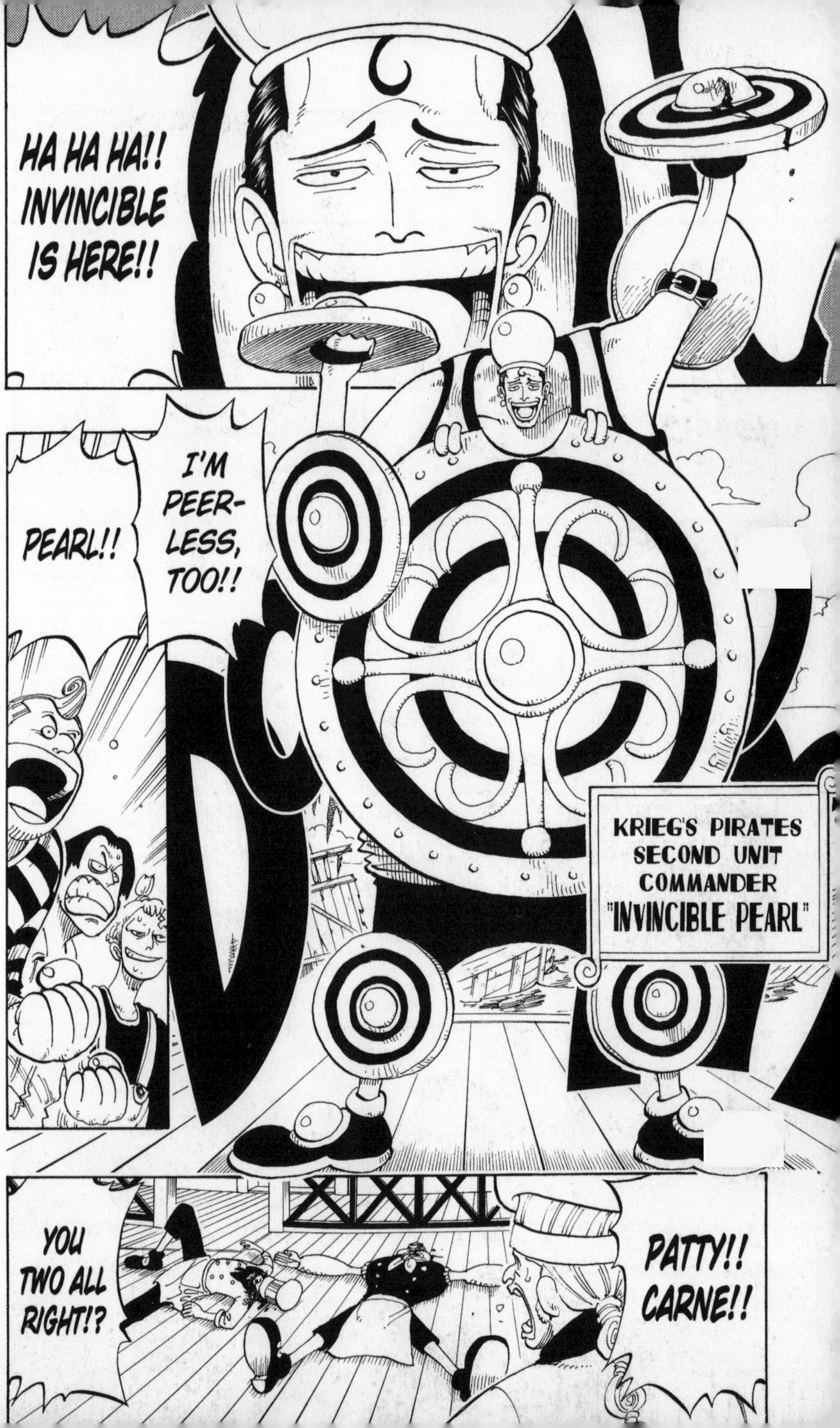
HA HA HA!! INVINCIBLE IS HERE!!
I'M PEER-LESS, TOO!!
PEARL!!
KRIEG'S PIRATES SECOND UNIT COMMANDER "INVINCIBLE PEARL"
PATTY!! CARNE!!
YOU TWO ALL RIGHT!?

READ THIS WAY

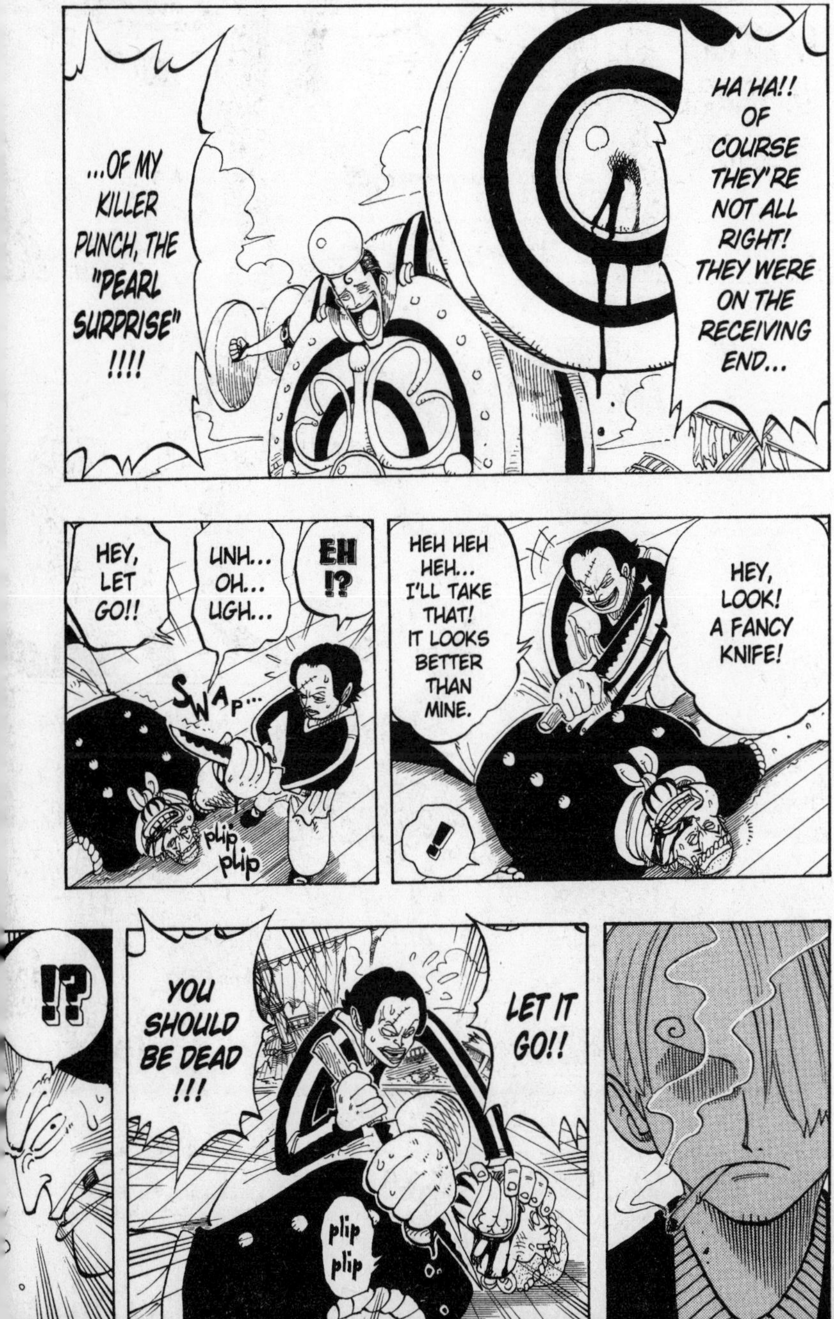
HA HA!! OF COURSE THEY'RE NOT ALL RIGHT! THEY WERE ON THE RECEIVING END...
...OF MY KILLER PUNCH, THE "PEARL SURPRISE" !!!!
HEY, LOOK! A FANCY KNIFE!
HEH HEH HEH... I'LL TAKE THAT! IT LOOKS BETTER THAN MINE.
!
EH !?
UNH... OH... UGH...
HEY, LET GO!!
SWAP...
plip plip
LET IT GO!!
YOU SHOULD BE DEAD !!!
plip plip
!?

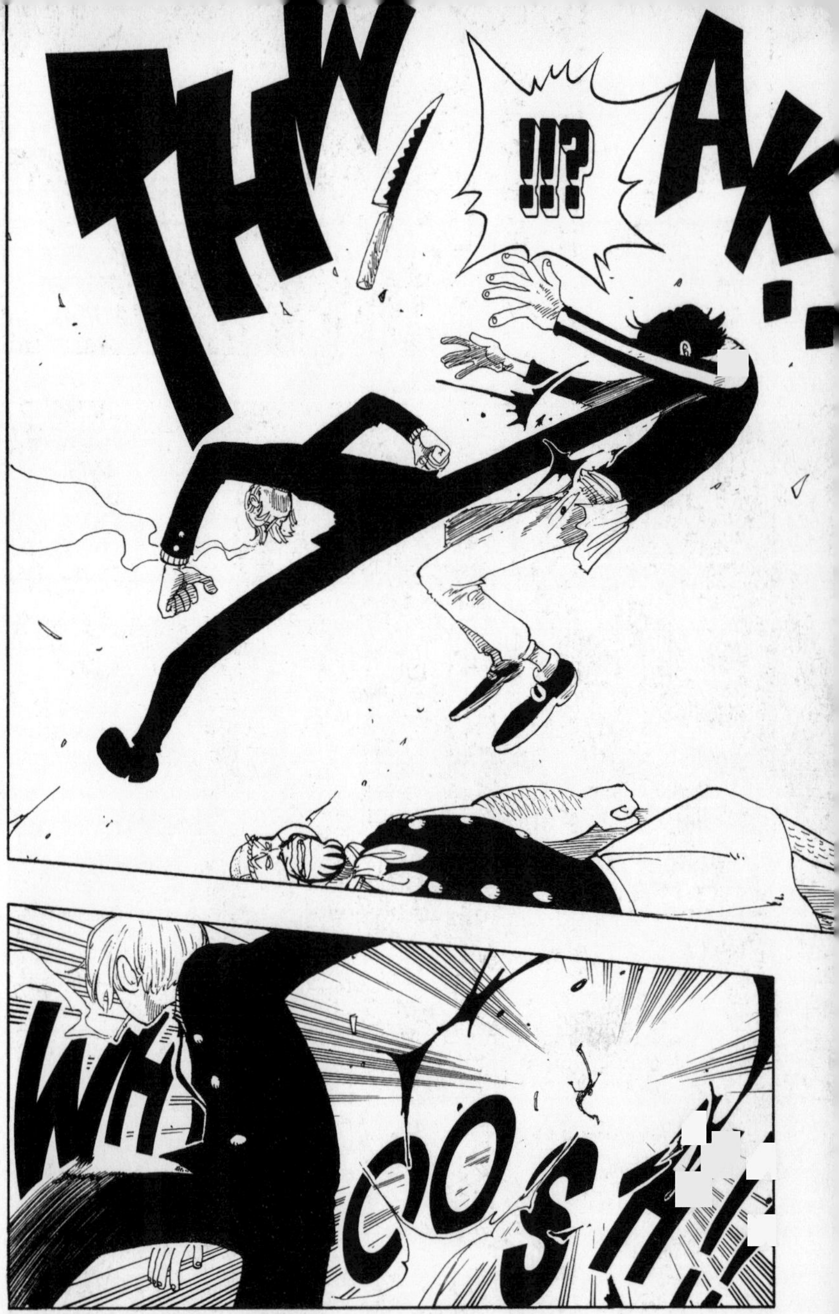
THWAK
!!?
WHOOSH!!

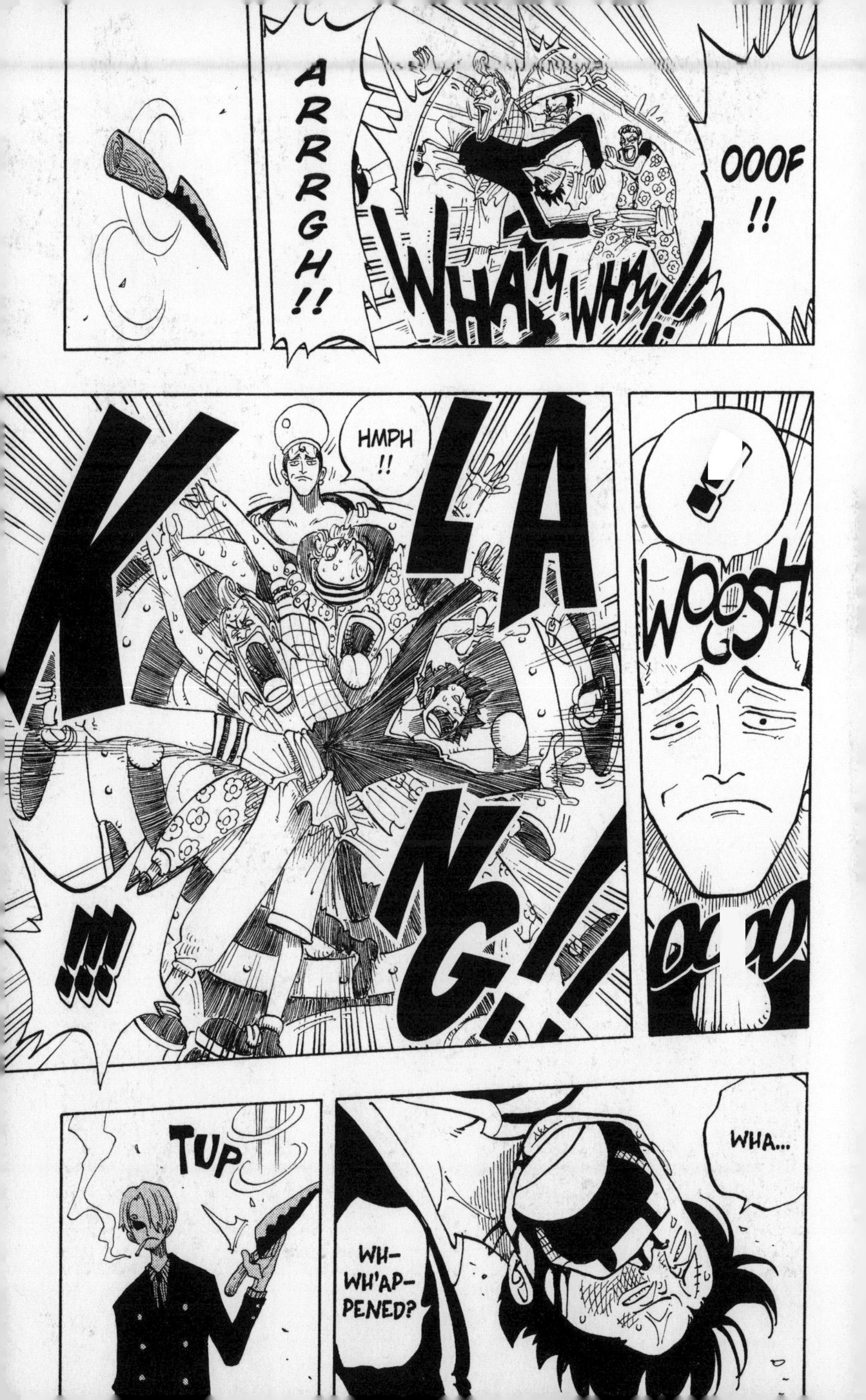
OOOF !!
ARRRGH!!
WHAM WHAM!!
!
WOOSH
HMPH !!
KLANG!!
!!!
WHA...
WH-WH'AP-PENED?
TUP

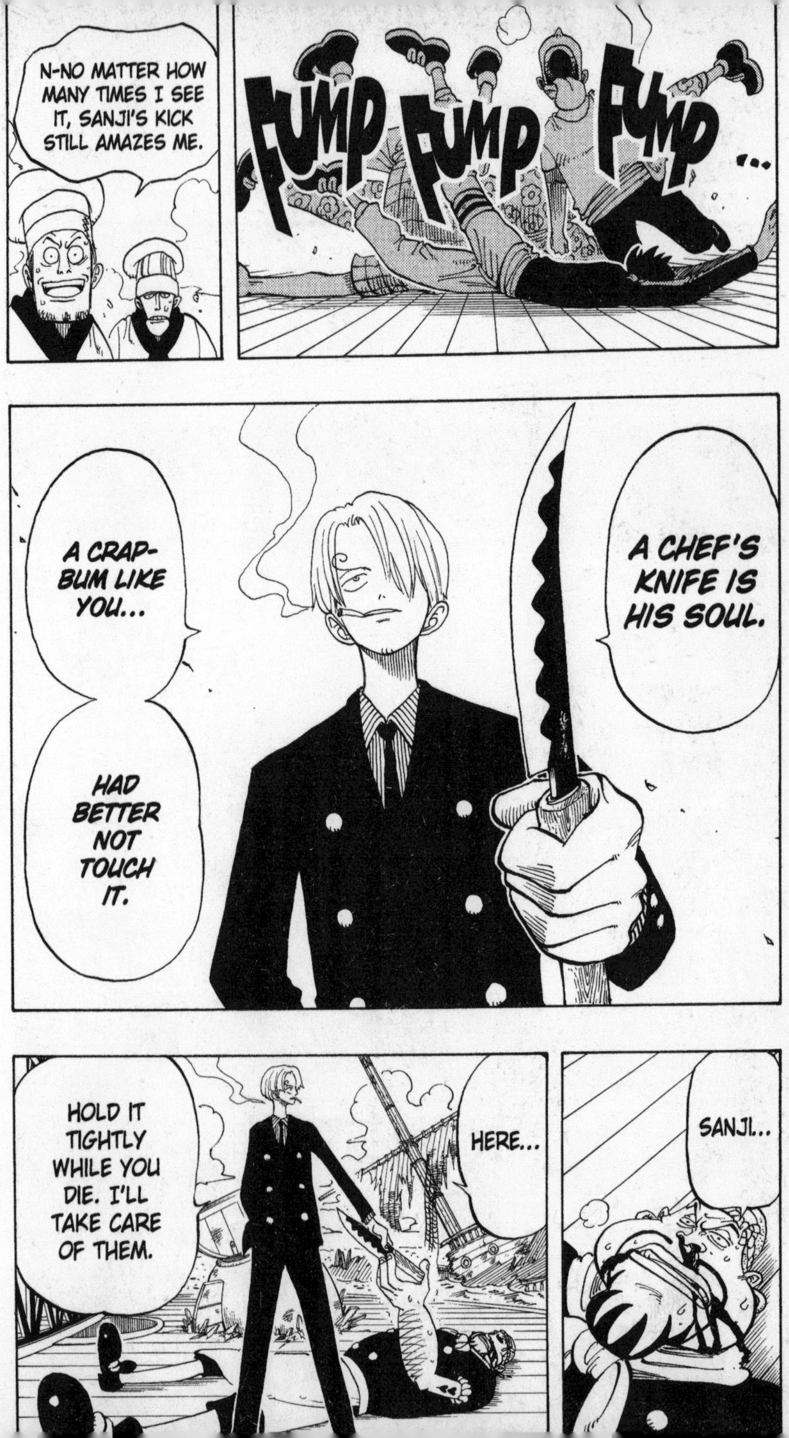
FUMP FUMP FUMP...
N-NO MATTER HOW MANY TIMES I SEE IT, SANJI'S KICK STILL AMAZES ME.
A CHEF'S KNIFE IS HIS SOUL.
A CRAP-BUM LIKE YOU...
HAD BETTER NOT TOUCH IT.
SANJI...
HERE...
HOLD IT TIGHTLY WHILE YOU DIE. I'LL TAKE CARE OF THEM.

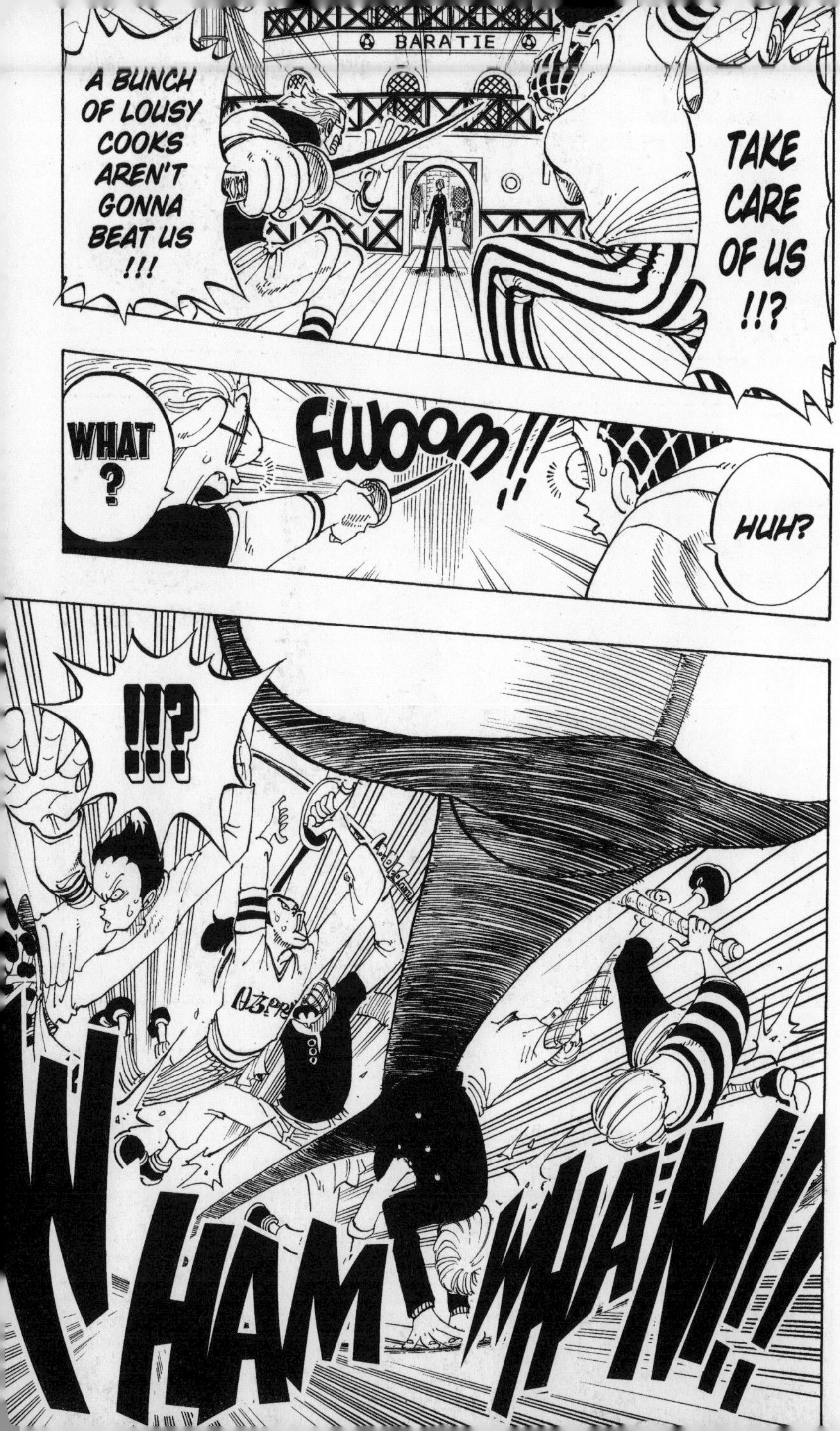
TAKE CARE OF US !!?
A BUNCH OF LOUSY COOKS AREN'T GONNA BEAT US !!!
BARATIE
HUH?
FWOOM !!
WHAT ?
!!?
WHAM WHAM!!

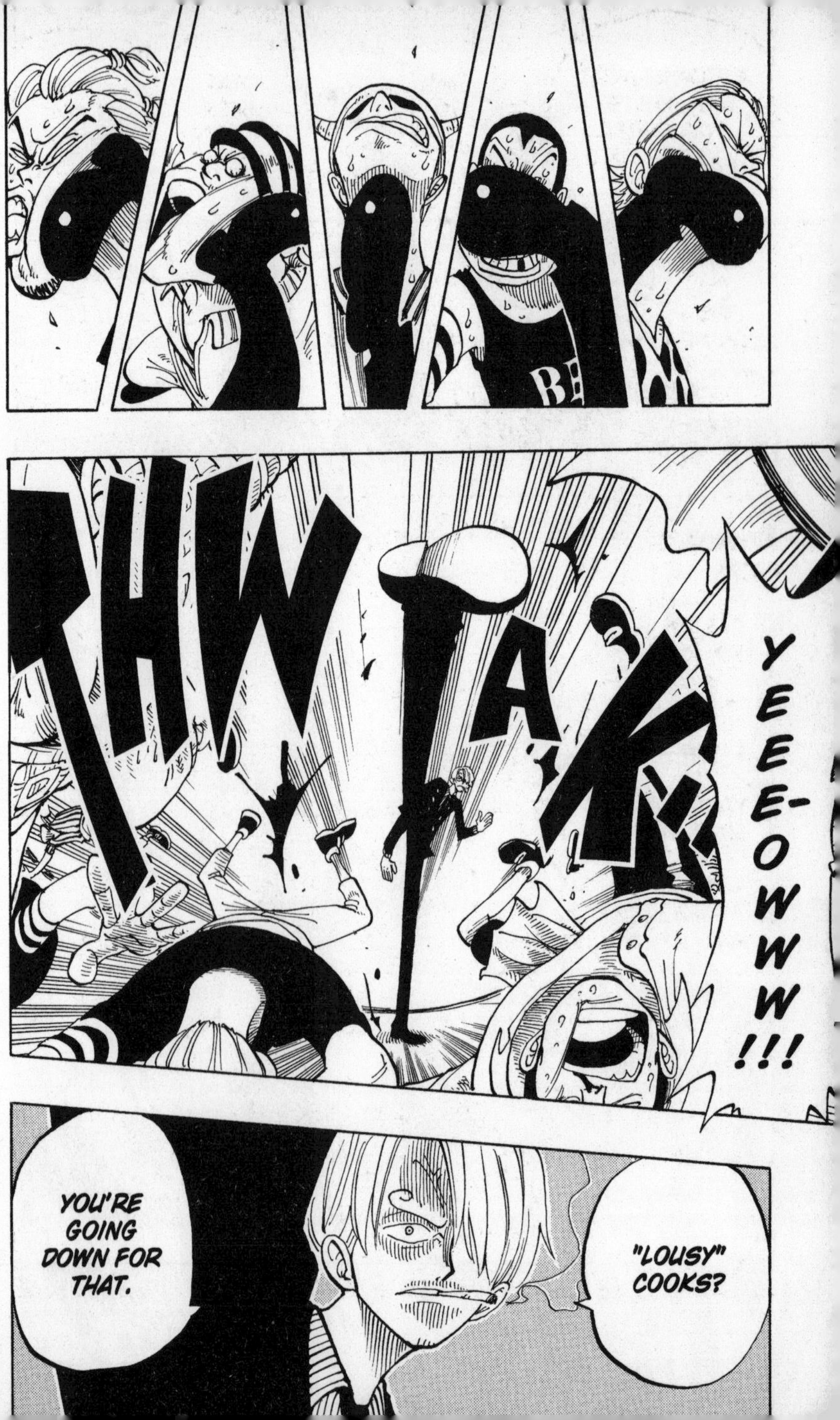
THWAK
YEEEE-OWWWW!!!
"LOUSY" COOKS?
YOU'RE GOING DOWN FOR THAT.

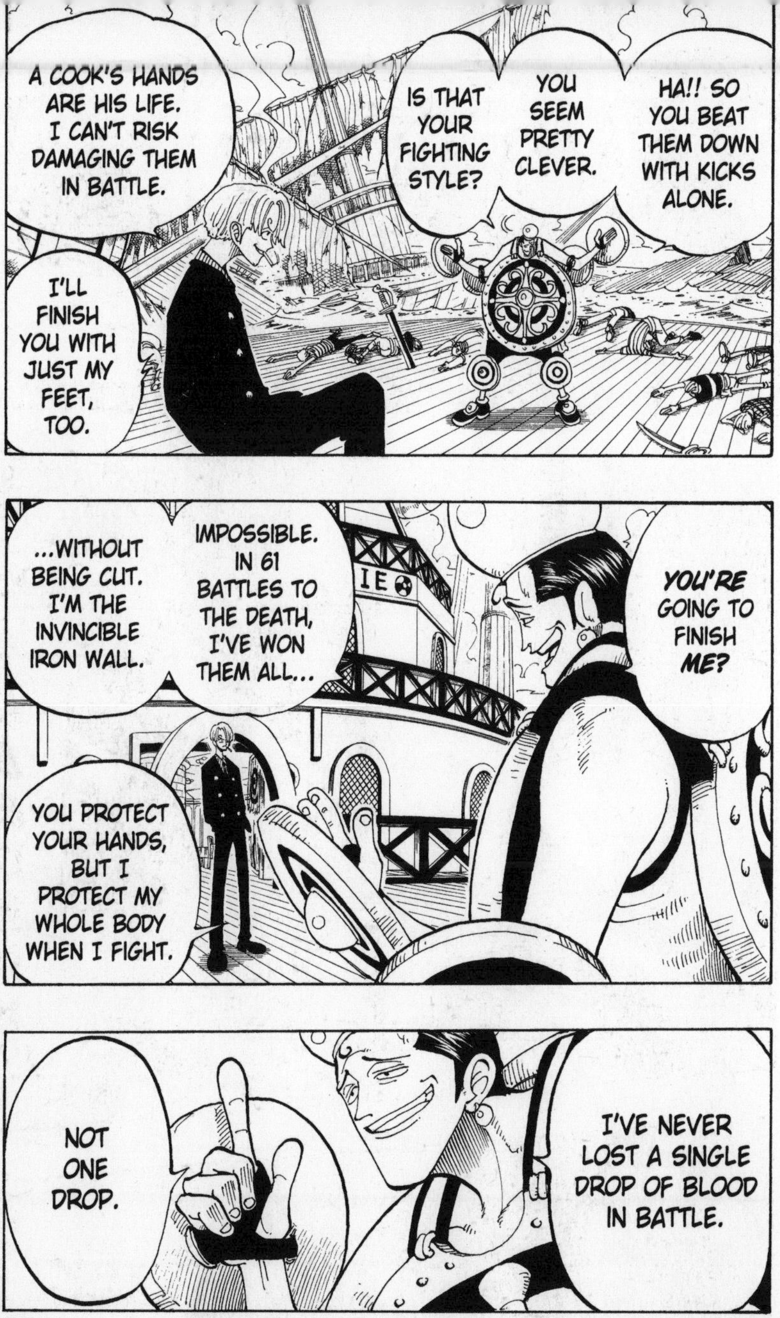
HA!! SO YOU BEAT THEM DOWN WITH KICKS ALONE.
YOU SEEM PRETTY CLEVER.
IS THAT YOUR FIGHTING STYLE?
A COOK'S HANDS ARE HIS LIFE. I CAN'T RISK DAMAGING THEM IN BATTLE.
I'LL FINISH YOU WITH JUST MY FEET, TOO.
YOU'RE GOING TO FINISH *ME?*
IMPOSSIBLE. IN 61 BATTLES TO THE DEATH, I'VE WON THEM ALL...
...WITHOUT BEING CUT. I'M THE INVINCIBLE IRON WALL.
YOU PROTECT YOUR HANDS, BUT I PROTECT MY WHOLE BODY WHEN I FIGHT.
I'VE NEVER LOST A SINGLE DROP OF BLOOD IN BATTLE.
NOT ONE DROP.

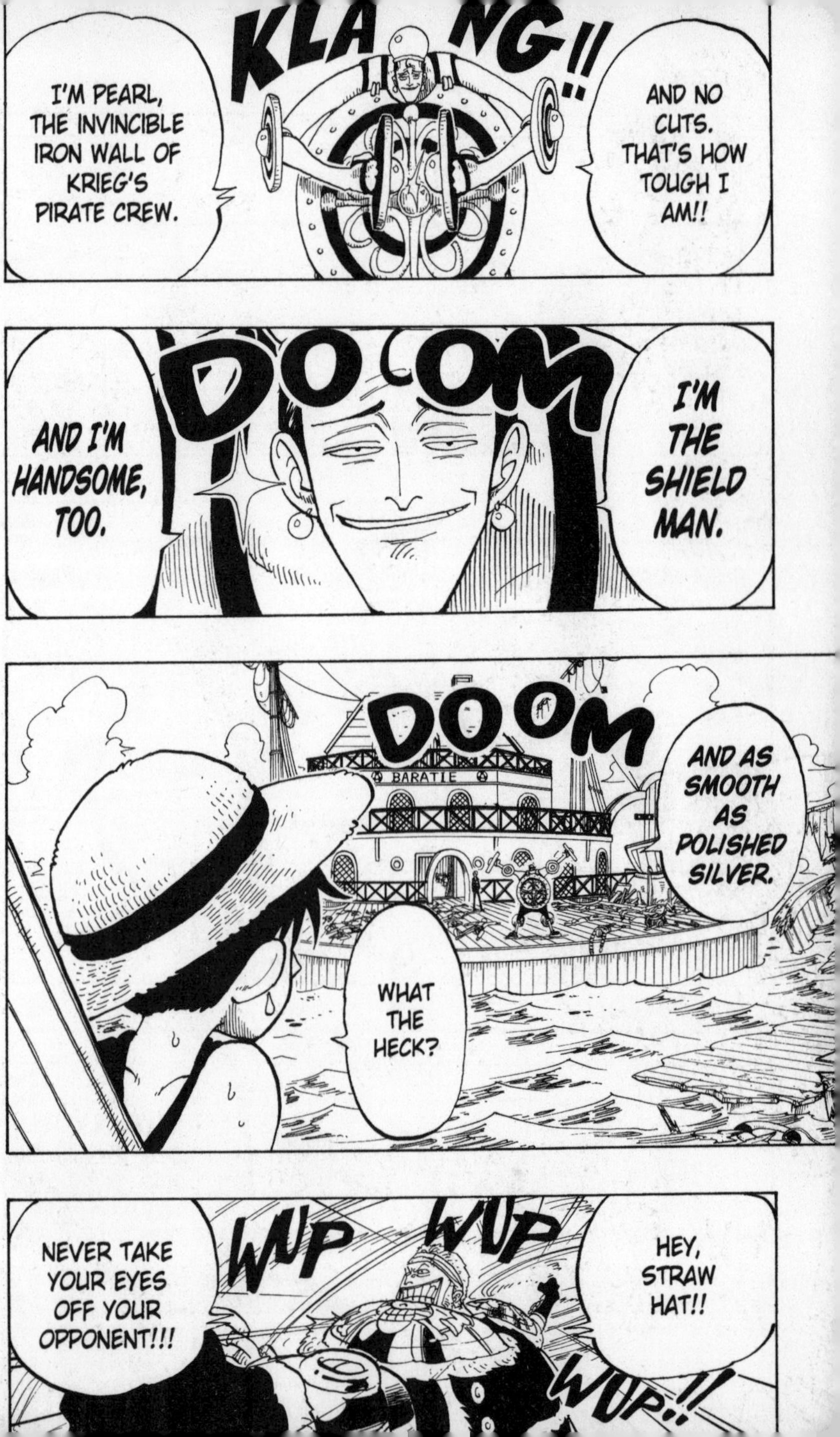
KLANG!!
AND NO CUTS. THAT'S HOW TOUGH I AM!!
I'M PEARL, THE INVINCIBLE IRON WALL OF KRIEG'S PIRATE CREW.
DOOM
I'M THE SHIELD MAN.
AND I'M HANDSOME, TOO.
DOOM
AND AS SMOOTH AS POLISHED SILVER.
BARATIE
WHAT THE HECK?
HEY, STRAW HAT!!
WUP WUP
NEVER TAKE YOUR EYES OFF YOUR OPPONENT!!!
WUP!!

READ THIS WAY

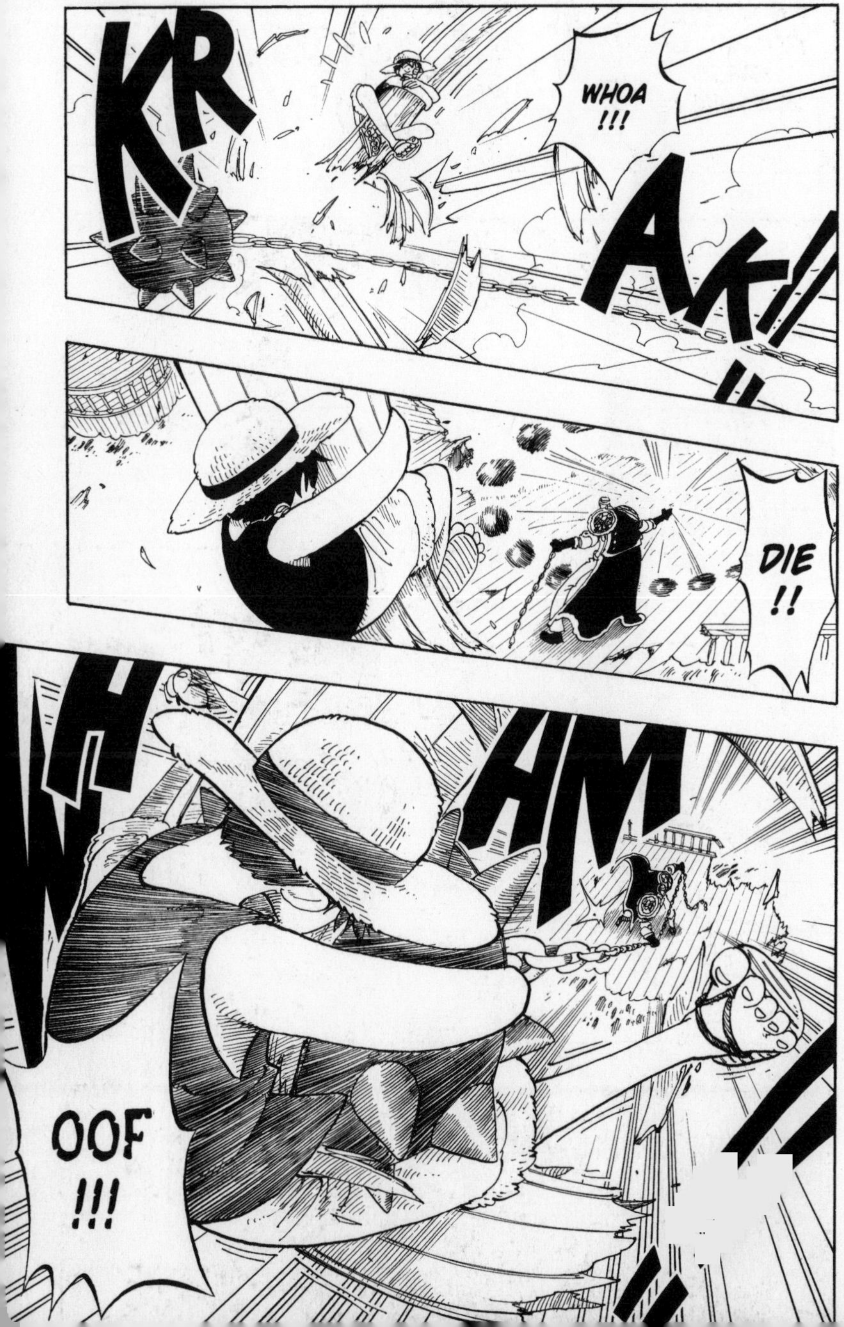
WHOA !!!
KR
AK!!
DIE !!
WH
AM
OOF !!!

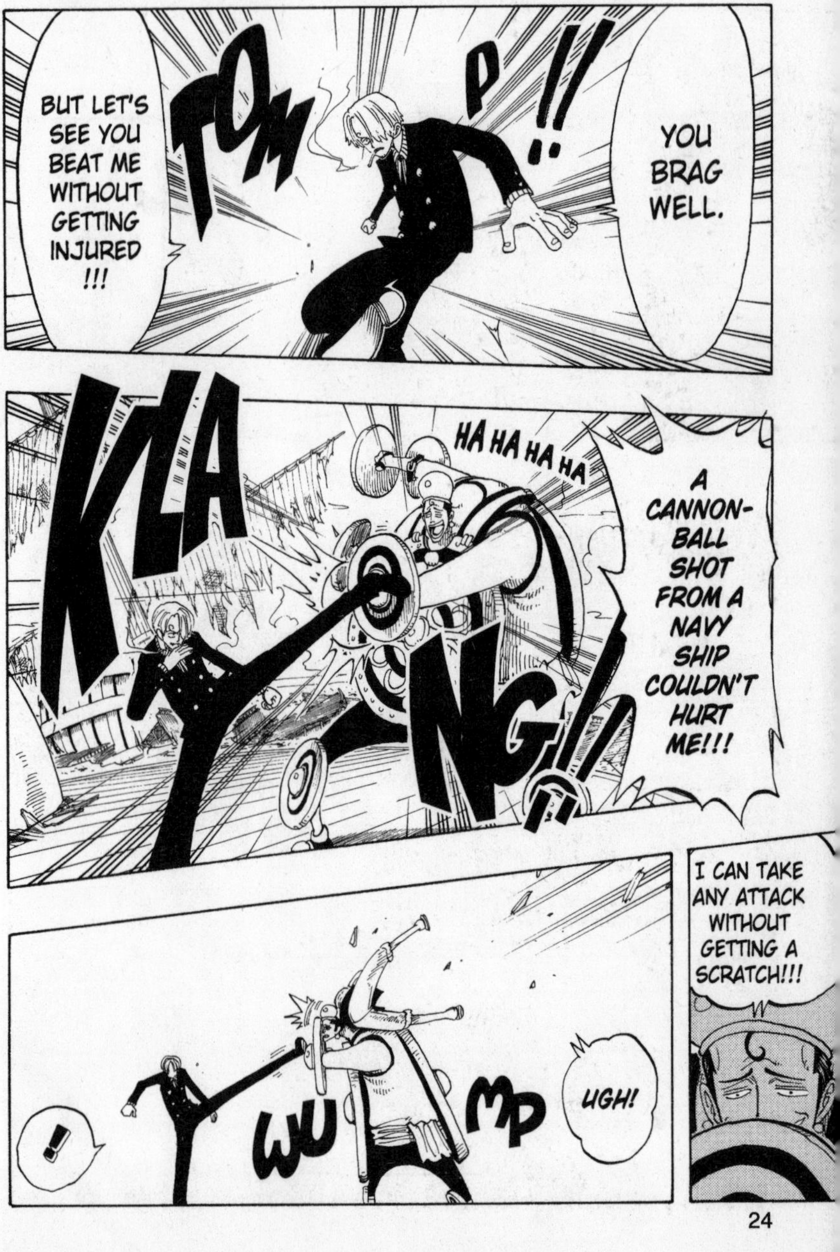
YOU BRAG WELL.
TOMP!!
BUT LET'S SEE YOU BEAT ME WITHOUT GETTING INJURED!!!
A CANNON-BALL SHOT FROM A NAVY SHIP COULDN'T HURT ME!!!
HA HA HA HA
KLANG!!
I CAN TAKE ANY ATTACK WITHOUT GETTING A SCRATCH!!!
UGH!
WUMP
!

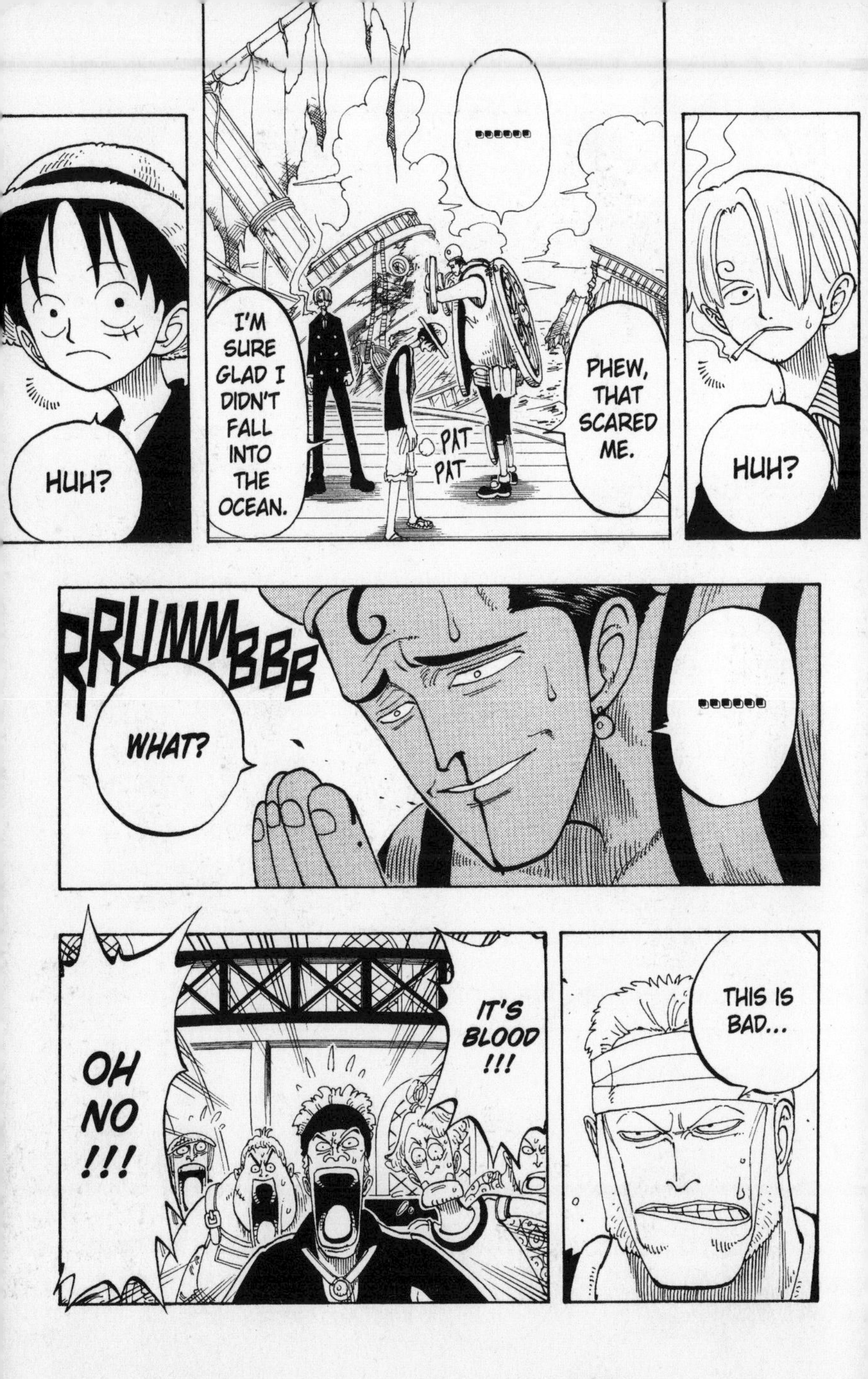
HUH?
......
PHEW, THAT SCARED ME.
PAT PAT
I'M SURE GLAD I DIDN'T FALL INTO THE OCEAN.
HUH?
......
RRUMMBBB
WHAT?
THIS IS BAD...
IT'S BLOOD!!!
OH NO!!!

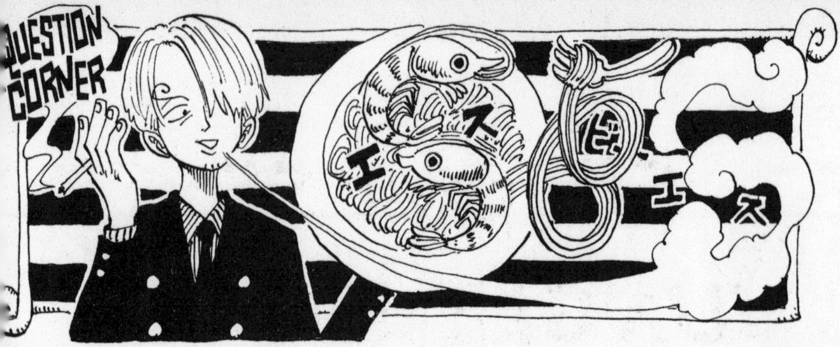
QUESTION CORNER

Q: (Question) Master Ei, what time is it now?

A: (Oda's answer) Um, nine past...midnight! It's time for Question Corner!!

Q: Does Shanks like me?

A: I don't know.

Q: Oda Sensei! The other day a friend said, "I've got the perfect Devil Fruit for you" and he gave me some strange-looking fruit and I ate it. It might be my imagination, but ever since then, I feel like all the jokes I tell are flops.

A: Oh...You ate that one, eh? Yes, I know that one. It's definitely a Samu-Samu (chilly-chilly) Fruit. When you eat that fruit, only really bad (chilly) jokes come out of your mouth. And you can't swim, of course. It's kind of like being stepped on...and then kicked. Ha ha ha ha! Laugh. Go on, laugh! Ha ha ha ha.

Q: In volume 1, when the mountain bandits enter the tavern, they break down the door, so why is it fixed when they leave?

A: That's Mr. Minatomo, the carpenter's doing. He's very impatient, so if he sees something like a broken door, he has to fix it right away. It was certainly not a mistake on my part.

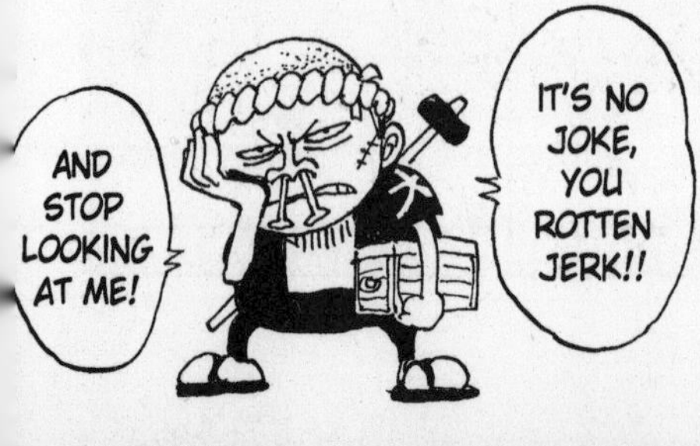
IT'S NO JOKE, YOU ROTTEN JERK!!
AND STOP LOOKING AT ME!

Chapter 55: JUNGLE BLOOD

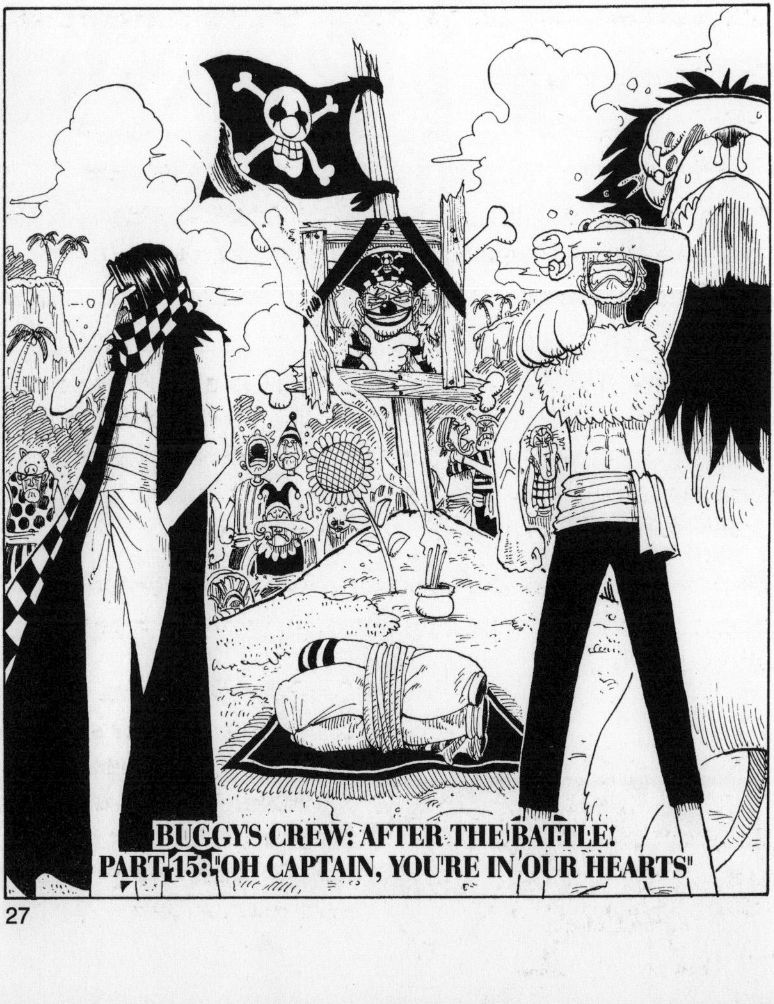
BUGGY'S CREW: AFTER THE BATTLE!
PART 15: "OH CAPTAIN, YOU'RE IN OUR HEARTS"

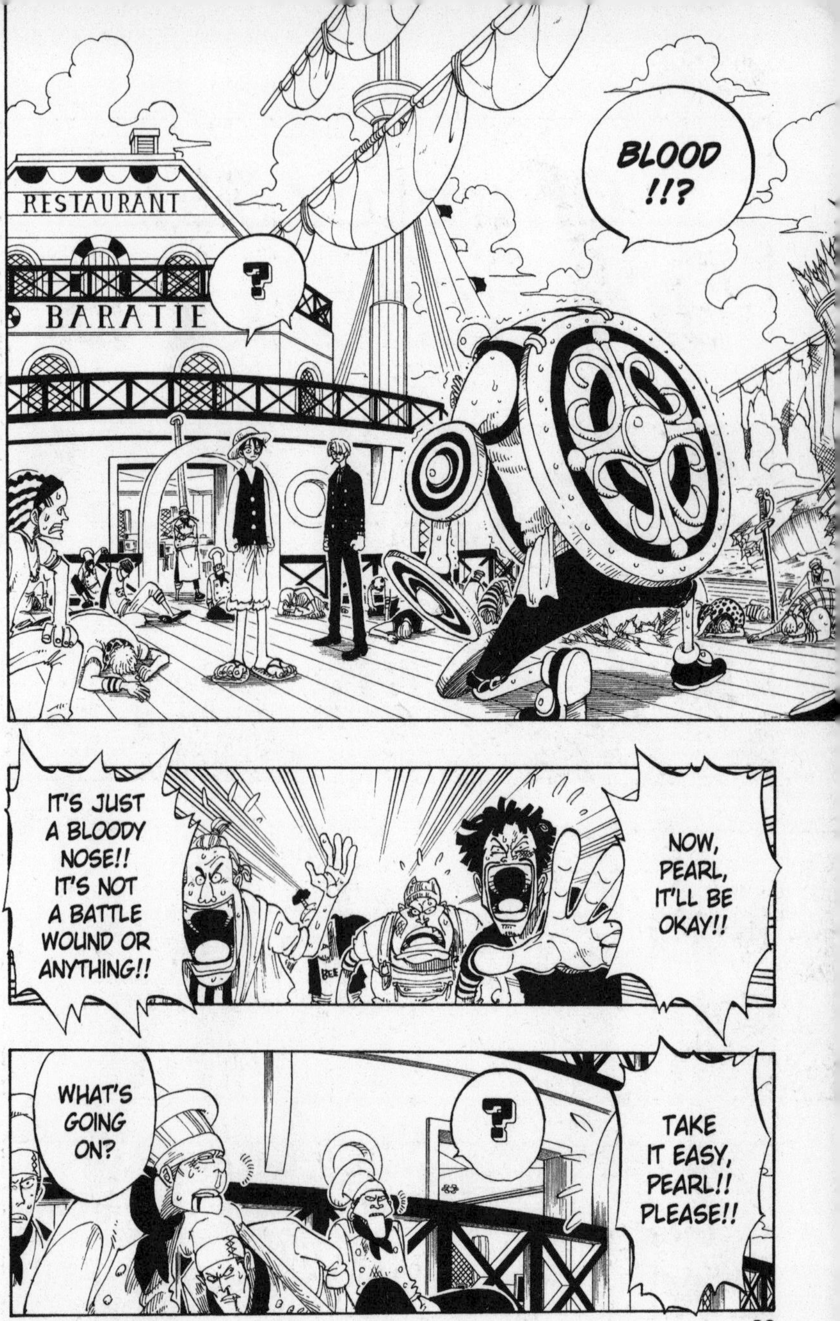
BLOOD !!?
?
RESTAURANT
BARATIE
NOW, PEARL, IT'LL BE OKAY!!
IT'S JUST A BLOODY NOSE!! IT'S NOT A BATTLE WOUND OR ANYTHING!!
TAKE IT EASY, PEARL!! PLEASE!!
?
WHAT'S GOING ON?

READ THIS WAY

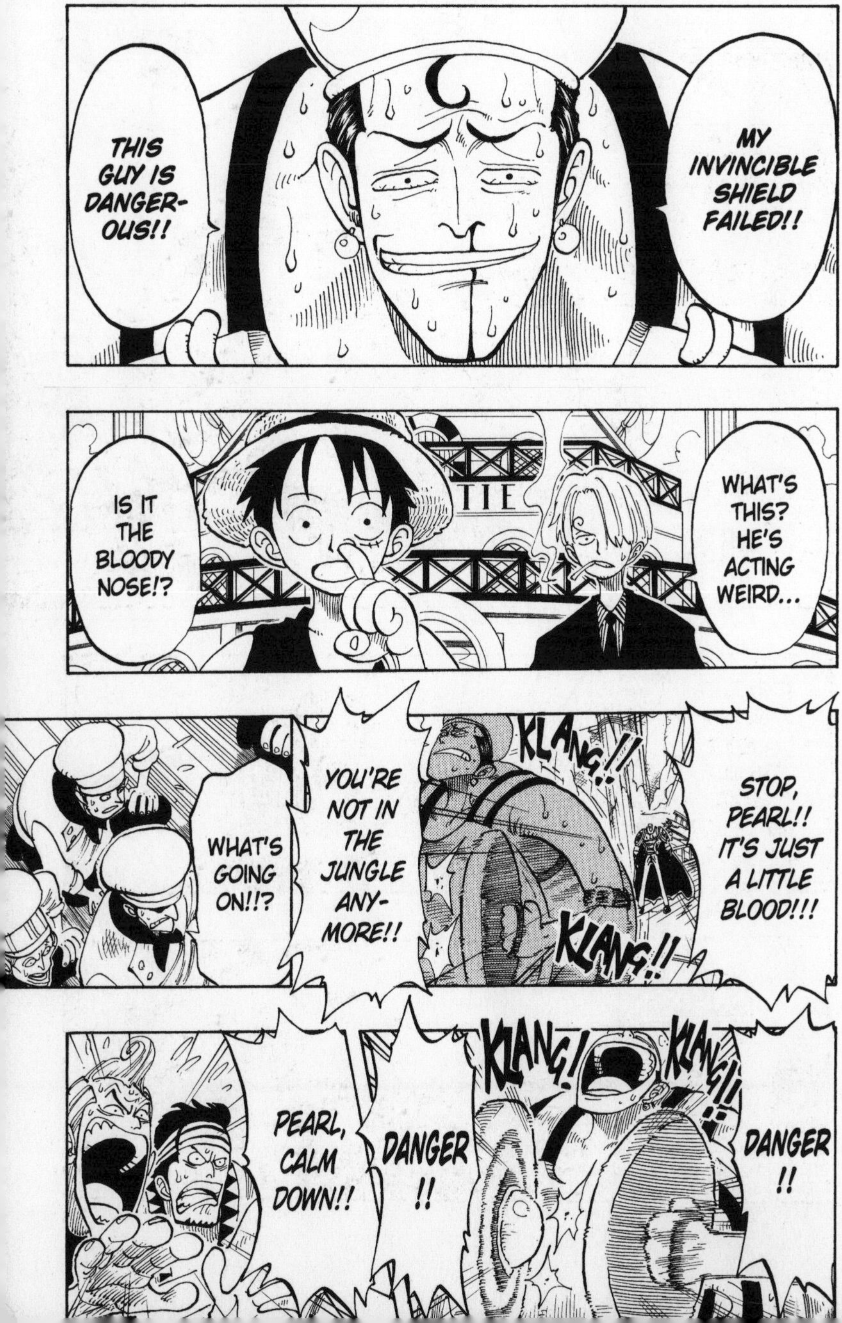
MY INVINCIBLE SHIELD FAILED!!
THIS GUY IS DANGER-OUS!!
WHAT'S THIS? HE'S ACTING WEIRD...
IS IT THE BLOODY NOSE!?
STOP, PEARL!! IT'S JUST A LITTLE BLOOD!!!
KLANG!!
KLANG!!
YOU'RE NOT IN THE JUNGLE ANY-MORE!!
WHAT'S GOING ON!!?
DANGER!!
KLANG!!
KLANG!
DANGER!!
PEARL, CALM DOWN!!

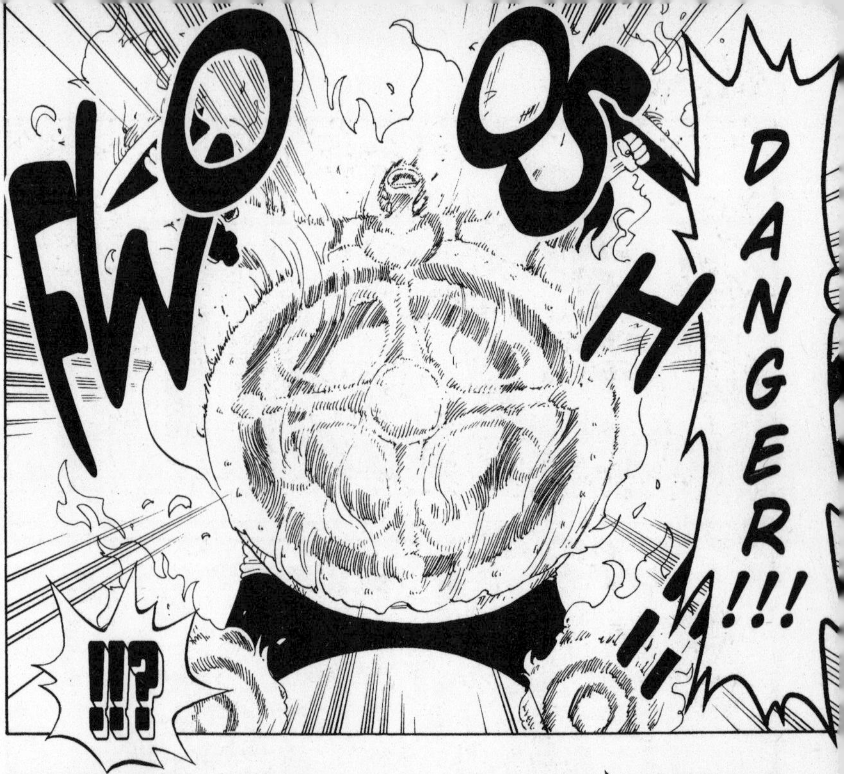
DANGER!!!
FWOOSH!!
!!?

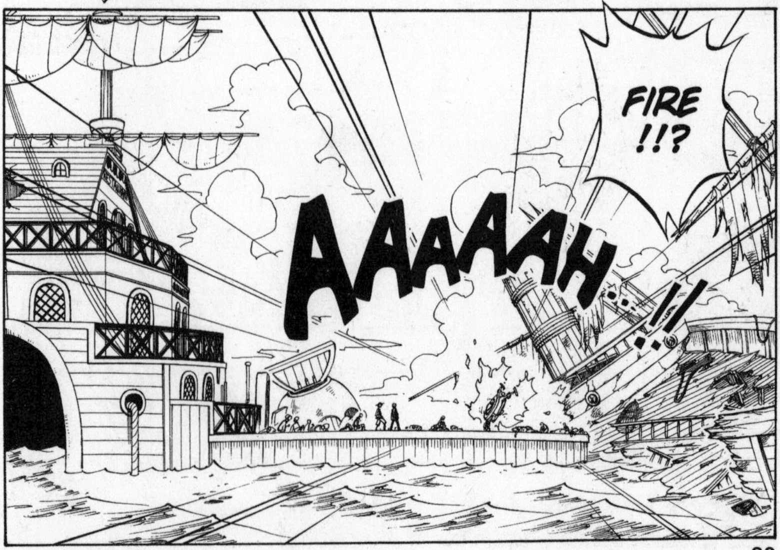
FIRE !!?
AAAAAH...!!

READ THIS WAY

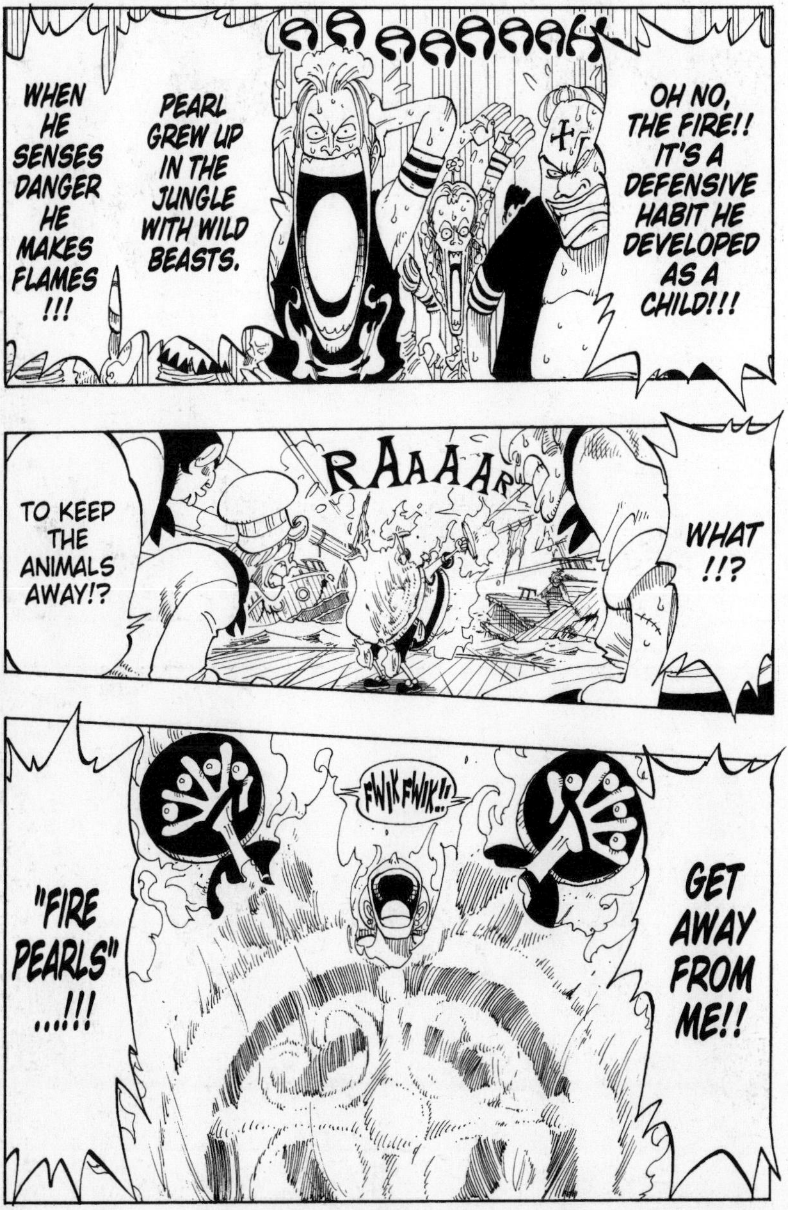
AAAAAAAAH
OH NO, THE FIRE!! IT'S A DEFENSIVE HABIT HE DEVELOPED AS A CHILD!!!
PEARL GREW UP IN THE JUNGLE WITH WILD BEASTS.
WHEN HE SENSES DANGER HE MAKES FLAMES!!!
WHAT!!?
RAAAAR
TO KEEP THE ANIMALS AWAY!?
GET AWAY FROM ME!!
FWIK FWIK!!
"FIRE PEARLS"...!!!

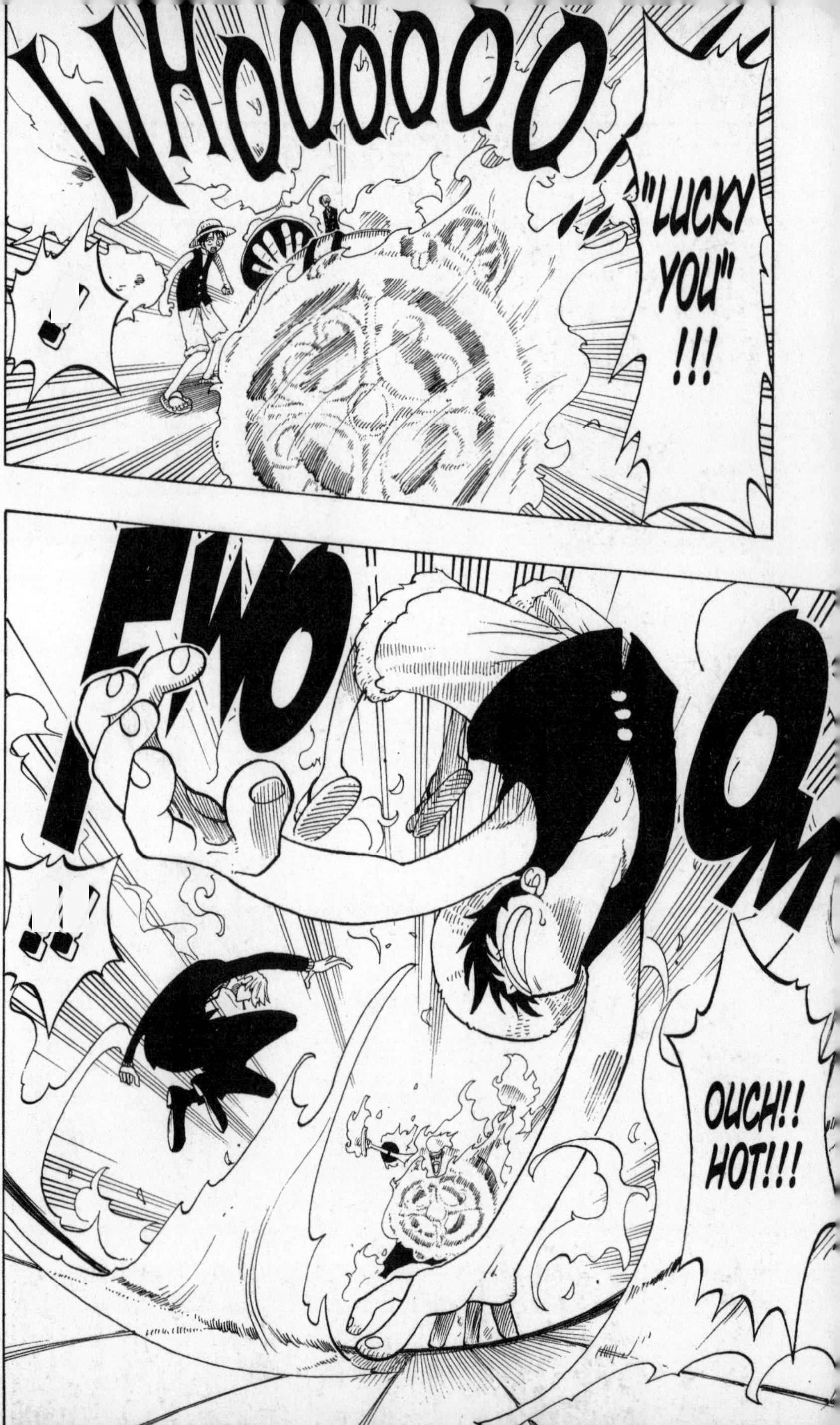
WHOOOOOO
"LUCKY YOU"!!!
FWOOM
OUCH!! HOT!!!

READ THIS WAY

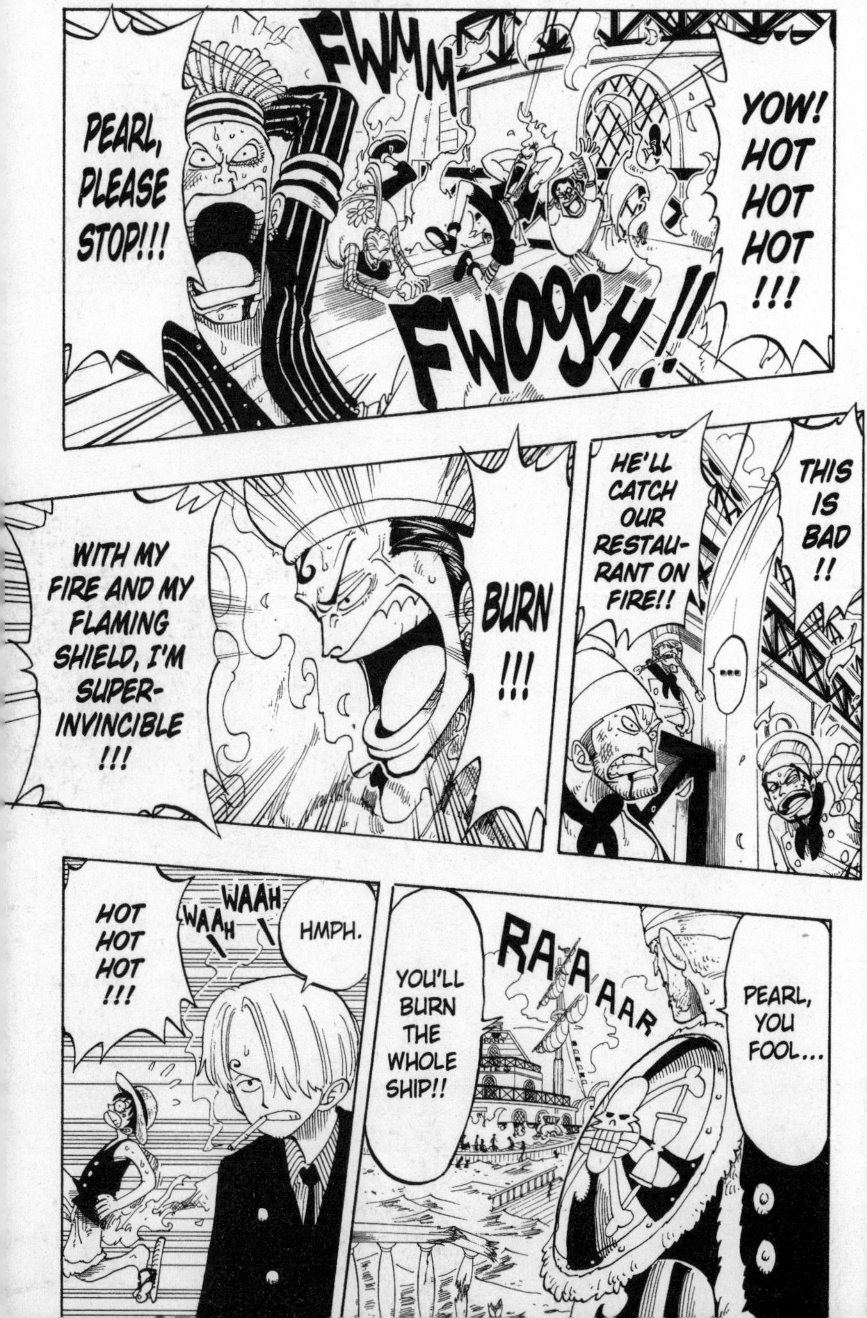
YOW! HOT HOT HOT!!!
FWMM
FWOOSH!!
PEARL, PLEASE STOP!!!
THIS IS BAD!!
HE'LL CATCH OUR RESTAURANT ON FIRE!!
...
BURN!!!
WITH MY FIRE AND MY FLAMING SHIELD, I'M SUPER-INVINCIBLE!!!
PEARL, YOU FOOL...
RAAAAR
YOU'LL BURN THE WHOLE SHIP!!
HMPH.
WAAH
WAAH
HOT HOT HOT!!!

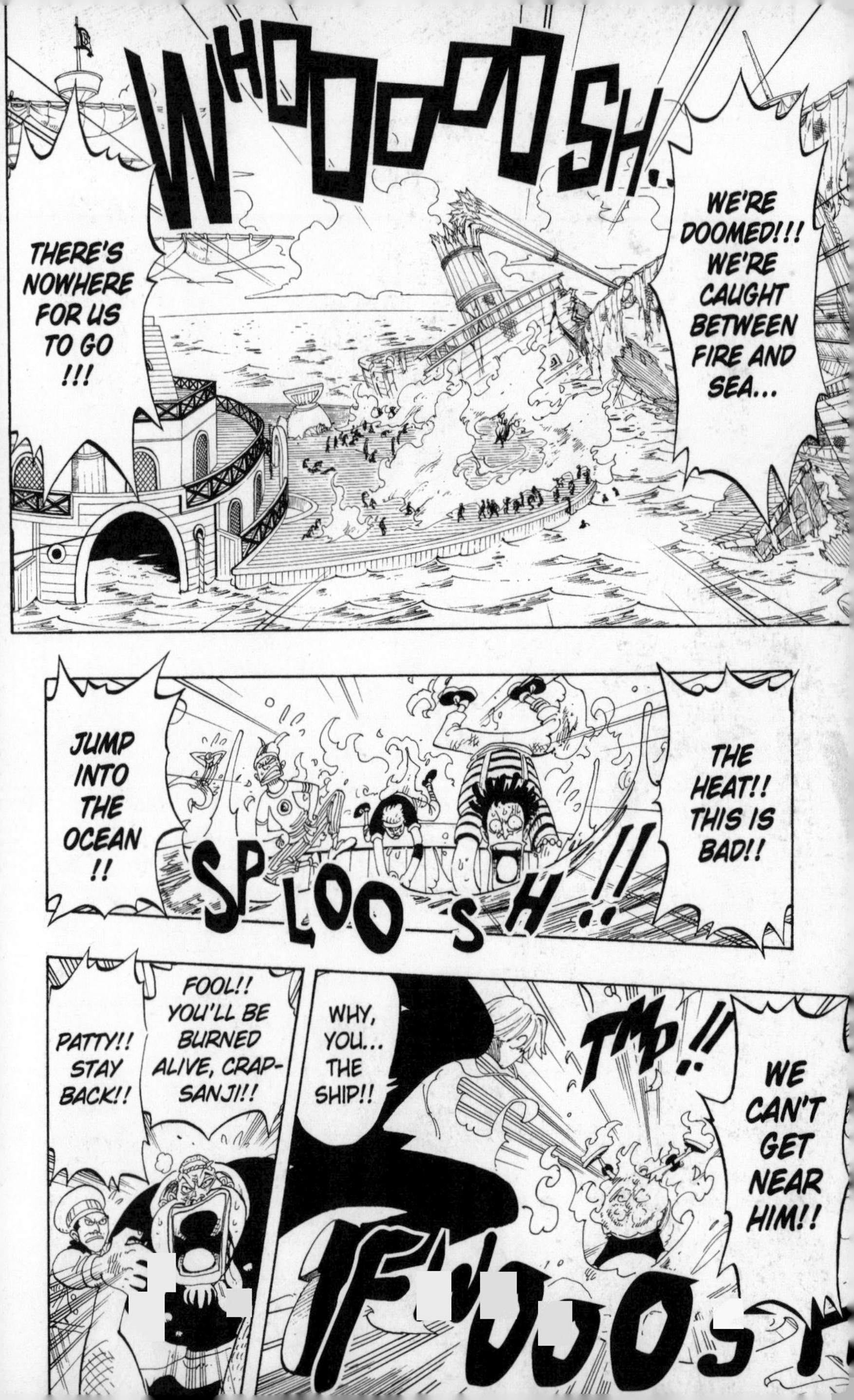
WE'RE DOOMED!!! WE'RE CAUGHT BETWEEN FIRE AND SEA...
WHOOOOOSH
THERE'S NOWHERE FOR US TO GO!!!
THE HEAT!! THIS IS BAD!!
SPLOOSH!!
JUMP INTO THE OCEAN!!
WE CAN'T GET NEAR HIM!!
TMP!!
WHY, YOU... THE SHIP!!
FOOL!! YOU'LL BE BURNED ALIVE, CRAP-SANJI!!
PATTY!! STAY BACK!!

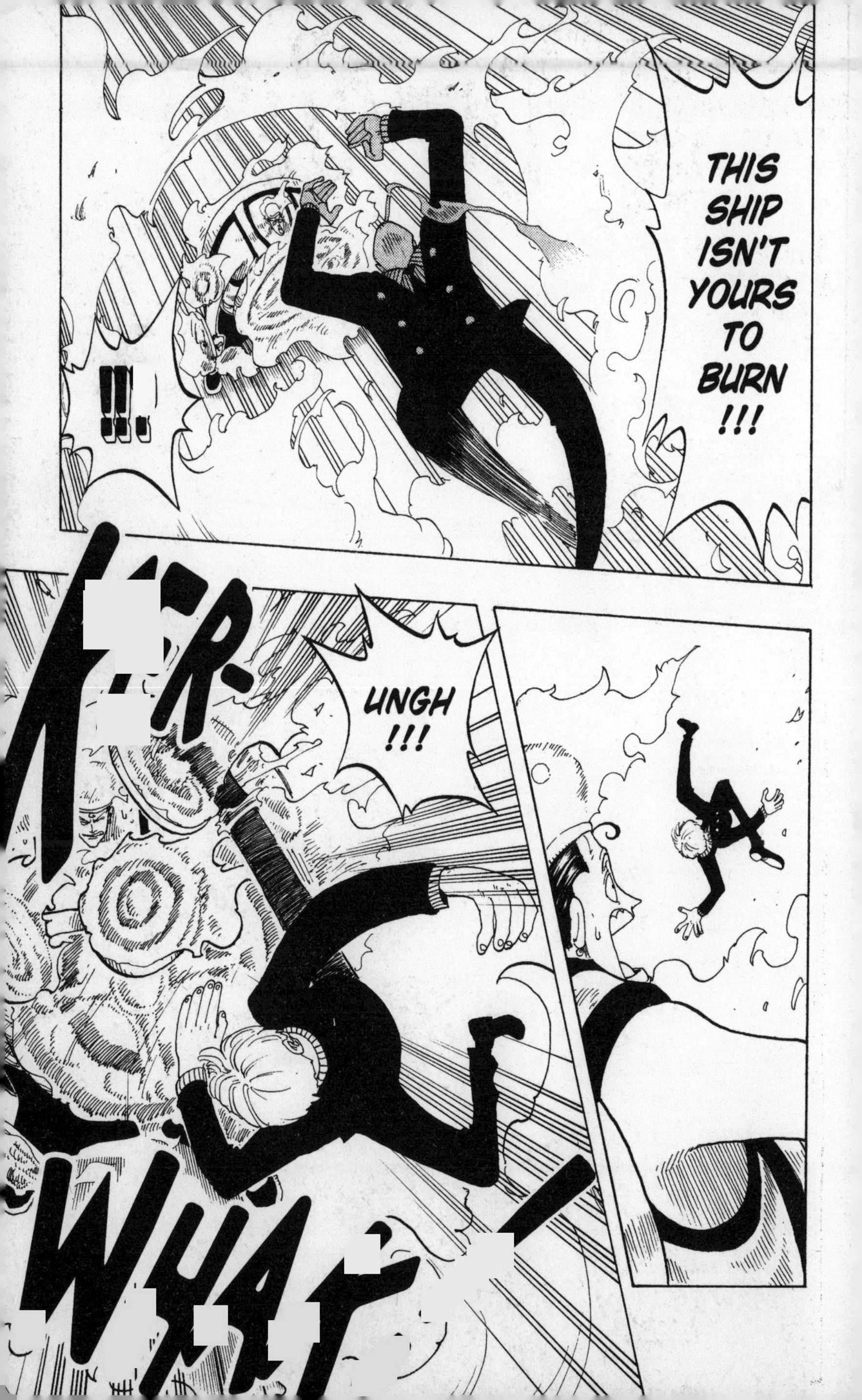
THIS SHIP ISN'T YOURS TO BURN!!!
!!
UNGH!!!

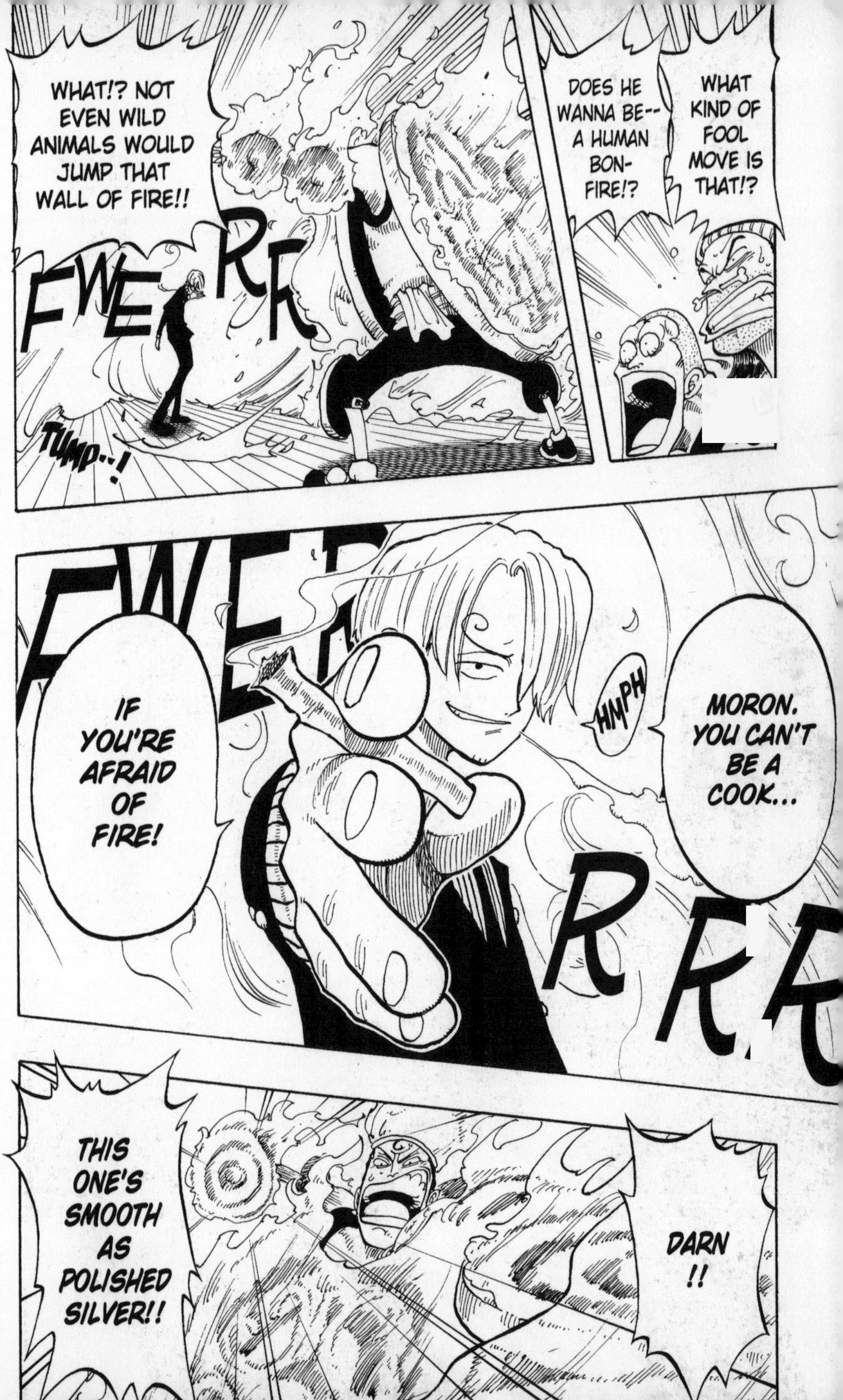
WHAT KIND OF FOOL MOVE IS THAT!?
DOES HE WANNA BE-- A HUMAN BONFIRE!?
WHAT!? NOT EVEN WILD ANIMALS WOULD JUMP THAT WALL OF FIRE!!
FWERRR
TUMP..!
HMPH
MORON. YOU CAN'T BE A COOK...
FWER
IF YOU'RE AFRAID OF FIRE!
RRR
DARN !!
THIS ONE'S SMOOTH AS POLISHED SILVER!!

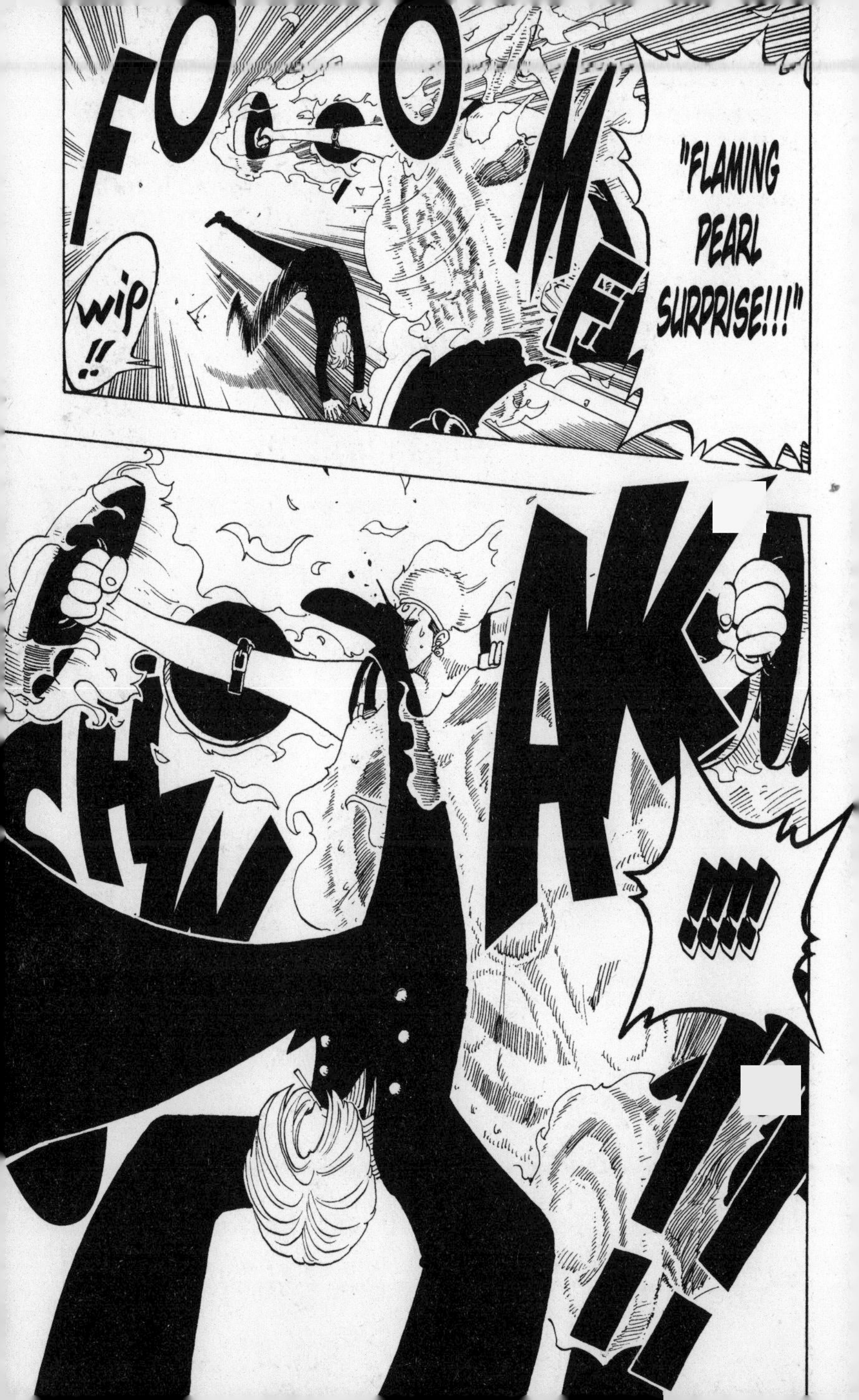
"FLAMING PEARL SURPRISE!!!"
wip !!

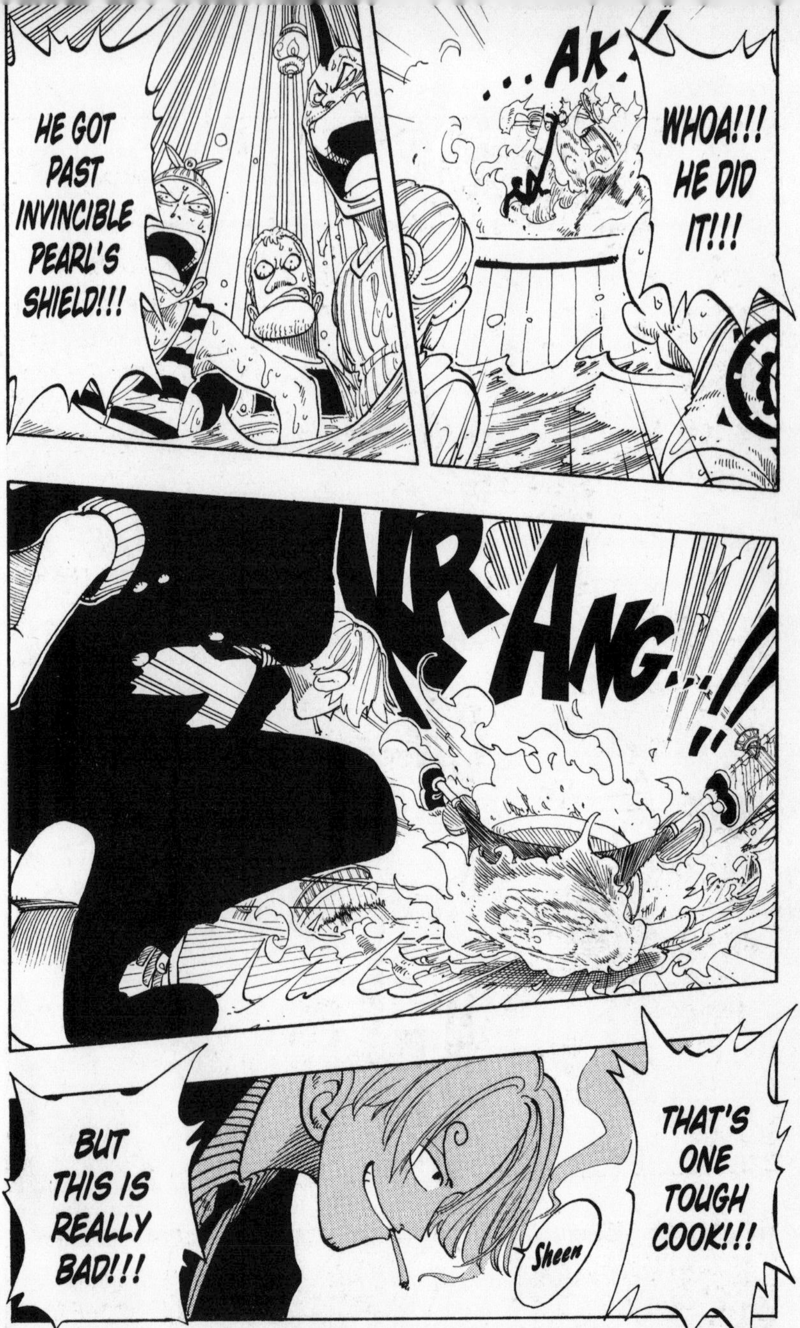
...AK
WHOA!!! HE DID IT!!!
HE GOT PAST INVINCIBLE PEARL'S SHIELD!!!
VRANG...!!
THAT'S ONE TOUGH COOK!!!
Sheen
BUT THIS IS REALLY BAD!!!

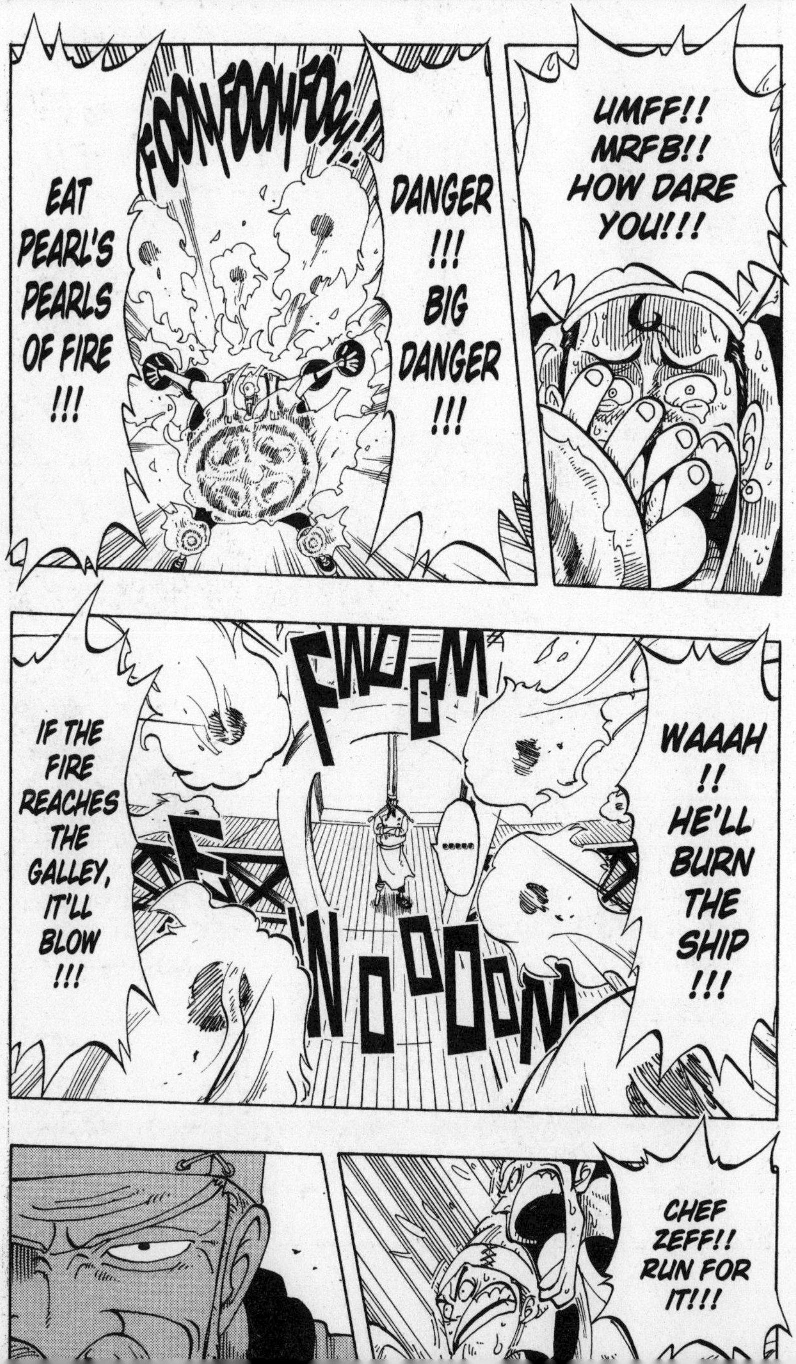
UMFF!! MRFB!! HOW DARE YOU!!!
FOOMFOOMFOOM!!
DANGER!!! BIG DANGER!!!
EAT PEARL'S PEARLS OF FIRE!!!
WAAAH!! HE'LL BURN THE SHIP!!!
FWOOM
.....
WOOOOM
IF THE FIRE REACHES THE GALLEY, IT'LL BLOW!!!
CHEF ZEFF!! RUN FOR IT!!!

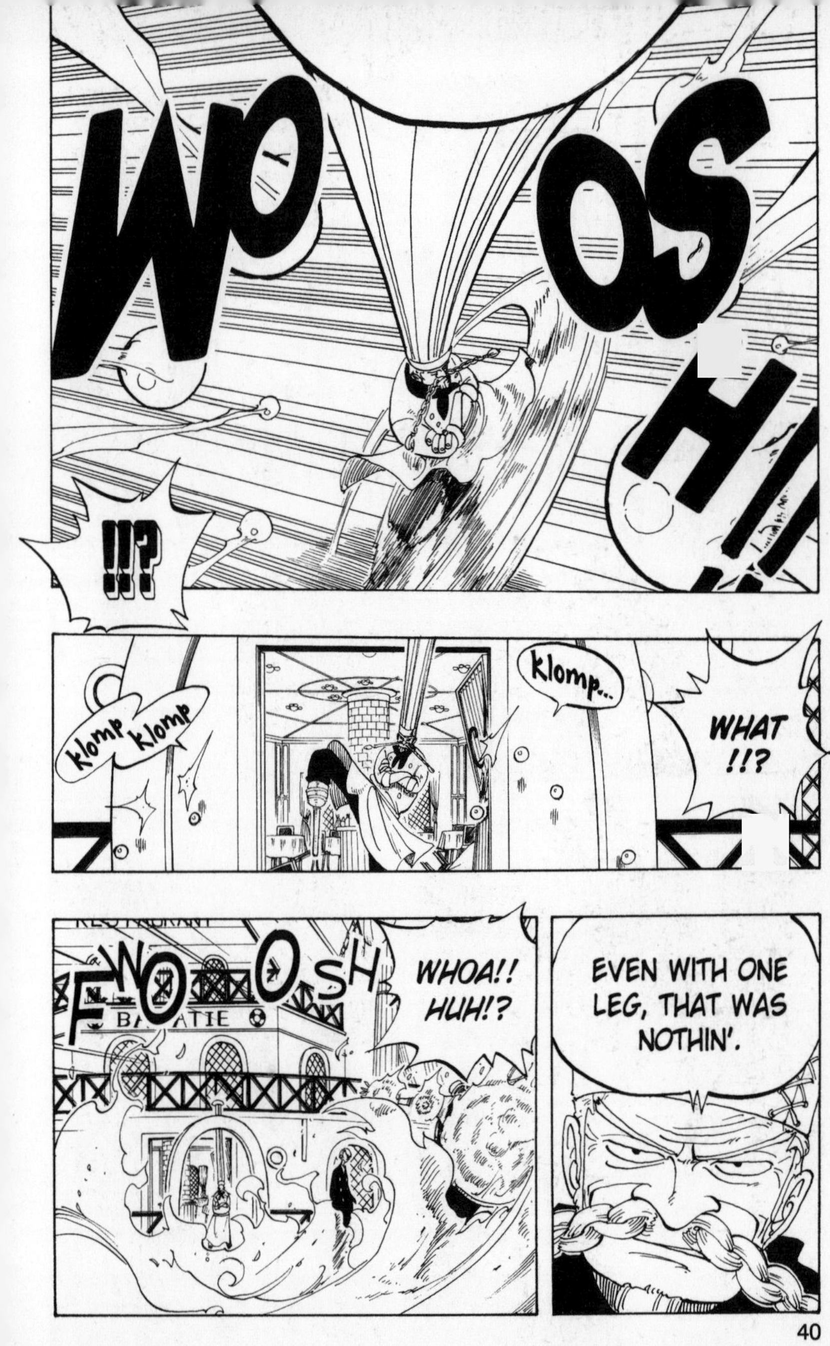
WOOSH!!
!!?
WHAT !!?
klomp...
klomp klomp
EVEN WITH ONE LEG, THAT WAS NOTHIN'.
WHOA!! HUH!?
FWOOOSH

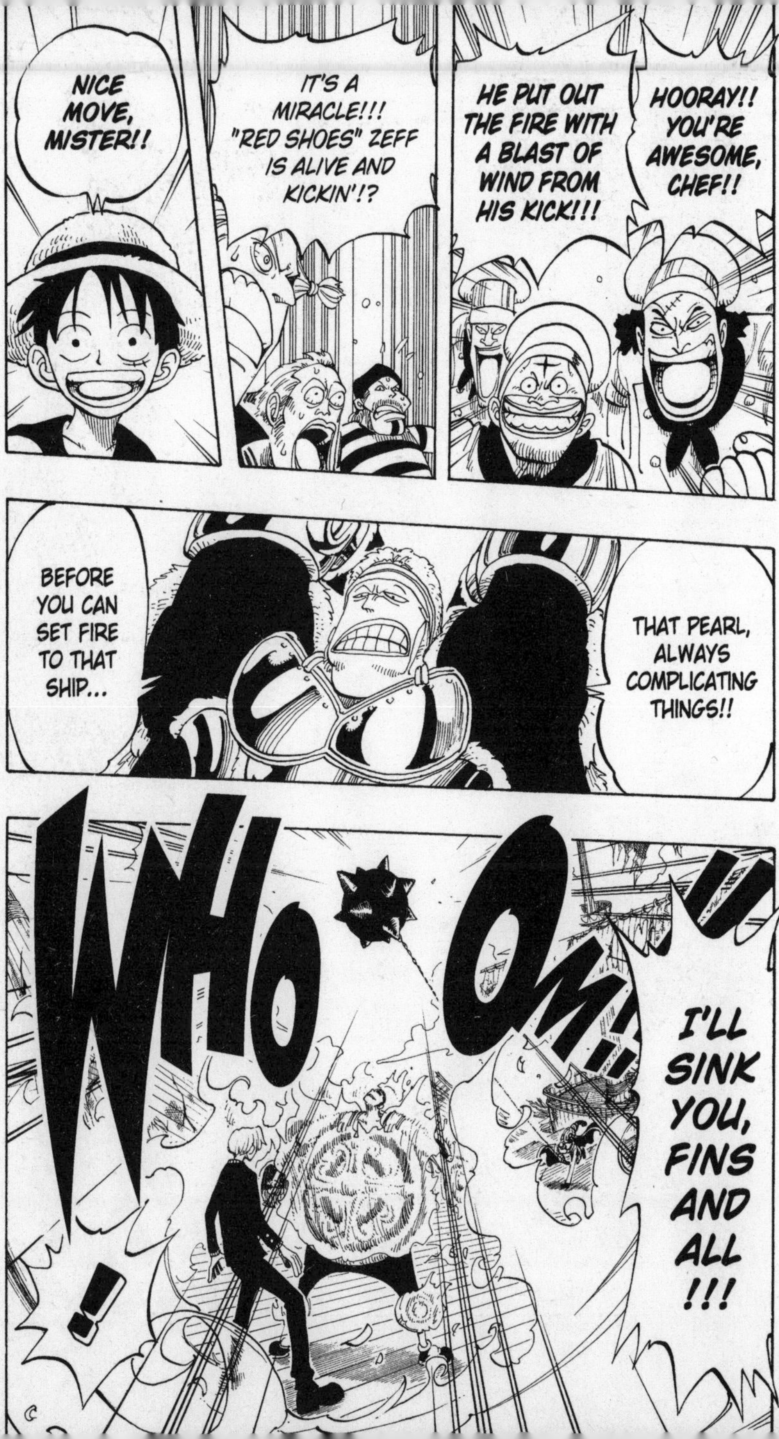
HOORAY!! YOU'RE AWESOME, CHEF!!
HE PUT OUT THE FIRE WITH A BLAST OF WIND FROM HIS KICK!!!
IT'S A MIRACLE!!! "RED SHOES" ZEFF IS ALIVE AND KICKIN'!?
NICE MOVE, MISTER!!
THAT PEARL, ALWAYS COMPLICATING THINGS!!
BEFORE YOU CAN SET FIRE TO THAT SHIP...
WHOOM!!
I'LL SINK YOU, FINS AND ALL!!!
!

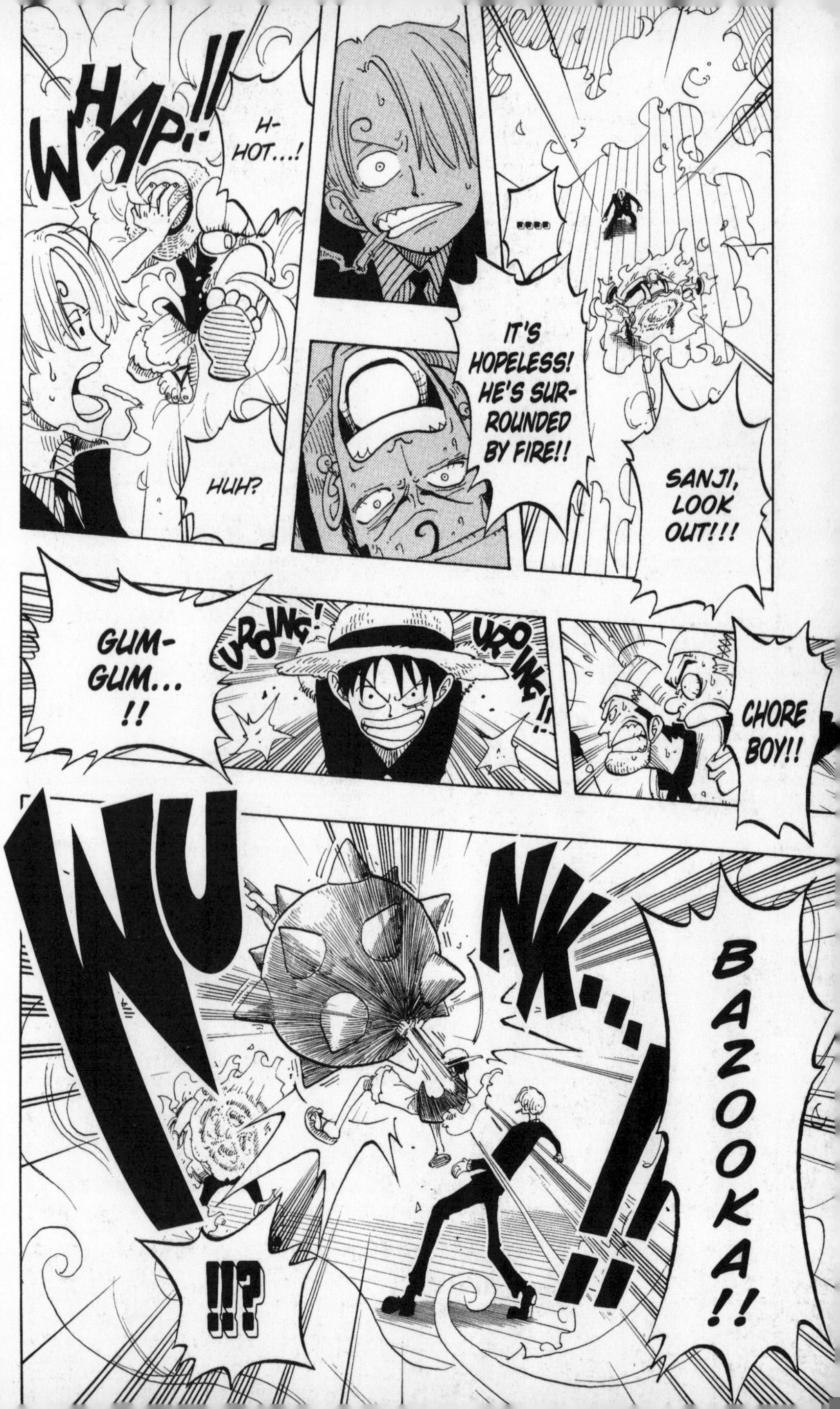
....
SANJI, LOOK OUT!!!
IT'S HOPELESS! HE'S SURROUNDED BY FIRE!!
WHAP!!
H-HOT...!
HUH?
CHORE BOY!!
UROONG!
UROWNG!!
GUM-GUM...!!
WUNK...!!
BAZOOKA!!
!!?

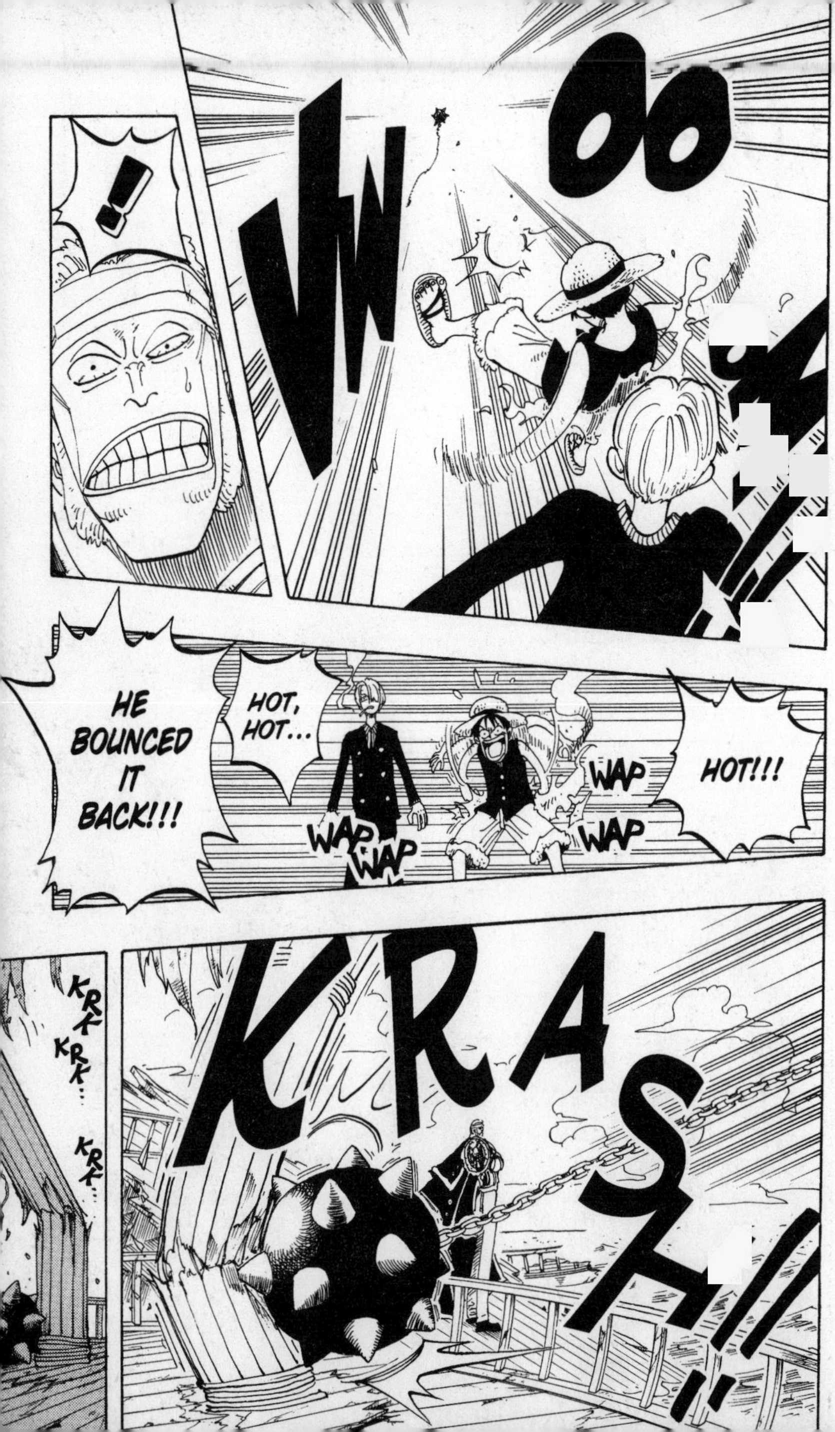
VWOO
!
HOT!!!
WAP
WAP
HOT, HOT...
WAP
WAP
HE BOUNCED IT BACK!!!
KRASH!!
KRK KRK...
KRK...

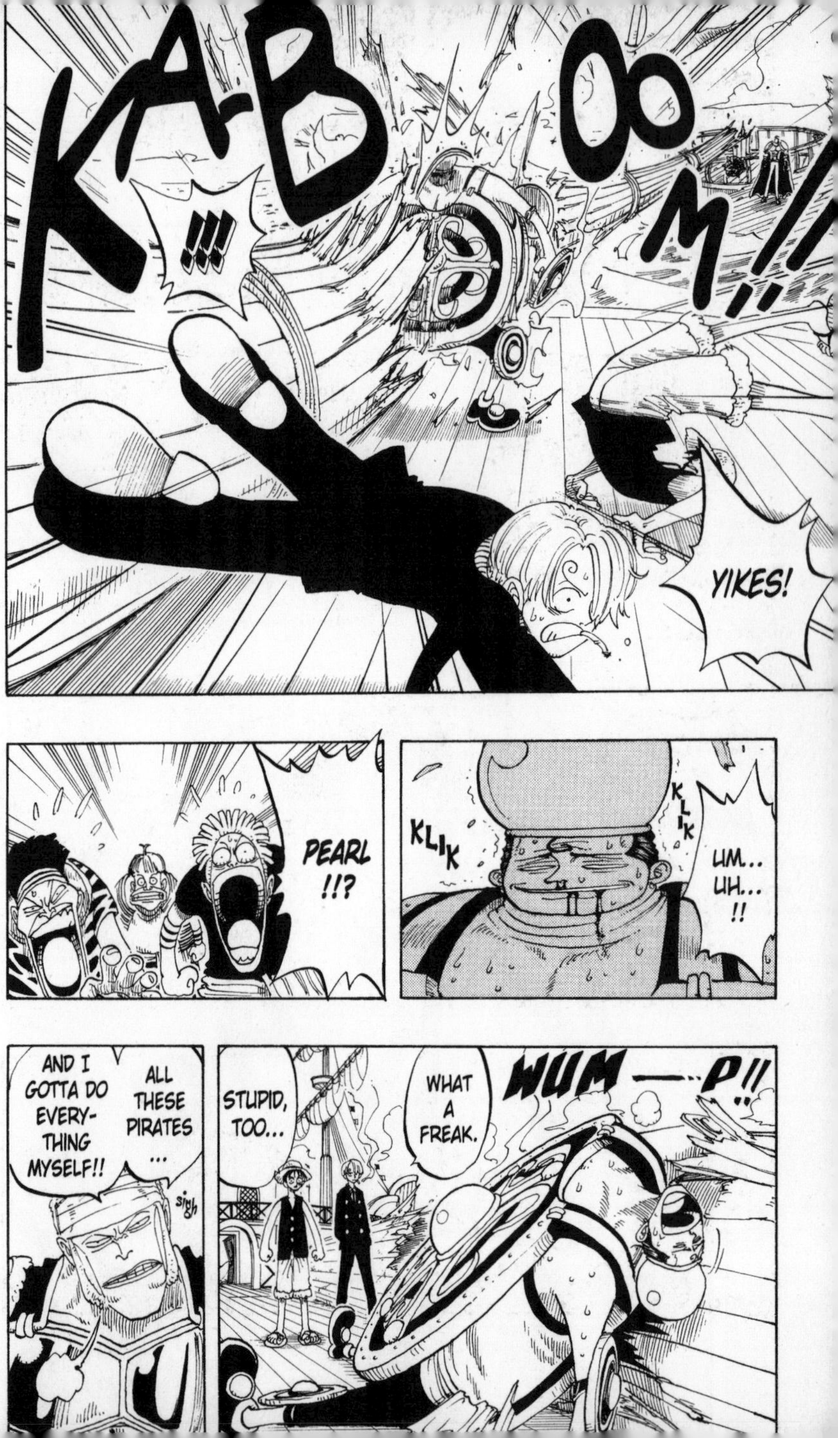
KA-BOOOM!!
!!!
YIKES!
KLIK
KLIK
UM... UH... !!
PEARL !!?
WUM——P!!
WHAT A FREAK.
STUPID, TOO...
ALL THESE PIRATES...
AND I GOTTA DO EVERYTHING MYSELF!!
sigh

HOLD IT RIGHT THERE, SANJI.

ARGH!!

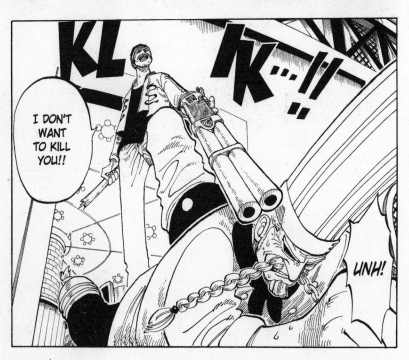

I DON'T WANT TO KILL YOU!!

UNH!

GIN! WHY, YOU...!!!

GIN!!

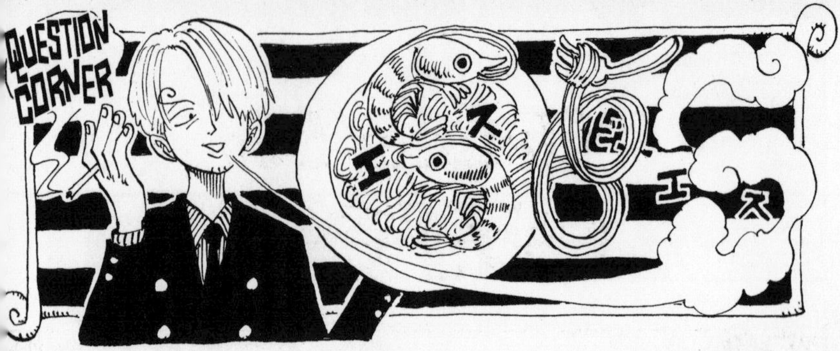
QUESTION CORNER

Q: Why do Sanji's eyebrows circle up at the ends? Is it a fashion statement? If you ask me, it's lame!!

A: Hey!! Sit down, now!! Listen!! All people owe their lives to circling!! The Sun and the Moon and the Earth all go around in circles. What if the circling of the Earth suddenly stopped!! The whole world would be deluged by gigantic waves and there would be a terrible disaster!! So remember that Sanji's eyebrows have that kind of energy!! Repent!! Dismissed!!

Q: A question. How old is Sanji?

A: 19 years old--just like Zolo.

Q: Nami, Nami, Nami, Nami! I love Nami!
I won't give Nami up to the likes of Sanji!! Therefore, I challenge him to a duel for Nami. Tomorrow afternoon at 3:00, on the Red Line. Don't you run from me! Is that okay, Oda Sensei?

A: Okay!! Fight!!

Q: How many assistants do you have? What kind of things do they do?

A: I have four. They help with the backgrounds and stuff like that. They come to help for two nights and three days each week, sleeping over. Frankly, without these people it would be impossible to complete a script in a week. But it's a really goofy workplace, so we have a lot of fun working on the manga.

Chapter 56:
I REFUSE

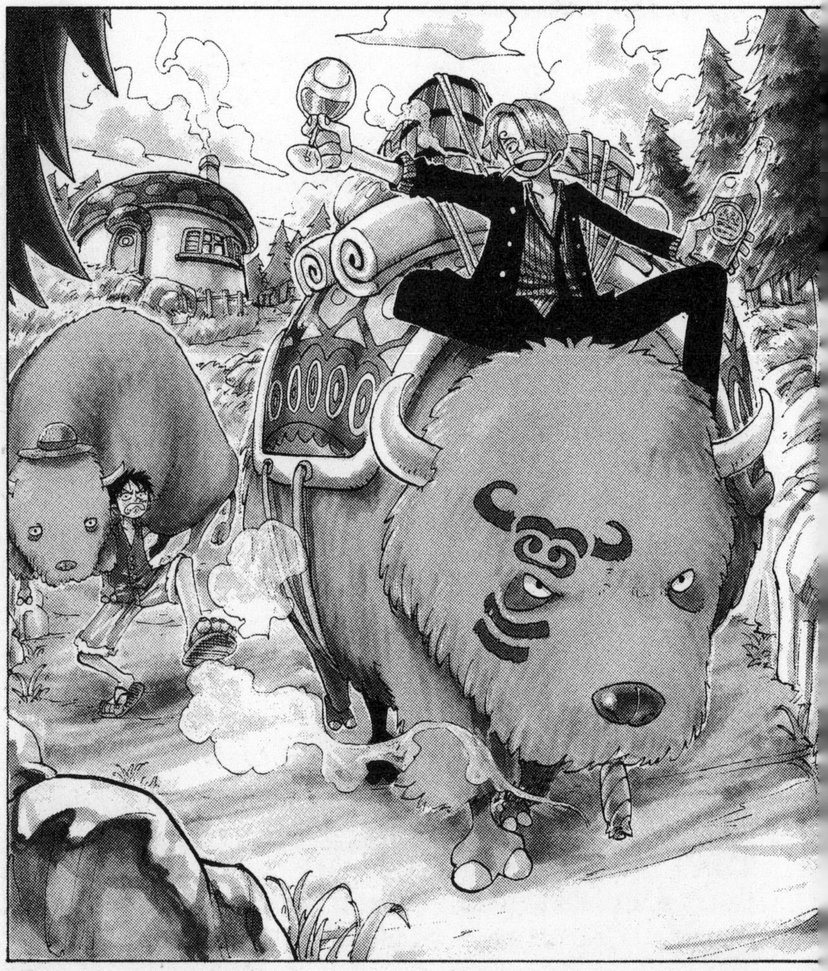

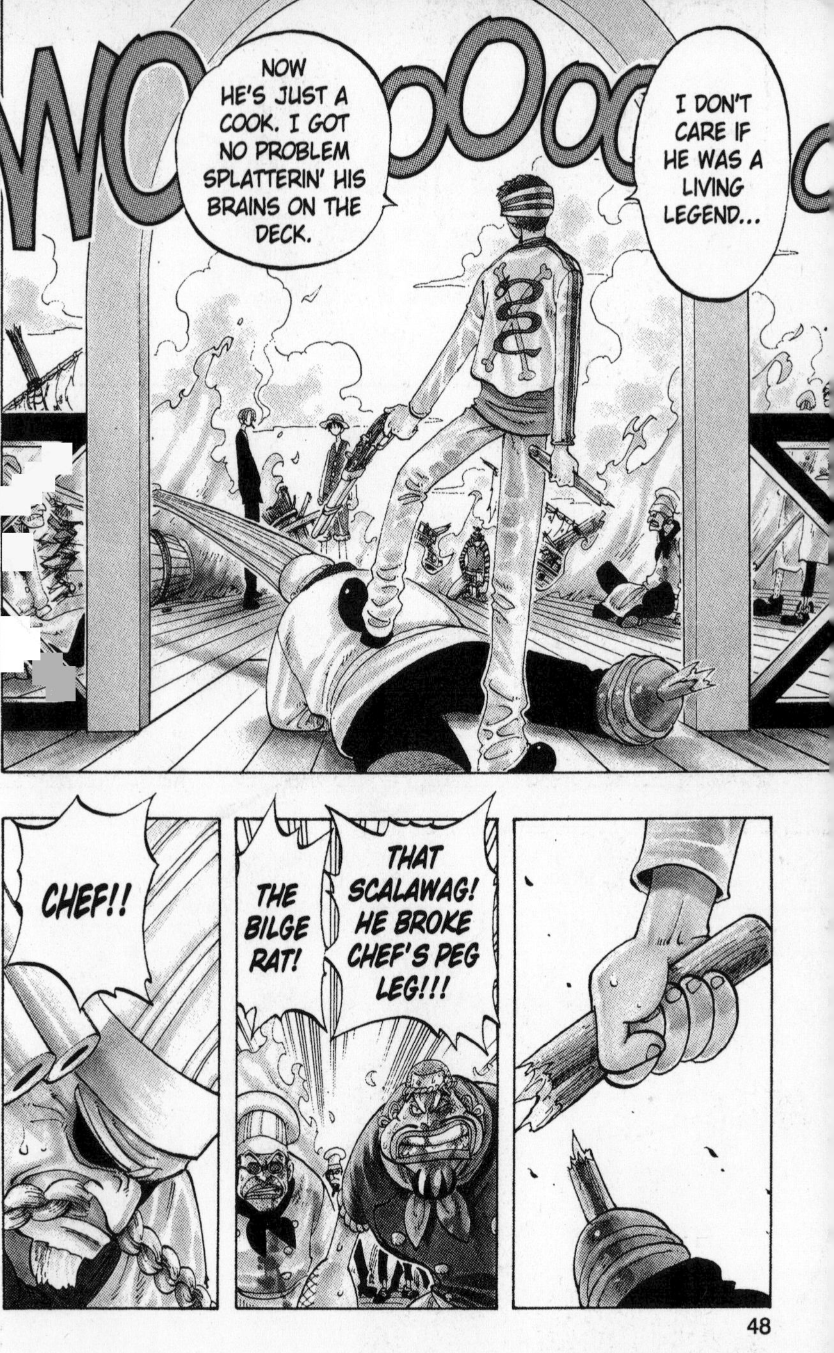
I DON'T CARE IF HE WAS A LIVING LEGEND...
NOW HE'S JUST A COOK. I GOT NO PROBLEM SPLATTERIN' HIS BRAINS ON THE DECK.
THAT SCALAWAG! HE BROKE CHEF'S PEG LEG!!!
THE BILGE RAT!
CHEF!!

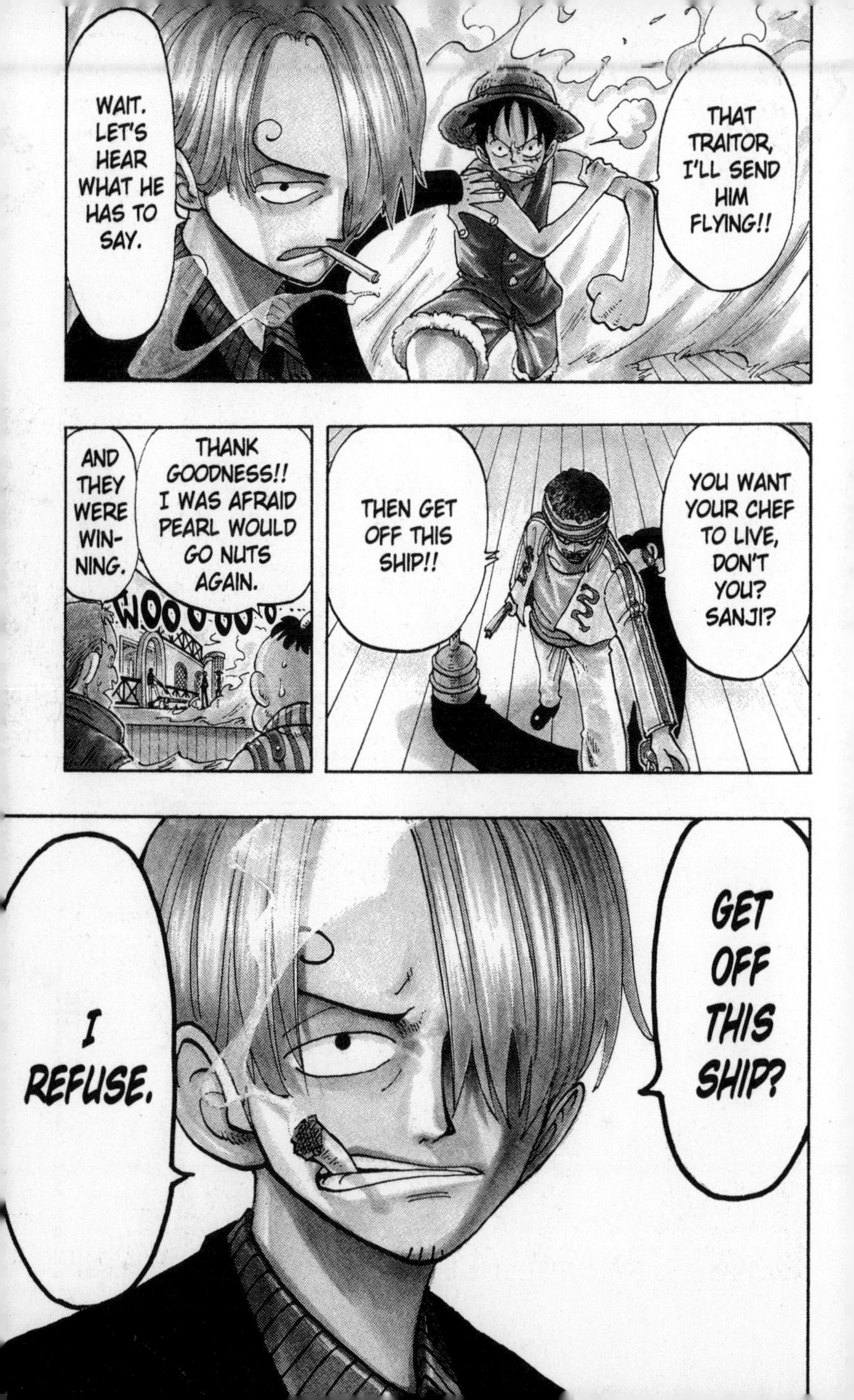
THAT TRAITOR, I'LL SEND HIM FLYING!!
WAIT. LET'S HEAR WHAT HE HAS TO SAY.
YOU WANT YOUR CHEF TO LIVE, DON'T YOU? SANJI?
THEN GET OFF THIS SHIP!!
THANK GOODNESS!! I WAS AFRAID PEARL WOULD GO NUTS AGAIN.
AND THEY WERE WIN-NING.
WOOOOOO
GET OFF THIS SHIP?
I REFUSE.

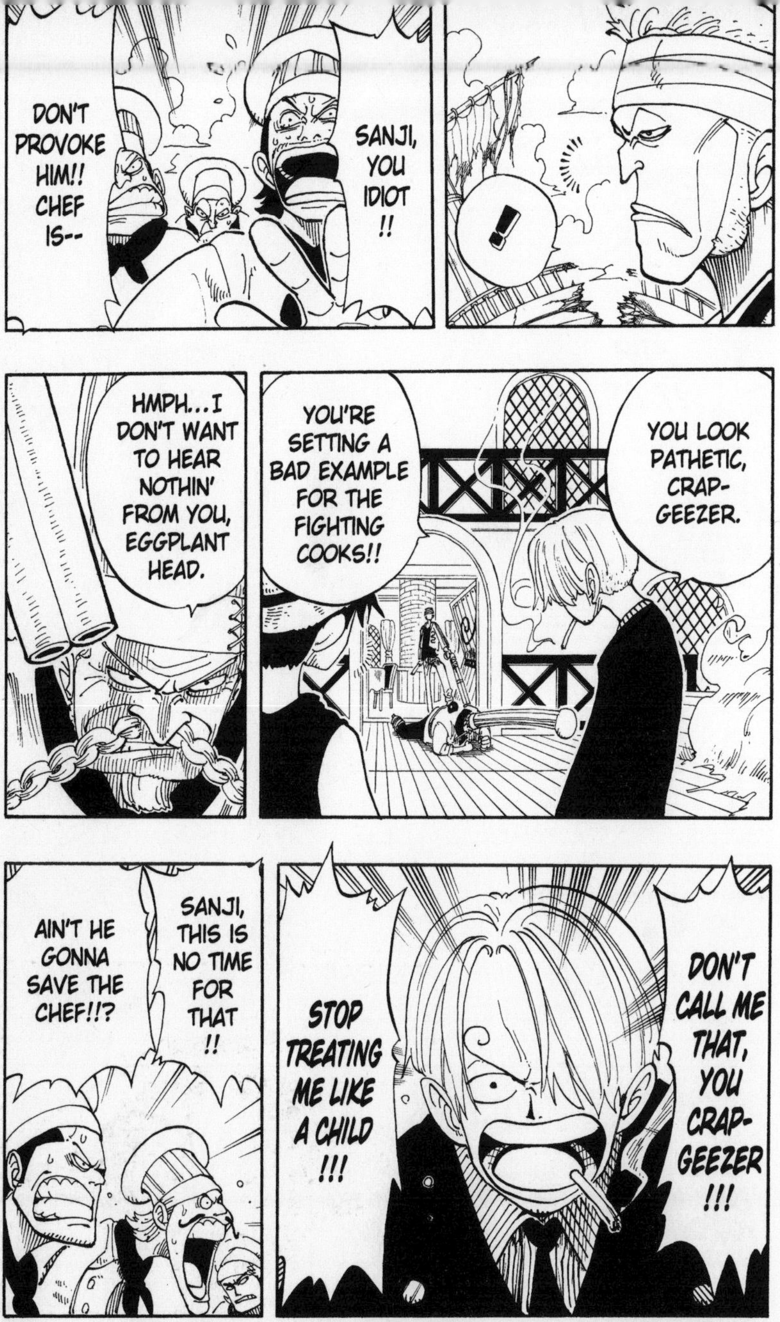
!
SANJI, YOU IDIOT!!
DON'T PROVOKE HIM!! CHEF IS--
YOU LOOK PATHETIC, CRAP-GEEZER.
YOU'RE SETTING A BAD EXAMPLE FOR THE FIGHTING COOKS!!
HMPH...I DON'T WANT TO HEAR NOTHIN' FROM YOU, EGGPLANT HEAD.
DON'T CALL ME THAT, YOU CRAP-GEEZER!!!
STOP TREATING ME LIKE A CHILD!!!
SANJI, THIS IS NO TIME FOR THAT!!
AIN'T HE GONNA SAVE THE CHEF!!?

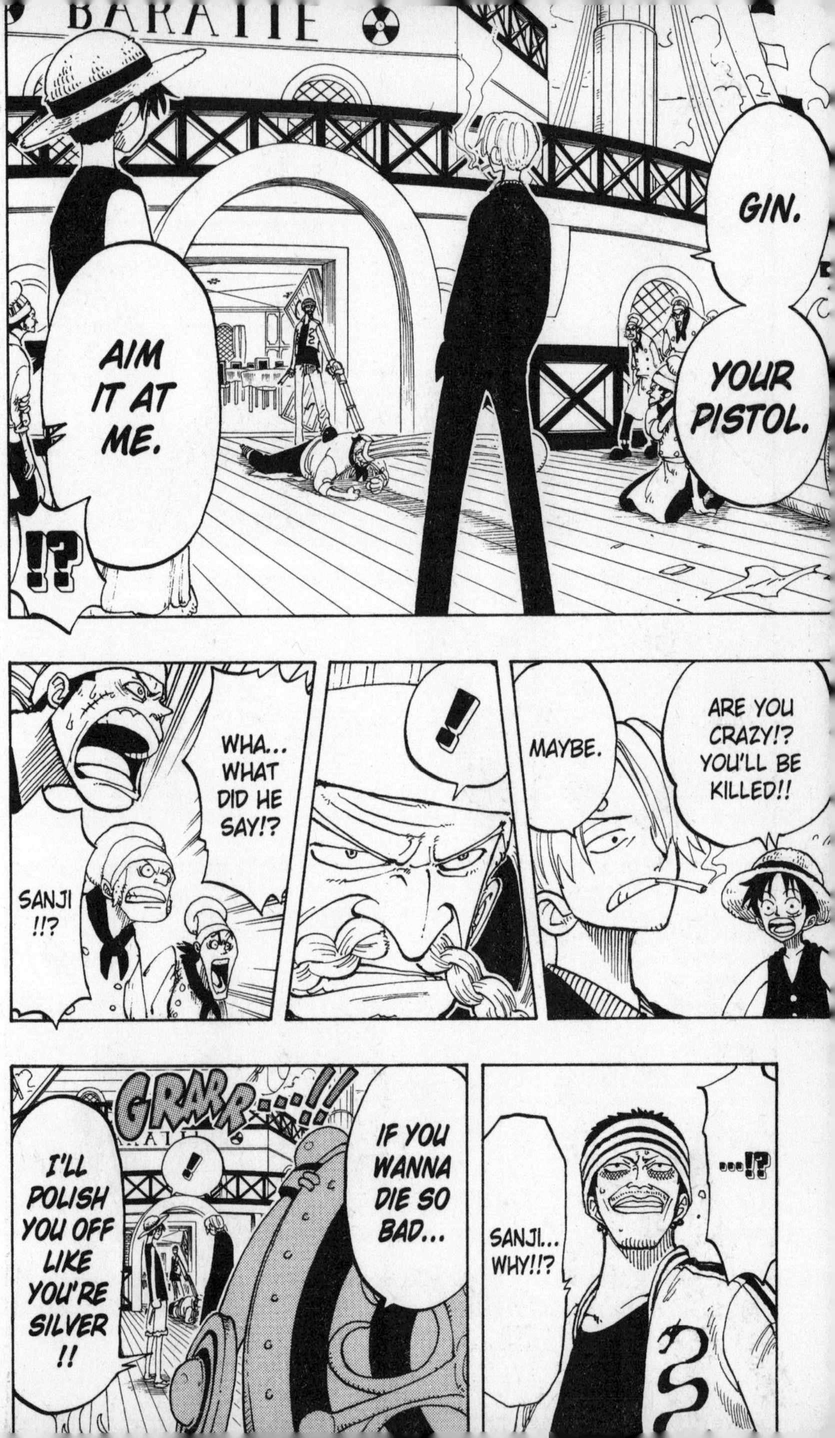
BARATIE
GIN.
YOUR PISTOL.
AIM IT AT ME.
!?
ARE YOU CRAZY!? YOU'LL BE KILLED!!
MAYBE.
!
WHA... WHAT DID HE SAY!?
SANJI !!?
...!?
SANJI... WHY!!?
IF YOU WANNA DIE SO BAD...
GRARR...!!
!
I'LL POLISH YOU OFF LIKE YOU'RE SILVER !!

READ THIS WAY

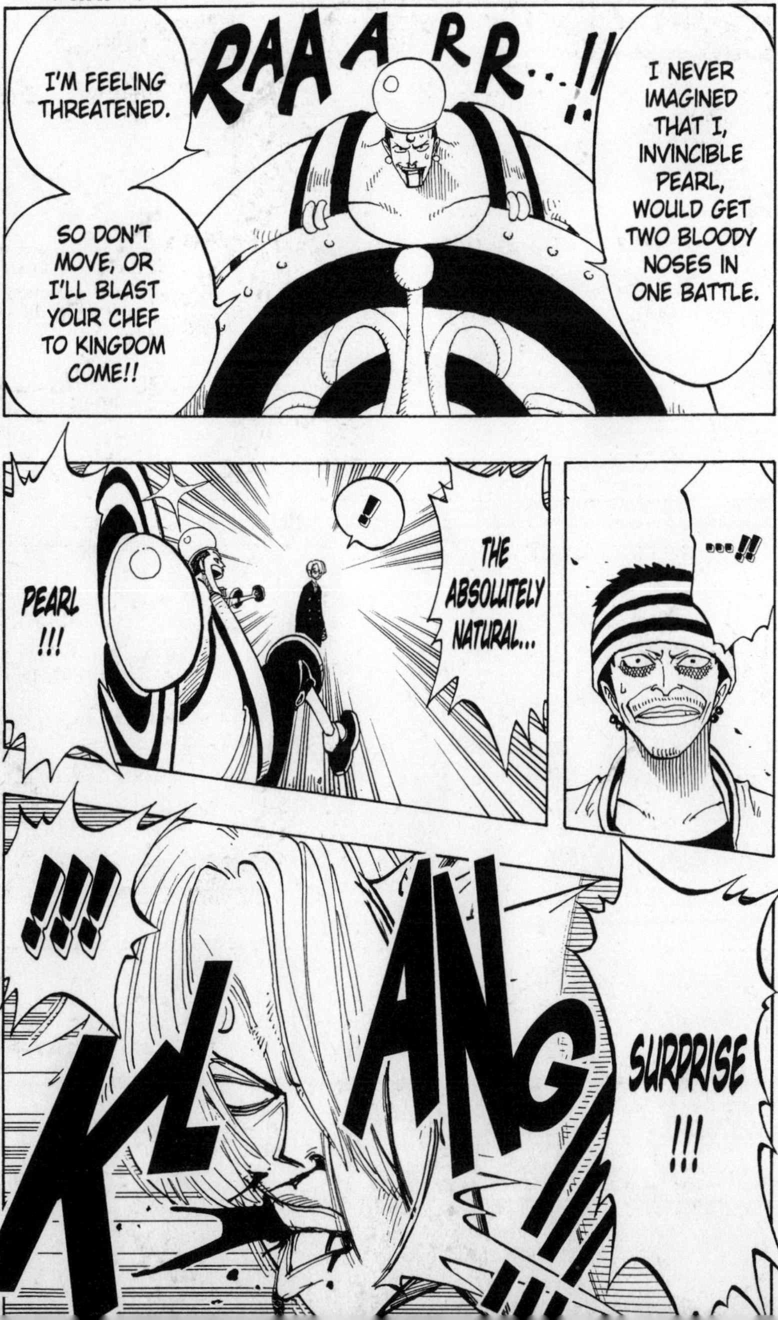

I NEVER IMAGINED THAT I, INVINCIBLE PEARL, WOULD GET TWO BLOODY NOSES IN ONE BATTLE.
RAAARR...!!
I'M FEELING THREATENED.
SO DON'T MOVE, OR I'LL BLAST YOUR CHEF TO KINGDOM COME!!
...!!
THE ABSOLUTELY NATURAL...
!
PEARL !!!
SURPRISE !!!
KLANG
!!!

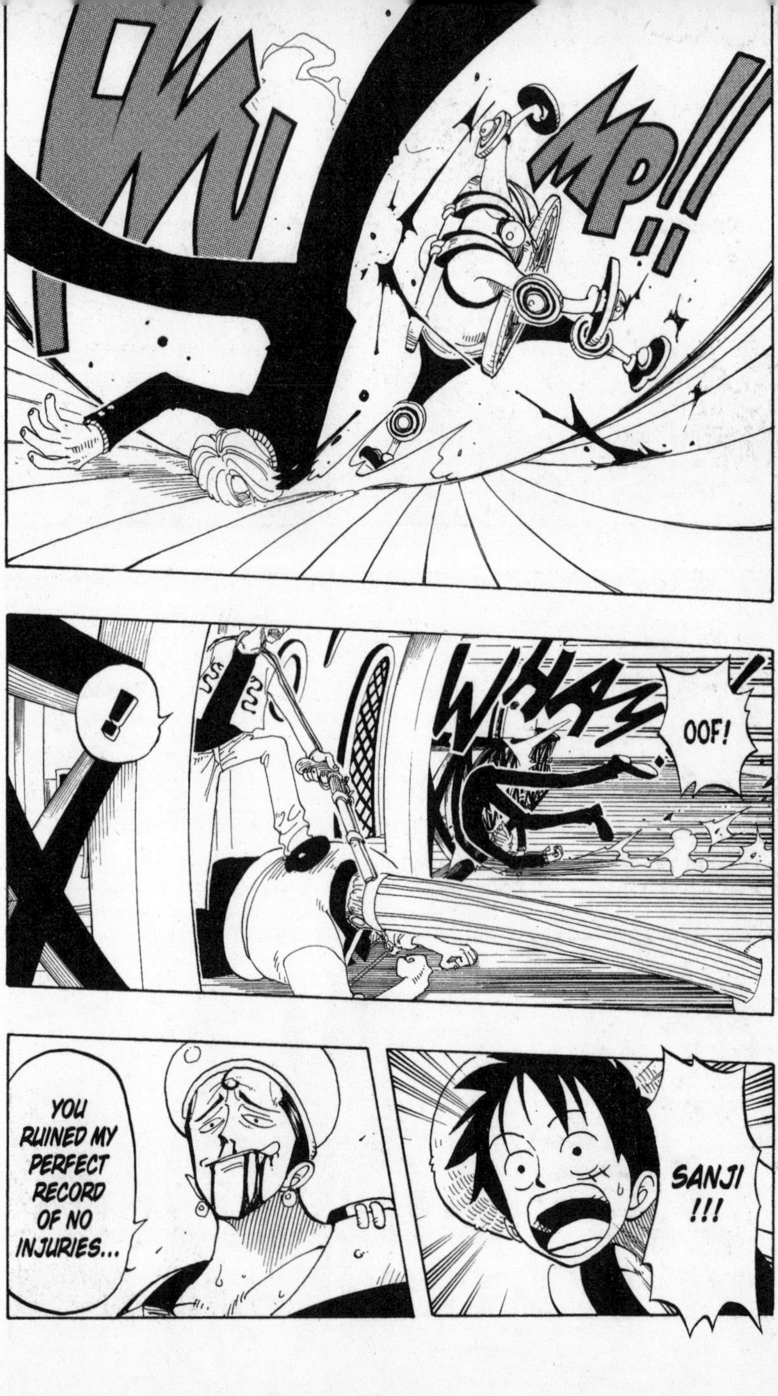
WHUMP!!
OOF!
WHAM
!
SANJI!!!
YOU RUINED MY PERFECT RECORD OF NO INJURIES...

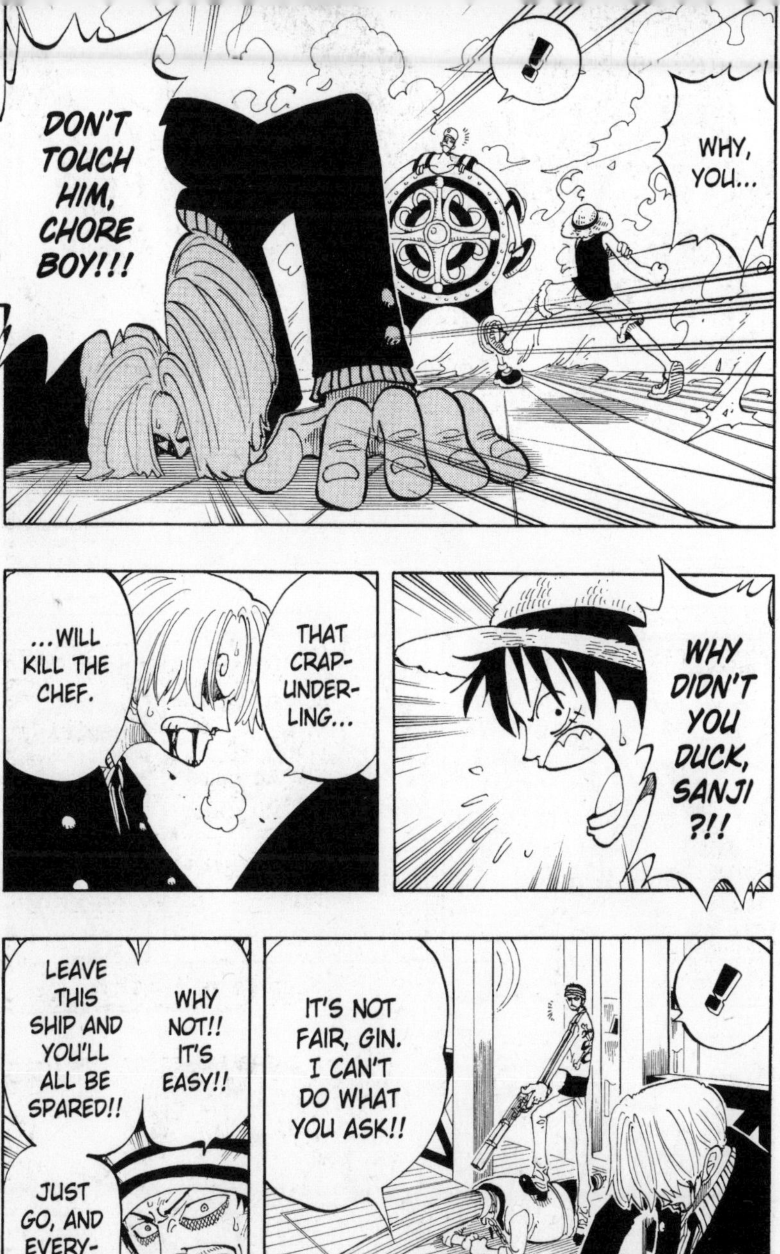
WHY, YOU...
!
DON'T TOUCH HIM, CHORE BOY!!!
WHY DIDN'T YOU DUCK, SANJI ?!!
THAT CRAP-UNDERLING...
...WILL KILL THE CHEF.
!
IT'S NOT FAIR, GIN. I CAN'T DO WHAT YOU ASK!!
WHY NOT!! IT'S EASY!!
LEAVE THIS SHIP AND YOU'LL ALL BE SPARED!!
JUST GO, AND EVERYBODY...

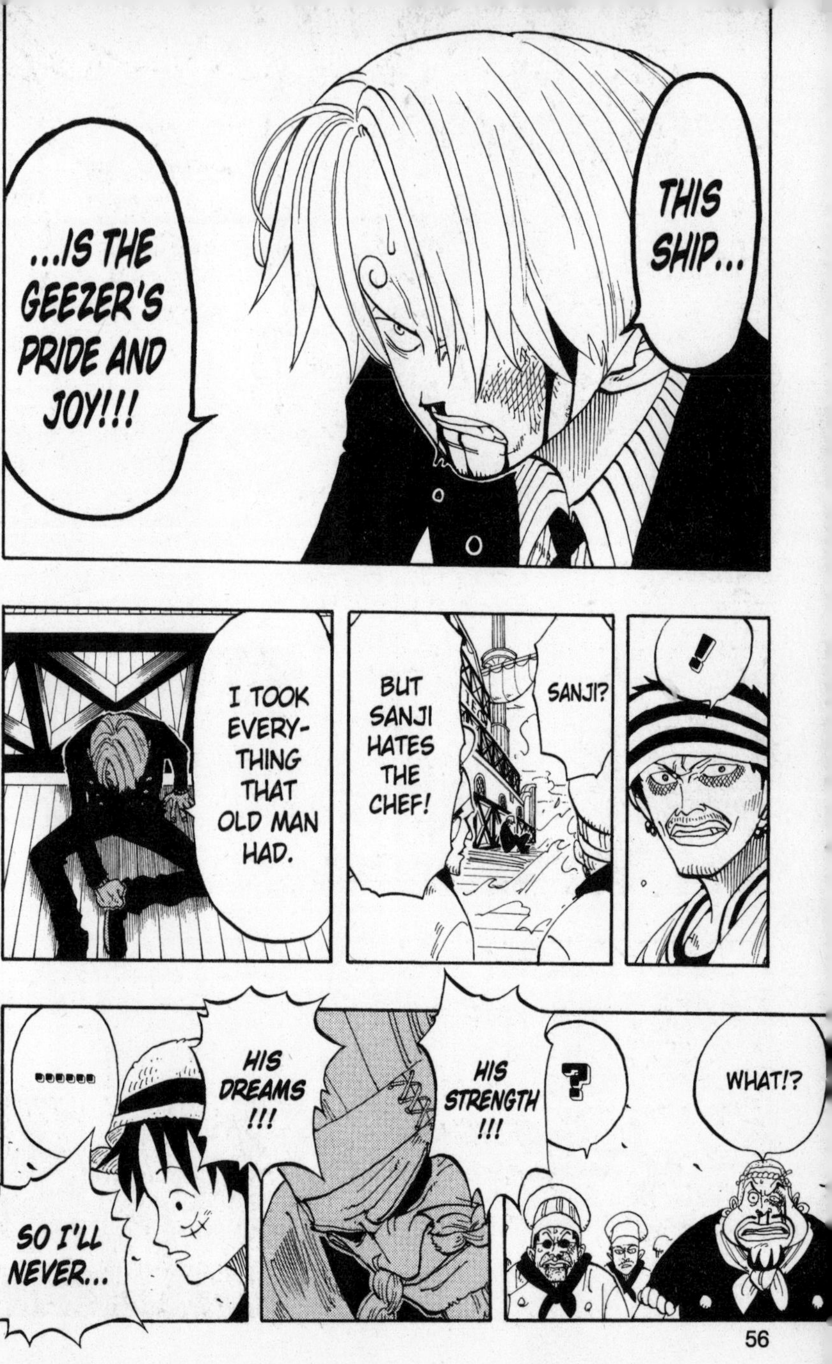
THIS SHIP...
...IS THE GEEZER'S PRIDE AND JOY!!!
!
SANJI?
BUT SANJI HATES THE CHEF!
I TOOK EVERY-THING THAT OLD MAN HAD.
WHAT!?
?
HIS STRENGTH!!!
HIS DREAMS!!!
......
SO I'LL NEVER...

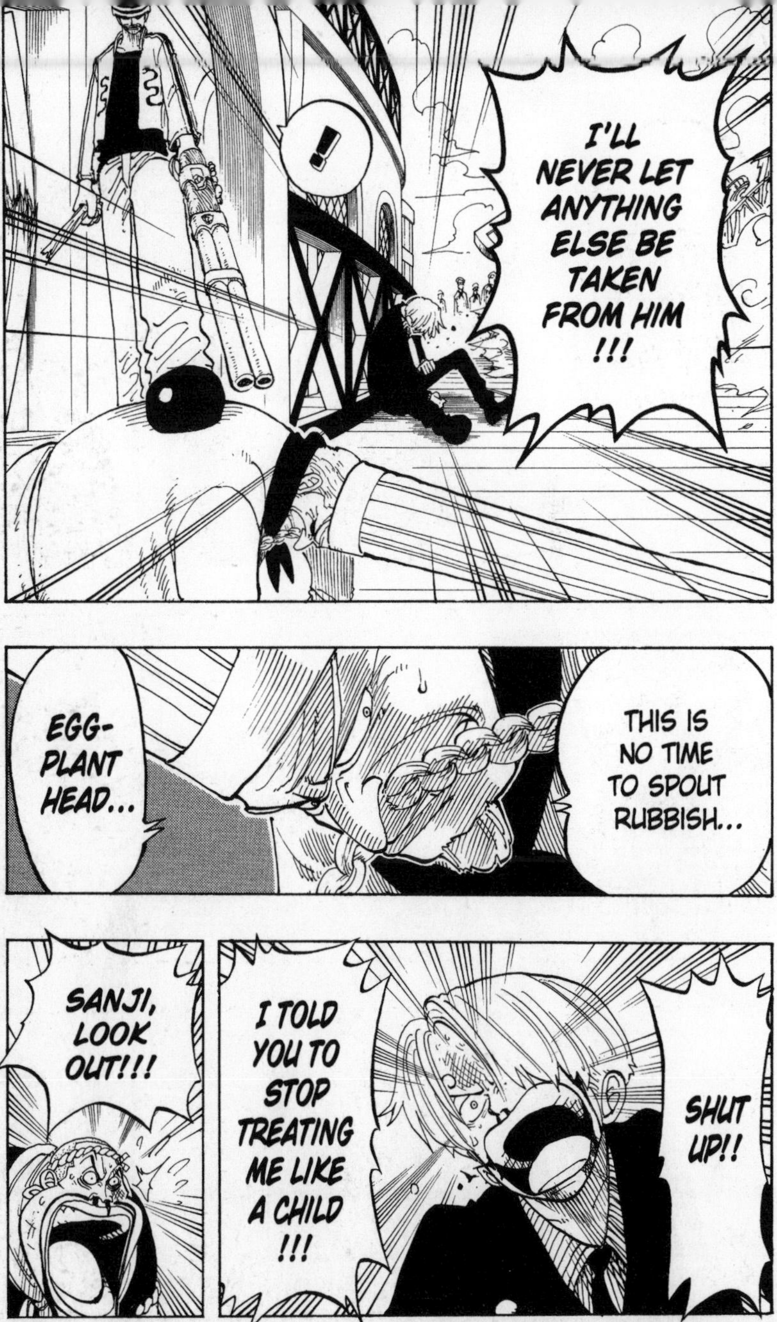
I'LL NEVER LET ANYTHING ELSE BE TAKEN FROM HIM !!!
!
THIS IS NO TIME TO SPOUT RUBBISH...
EGG-PLANT HEAD...
SHUT UP!!
I TOLD YOU TO STOP TREATING ME LIKE A CHILD !!!
SANJI, LOOK OUT!!!

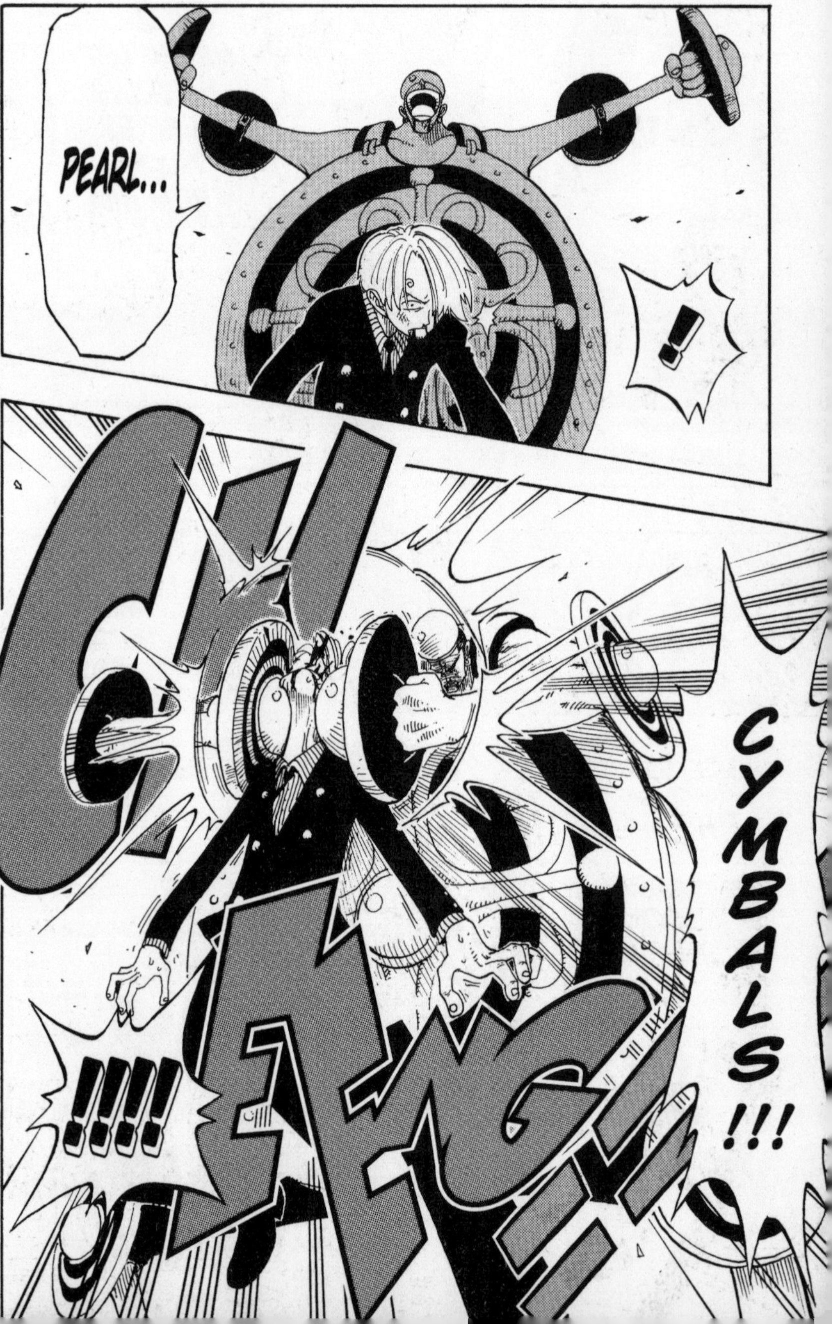
!
PEARL...
CYMBALS !!!
!!!!

READ THIS WAY

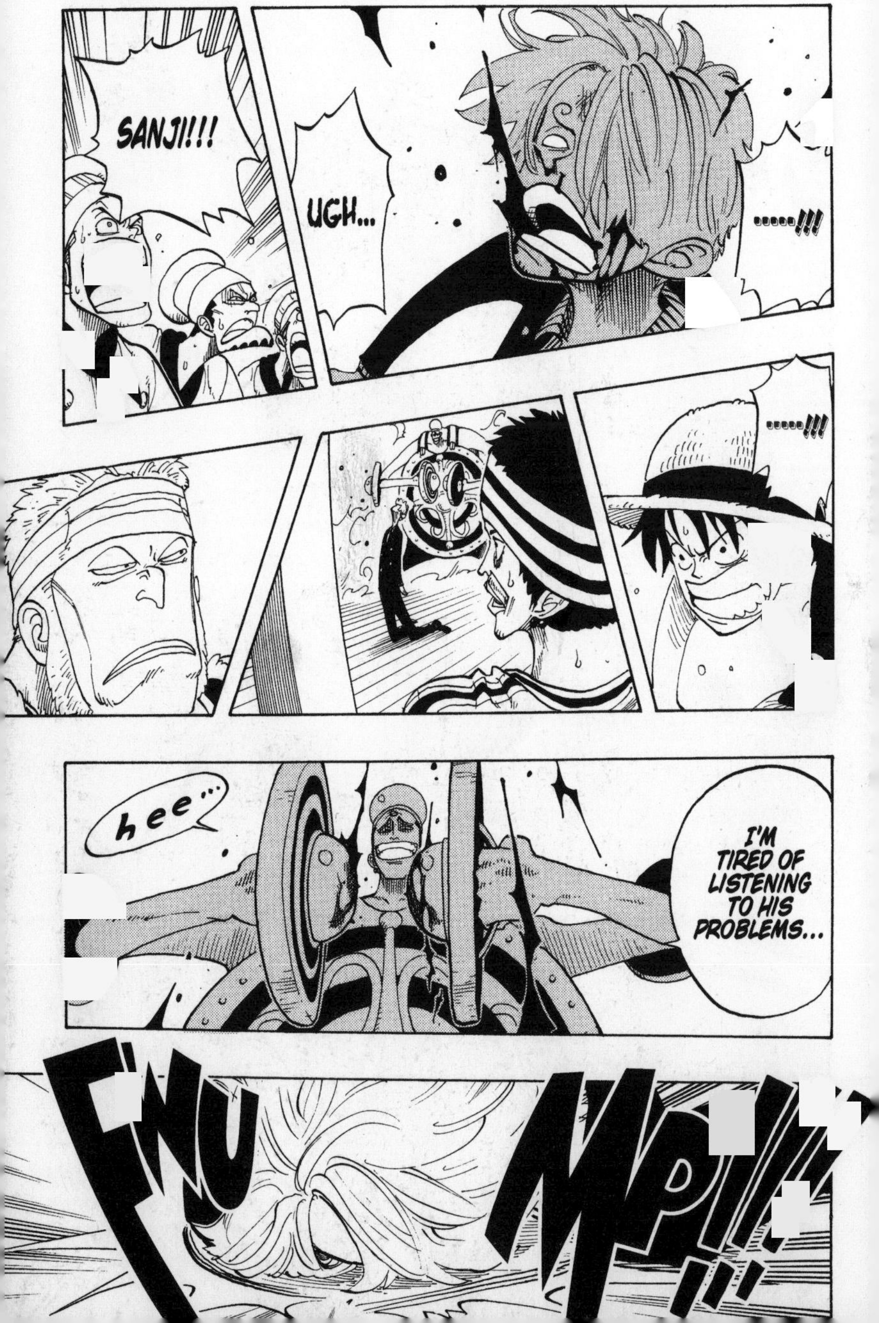
......!!!
UGH...
SANJI!!!
......!!!
I'M TIRED OF LISTENING TO HIS PROBLEMS...
hee...
FWUMP!!!

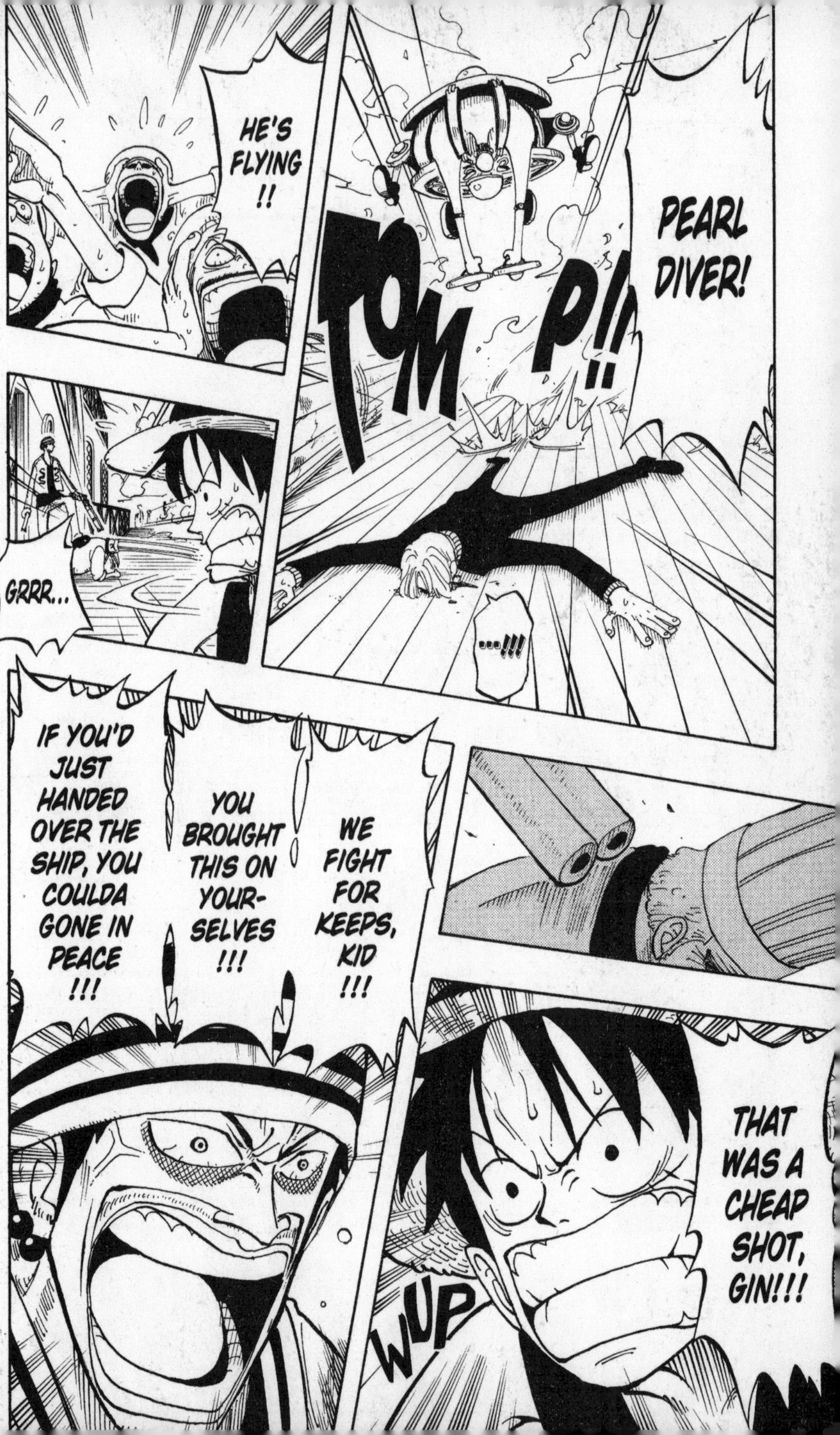
PEARL DIVER!
TOMP!!
...!!!
HE'S FLYING !!
GRRR...
THAT WAS A CHEAP SHOT, GIN!!!
WUP
WE FIGHT FOR KEEPS, KID !!!
YOU BROUGHT THIS ON YOURSELVES !!!
IF YOU'D JUST HANDED OVER THE SHIP, YOU COULDA GONE IN PEACE !!!

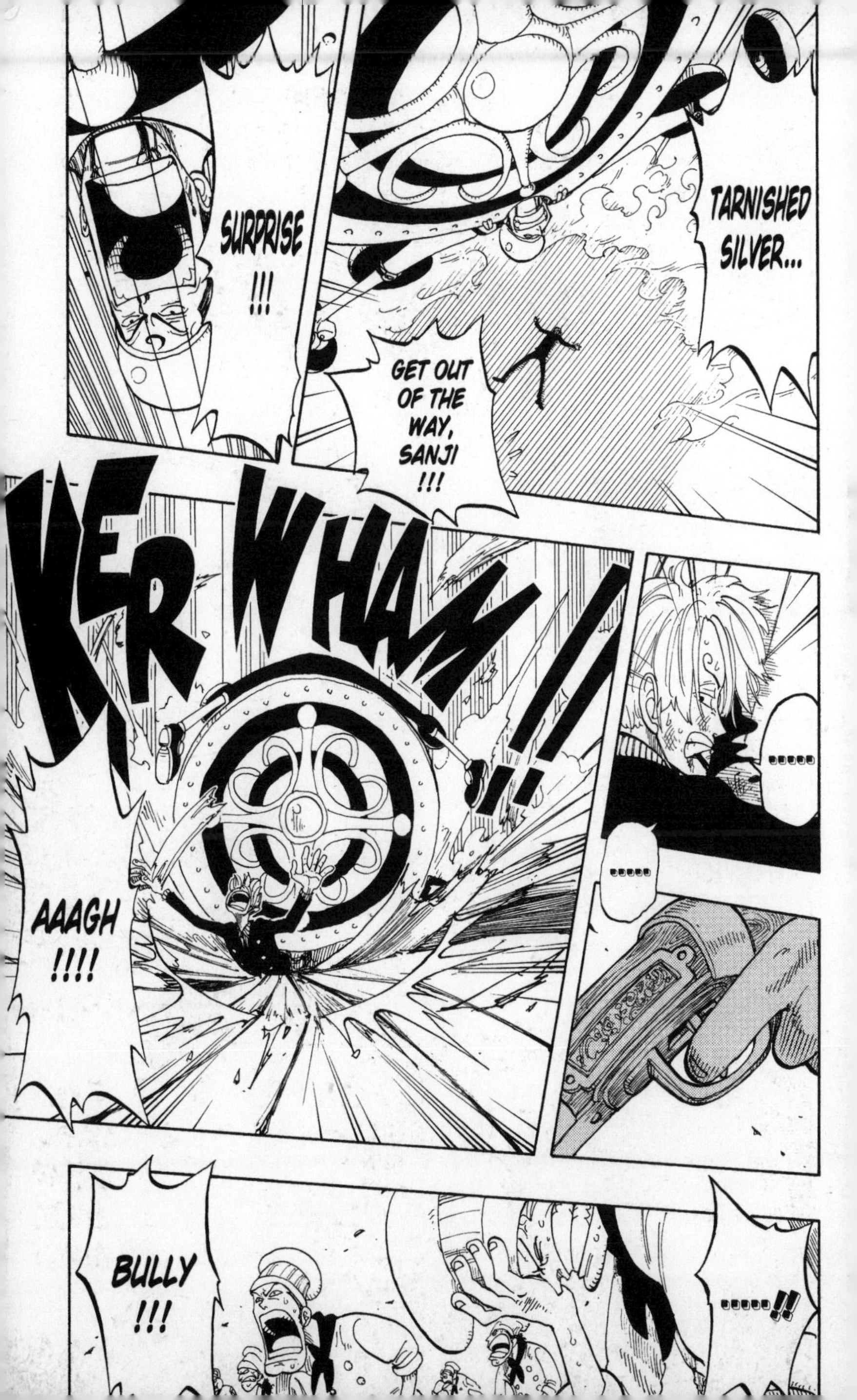
TARNISHED SILVER...
SURPRISE !!!
GET OUT OF THE WAY, SANJI !!!
KER WHAM!!
.....
.....
AAAGH !!!!
.....!!
BULLY !!!

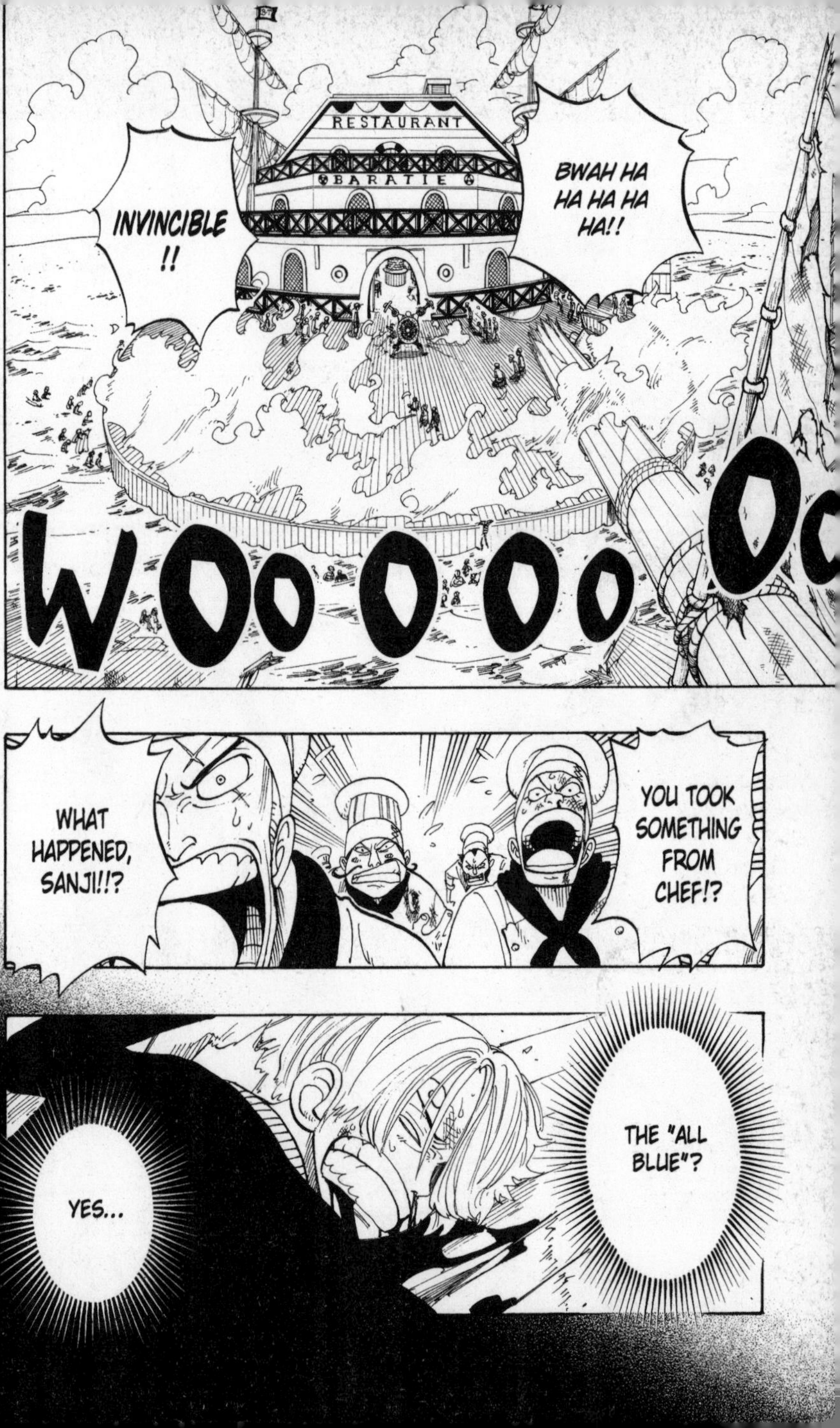
RESTAURANT
BARATIE
BWAH HA HA HA HA HA!!
INVINCIBLE !!
WOOOOOOO
YOU TOOK SOMETHING FROM CHEF!?
WHAT HAPPENED, SANJI!!?
THE "ALL BLUE"?
YES...

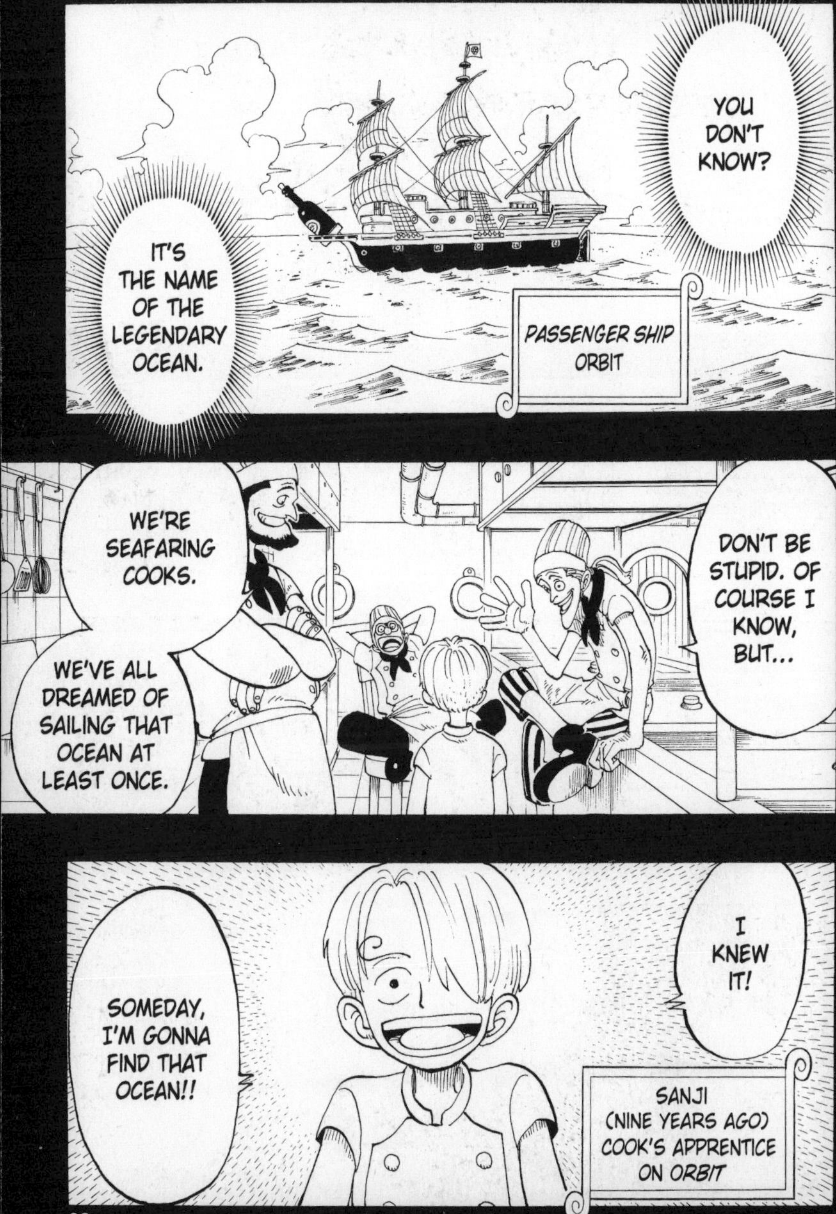
YOU DON'T KNOW?
PASSENGER SHIP ORBIT
IT'S THE NAME OF THE LEGENDARY OCEAN.
DON'T BE STUPID. OF COURSE I KNOW, BUT...
WE'RE SEAFARING COOKS.
WE'VE ALL DREAMED OF SAILING THAT OCEAN AT LEAST ONCE.
I KNEW IT!
SANJI (NINE YEARS AGO) COOK'S APPRENTICE ON ORBIT
SOMEDAY, I'M GONNA FIND THAT OCEAN!!

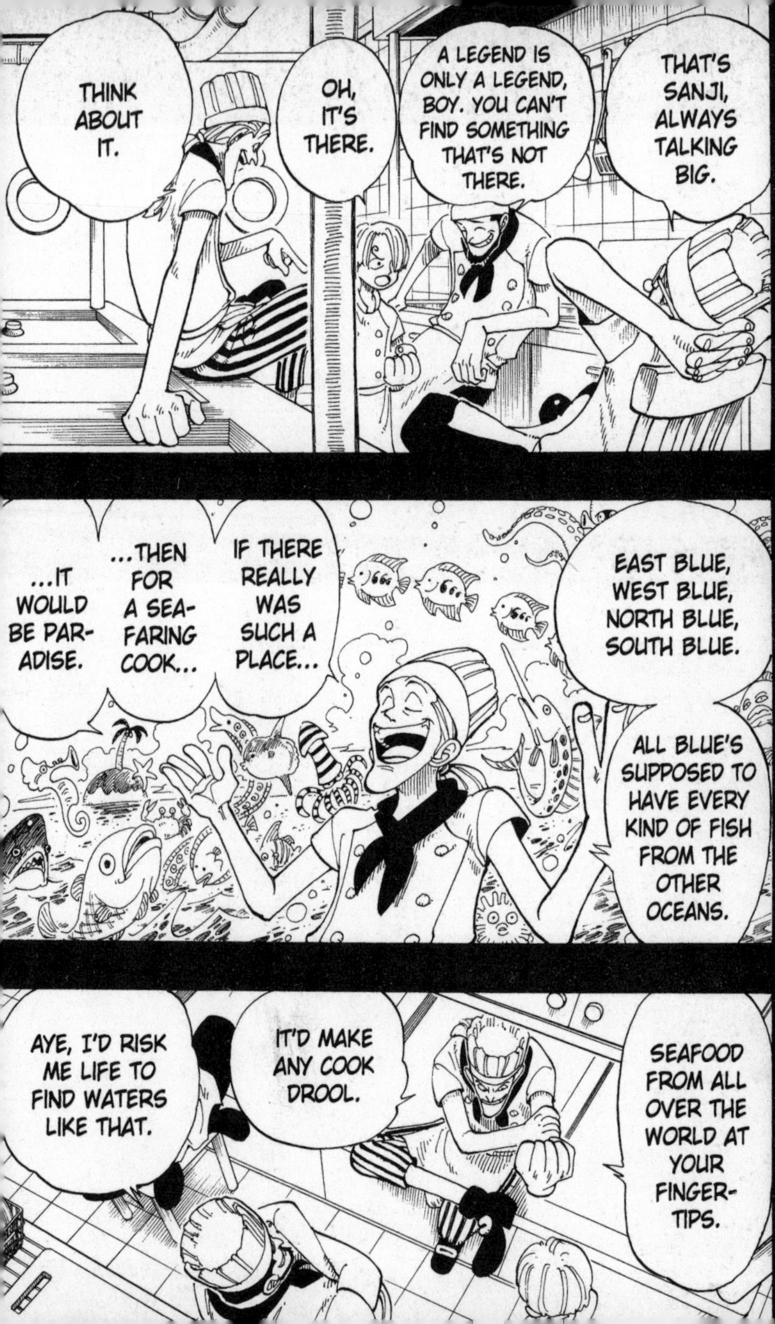
THAT'S SANJI, ALWAYS TALKING BIG.
A LEGEND IS ONLY A LEGEND, BOY. YOU CAN'T FIND SOMETHING THAT'S NOT THERE.
OH, IT'S THERE.
THINK ABOUT IT.
EAST BLUE, WEST BLUE, NORTH BLUE, SOUTH BLUE.
ALL BLUE'S SUPPOSED TO HAVE EVERY KIND OF FISH FROM THE OTHER OCEANS.
IF THERE REALLY WAS SUCH A PLACE...
...THEN FOR A SEA-FARING COOK...
...IT WOULD BE PAR-ADISE.
SEAFOOD FROM ALL OVER THE WORLD AT YOUR FINGER-TIPS.
IT'D MAKE ANY COOK DROOL.
AYE, I'D RISK ME LIFE TO FIND WATERS LIKE THAT.

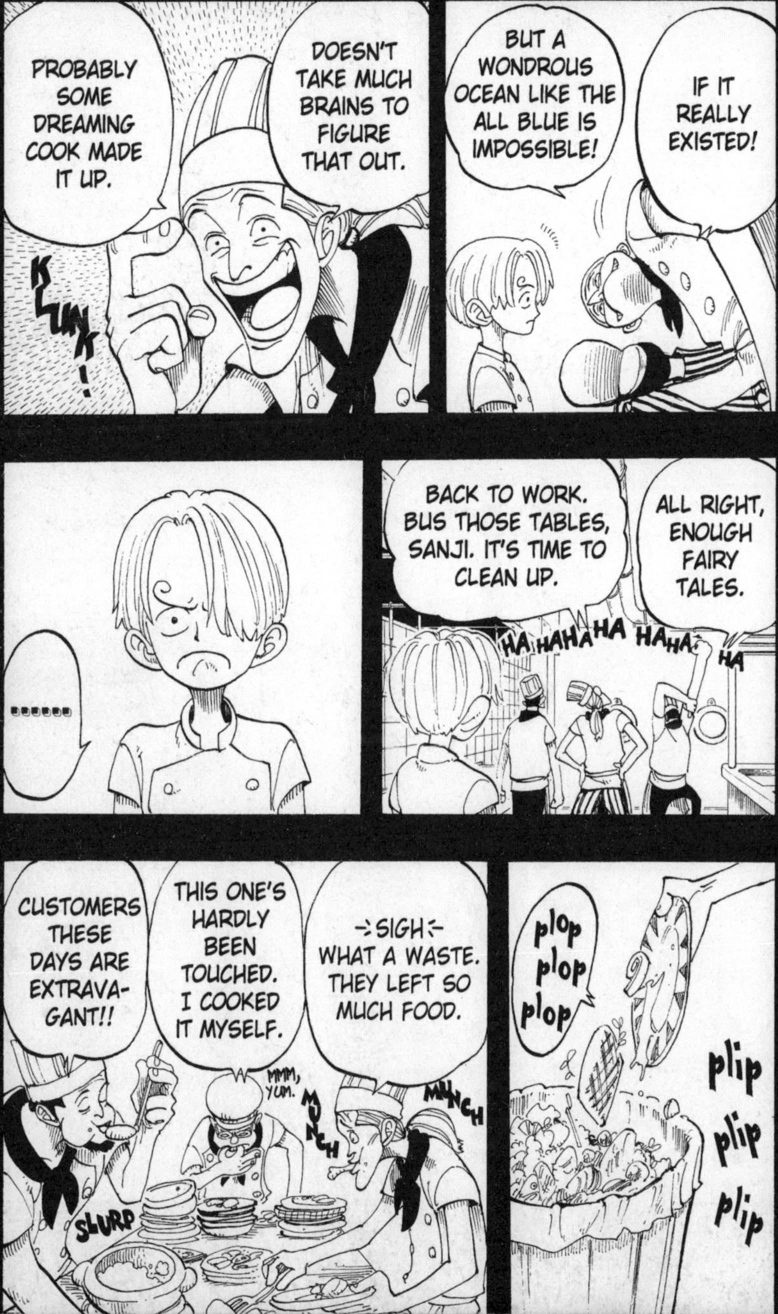
IF IT REALLY EXISTED!
BUT A WONDROUS OCEAN LIKE THE ALL BLUE IS IMPOSSIBLE!
DOESN'T TAKE MUCH BRAINS TO FIGURE THAT OUT.
PROBABLY SOME DREAMING COOK MADE IT UP.
KLUNK!!
ALL RIGHT, ENOUGH FAIRY TALES.
BACK TO WORK. BUS THOSE TABLES, SANJI. IT'S TIME TO CLEAN UP.
HA HAHAHA HA HAHA HA
......
plop plop plop
plip plip plip
SIGH WHAT A WASTE. THEY LEFT SO MUCH FOOD.
MUNCH
THIS ONE'S HARDLY BEEN TOUCHED. I COOKED IT MYSELF.
MMM, YUM.
MUNCH
CUSTOMERS THESE DAYS ARE EXTRAVA-GANT!!
SLURP

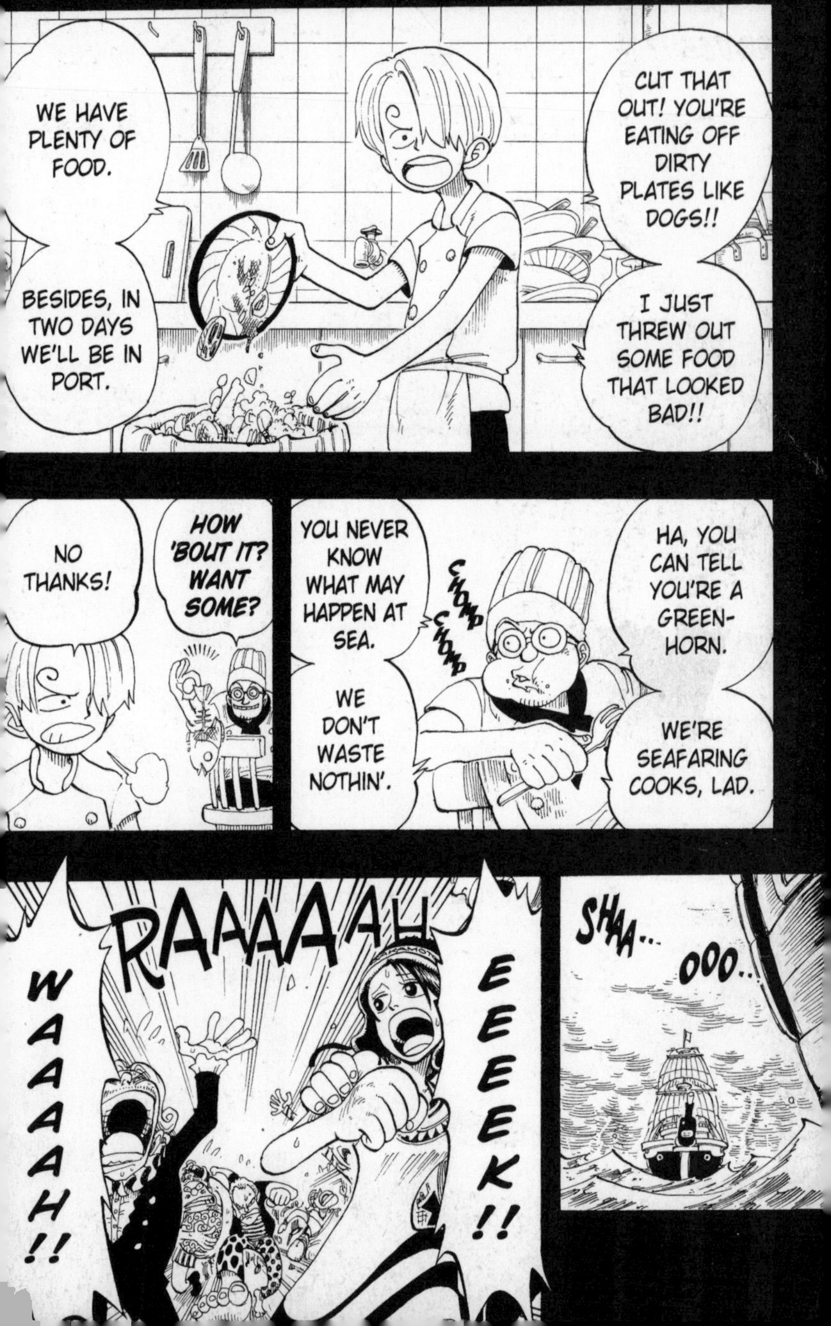
CUT THAT OUT! YOU'RE EATING OFF DIRTY PLATES LIKE DOGS!!
I JUST THREW OUT SOME FOOD THAT LOOKED BAD!!
WE HAVE PLENTY OF FOOD.
BESIDES, IN TWO DAYS WE'LL BE IN PORT.
HA, YOU CAN TELL YOU'RE A GREEN-HORN.
WE'RE SEAFARING COOKS, LAD.
CHOMP CHOMP
YOU NEVER KNOW WHAT MAY HAPPEN AT SEA.
WE DON'T WASTE NOTHIN'.
HOW 'BOUT IT? WANT SOME?
NO THANKS!
SHAA... OOO...
RAAAAAH
EEEEEK!!
WAAAAAH!!

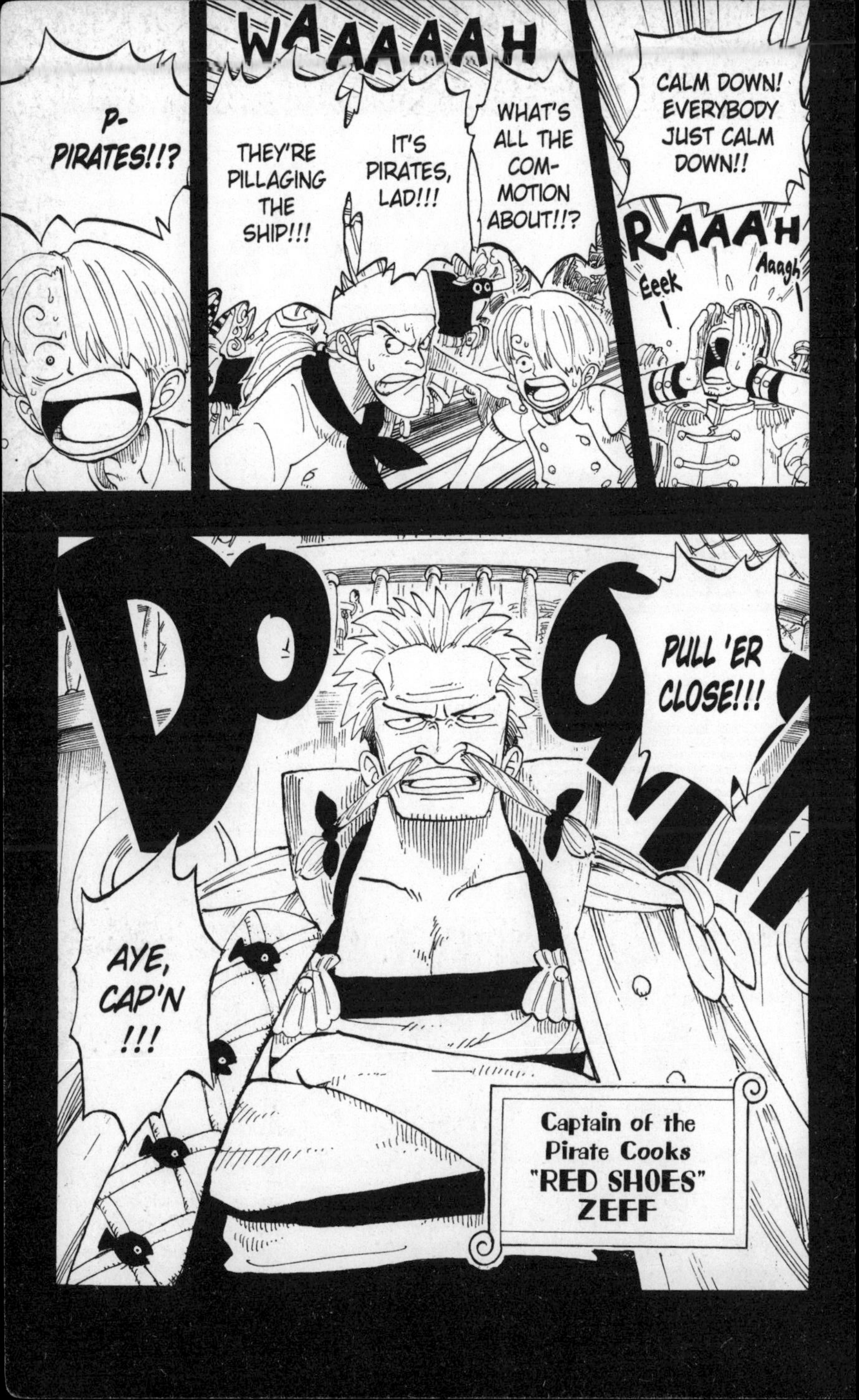
CALM DOWN! EVERYBODY JUST CALM DOWN!!
RAAAH
Aaagh
Eeek
WAAAAAH
WHAT'S ALL THE COM-MOTION ABOUT!!?
IT'S PIRATES, LAD!!!
THEY'RE PILLAGING THE SHIP!!!
P-PIRATES!!?
PULL 'ER CLOSE!!!
AYE, CAP'N!!!
Captain of the Pirate Cooks "RED SHOES" ZEFF

☆ THIS IS "THE MYSTERY OF **ULTIMATE MUSCLE 77**."
I DREW IT FOR THE SHUEISHA **JUMP COMICS** SELECTION
NEW SUPERHERO CONTEST.

ENTRY NUMBER 12
PANDA MAN

Conceived by

Eiichiro Oda Sensei

Panda Man, who somehow looks cool despite having a panda face, is the new superhero from Oda Sensei, whose popular ONE PIECE also runs in *Shonen Jump* magazine.

D A T A
Name: Panda Man
Origin: Tibet
Age: He doesn't know
Height: 6 ft. 6 in.
Weight: 270 lbs.
Superhero strength: After eating bamboo, 3,300,000 power. Before meals, 3,300,000 power.
Mortal blow techniques: S.P.D.-- Bamboo Leaves Panda Drop, Giant Panda Deathlock.

EXPLANATION: ABANDONED IN A BAMBOO THICKET AS AN INFANT, PANDA MAN WAS RAISED BY GIANT PANDAS. HE IS A DEMON SUPERHERO WHO RESOLVED TO BECOME STRONG BECAUSE WHEN HE TOLD PEOPLE HE HAD SEEN KAGUYAHIME, THEY DIDN'T BELIEVE HIM AND PICKED ON HIM. (KAGUYAHIME WAS A PRINCESS WHO WAS FOUND AS A BABY INSIDE A BAMBOO STUMP.)

Chapter 57:
IF YOU HAVE A DREAM

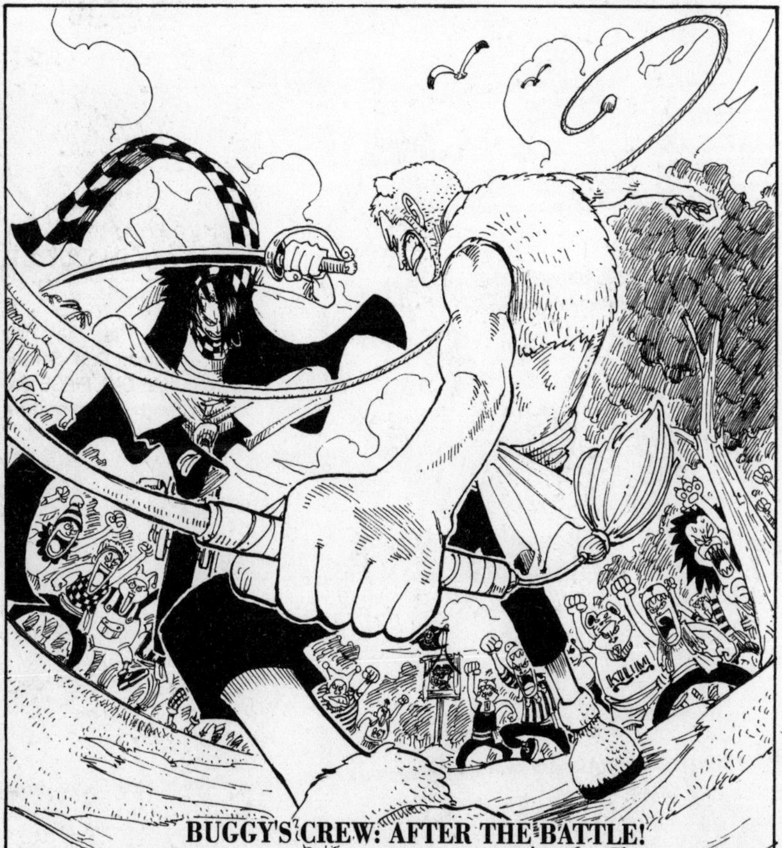
BUGGY'S CREW: AFTER THE BATTLE!
PART 16: "DUEL TO DECIDE THE NEXT CAPTAIN"

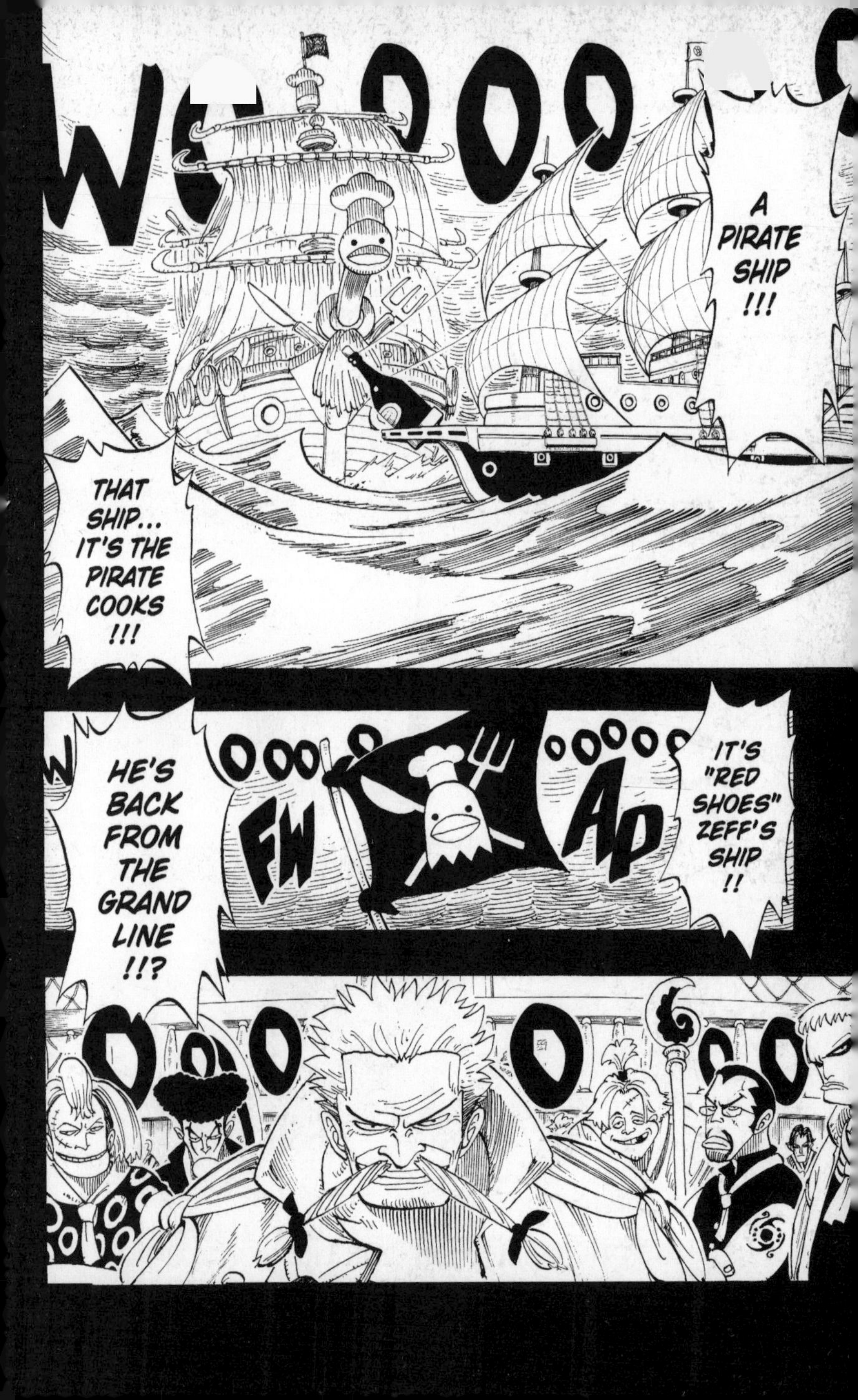
A PIRATE SHIP !!!
THAT SHIP... IT'S THE PIRATE COOKS !!!
IT'S "RED SHOES" ZEFF'S SHIP !!
FWAP
HE'S BACK FROM THE GRAND LINE !!?

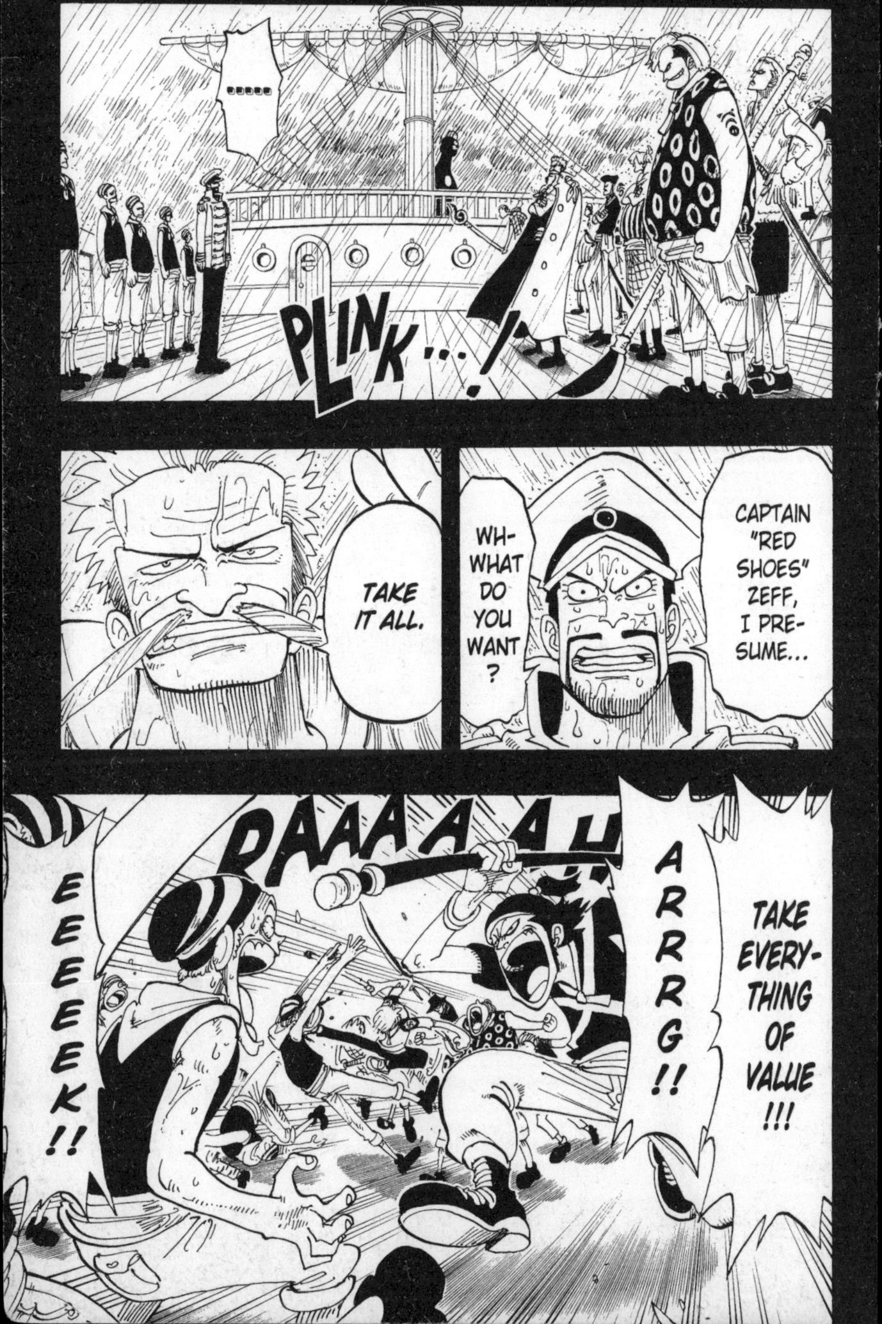
PLINK...!
CAPTAIN "RED SHOES" ZEFF, I PRESUME...
WH-WHAT DO YOU WANT?
TAKE IT ALL.
TAKE EVERY-THING OF VALUE!!!
ARRRG!!
DAAAAAH
EEEEEEK!!

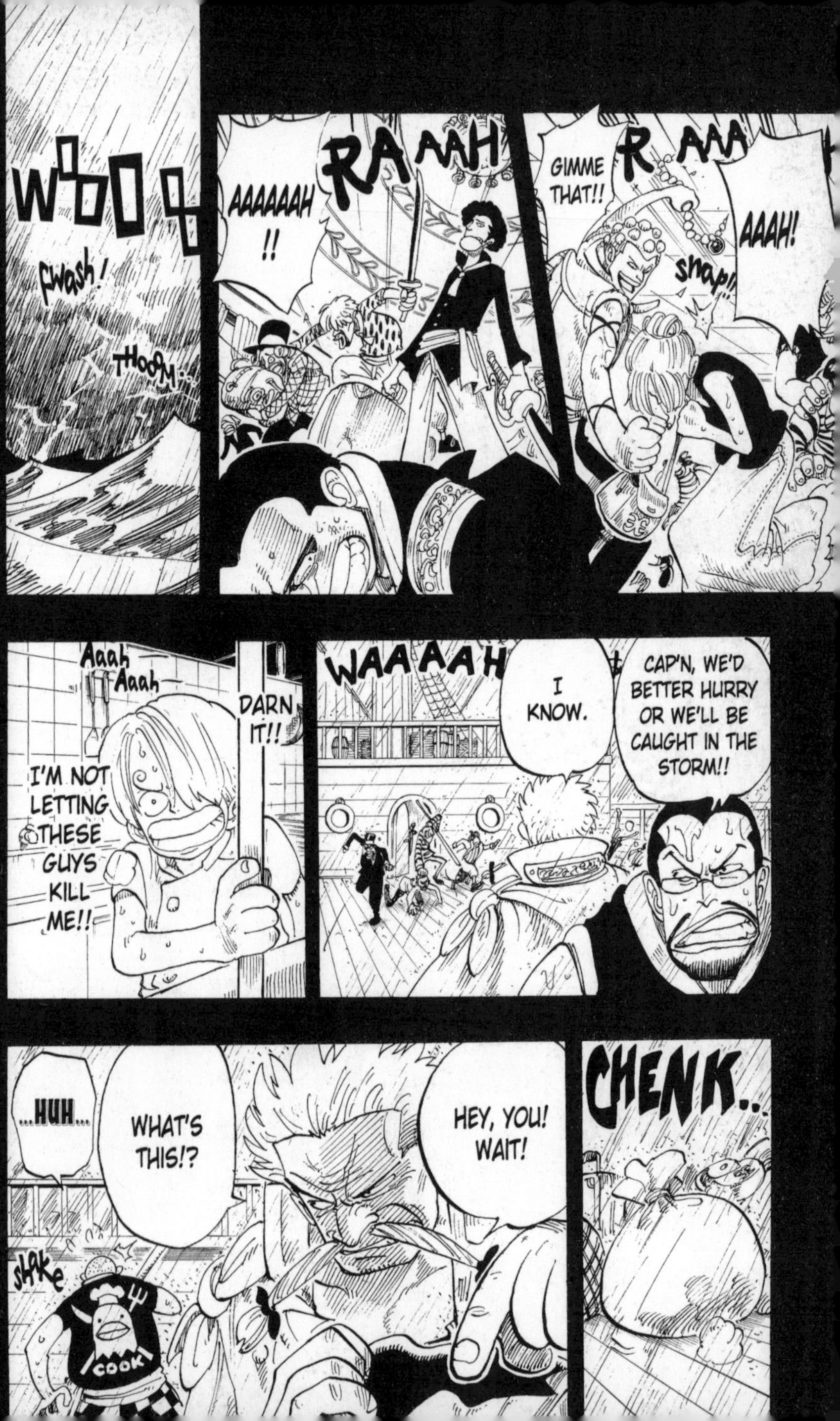
R AAA
GIMME THAT!!
AAAH!
snap!!
RA AAH
AAAAAAH !!
WOOOO
fwash!
THOOM...
CAP'N, WE'D BETTER HURRY OR WE'LL BE CAUGHT IN THE STORM!!
I KNOW.
WAAAAH
Aaah Aaah
DARN IT!!
I'M NOT LETTING THESE GUYS KILL ME!!
CHENK..
HEY, YOU! WAIT!
WHAT'S THIS!?
...HUH...
shake
COOK

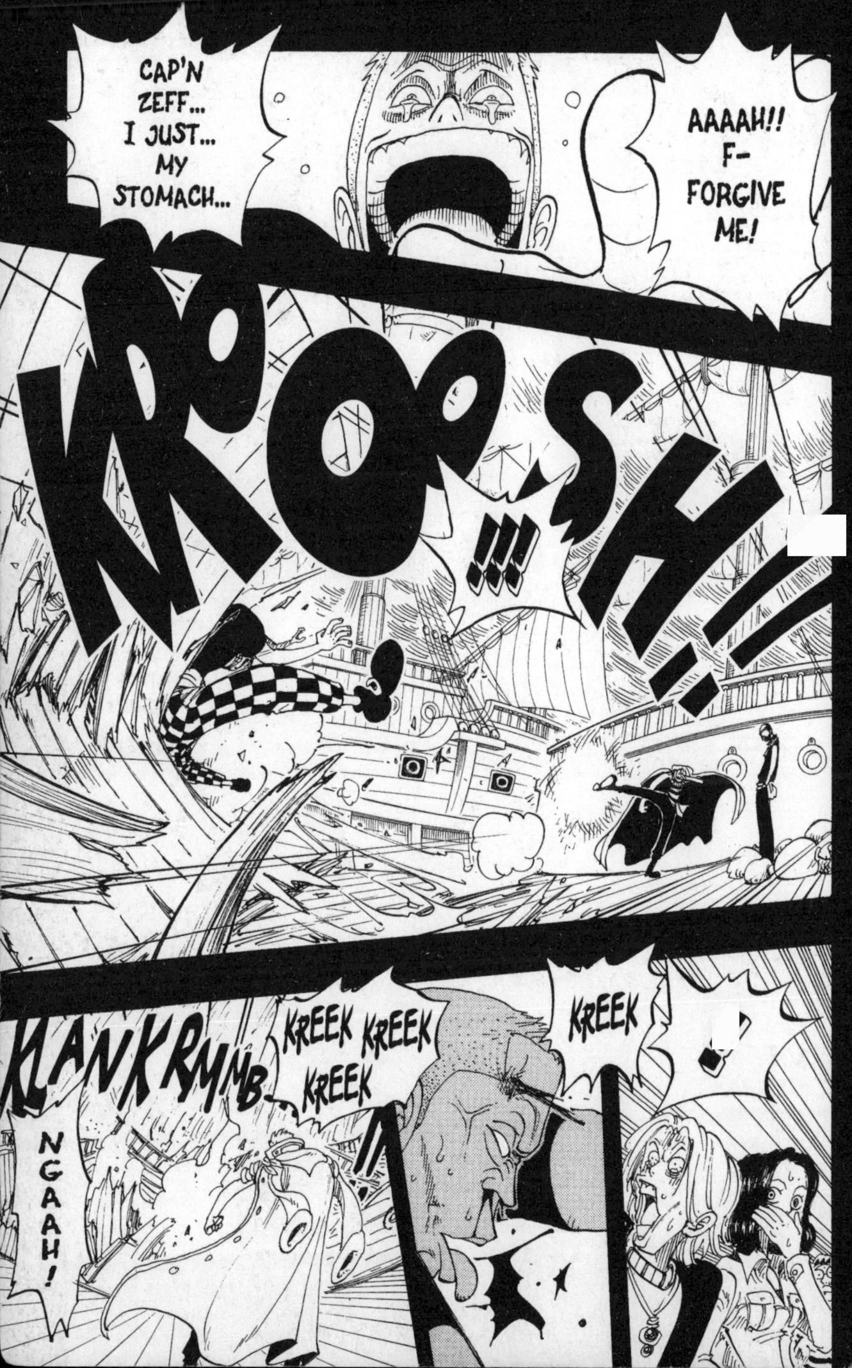

AAAAH!! F-FORGIVE ME!
CAP'N ZEFF... I JUST... MY STOMACH...
KROOSH!!!
KREEK
KREEK KREEK KREEK
KLANKRYMB
NGAAH!

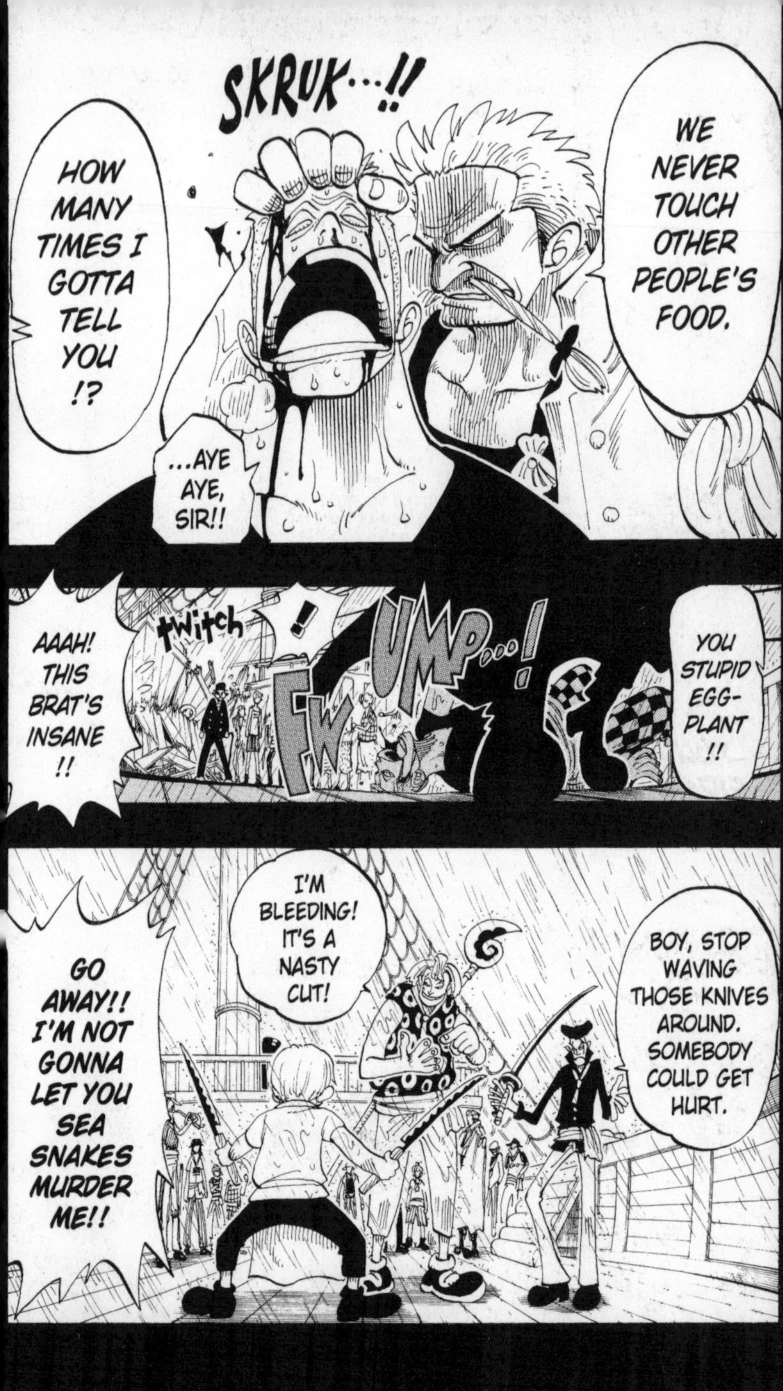
SKRUK...!!
WE NEVER TOUCH OTHER PEOPLE'S FOOD.
HOW MANY TIMES I GOTTA TELL YOU !?
...AYE AYE, SIR!!
YOU STUPID EGG-PLANT !!
FWUMP...!
twitch
AAAH! THIS BRAT'S INSANE !!
BOY, STOP WAVING THOSE KNIVES AROUND. SOMEBODY COULD GET HURT.
I'M BLEEDING! IT'S A NASTY CUT!
GO AWAY!! I'M NOT GONNA LET YOU SEA SNAKES MURDER ME!!

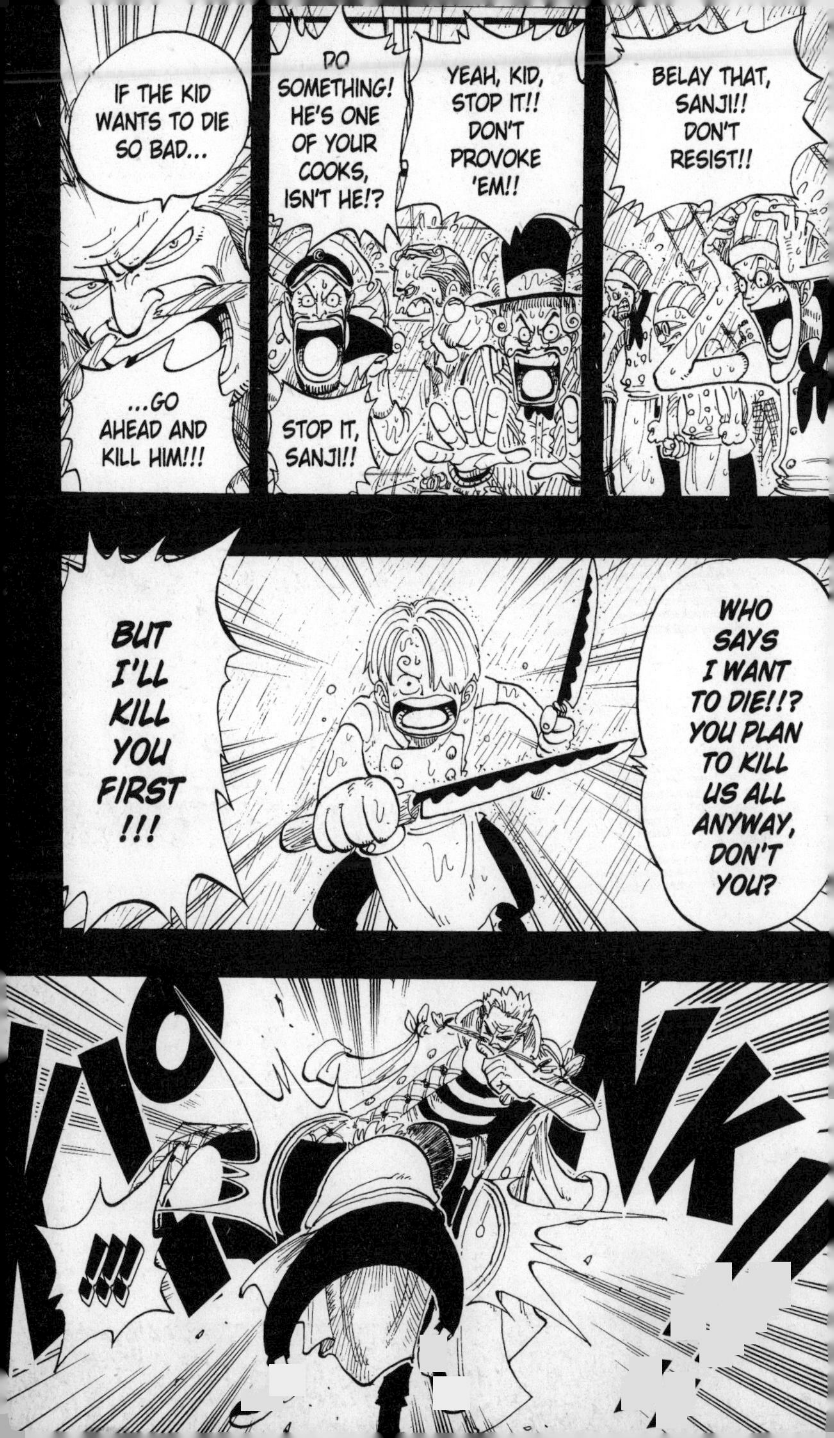
BELAY THAT, SANJI!! DON'T RESIST!!
YEAH, KID, STOP IT!! DON'T PROVOKE 'EM!!
DO SOMETHING! HE'S ONE OF YOUR COOKS, ISN'T HE!?
STOP IT, SANJI!!
IF THE KID WANTS TO DIE SO BAD...
...GO AHEAD AND KILL HIM!!!
WHO SAYS I WANT TO DIE!!? YOU PLAN TO KILL US ALL ANYWAY, DON'T YOU?
BUT I'LL KILL YOU FIRST!!!

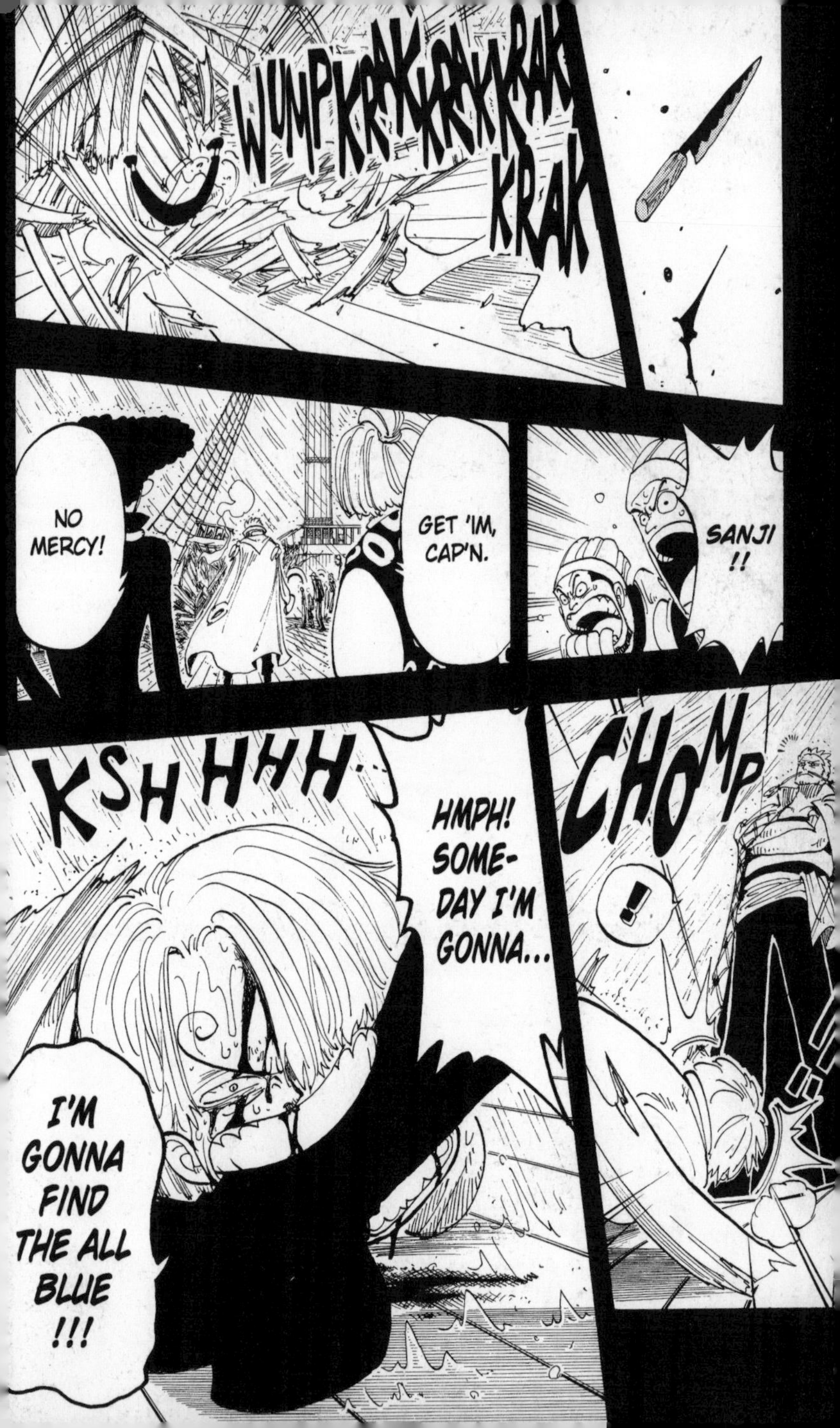
WUMP KRAK KRAK KRAK KRAK
KRAK
SANJI !!
GET 'IM, CAP'N.
NO MERCY!
CHOMP
!
KSHHHH...
HMPH! SOME-DAY I'M GONNA...
I'M GONNA FIND THE ALL BLUE !!!

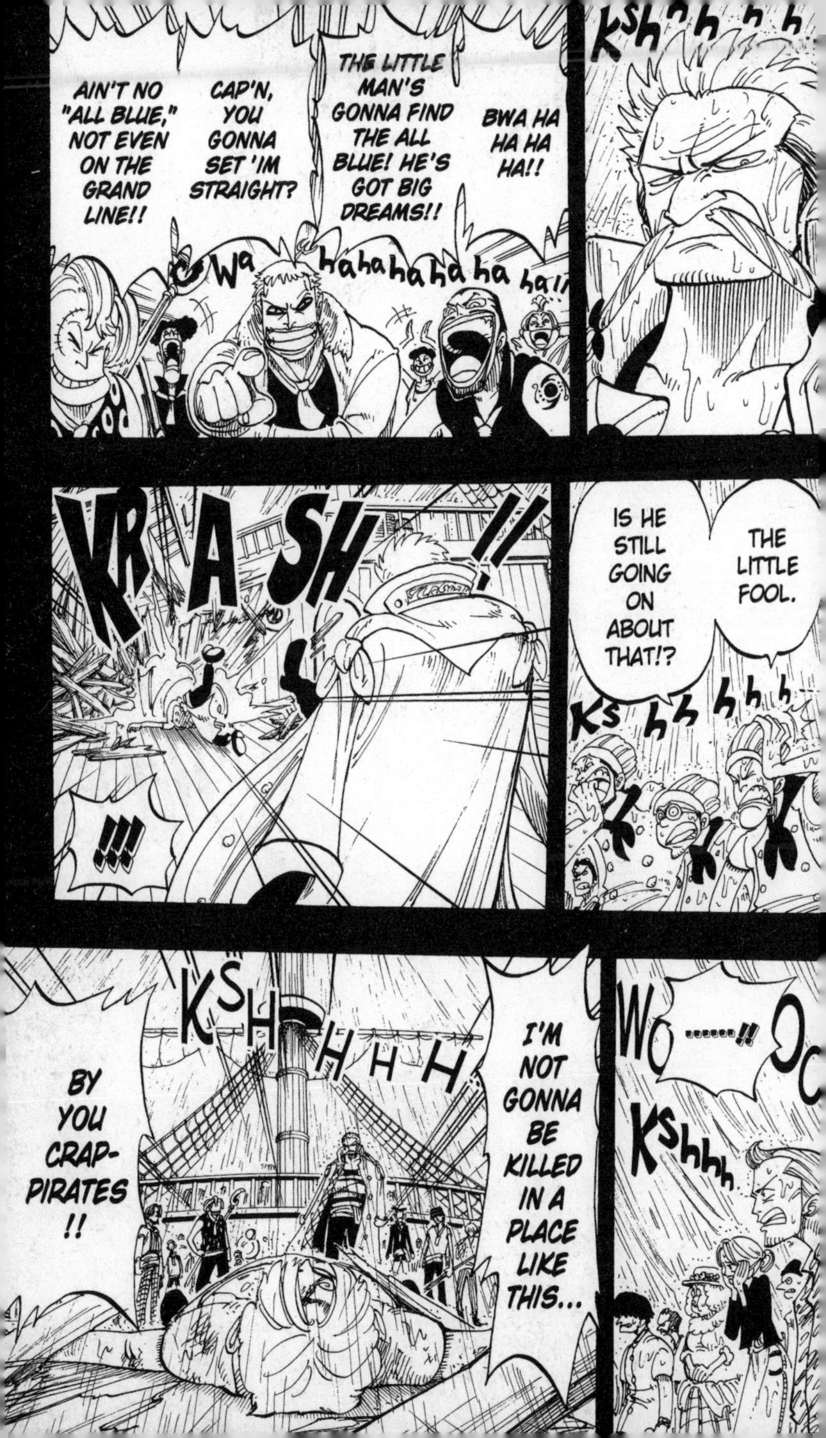
KShhhhh
BWA HA HA HA HA!!
THE LITTLE MAN'S GONNA FIND THE ALL BLUE! HE'S GOT BIG DREAMS!!
CAP'N, YOU GONNA SET 'IM STRAIGHT?
AIN'T NO "ALL BLUE," NOT EVEN ON THE GRAND LINE!!
Wa hahahahaha ha ha!!
THE LITTLE FOOL.
IS HE STILL GOING ON ABOUT THAT!?
Kshhhhh
KRASH!!
!!!!
WO......!!
Kshhhh
I'M NOT GONNA BE KILLED IN A PLACE LIKE THIS...
BY YOU CRAP-PIRATES!!
KSHHHH

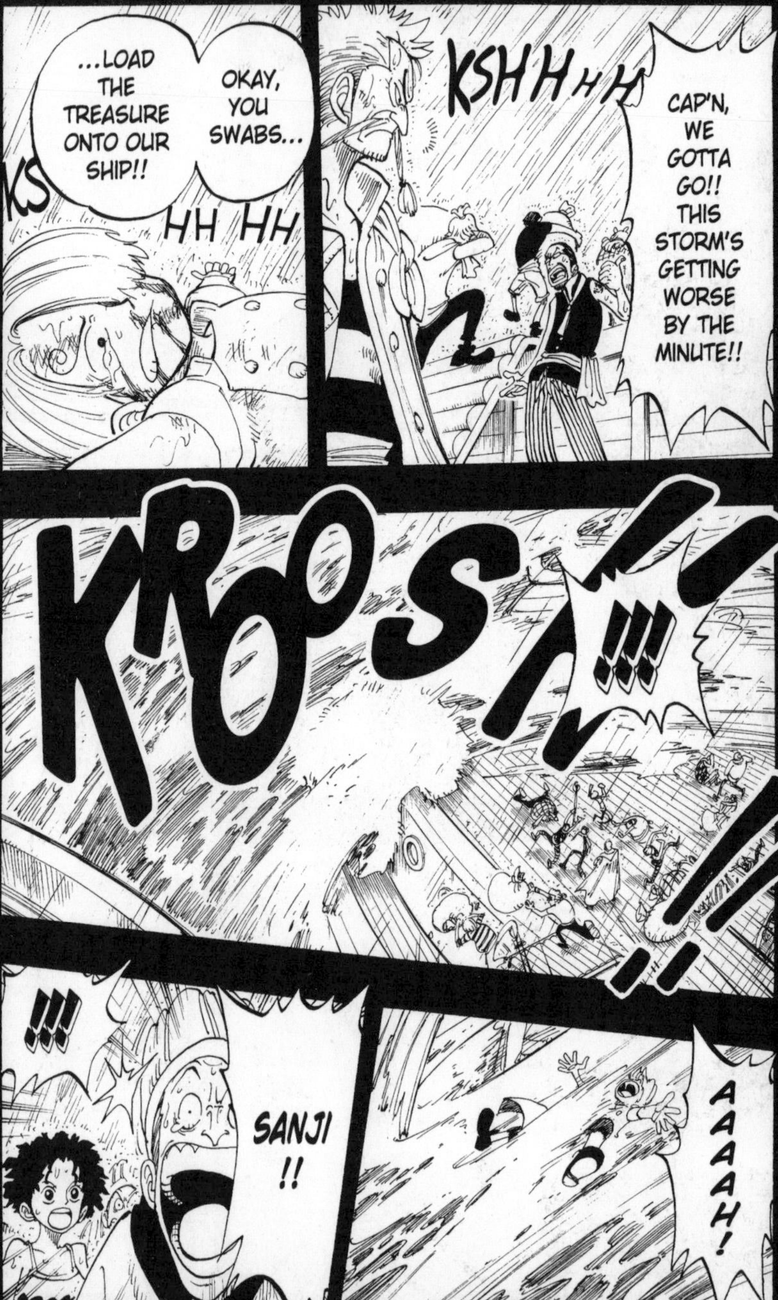
KSHHHHH
CAP'N, WE GOTTA GO!! THIS STORM'S GETTING WORSE BY THE MINUTE!!
KSHH HH HH
OKAY, YOU SWABS...
...LOAD THE TREASURE ONTO OUR SHIP!!
KROOSH!!!
AAAAAH!
!!!!
SANJI!!

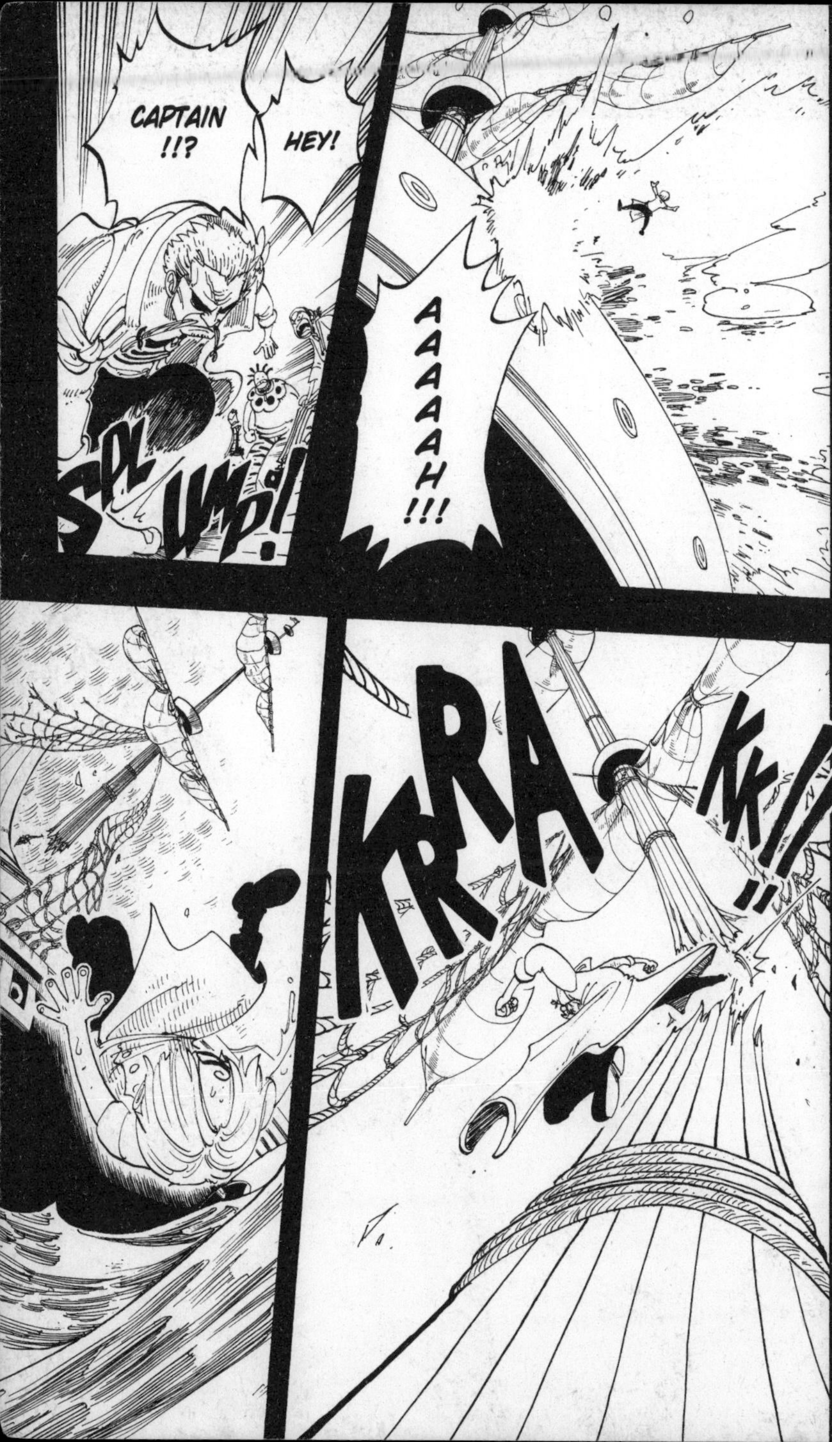
AAAAAAH!!!
HEY!
CAPTAIN !!?
SPLUMP!
KRRAKK!!

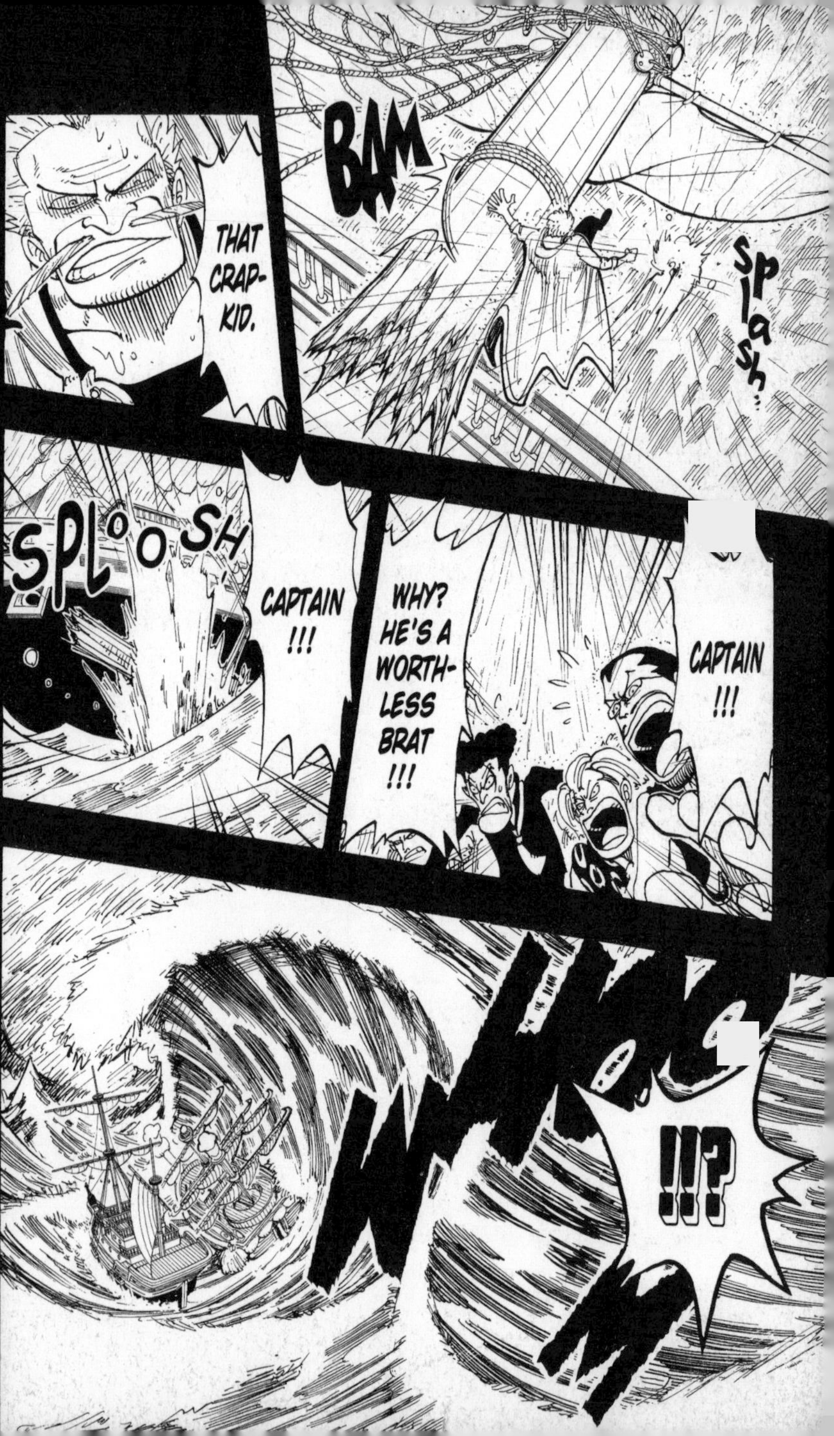
BAM
Splash..
THAT CRAP-KID.
CAPTAIN !!!
WHY? HE'S A WORTHLESS BRAT !!!
SPLOOSH
CAPTAIN !!!
!!?

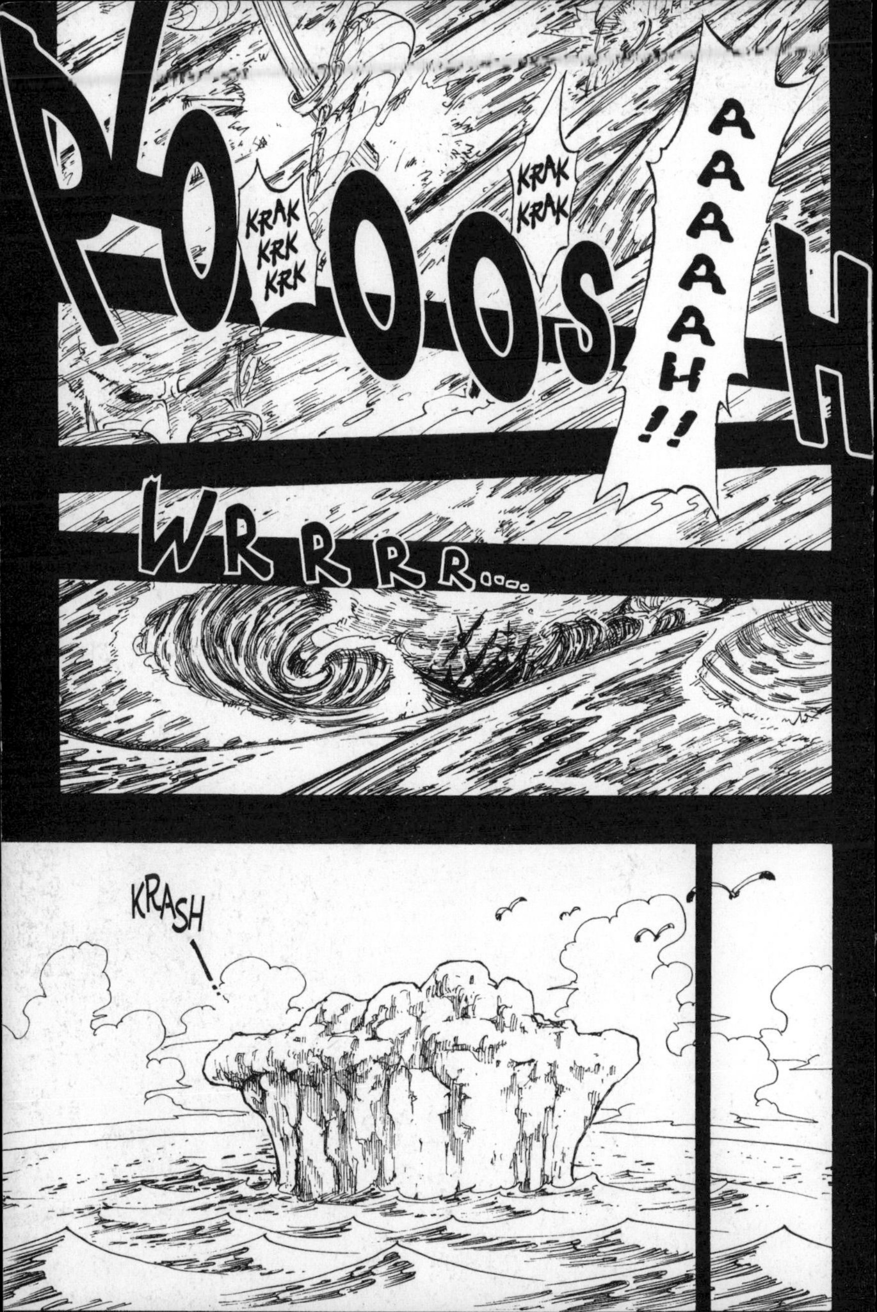
AAAAAAH!!
KRAK KRAK
ROOOSH
KRAK KRK KRK
WR R R R....
KRASH

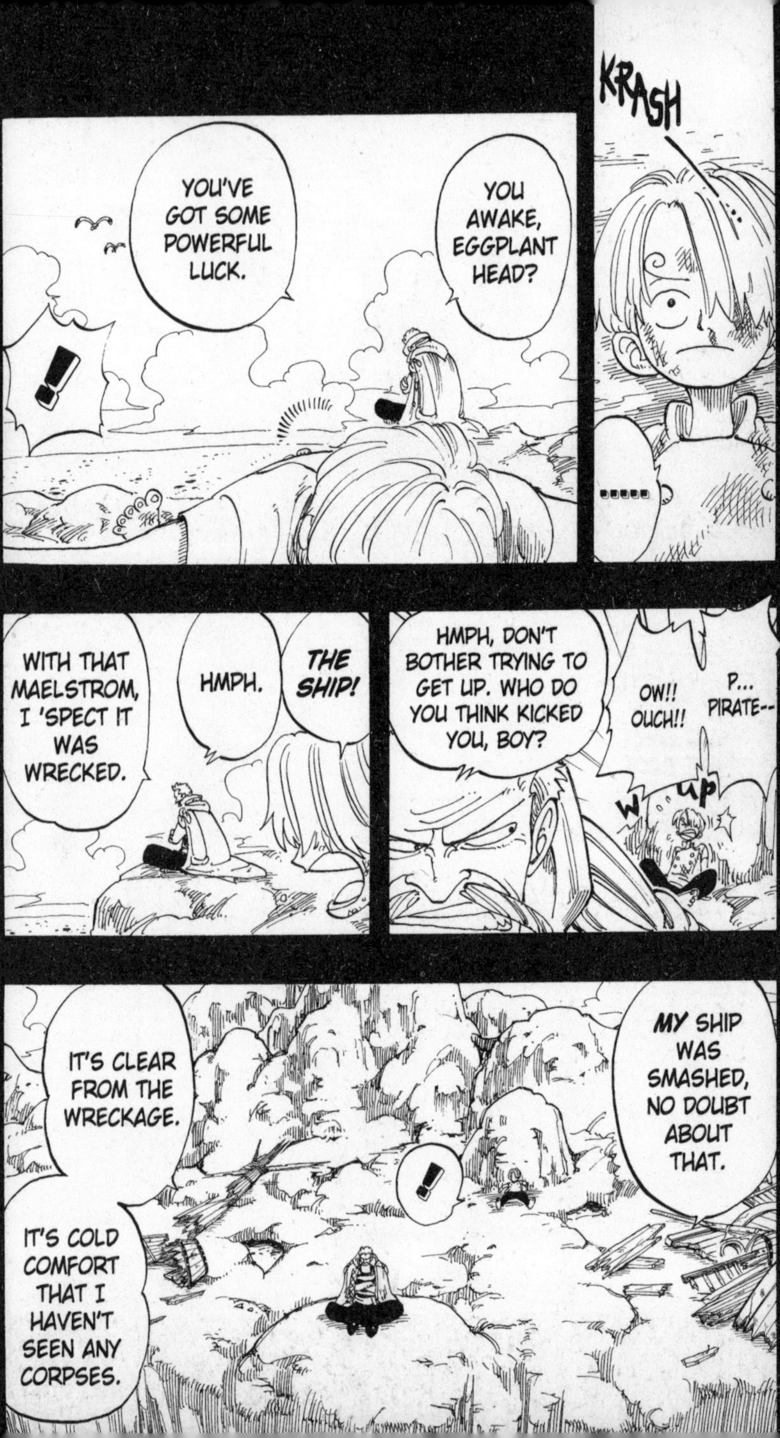
KRASH
.....
YOU AWAKE, EGGPLANT HEAD?
YOU'VE GOT SOME POWERFUL LUCK.
!
P... PIRATE--
OW!! OUCH!!
HMPH, DON'T BOTHER TRYING TO GET UP. WHO DO YOU THINK KICKED YOU, BOY?
WUP
THE SHIP!
HMPH.
WITH THAT MAELSTROM, I 'SPECT IT WAS WRECKED.
MY SHIP WAS SMASHED, NO DOUBT ABOUT THAT.
IT'S CLEAR FROM THE WRECKAGE.
!
IT'S COLD COMFORT THAT I HAVEN'T SEEN ANY CORPSES.

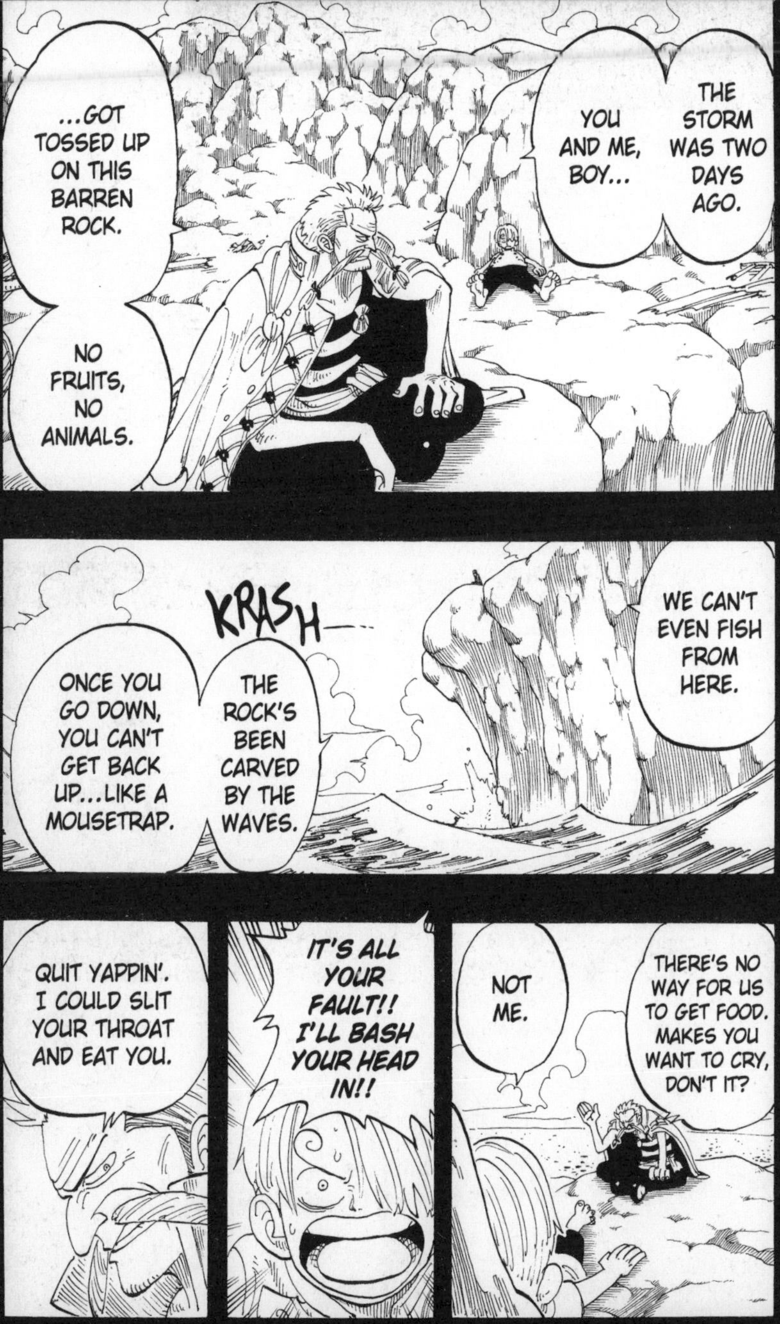
THE STORM WAS TWO DAYS AGO.
YOU AND ME, BOY...
...GOT TOSSED UP ON THIS BARREN ROCK.
NO FRUITS, NO ANIMALS.
WE CAN'T EVEN FISH FROM HERE.
KRASH
THE ROCK'S BEEN CARVED BY THE WAVES.
ONCE YOU GO DOWN, YOU CAN'T GET BACK UP...LIKE A MOUSETRAP.
THERE'S NO WAY FOR US TO GET FOOD. MAKES YOU WANT TO CRY, DON'T IT?
NOT ME.
IT'S ALL YOUR FAULT!! I'LL BASH YOUR HEAD IN!!
QUIT YAPPIN'. I COULD SLIT YOUR THROAT AND EAT YOU.

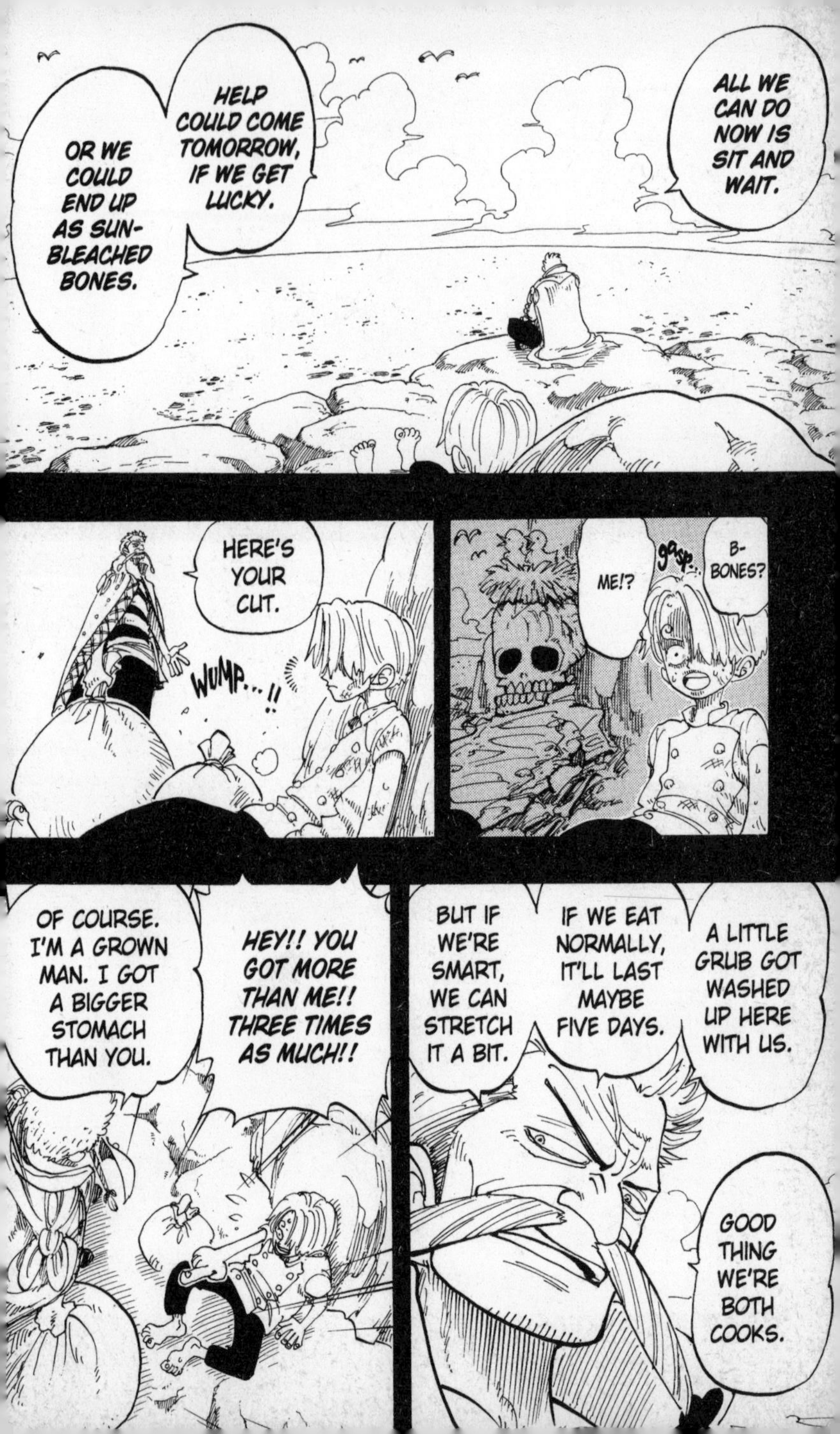
ALL WE CAN DO NOW IS SIT AND WAIT.
HELP COULD COME TOMORROW, IF WE GET LUCKY.
OR WE COULD END UP AS SUN-BLEACHED BONES.
B-BONES?
gasp...
ME!?
HERE'S YOUR CUT.
WUMP...!!
A LITTLE GRUB GOT WASHED UP HERE WITH US.
IF WE EAT NORMALLY, IT'LL LAST MAYBE FIVE DAYS.
BUT IF WE'RE SMART, WE CAN STRETCH IT A BIT.
GOOD THING WE'RE BOTH COOKS.
HEY!! YOU GOT MORE THAN ME!! THREE TIMES AS MUCH!!
OF COURSE. I'M A GROWN MAN. I GOT A BIGGER STOMACH THAN YOU.

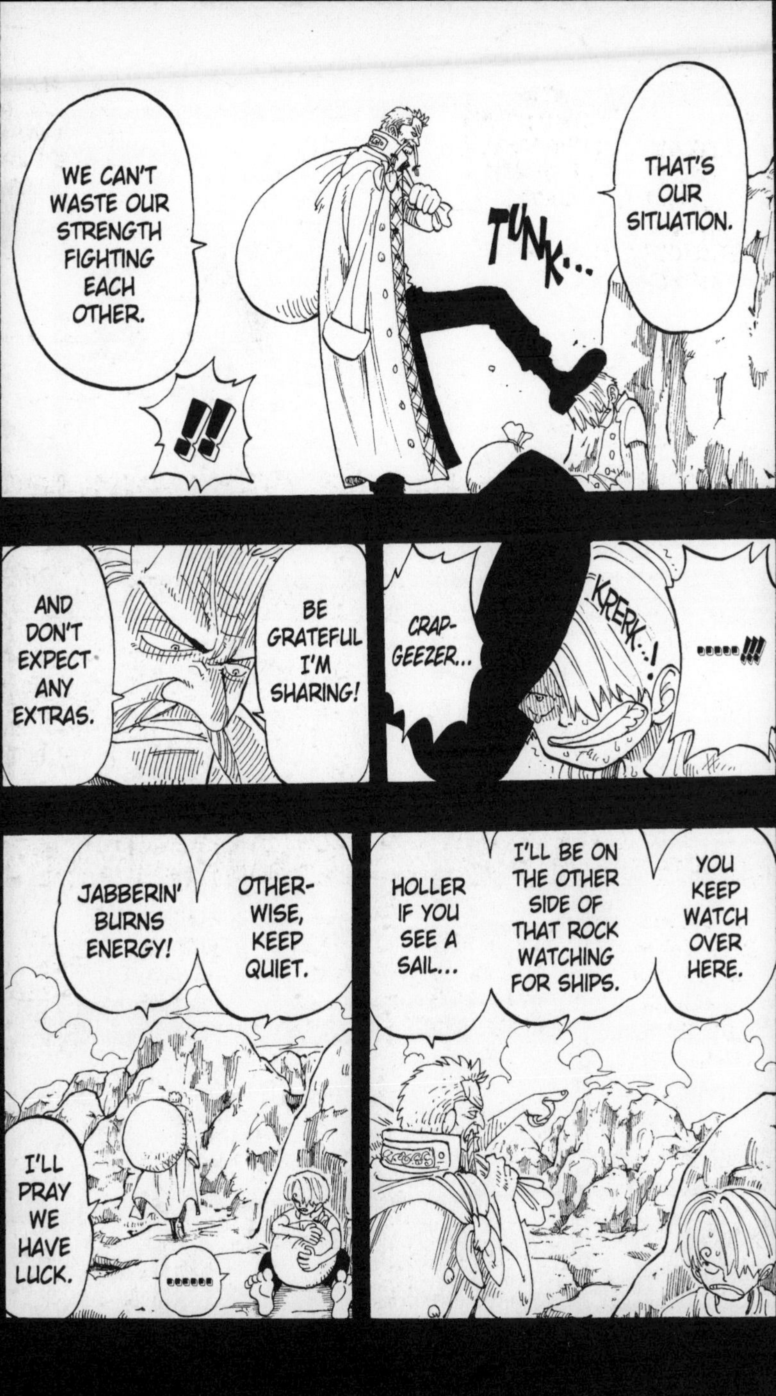

THAT'S OUR SITUATION.
TUNK...
WE CAN'T WASTE OUR STRENGTH FIGHTING EACH OTHER.
!!
......!!!
KRERK...!
CRAP-GEEZER...
BE GRATEFUL I'M SHARING!
AND DON'T EXPECT ANY EXTRAS.
YOU KEEP WATCH OVER HERE.
I'LL BE ON THE OTHER SIDE OF THAT ROCK WATCHING FOR SHIPS.
HOLLER IF YOU SEE A SAIL...
OTHER-WISE, KEEP QUIET.
JABBERIN' BURNS ENERGY!
I'LL PRAY WE HAVE LUCK.
......

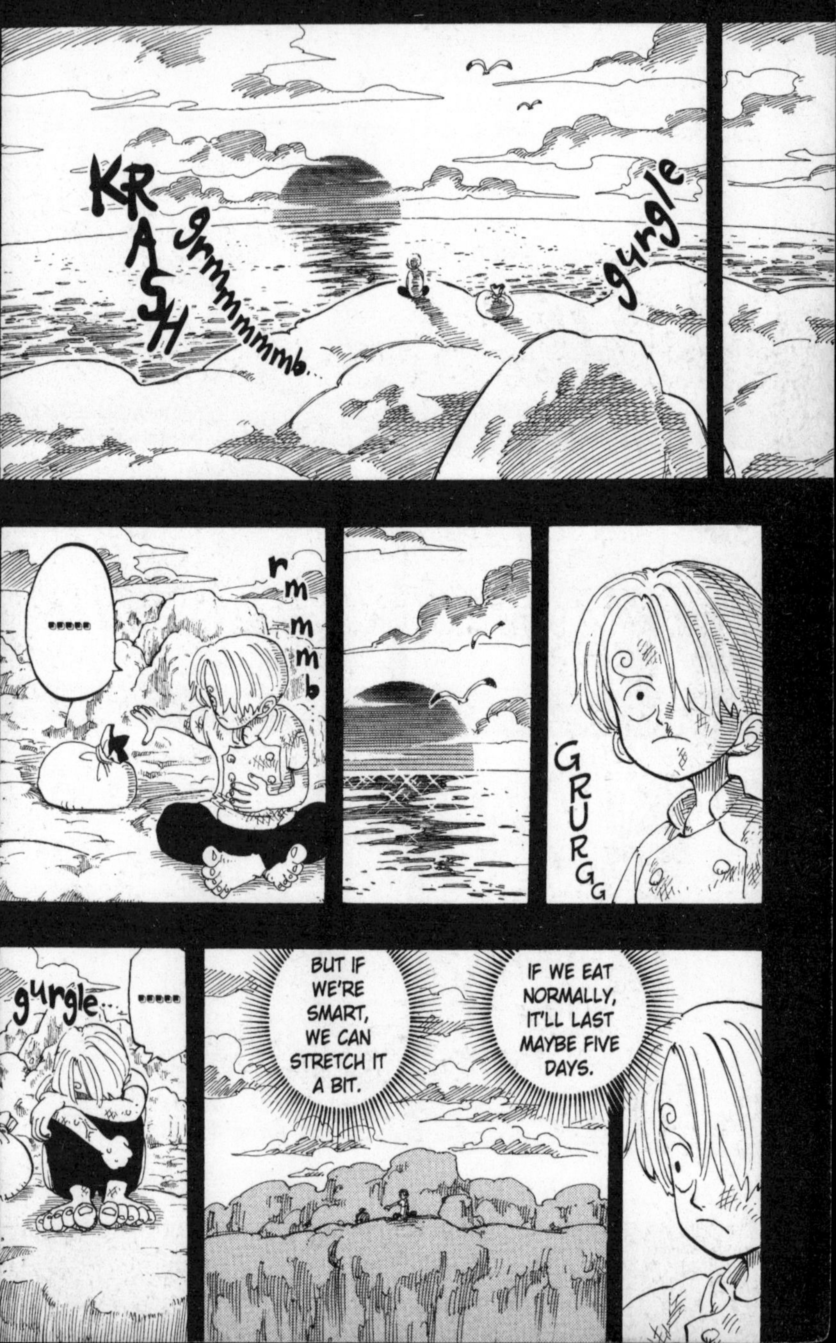
gurgle
grmmmmmmb...
KRASH
GRURGG
rmmmb...
.....
IF WE EAT NORMALLY, IT'LL LAST MAYBE FIVE DAYS.
BUT IF WE'RE SMART, WE CAN STRETCH IT A BIT.
.....
gurgle...

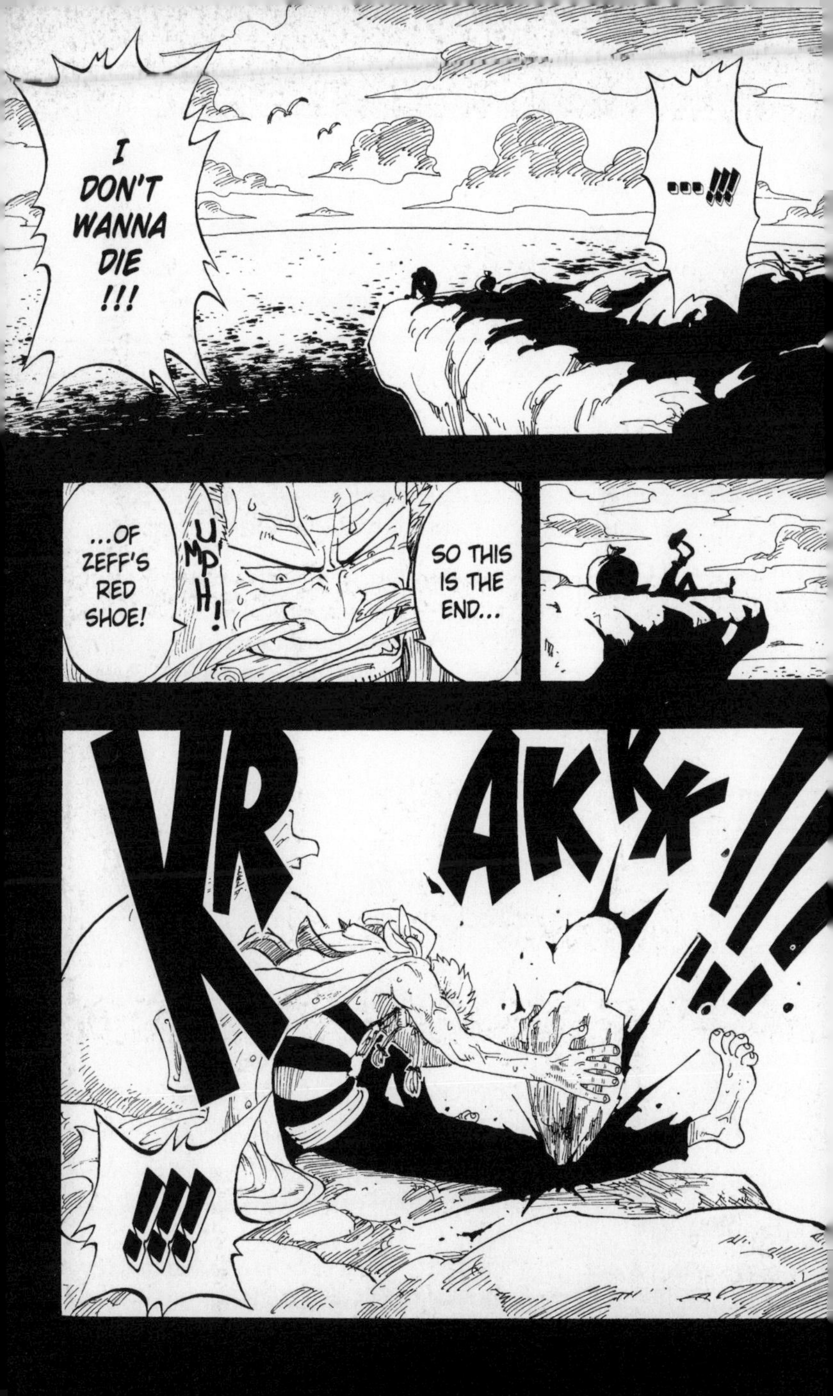
...!!!
I DON'T WANNA DIE !!!
SO THIS IS THE END...
UMPH!
...OF ZEFF'S RED SHOE!
KRAKK!!!
!!!

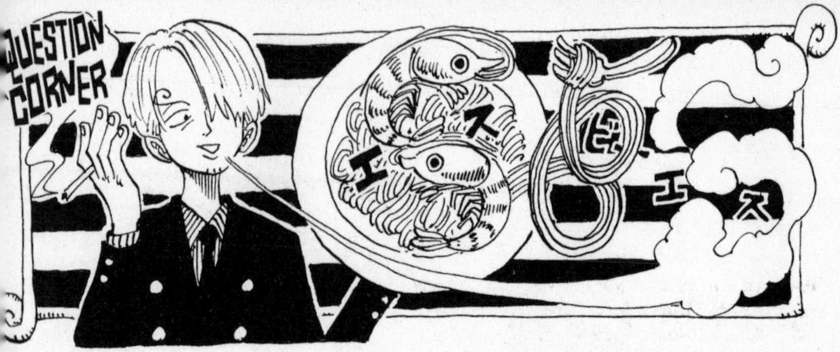
QUESTION CORNER

Q: Question. How fast can Captain Kuro run 100 meters?

A: To be honest, it's difficult to measure his speed accurately, but it would be less than, say, five seconds. Think in the four second range. Wow! A world record.

Q: Do Patty and Carne's names come from "*spaghetti*" and "*calzone*"?

A: Hmm! They come from cooking-related words to be sure, but not those. Patty comes from pâtissier, a pastry chef in charge of desserts. Carne comes directly from the Spanish word for meat dishes.

Q: If Luffy is 7,200 Funky Gum-Gums, then is Sanji about 8,500 Funky Ero-Ero?

A: No, not quite. More like 930 märchen Ero-Ero.

Q: Can't the *One Piece* graphic novel be a little cheaper? (About 100 yen...)

A: Right now it's 410 yen per volume, right? And Jump is 220 yen... When I was in elementary school, graphic novels cost 360 yen per volume and Jump cost 170 yen. But the price of all goods has risen, so it can't be helped. Everyone is in the same boat. 100 yen just isn't possible.

Q: Sensei! When you are drawing *One Piece* characters and Luffy is mad, does your face look mad or tense too? Tell me!! Mine does.

A: It does, yes. I make lots of faces when I draw. When I drew the double-page spread of the breakup of Usopp's pirate crew, my face got very tired. I was making a crying face the whole time I drew it, and my face started to cramp.

Chapter 58: THE CRAP-GEEZER

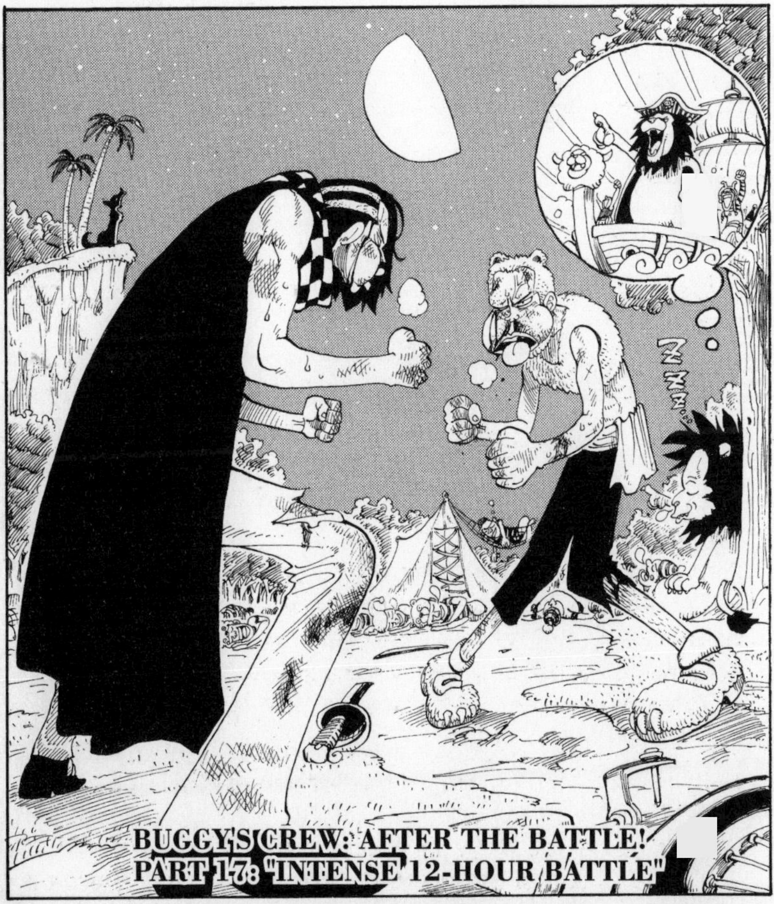
BUGGY'S CREW: AFTER THE BATTLE!
PART 17: "INTENSE 12-HOUR BATTLE"

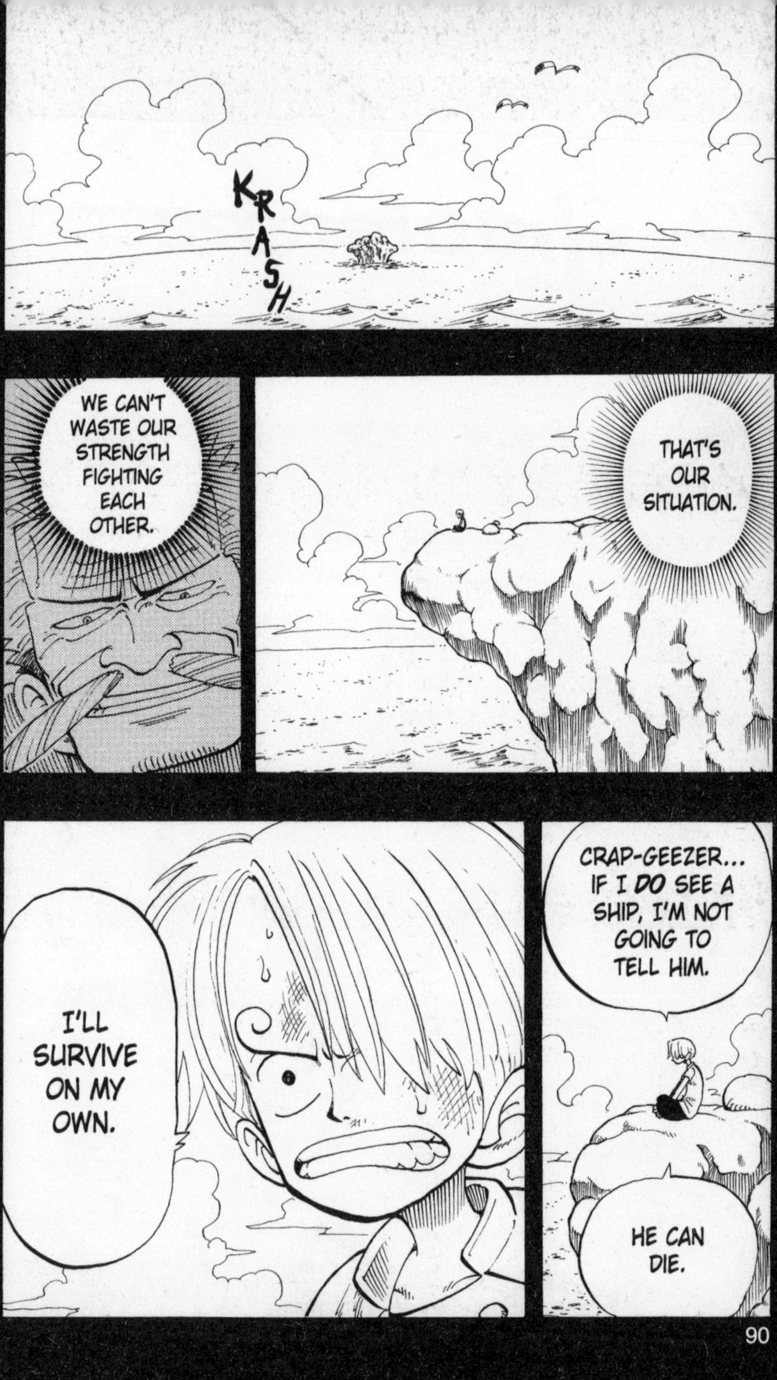
KRASH
THAT'S OUR SITUATION.
WE CAN'T WASTE OUR STRENGTH FIGHTING EACH OTHER.
CRAP-GEEZER... IF I *DO* SEE A SHIP, I'M NOT GOING TO TELL HIM.
HE CAN DIE.
I'LL SURVIVE ON MY OWN.

READ THIS WAY

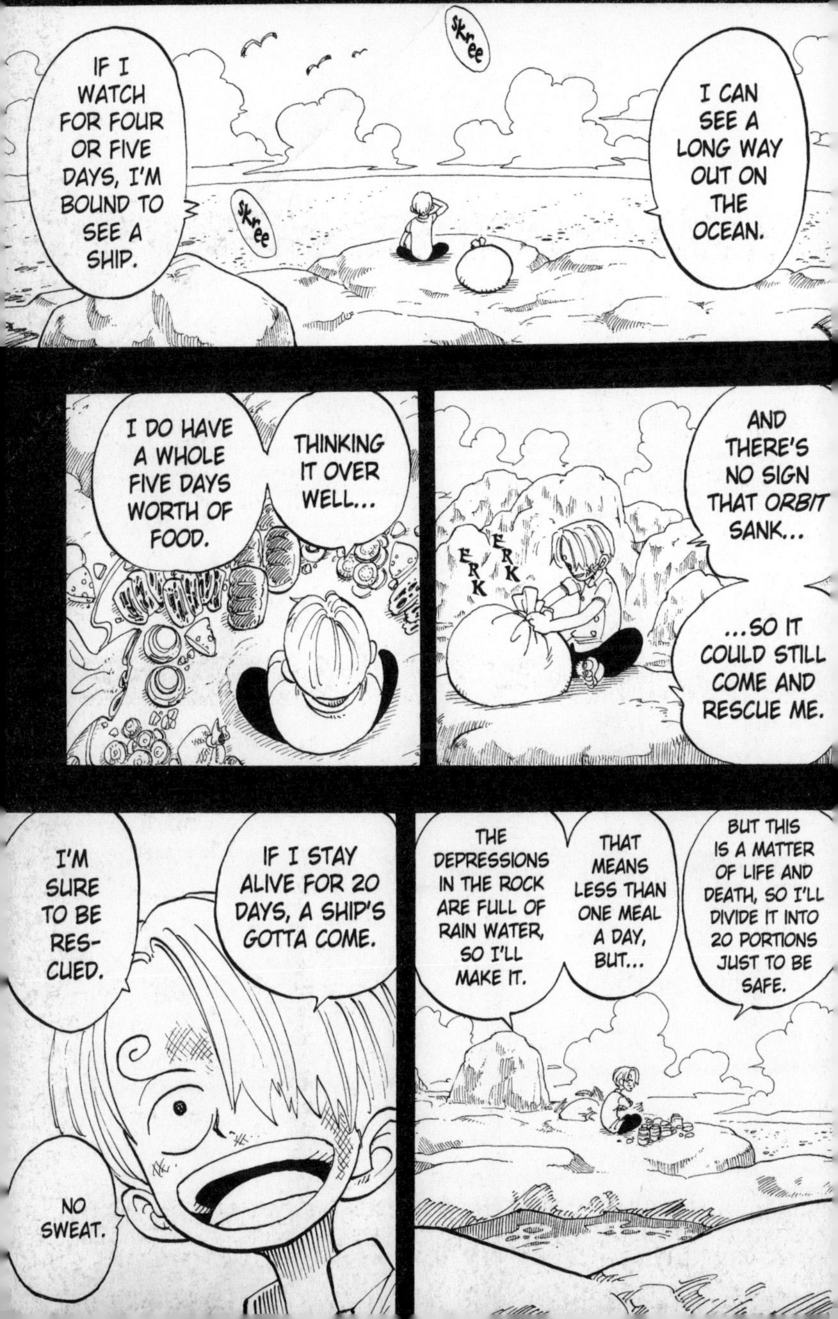
I CAN SEE A LONG WAY OUT ON THE OCEAN.
IF I WATCH FOR FOUR OR FIVE DAYS, I'M BOUND TO SEE A SHIP.
Skree
Skree
AND THERE'S NO SIGN THAT *ORBIT* SANK...
...SO IT COULD STILL COME AND RESCUE ME.
ERK ERK
THINKING IT OVER WELL...
I DO HAVE A WHOLE FIVE DAYS WORTH OF FOOD.
BUT THIS IS A MATTER OF LIFE AND DEATH, SO I'LL DIVIDE IT INTO 20 PORTIONS JUST TO BE SAFE.
THAT MEANS LESS THAN ONE MEAL A DAY, BUT...
THE DEPRESSIONS IN THE ROCK ARE FULL OF RAIN WATER, SO I'LL MAKE IT.
IF I STAY ALIVE FOR 20 DAYS, A SHIP'S GOTTA COME.
I'M SURE TO BE RES- CUED.
NO SWEAT.

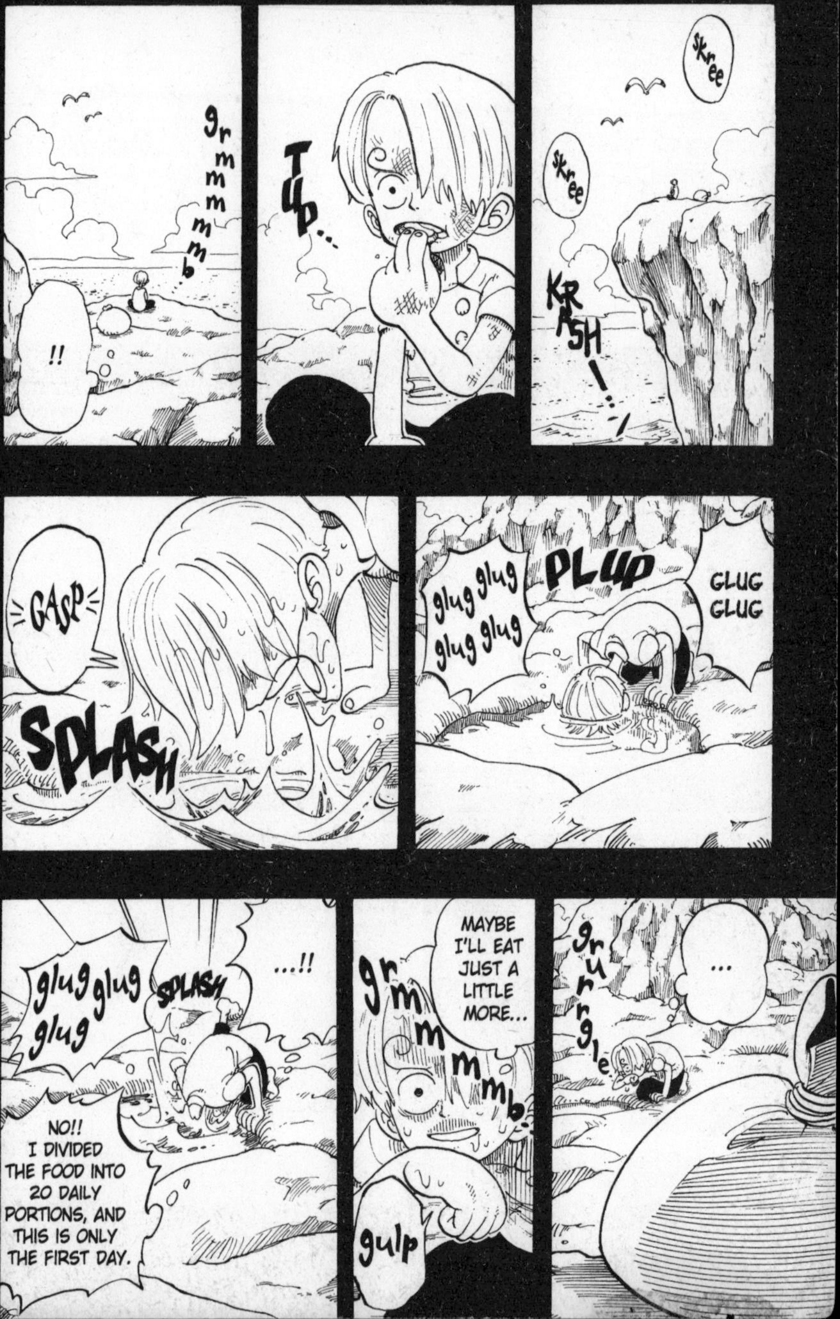
skree
skree
KRRSH...!
TUP...
grmmmmmb...
!!
glug glug glug glug
PLUP
GLUG GLUG
GASP
SPLASH
...
grurrgle...
MAYBE I'LL EAT JUST A LITTLE MORE...
grmmmmmb...
gulp
...!!
glug glug glug
SPLASH
NO!! I DIVIDED THE FOOD INTO 20 DAILY PORTIONS, AND THIS IS ONLY THE FIRST DAY.

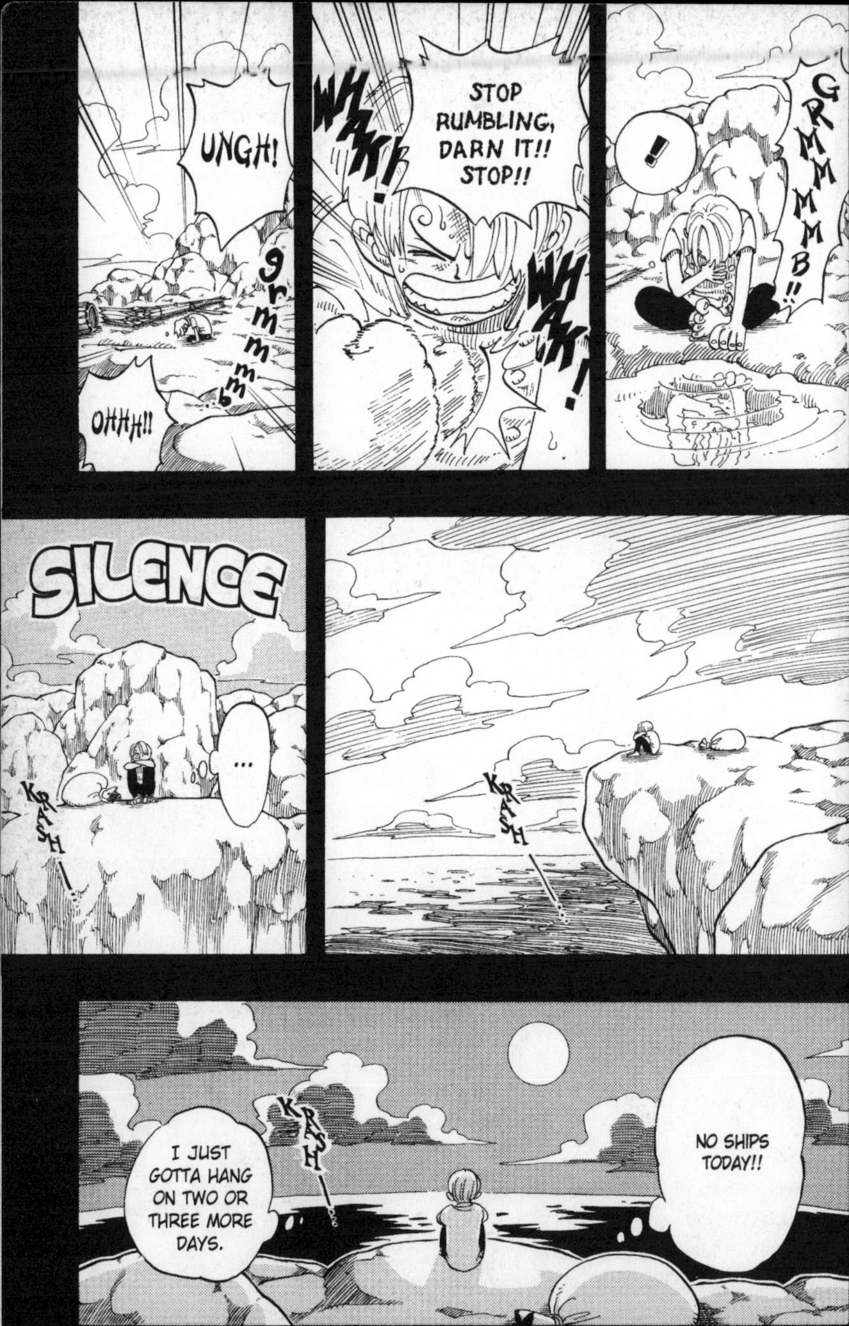
!
GRMMMB!!
WHAK!
STOP RUMBLING, DARN IT!! STOP!!
WHAK!
UNGH!
grmmmmb...
OHHH!!
KRASH...
SILENCE
...
KRASH...
NO SHIPS TODAY!!
KRASH...
I JUST GOTTA HANG ON TWO OR THREE MORE DAYS.

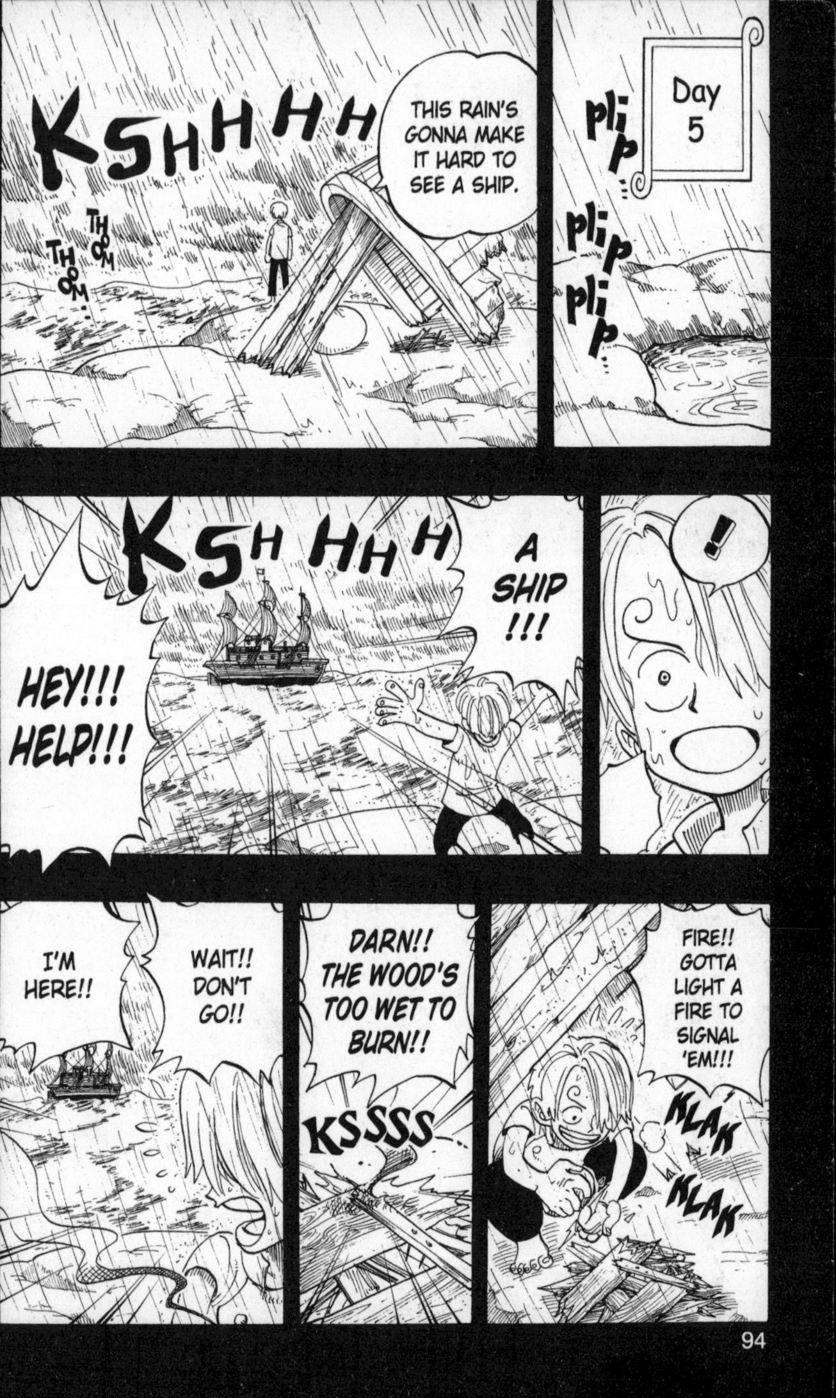
Day 5
plip
plip
plip
THIS RAIN'S GONNA MAKE IT HARD TO SEE A SHIP.
KSHHHH
THOOM
THOOM
!
A SHIP!!!
KSHHHH
HEY!!! HELP!!!
FIRE!! GOTTA LIGHT A FIRE TO SIGNAL 'EM!!!
KLAK
KLAK
DARN!! THE WOOD'S TOO WET TO BURN!!
KSSSS
WAIT!! DON'T GO!!
I'M HERE!!

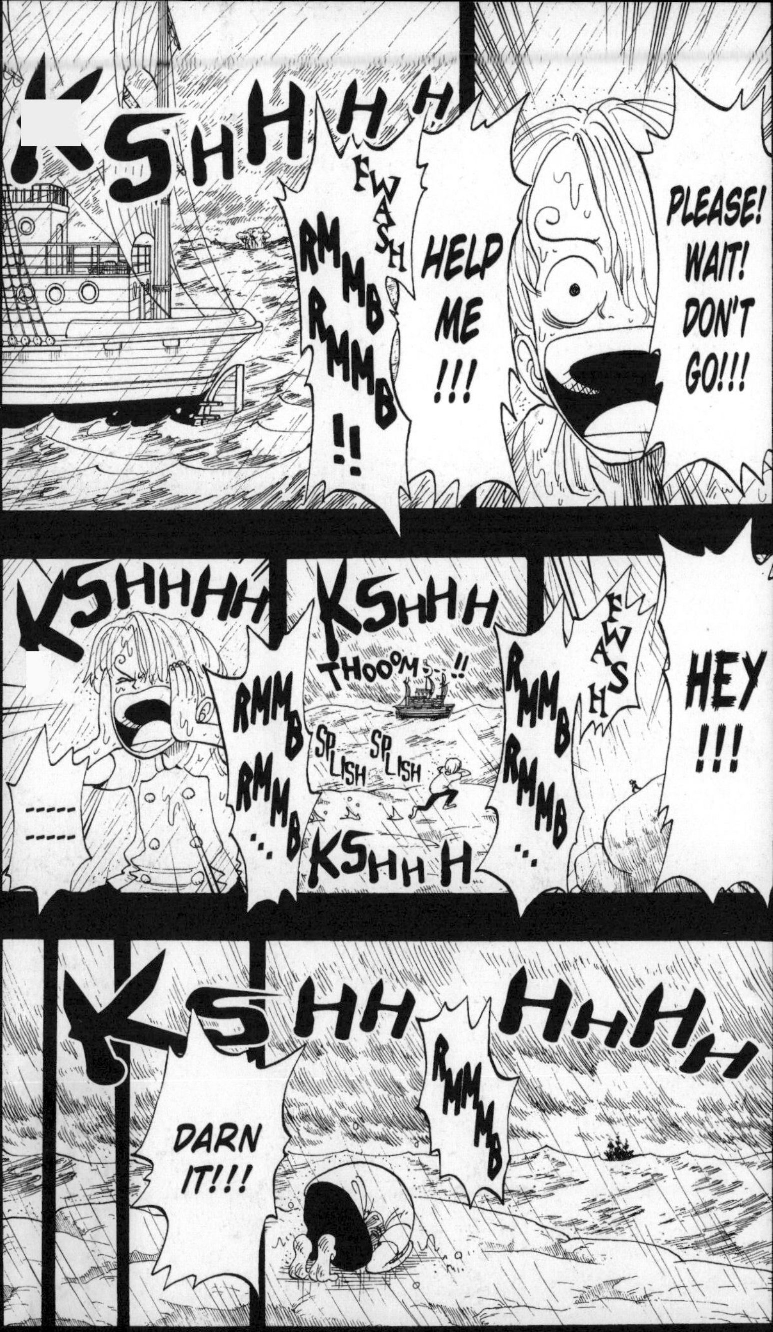
PLEASE! WAIT! DON'T GO!!!
HELP ME !!!
FWASH
RMMB RMMMB !!
KSHHHH
HEY !!!
FWASH
RMMB RMMMB ..
KSHHHH
THOOOM...!!
SPLISH SPLISH
KSHH H
RMMB RMMB ..

KSHHHHH
KSHHHHHHH
RMMMB
DARN IT!!!

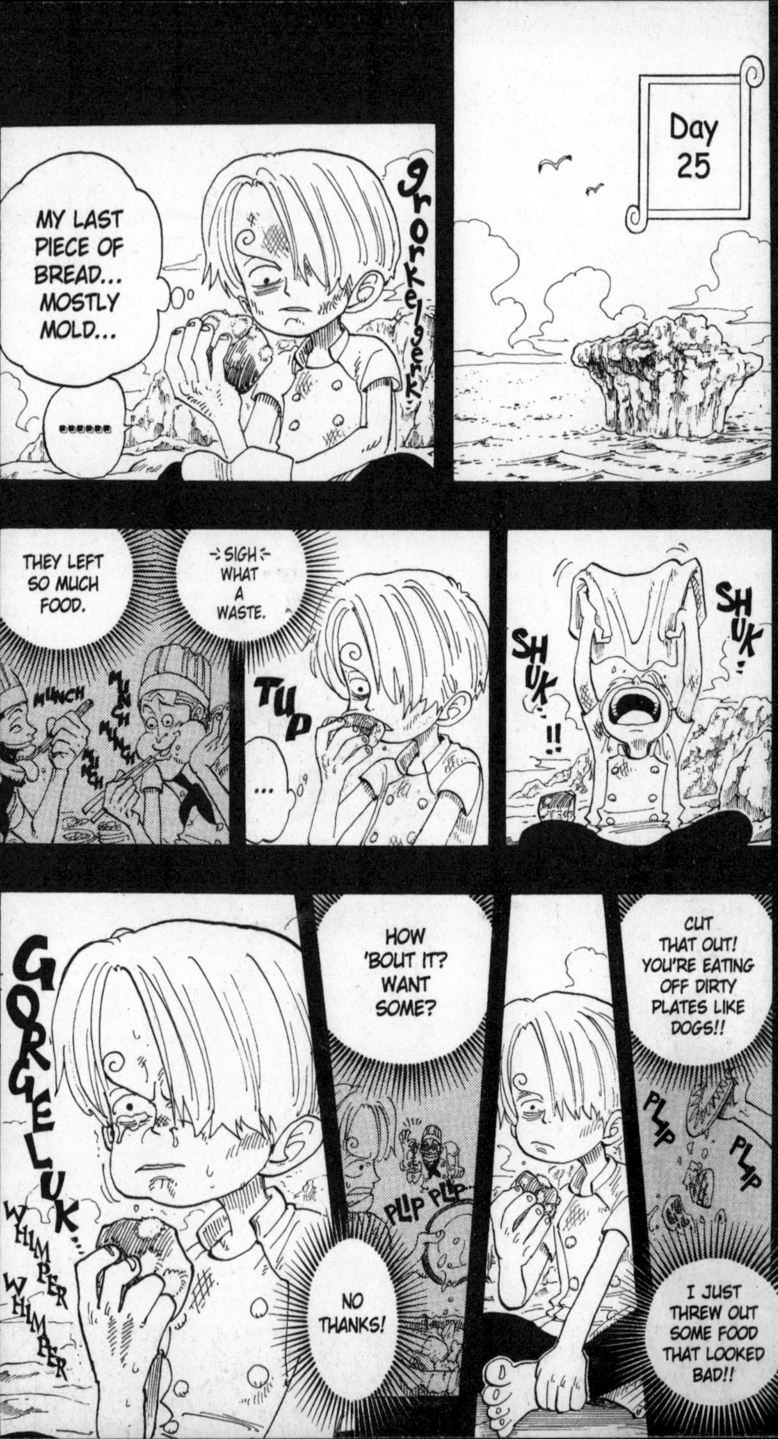
Day 25
MY LAST PIECE OF BREAD... MOSTLY MOLD...
grorkelgerk
......
SHUK
SHUK
!!
-SIGH- WHAT A WASTE.
TUP
...
THEY LEFT SO MUCH FOOD.
MUNCH
MUNCH MUNCH MUNCH
CUT THAT OUT! YOU'RE EATING OFF DIRTY PLATES LIKE DOGS!!
PLIP
PLIP
I JUST THREW OUT SOME FOOD THAT LOOKED BAD!!
HOW 'BOUT IT? WANT SOME?
PLIP PLIP
NO THANKS!
GORGELUK
WHIMPER
WHIMPER
WHIMPER

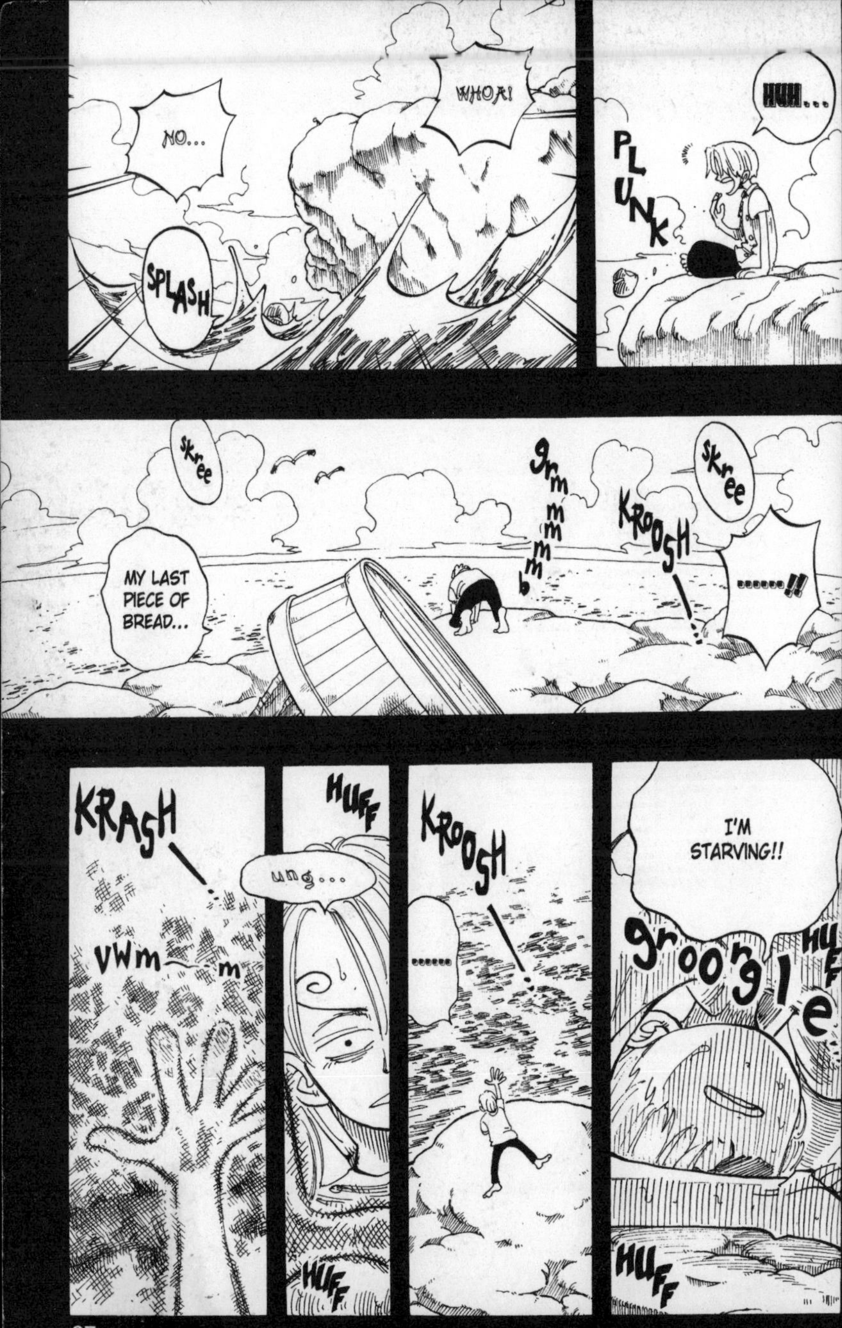
HUH...
PLUNK
WHOA!
NO...
SPLASH
skree
......!!
KROOSH
grmmmmb
skree
MY LAST PIECE OF BREAD...
I'M STARVING!!
HUFF
groogle
HUFF
KROOSH
......
HUFF
ung...
HUFF
KRASH
VWm~m

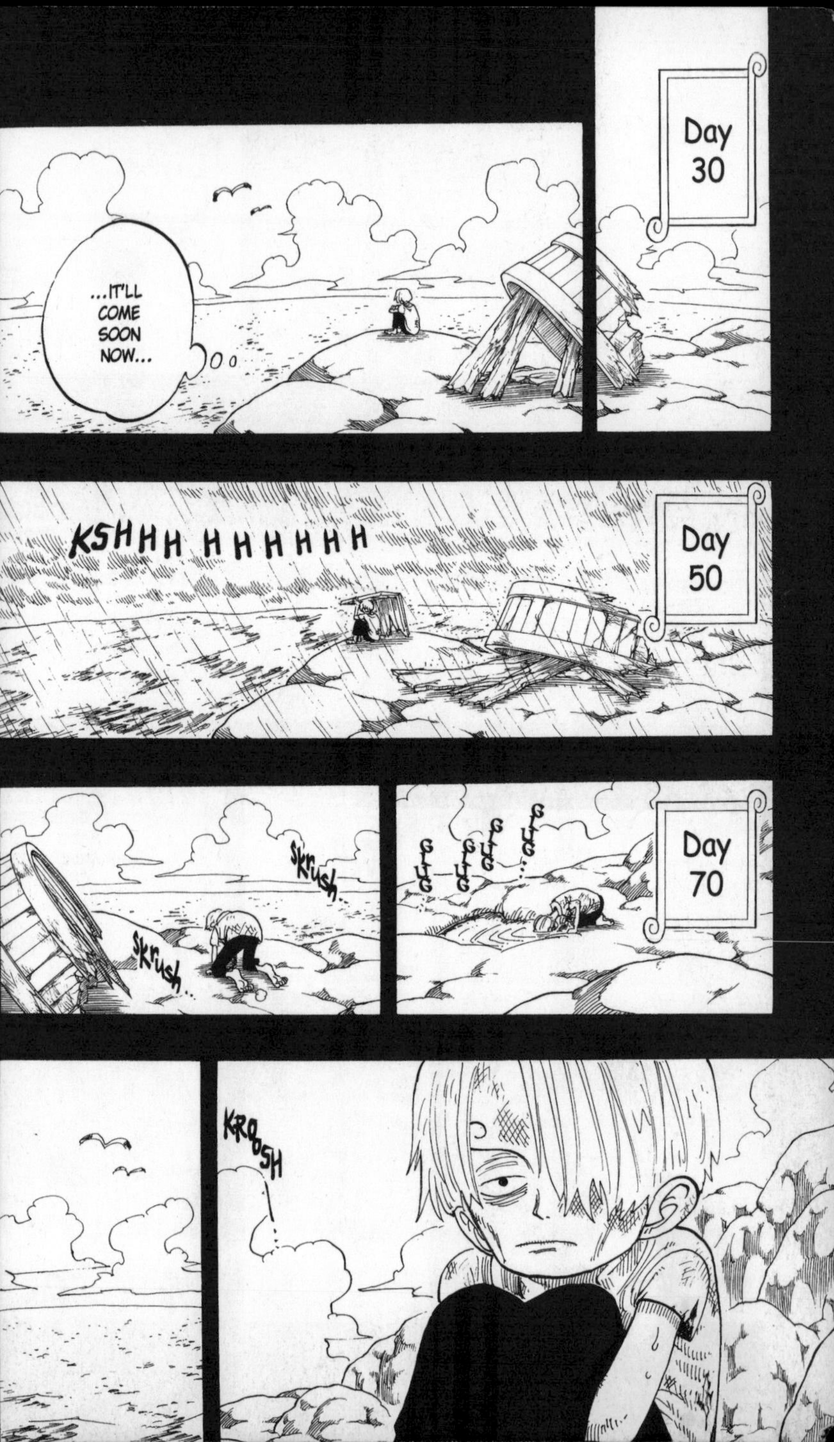
Day 30
...IT'LL COME SOON NOW...
Day 50
KSHHH HHHHHH
Day 70
GLUG GLUG GLUG GLUG...
SKRUSH...
SKRUSH...
KROOSH

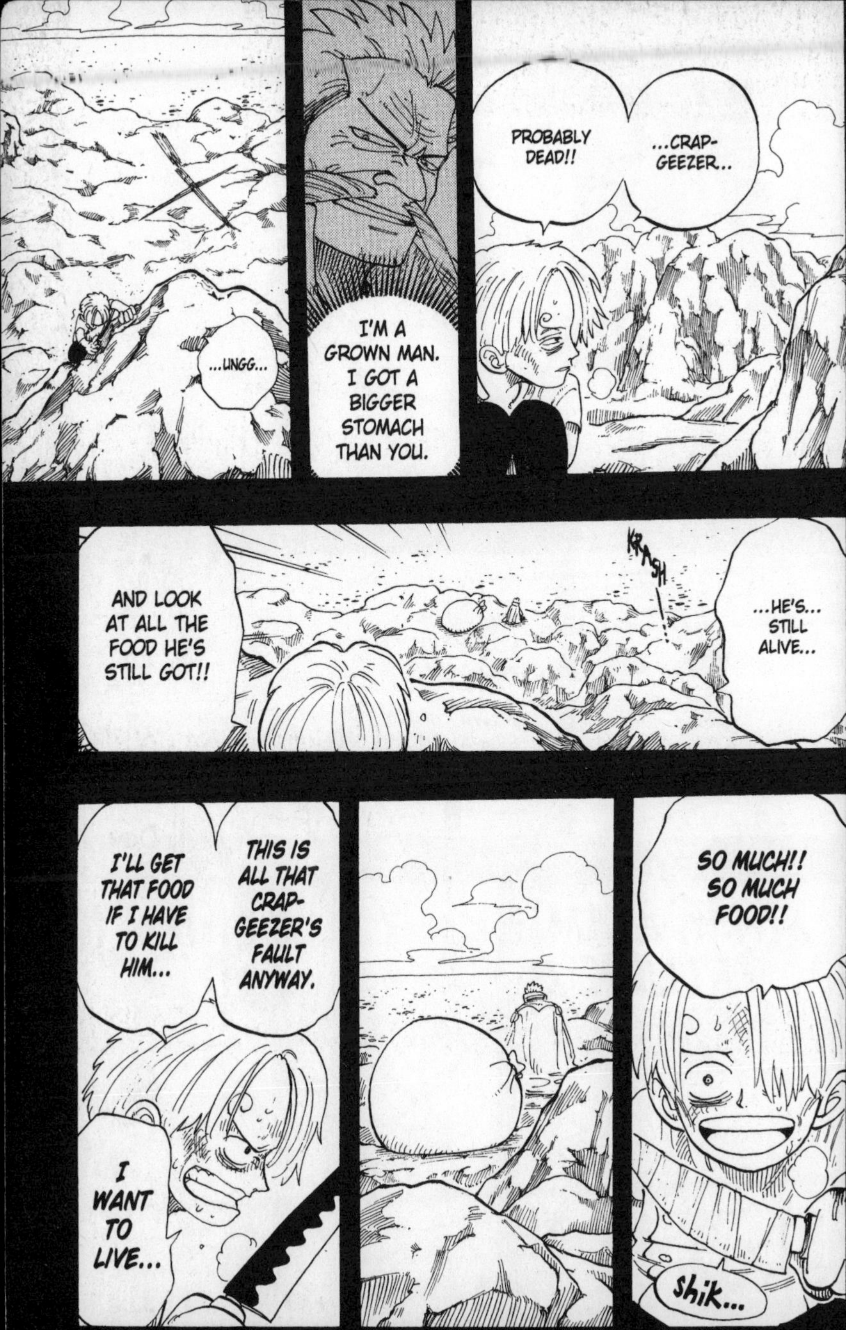
...CRAP-GEEZER...
PROBABLY DEAD!!
I'M A GROWN MAN. I GOT A BIGGER STOMACH THAN YOU.
...UNGG...
...HE'S... STILL ALIVE...
KRASH
AND LOOK AT ALL THE FOOD HE'S STILL GOT!!
SO MUCH!! SO MUCH FOOD!!
Shik...
THIS IS ALL THAT CRAP-GEEZER'S FAULT ANYWAY.
I'LL GET THAT FOOD IF I HAVE TO KILL HIM...
I WANT TO LIVE...

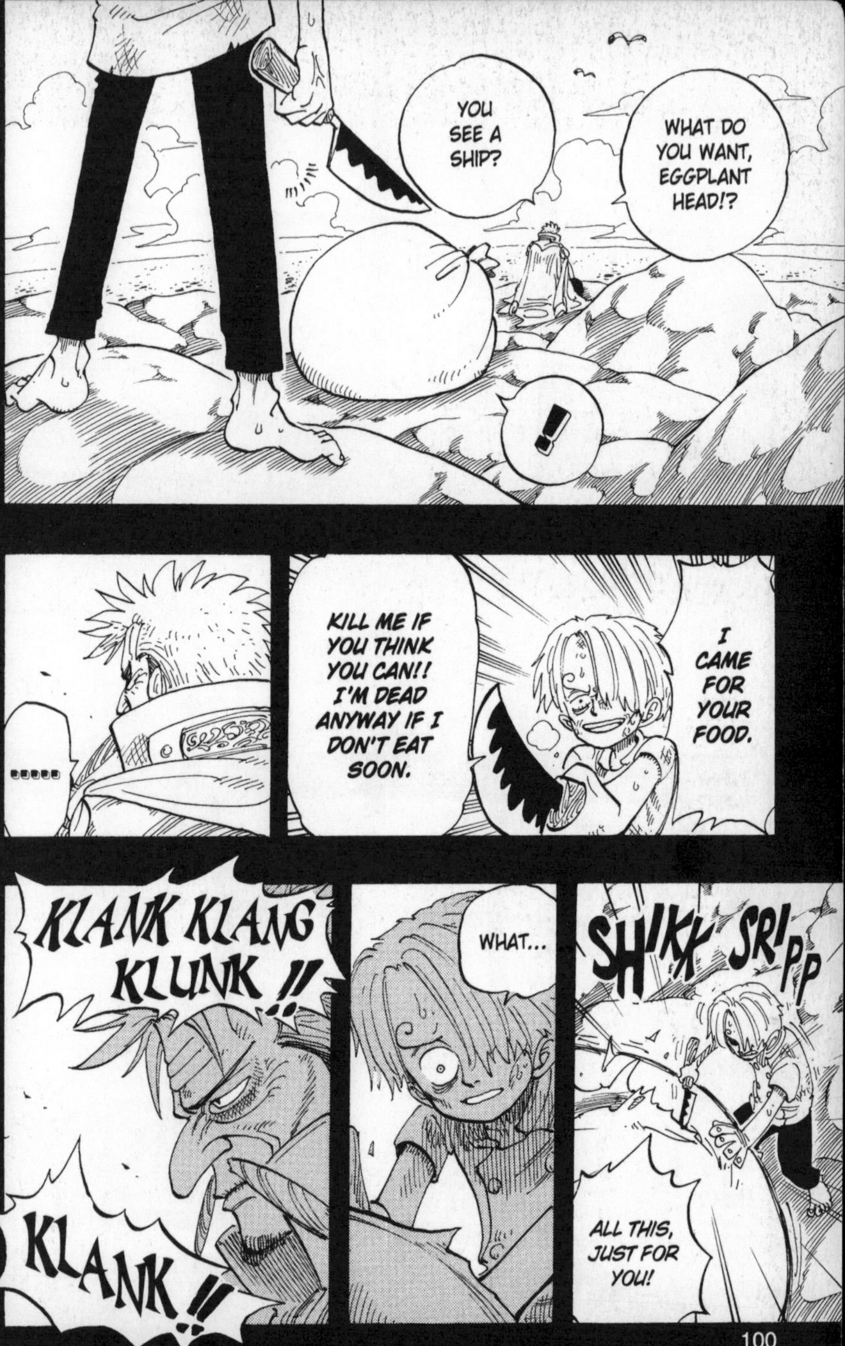

WHAT DO YOU WANT, EGGPLANT HEAD!?
YOU SEE A SHIP?
!
I CAME FOR YOUR FOOD.
KILL ME IF YOU THINK YOU CAN!! I'M DEAD ANYWAY IF I DON'T EAT SOON.
.....
SHIKK SRIPP
ALL THIS, JUST FOR YOU!
WHAT...
KLANK KLANG KLUNK!!
KLANK!!

READ THIS WAY

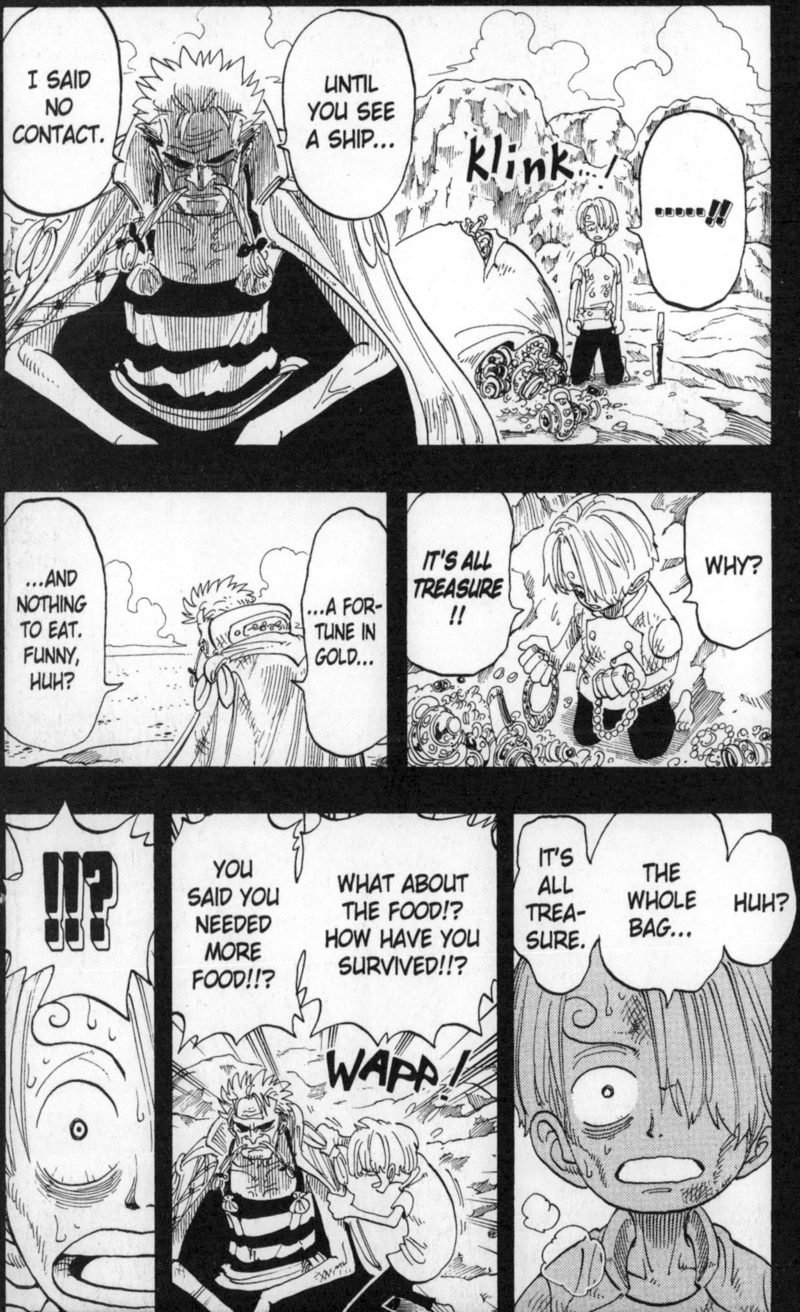

......!!
klink...!
UNTIL YOU SEE A SHIP...
I SAID NO CONTACT.
WHY?
IT'S ALL TREASURE !!
...A FORTUNE IN GOLD...
...AND NOTHING TO EAT. FUNNY, HUH?
HUH?
THE WHOLE BAG...
IT'S ALL TREASURE.
WHAT ABOUT THE FOOD!? HOW HAVE YOU SURVIVED!!?
YOU SAID YOU NEEDED MORE FOOD!!?
WAPP!
!!?

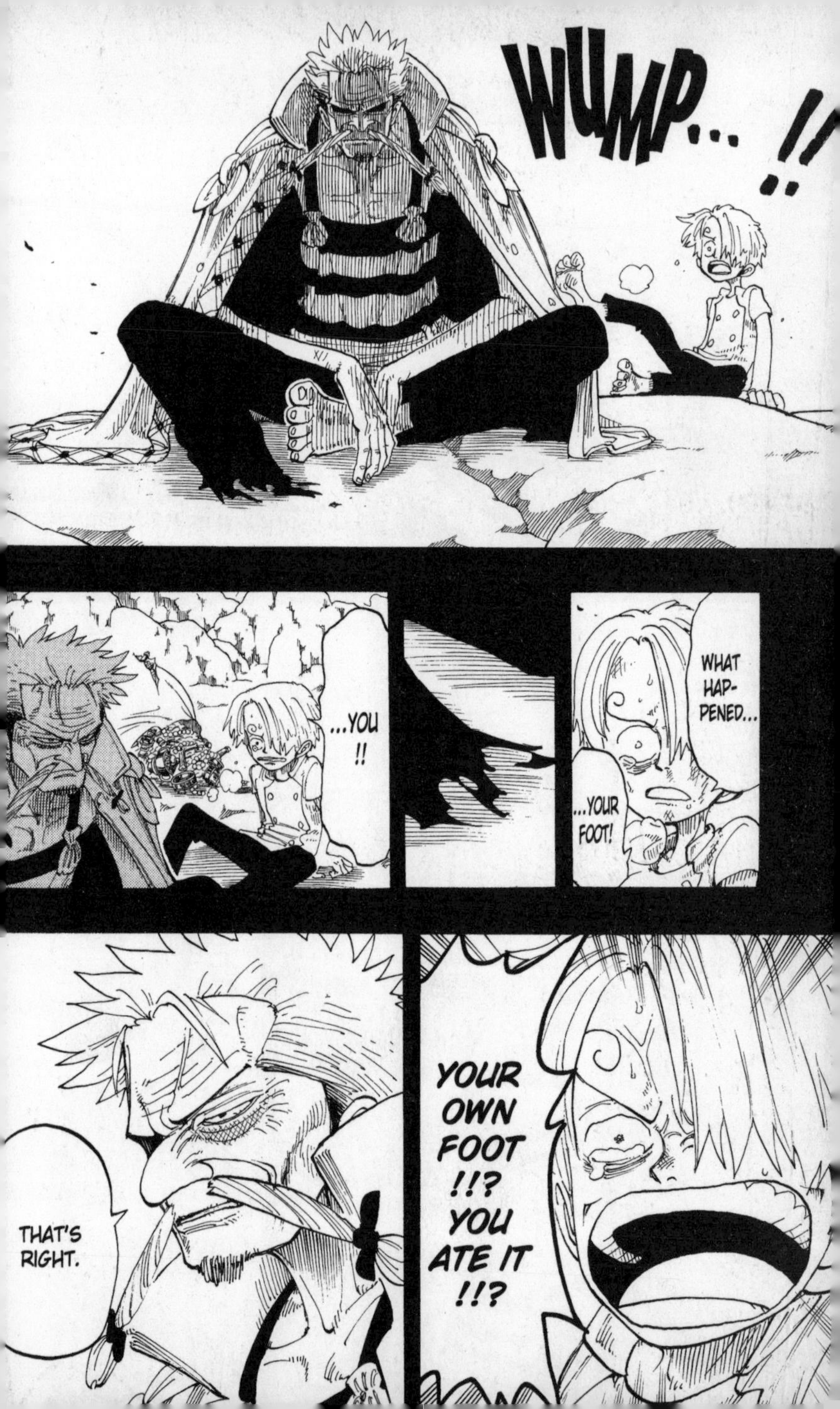
WUMP... !!
!!
WHAT HAP-PENED...
...YOUR FOOT!
...YOU !!
YOUR OWN FOOT !!? YOU ATE IT !!?
THAT'S RIGHT.

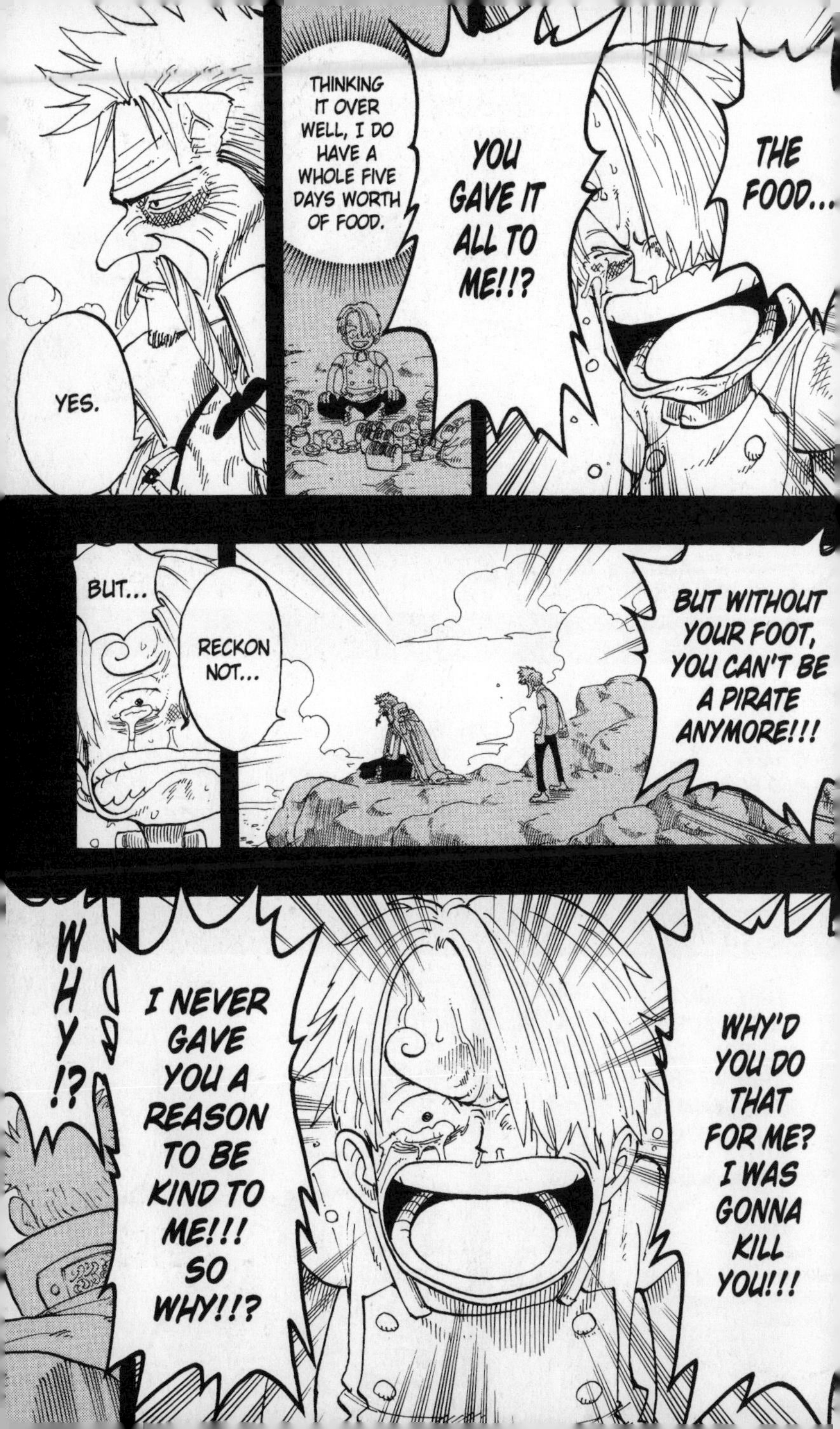
THE FOOD...
YOU GAVE IT ALL TO ME!!?
THINKING IT OVER WELL, I DO HAVE A WHOLE FIVE DAYS WORTH OF FOOD.
YES.
BUT WITHOUT YOUR FOOT, YOU CAN'T BE A PIRATE ANYMORE!!!
RECKON NOT...
BUT...
WHY'D YOU DO THAT FOR ME? I WAS GONNA KILL YOU!!!
I NEVER GAVE YOU A REASON TO BE KIND TO ME!!! SO WHY!!?
WHY!?

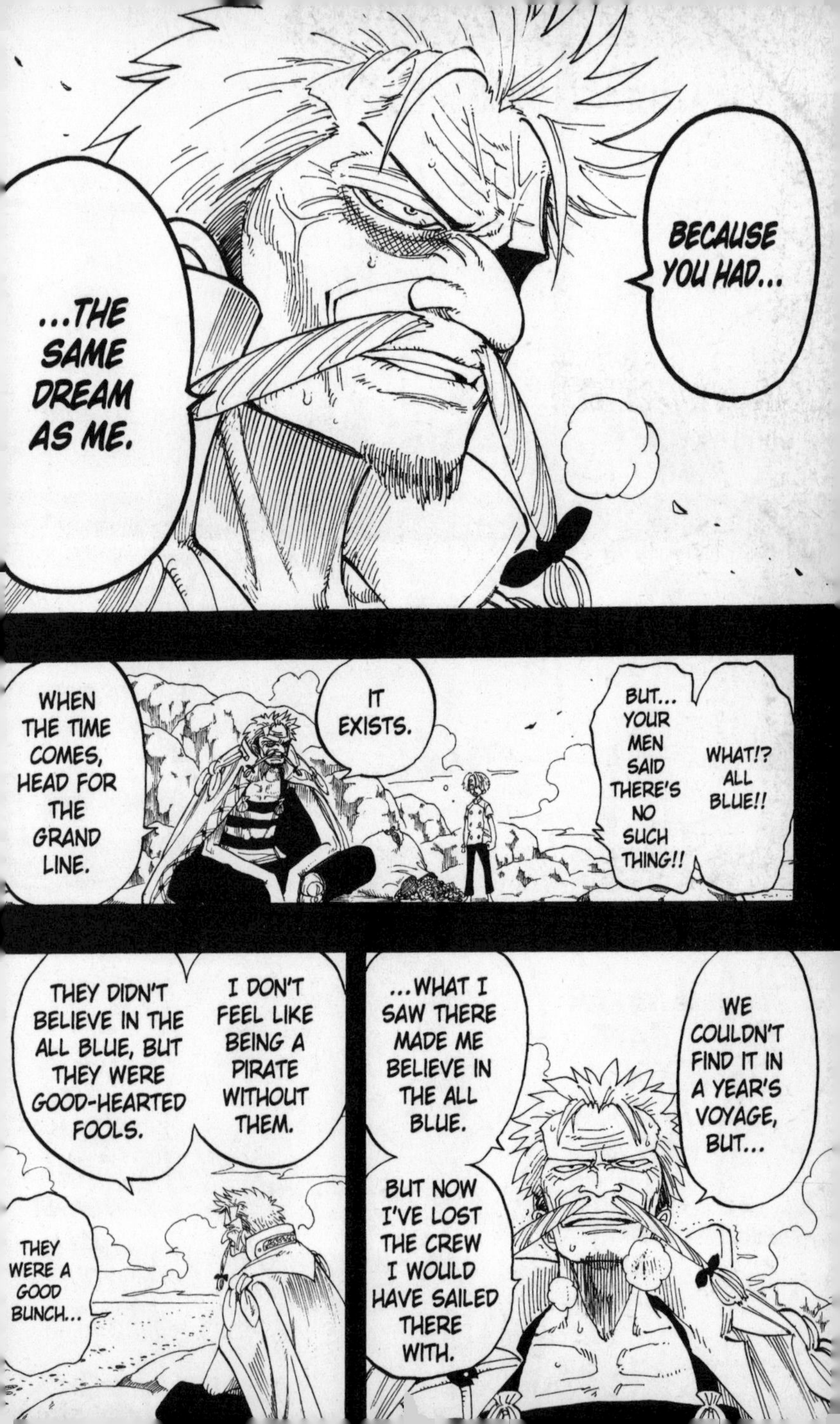
BECAUSE YOU HAD...
...THE SAME DREAM AS ME.
WHAT!? ALL BLUE!!
BUT... YOUR MEN SAID THERE'S NO SUCH THING!!
IT EXISTS.
WHEN THE TIME COMES, HEAD FOR THE GRAND LINE.
WE COULDN'T FIND IT IN A YEAR'S VOYAGE, BUT...
...WHAT I SAW THERE MADE ME BELIEVE IN THE ALL BLUE.
BUT NOW I'VE LOST THE CREW I WOULD HAVE SAILED THERE WITH.
I DON'T FEEL LIKE BEING A PIRATE WITHOUT THEM.
THEY DIDN'T BELIEVE IN THE ALL BLUE, BUT THEY WERE GOOD-HEARTED FOOLS.
THEY WERE A GOOD BUNCH...

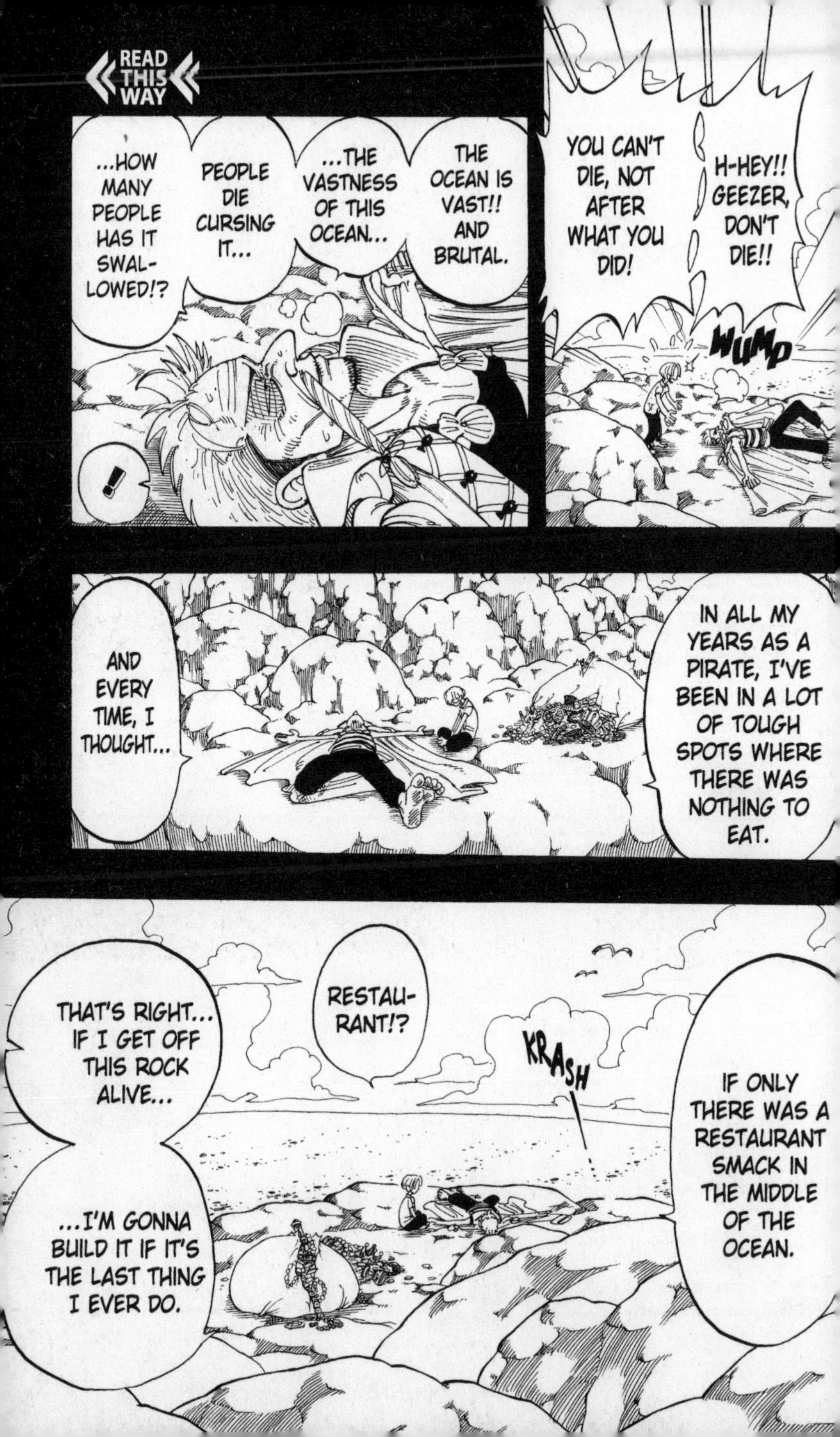
READ THIS WAY
H-HEY!! GEEZER, DON'T DIE!!
YOU CAN'T DIE, NOT AFTER WHAT YOU DID!
WUMP
THE OCEAN IS VAST!! AND BRUTAL.
...THE VASTNESS OF THIS OCEAN...
PEOPLE DIE CURSING IT...
...HOW MANY PEOPLE HAS IT SWAL-LOWED!?
!
IN ALL MY YEARS AS A PIRATE, I'VE BEEN IN A LOT OF TOUGH SPOTS WHERE THERE WAS NOTHING TO EAT.
AND EVERY TIME, I THOUGHT...
IF ONLY THERE WAS A RESTAURANT SMACK IN THE MIDDLE OF THE OCEAN.
KRASH
RESTAU-RANT!?
THAT'S RIGHT... IF I GET OFF THIS ROCK ALIVE...
...I'M GONNA BUILD IT IF IT'S THE LAST THING I EVER DO.

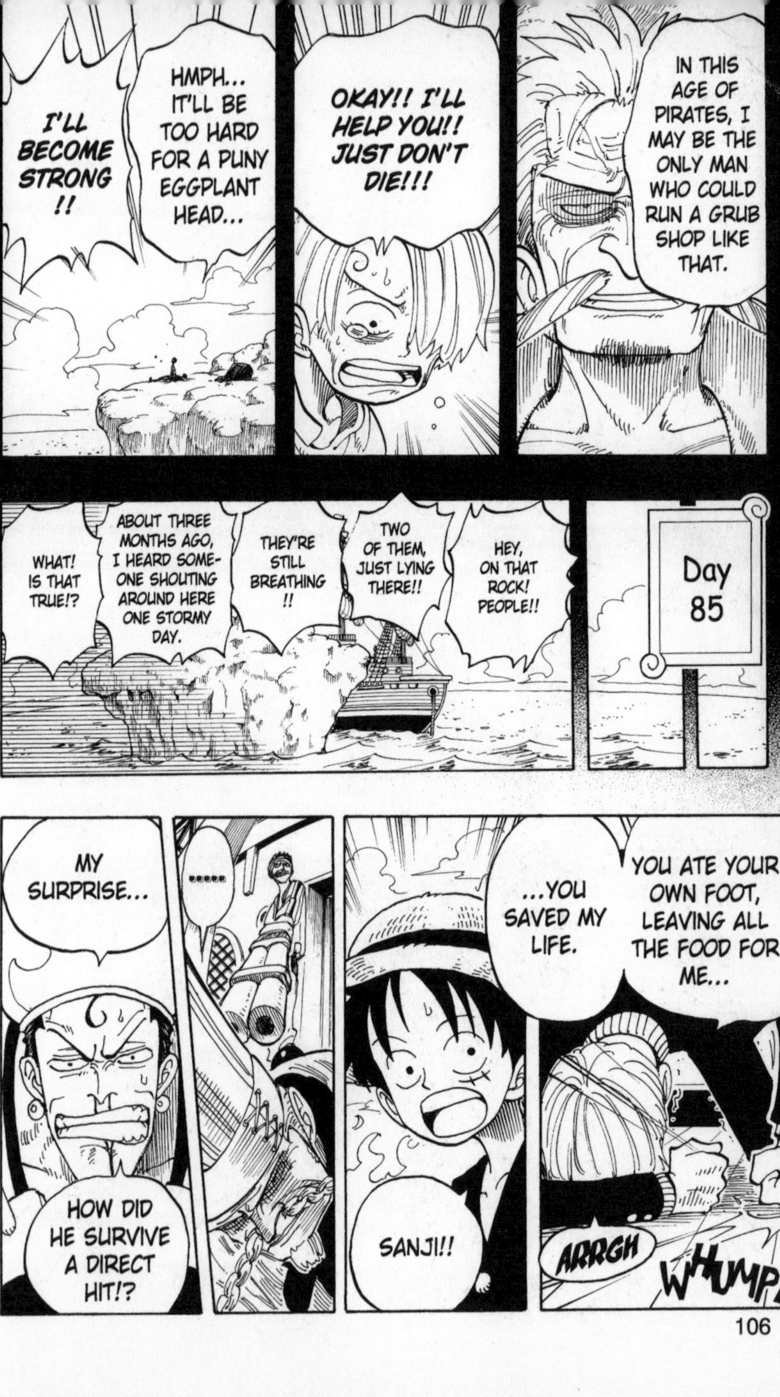
IN THIS AGE OF PIRATES, I MAY BE THE ONLY MAN WHO COULD RUN A GRUB SHOP LIKE THAT.
OKAY!! I'LL HELP YOU!! JUST DON'T DIE!!!
HMPH... IT'LL BE TOO HARD FOR A PUNY EGGPLANT HEAD...
I'LL BECOME STRONG !!
Day 85
HEY, ON THAT ROCK! PEOPLE!!
TWO OF THEM, JUST LYING THERE!!
THEY'RE STILL BREATHING !!
ABOUT THREE MONTHS AGO, I HEARD SOME-ONE SHOUTING AROUND HERE ONE STORMY DAY.
WHAT! IS THAT TRUE!?
YOU ATE YOUR OWN FOOT, LEAVING ALL THE FOOD FOR ME...
...YOU SAVED MY LIFE.
ARRGH
WHUMP!!
SANJI!!
.....
MY SURPRISE...
HOW DID HE SURVIVE A DIRECT HIT!?

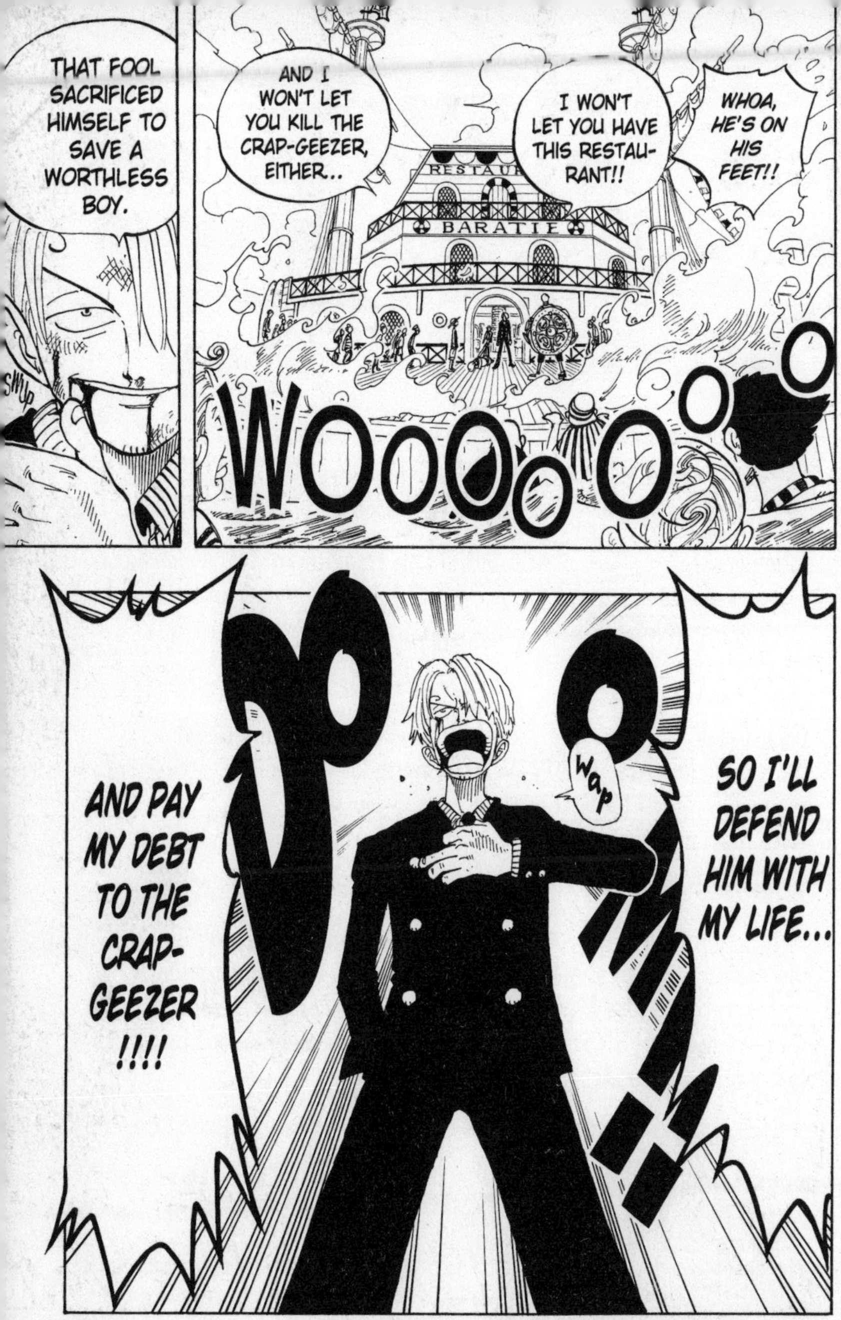
WHOA, HE'S ON HIS FEET!!
I WON'T LET YOU HAVE THIS RESTAURANT!!
AND I WON'T LET YOU KILL THE CRAP-GEEZER, EITHER...
RESTAU
BARATIE
WOOOOOOOOO
THAT FOOL SACRIFICED HIMSELF TO SAVE A WORTHLESS BOY.
SWUP
SO I'LL DEFEND HIM WITH MY LIFE...
Wap
AND PAY MY DEBT TO THE CRAP-GEEZER!!!!

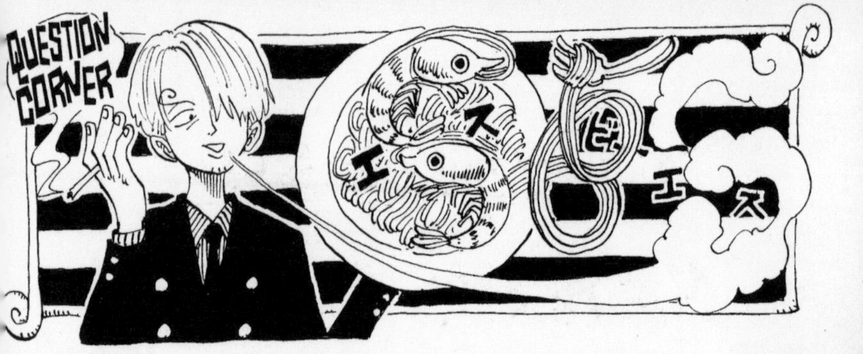
QUESTION CORNER

Q: Zeff of the oceangoing restaurant has braids under his nose. Is that a mustache? Nose hair? Fake hair?

A: They're "phony tails." The scientific name is "phonus bolognus tails."

Q: Oda Sensei, I'm Akinori! I thought of an amazing move! 1. Luffy stretches his arm. 2. Zolo cuts that arm off. 3. The arm goes flying. (Note: this technique can only be used twice!)

A: Hey hey hey...

Q: Dear Odakins ♡, I'm your fiancée. When are we going to get married? How about 11/1? We're going to kiss at the wedding, right!? Oooh, how exciting! ♡ Smack! ♡ Actually, I'm Namie Amuro's younger sister. ♡

A: Okay. I'll visit you in the hospital.

Q: This is to the guy who said that Zolo's sash made him look like an old man in the Question Corner in volume 4!! It's your problem, man!! At first, I also thought, "a cool guy like Zolo, in a sash?" but if that's part of Zolo, I accept it! Yes, I accept it!! So you should, too! Okay, let's be friends!

A: Wow! Friendship blossoming between my readers! How heartwarming.

Q: Buggy's top half can fly, right? (Or float, anyway.) Then it should be able to fly to the Grand Line. So why doesn't he?

A: He can't go that far. The powers of the Chop-Chop Fruit have limits. His body parts can only scatter up to a diameter of 200 Chop-Chops. Once this limit is exceeded, control is no longer possible.

Chapter 59: SANJI'S DEBT

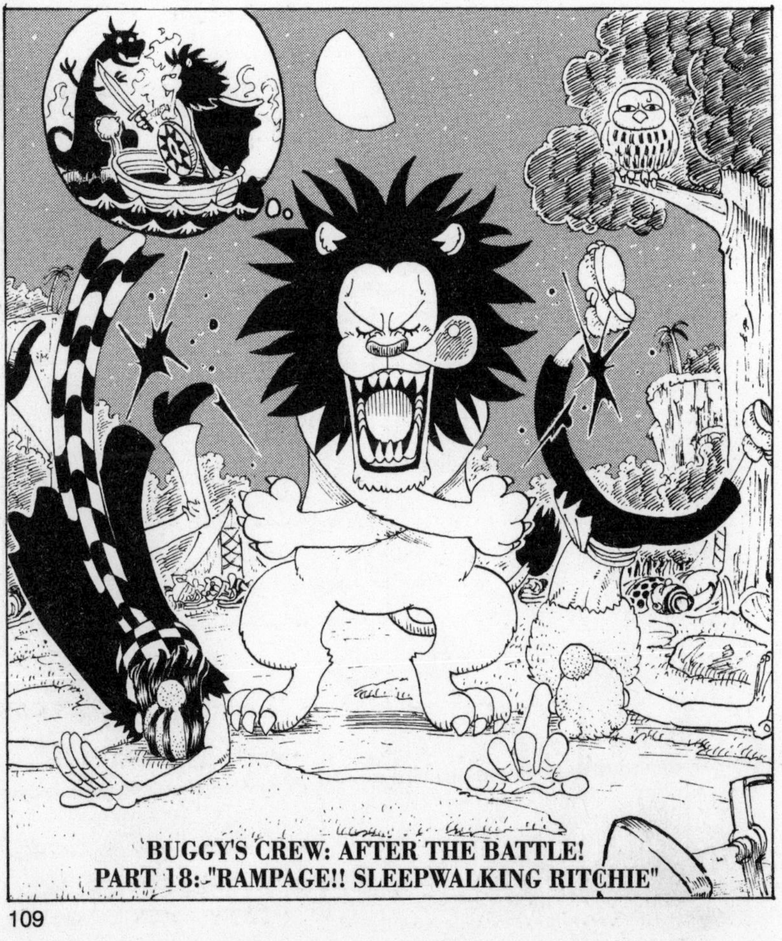
BUGGY'S CREW: AFTER THE BATTLE!
PART 18: "RAMPAGE!! SLEEPWALKING RITCHIE"

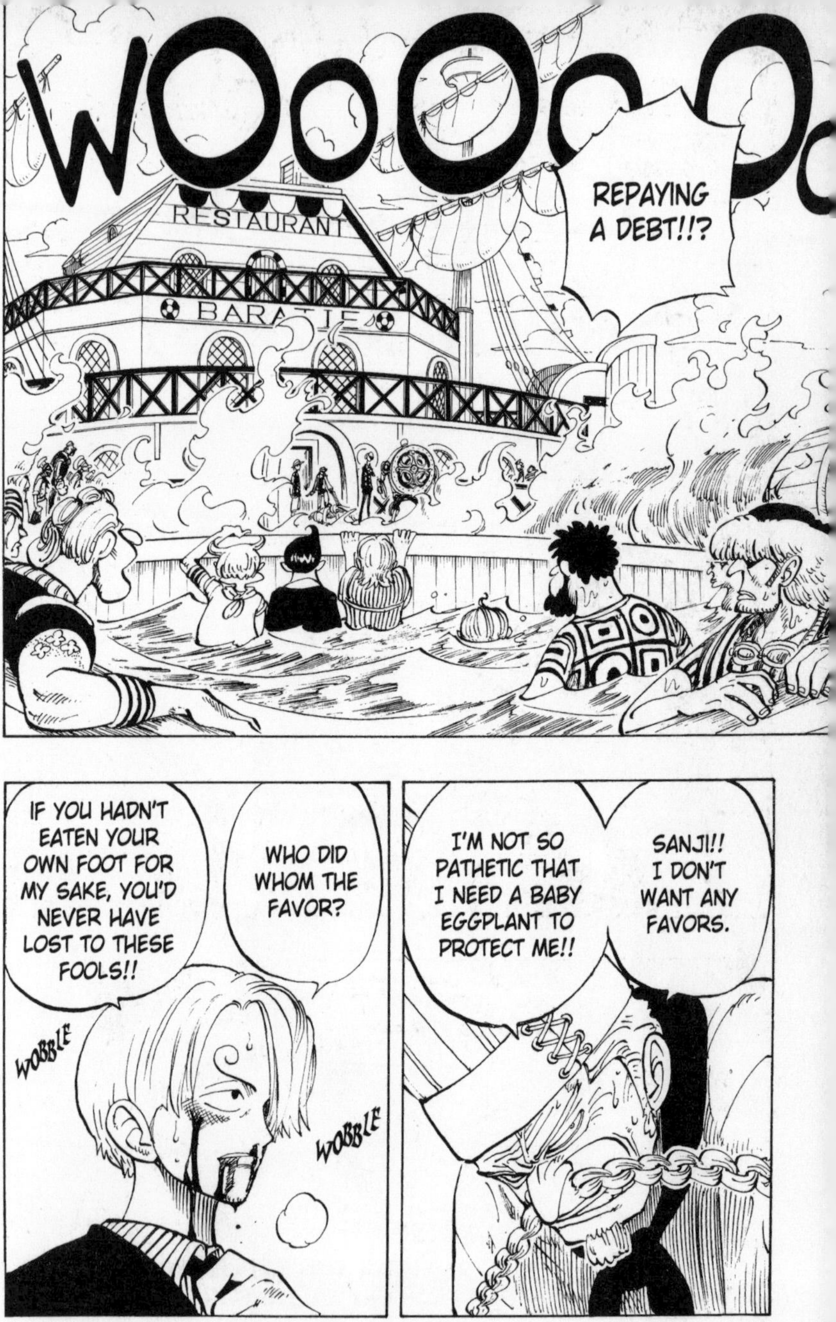
WOOOOO
REPAYING A DEBT!!?
SANJI!! I DON'T WANT ANY FAVORS.
I'M NOT SO PATHETIC THAT I NEED A BABY EGGPLANT TO PROTECT ME!!
WHO DID WHOM THE FAVOR?
IF YOU HADN'T EATEN YOUR OWN FOOT FOR MY SAKE, YOU'D NEVER HAVE LOST TO THESE FOOLS!!
WOBBLE
WOBBLE

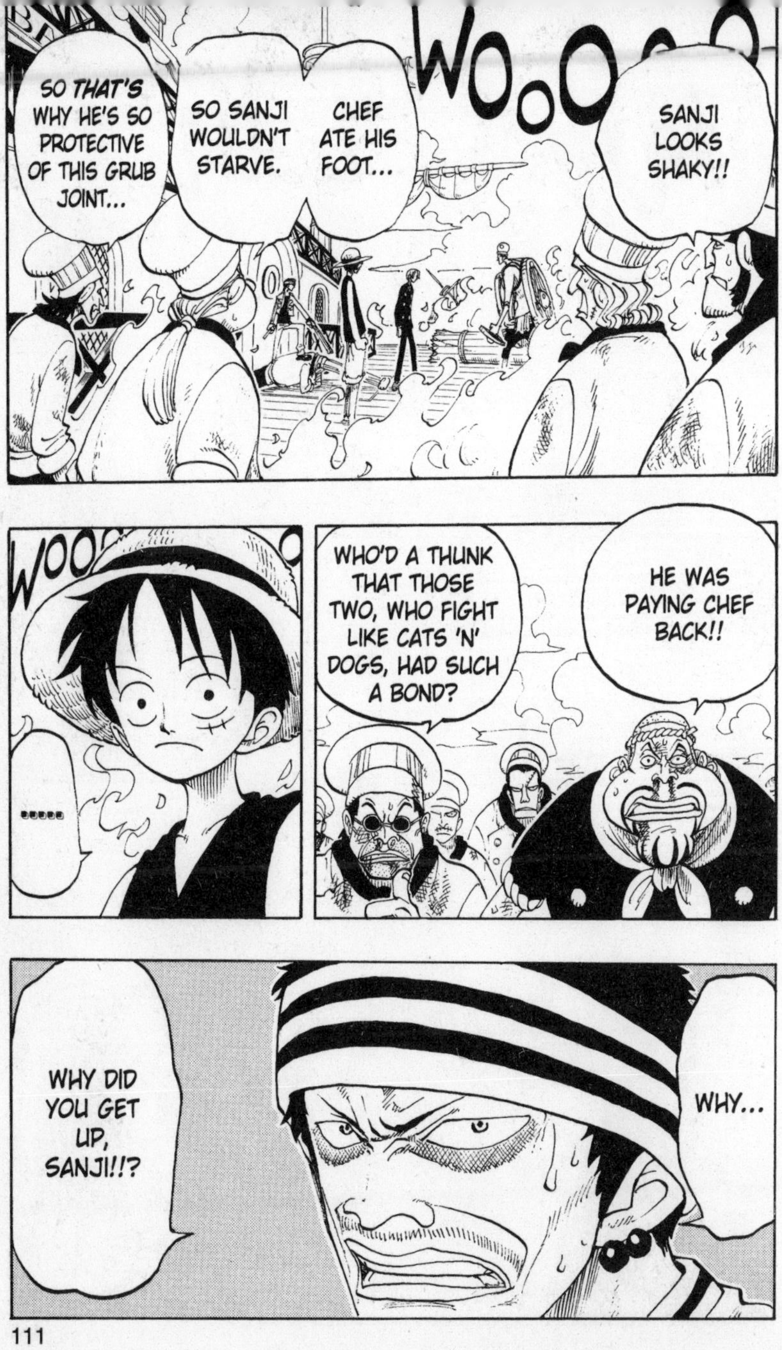
SANJI LOOKS SHAKY!!
WOoO
CHEF ATE HIS FOOT...
SO SANJI WOULDN'T STARVE.
SO *THAT'S* WHY HE'S SO PROTECTIVE OF THIS GRUB JOINT...
HE WAS PAYING CHEF BACK!!
WHO'D A THUNK THAT THOSE TWO, WHO FIGHT LIKE CATS 'N' DOGS, HAD SUCH A BOND?
WOO
.....
WHY...
WHY DID YOU GET UP, SANJI!!?

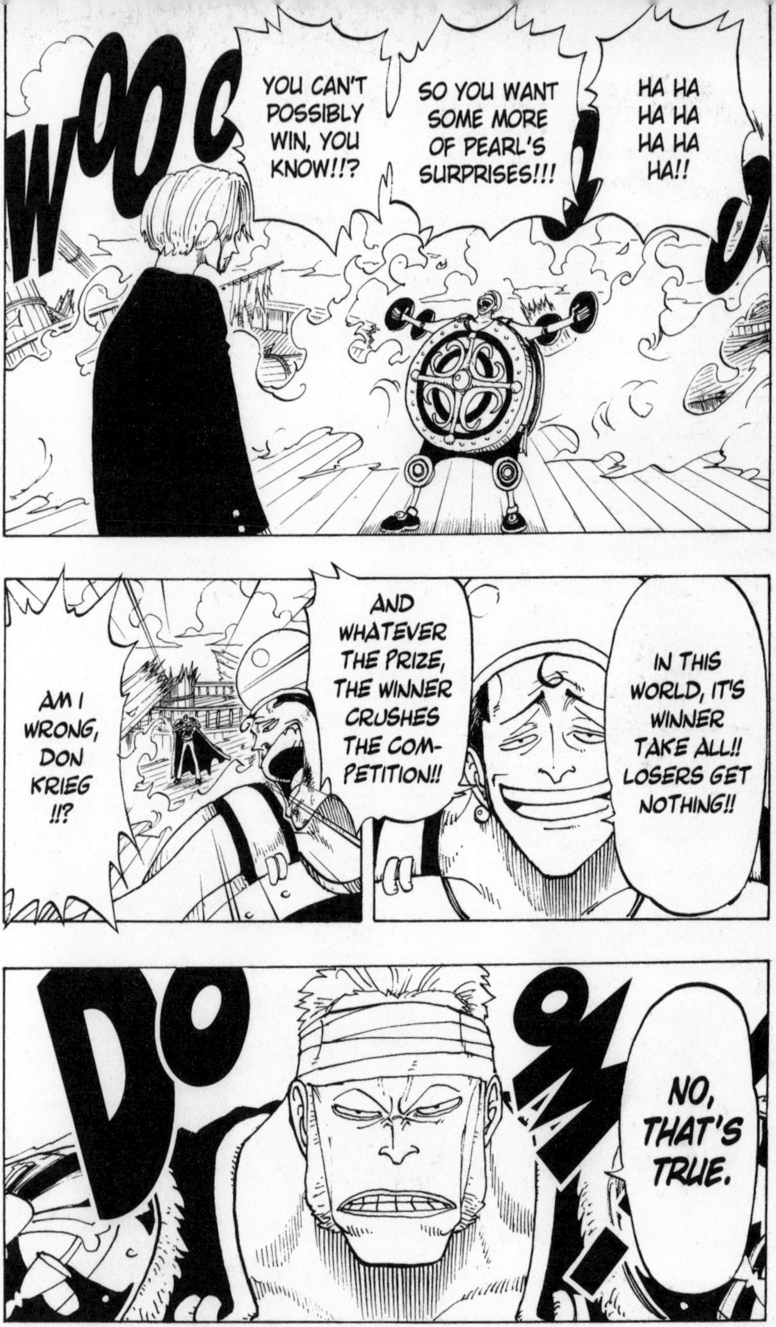
HA HA HA HA HA HA HA!!
SO YOU WANT SOME MORE OF PEARL'S SURPRISES!!!
YOU CAN'T POSSIBLY WIN, YOU KNOW!!?
IN THIS WORLD, IT'S WINNER TAKE ALL!! LOSERS GET NOTHING!!
AND WHATEVER THE PRIZE, THE WINNER CRUSHES THE COM-PETITION!!
AM I WRONG, DON KRIEG!!?
NO, THAT'S TRUE.

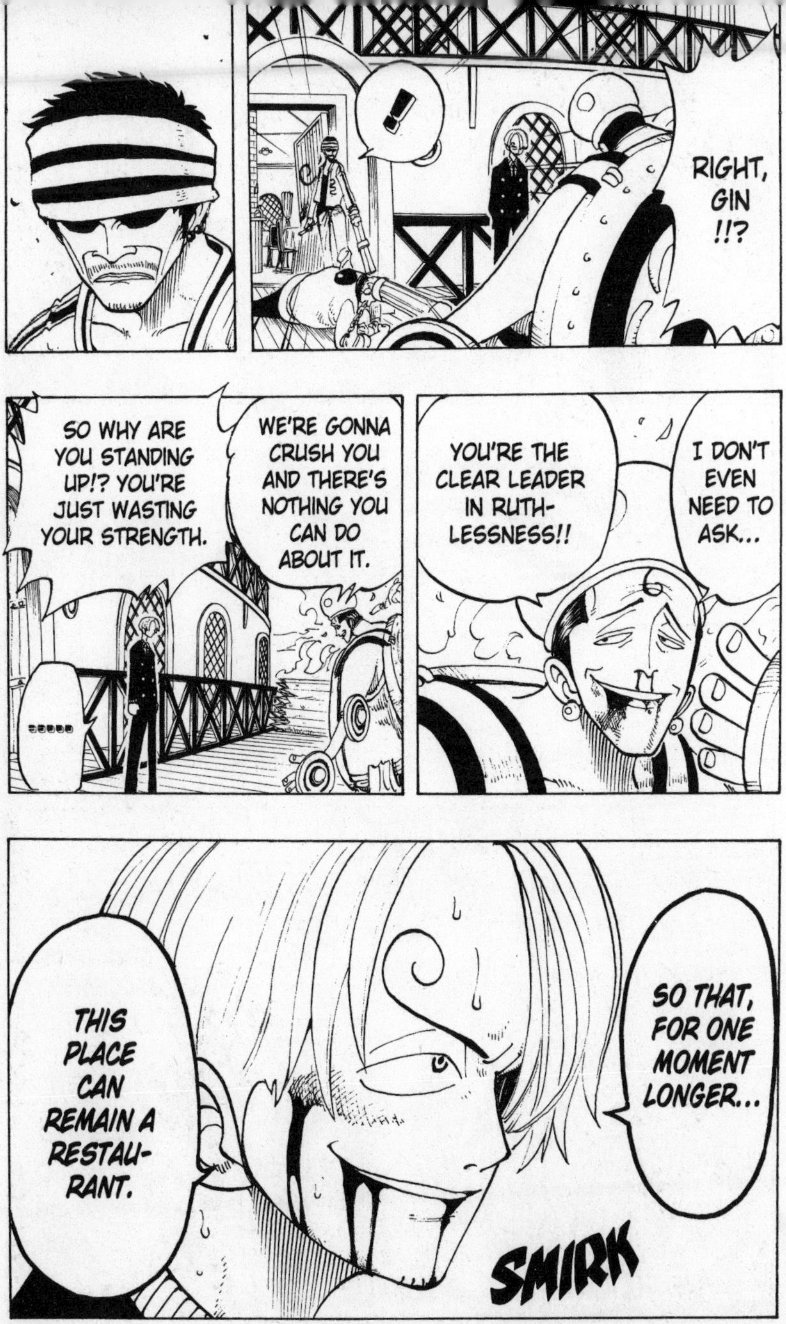
RIGHT, GIN !!?
!
I DON'T EVEN NEED TO ASK...
YOU'RE THE CLEAR LEADER IN RUTH-LESSNESS!!
WE'RE GONNA CRUSH YOU AND THERE'S NOTHING YOU CAN DO ABOUT IT.
SO WHY ARE YOU STANDING UP!? YOU'RE JUST WASTING YOUR STRENGTH.
.....
SO THAT, FOR ONE MOMENT LONGER...
THIS PLACE CAN REMAIN A RESTAU-RANT.
SMIRK

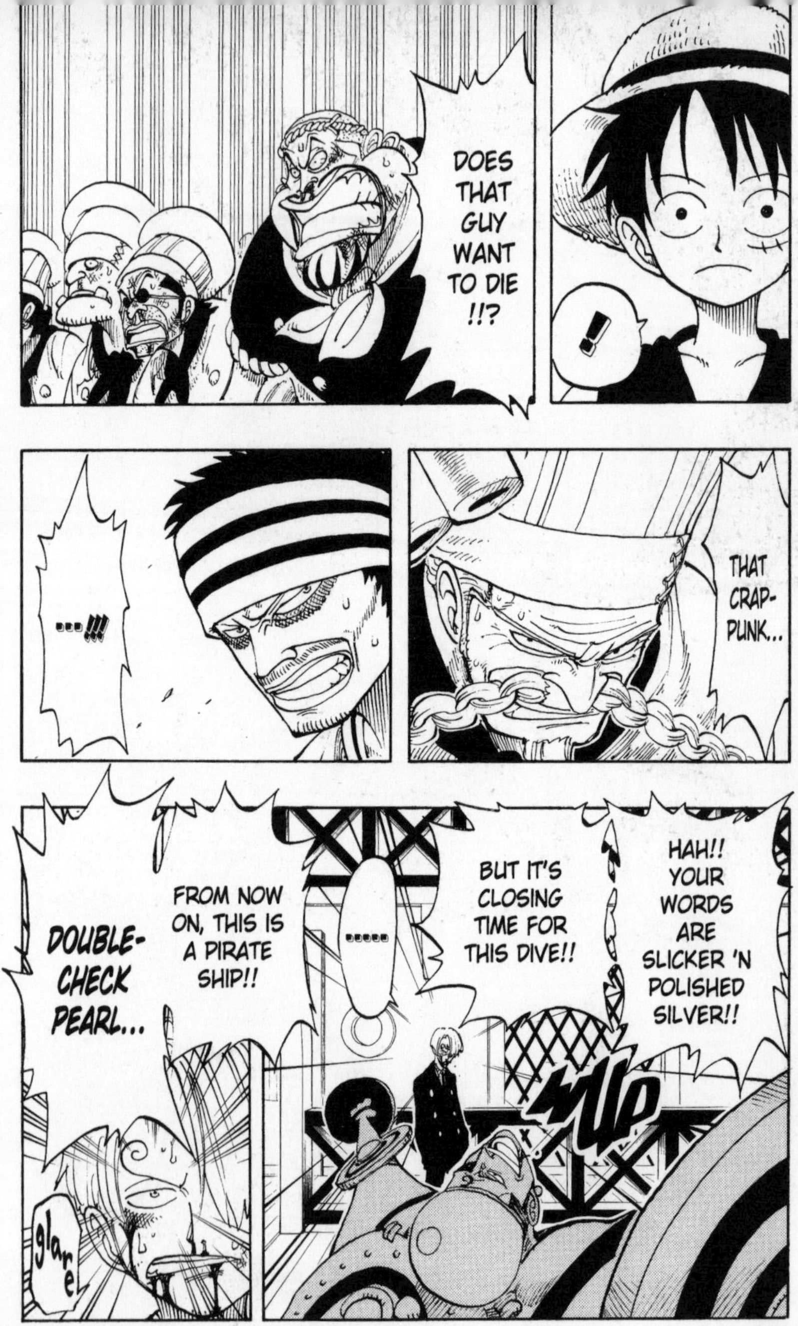
!
DOES THAT GUY WANT TO DIE !!?
THAT CRAP-PUNK...
...!!!
HAH!! YOUR WORDS ARE SLICKER 'N POLISHED SILVER!!
BUT IT'S CLOSING TIME FOR THIS DIVE!!
.....
FROM NOW ON, THIS IS A PIRATE SHIP!!
DOUBLE-CHECK PEARL...
glare

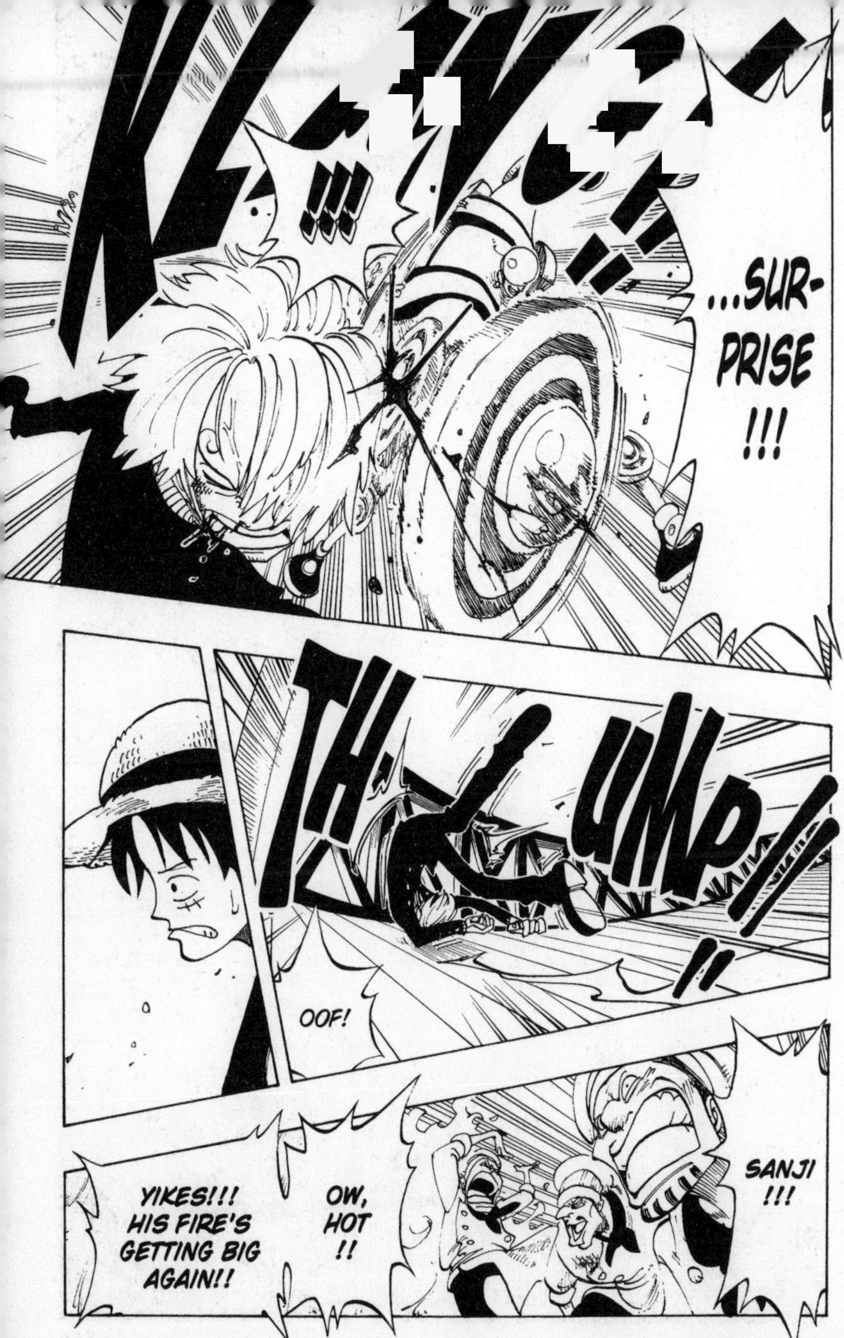
...SUR-
PRISE
!!!
THUMP!!
OOF!
SANJI
!!!
OW,
HOT
!!
YIKES!!!
HIS FIRE'S
GETTING BIG
AGAIN!!

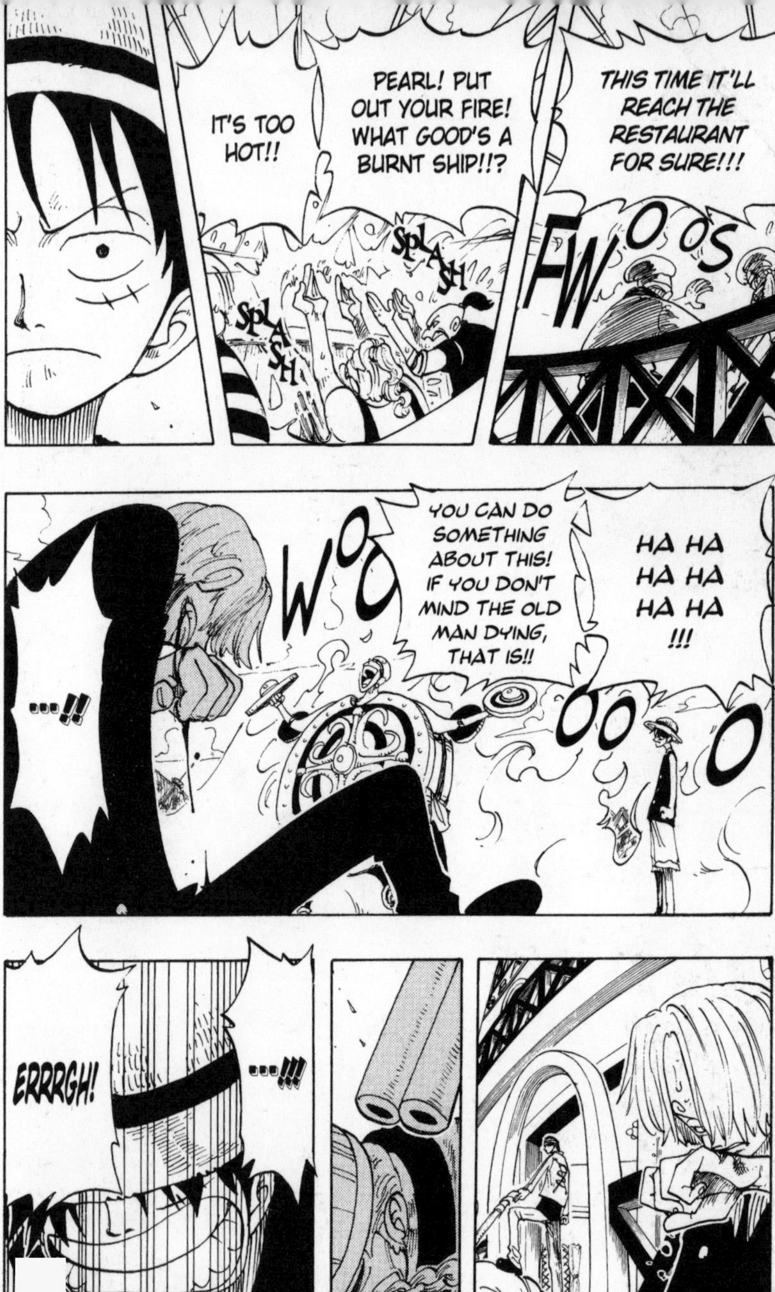
THIS TIME IT'LL REACH THE RESTAURANT FOR SURE!!!
FWOOOSH
PEARL! PUT OUT YOUR FIRE! WHAT GOOD'S A BURNT SHIP!!?
IT'S TOO HOT!!
SPLASH
SPLASH
HA HA HA HA HA HA !!!
YOU CAN DO SOMETHING ABOUT THIS! IF YOU DON'T MIND THE OLD MAN DYING, THAT IS!!
WOOOOOO
...!!
...!!!
ERRRGH!

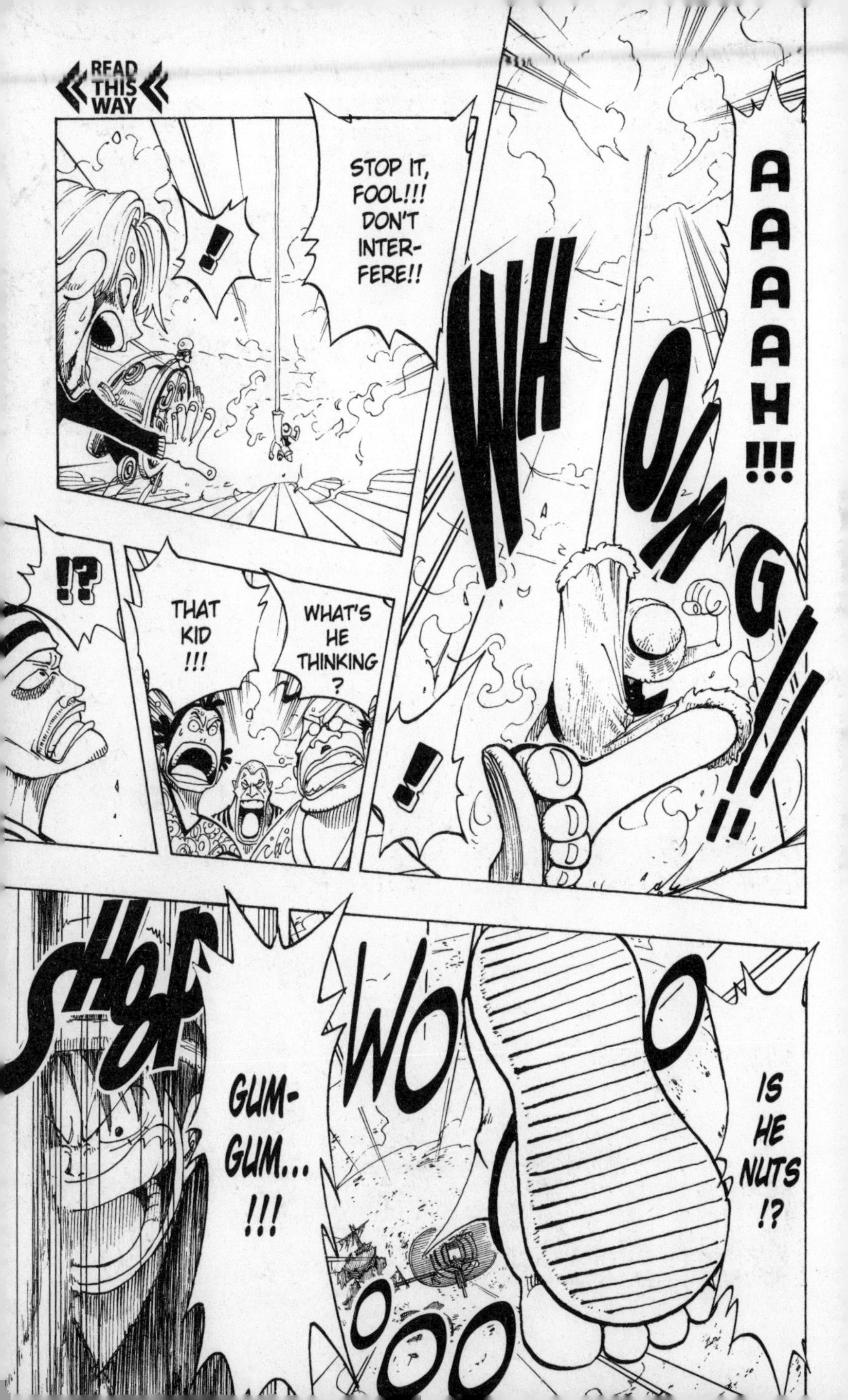
READ THIS WAY
AAAAAH!!!
WHOOONG!!
!
!
STOP IT, FOOL!!! DON'T INTERFERE!!
WHAT'S HE THINKING?
THAT KID!!!
!?
IS HE NUTS!?
WOOOOO
GUM-GUM...!!!

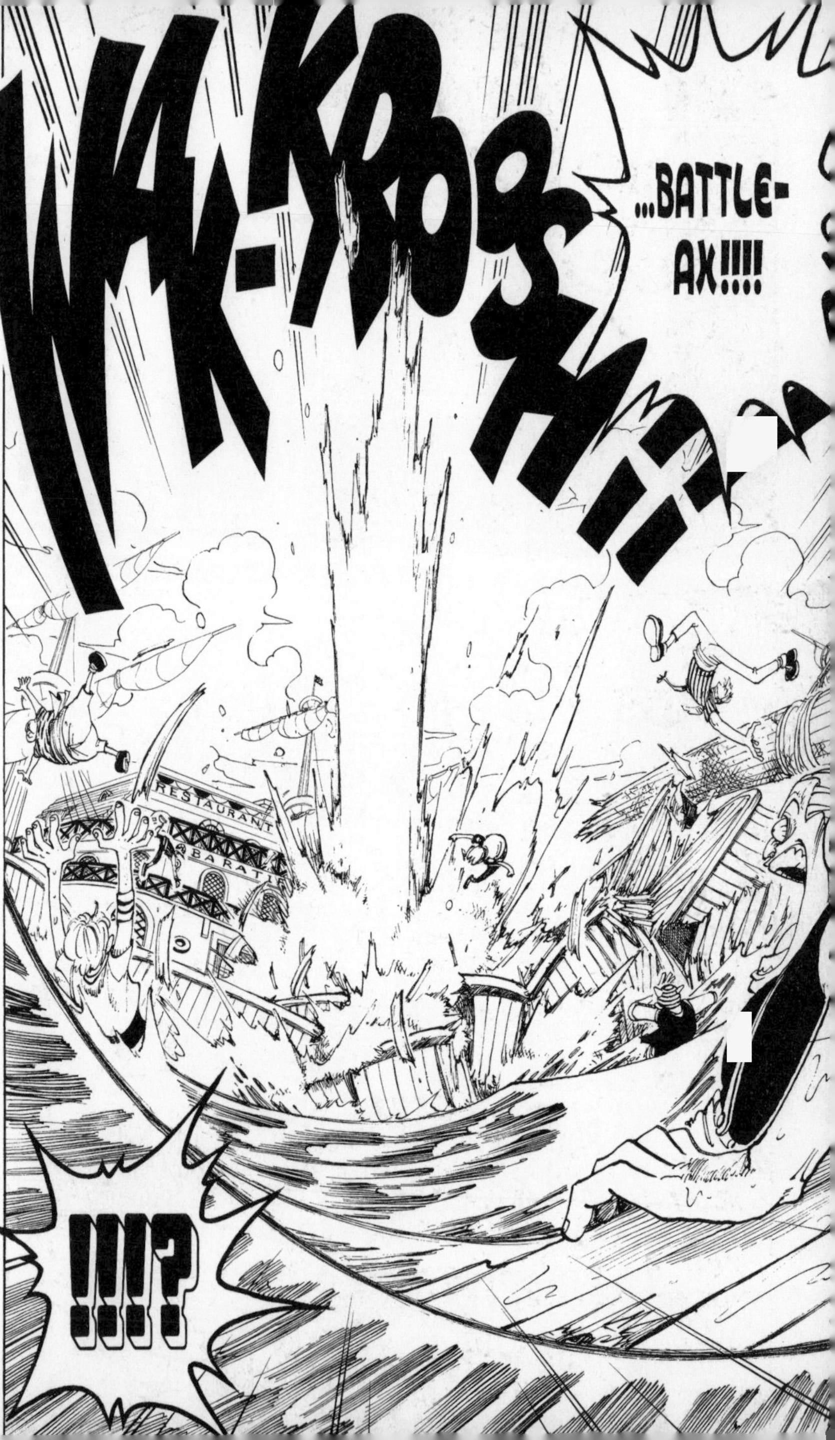

WAK-KRA-KOOSH!!
...BATTLE-AX!!!!
RESTAURANT BARATIE
!!!?

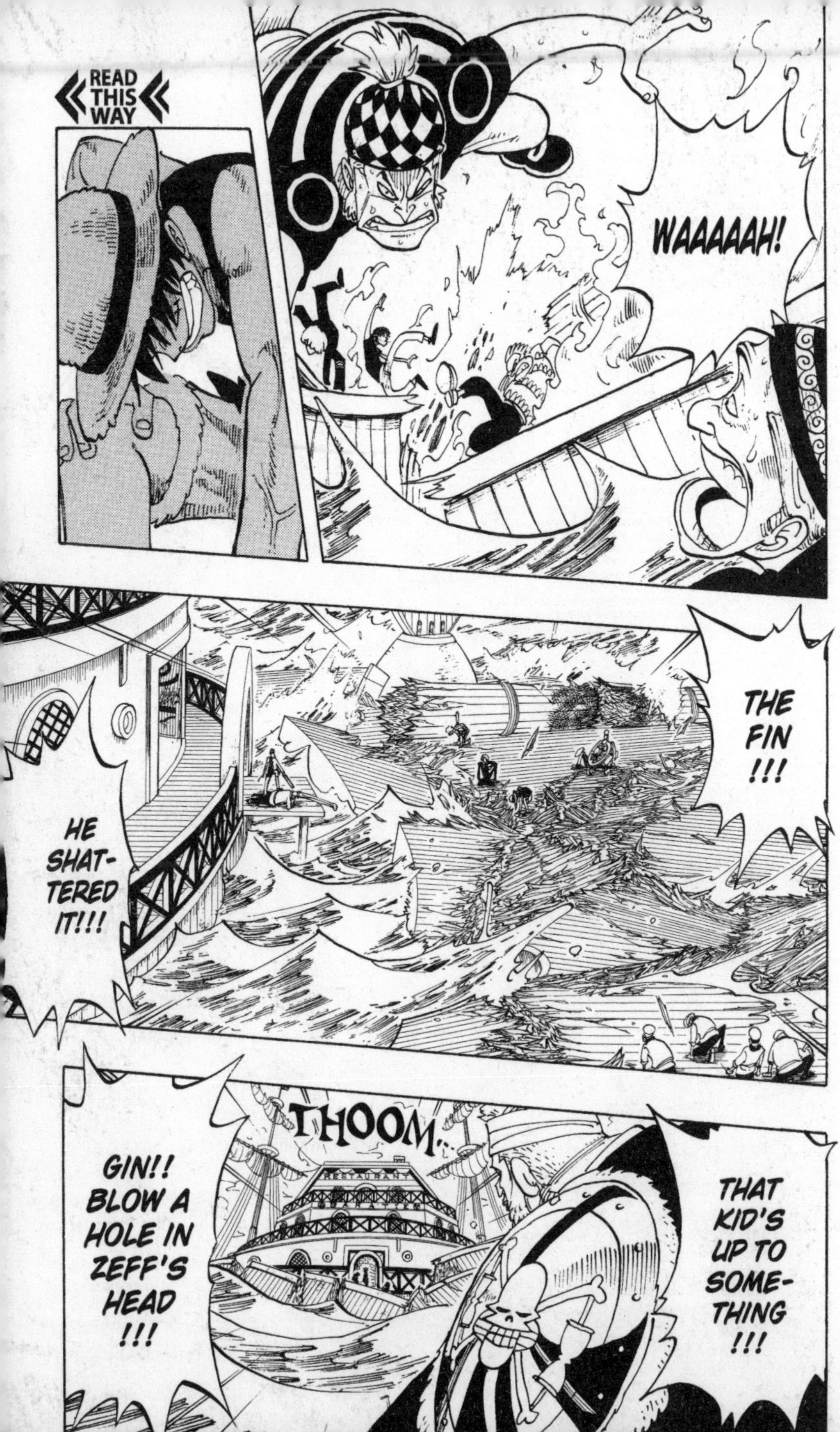
READ THIS WAY
WAAAAAH!
THE FIN!!!
HE SHATTERED IT!!!
THAT KID'S UP TO SOMETHING!!!
THOOM
GIN!! BLOW A HOLE IN ZEFF'S HEAD!!!
RESTAURANT BARATIE

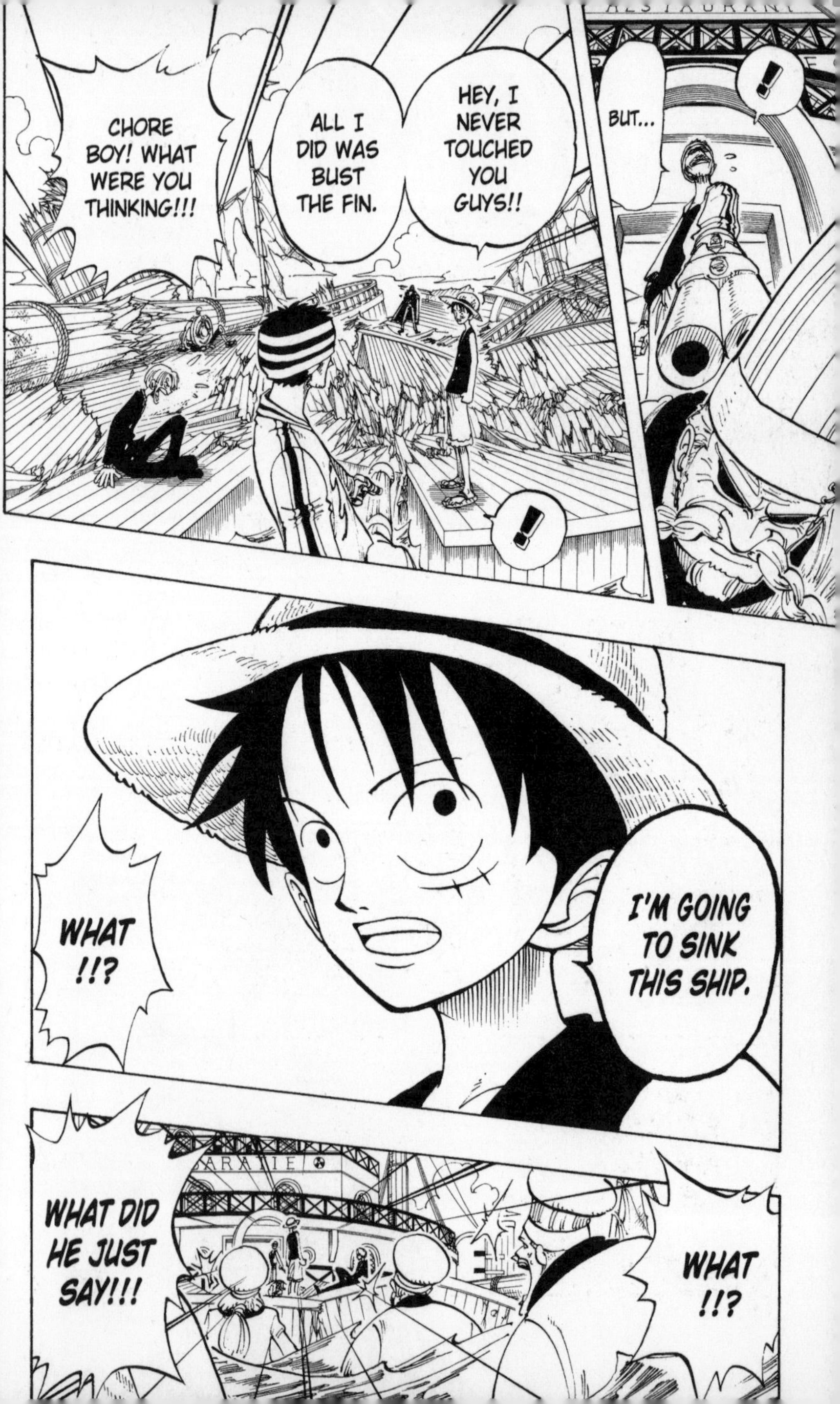
!
BUT...
HEY, I NEVER TOUCHED YOU GUYS!!
ALL I DID WAS BUST THE FIN.
CHORE BOY! WHAT WERE YOU THINKING!!!
!
I'M GOING TO SINK THIS SHIP.
WHAT !!?
WHAT !!?
WHAT DID HE JUST SAY!!!

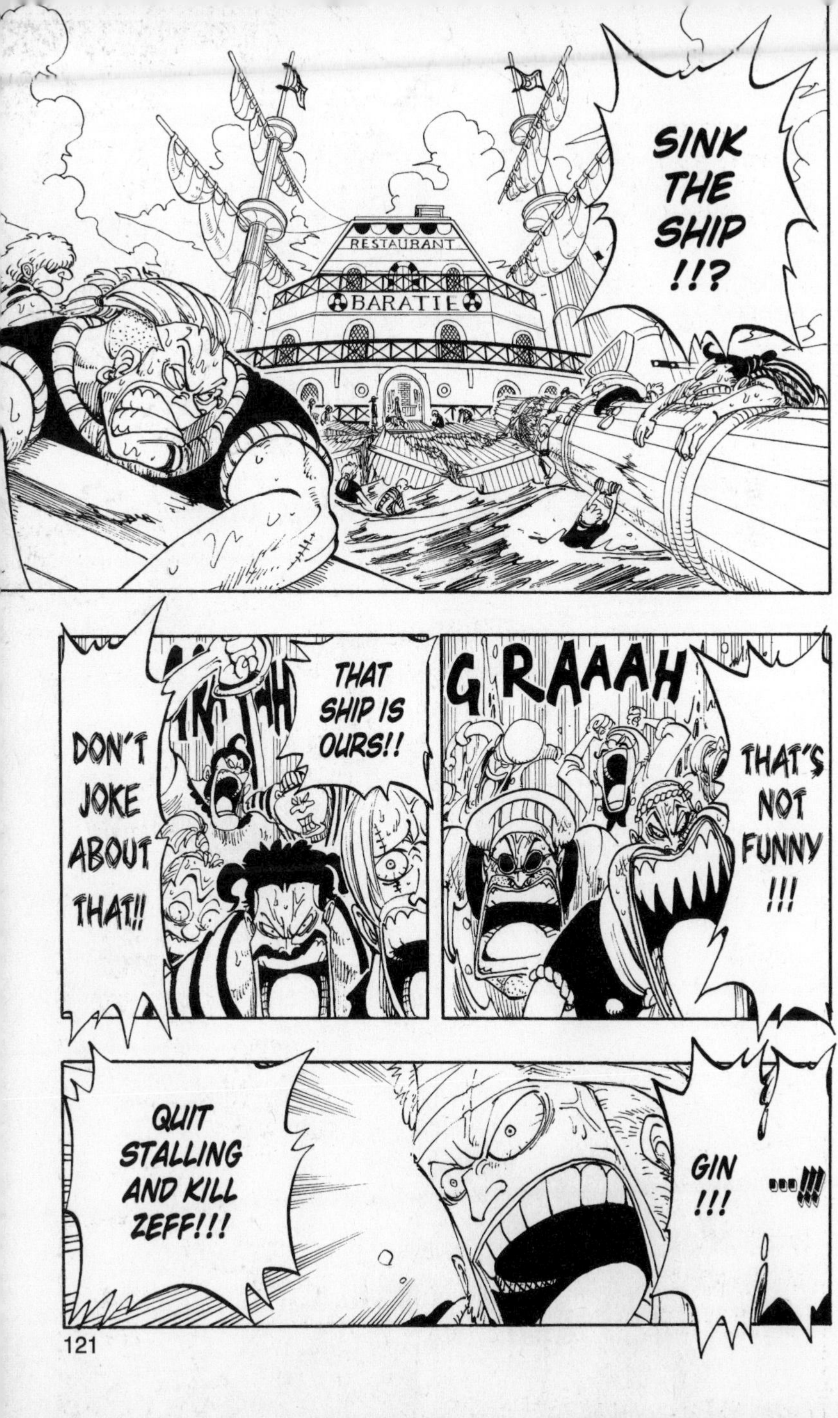
SINK THE SHIP!!?
RESTAURANT
BARATIE
GRAAAH
THAT'S NOT FUNNY!!!
THAT SHIP IS OURS!!
DON'T JOKE ABOUT THAT!!
...!!!
GIN!!!
QUIT STALLING AND KILL ZEFF!!!

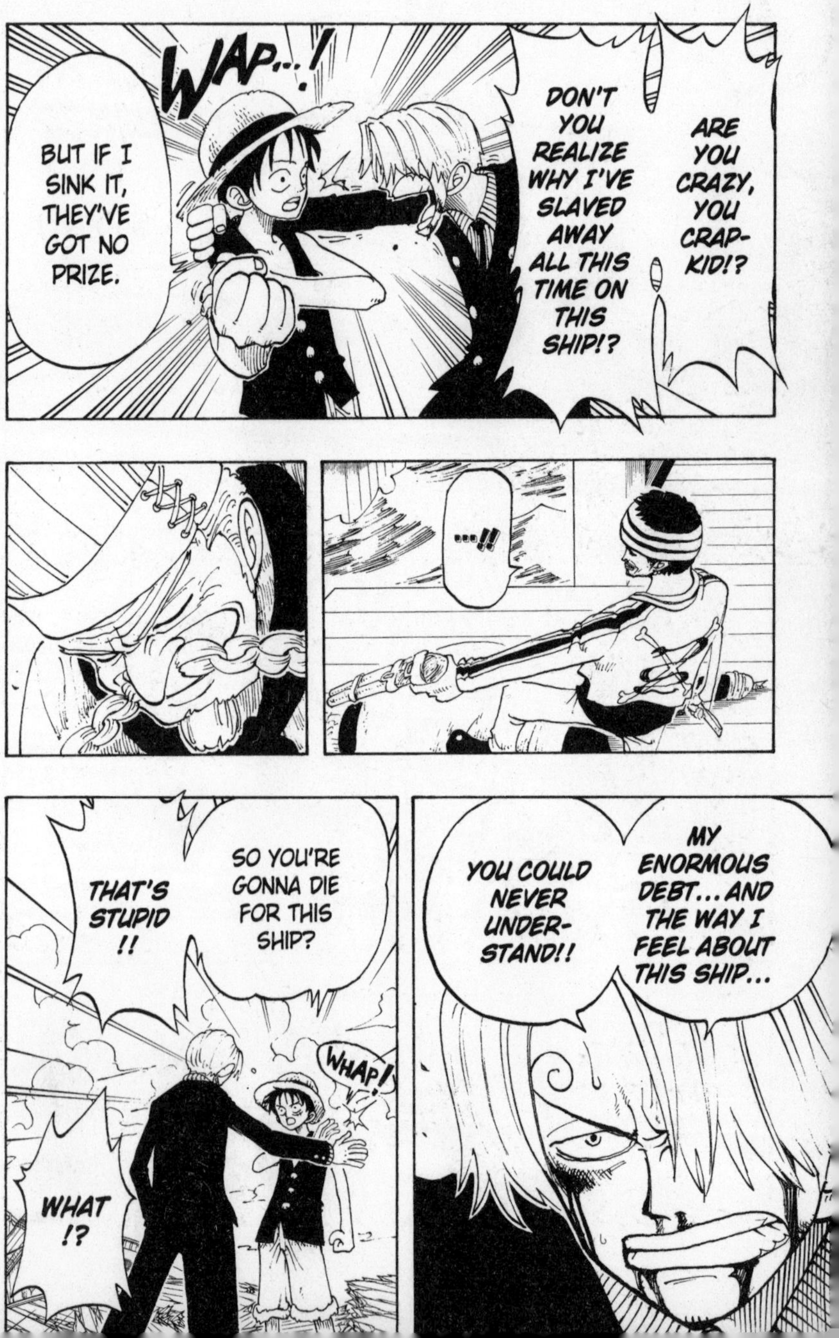
ARE YOU CRAZY, YOU CRAP-KID!?
DON'T YOU REALIZE WHY I'VE SLAVED AWAY ALL THIS TIME ON THIS SHIP!?
WAP...!
BUT IF I SINK IT, THEY'VE GOT NO PRIZE.
...!!
MY ENORMOUS DEBT...AND THE WAY I FEEL ABOUT THIS SHIP...
YOU COULD NEVER UNDER-STAND!!
SO YOU'RE GONNA DIE FOR THIS SHIP?
THAT'S STUPID!!
WHAP!
WHAT!?

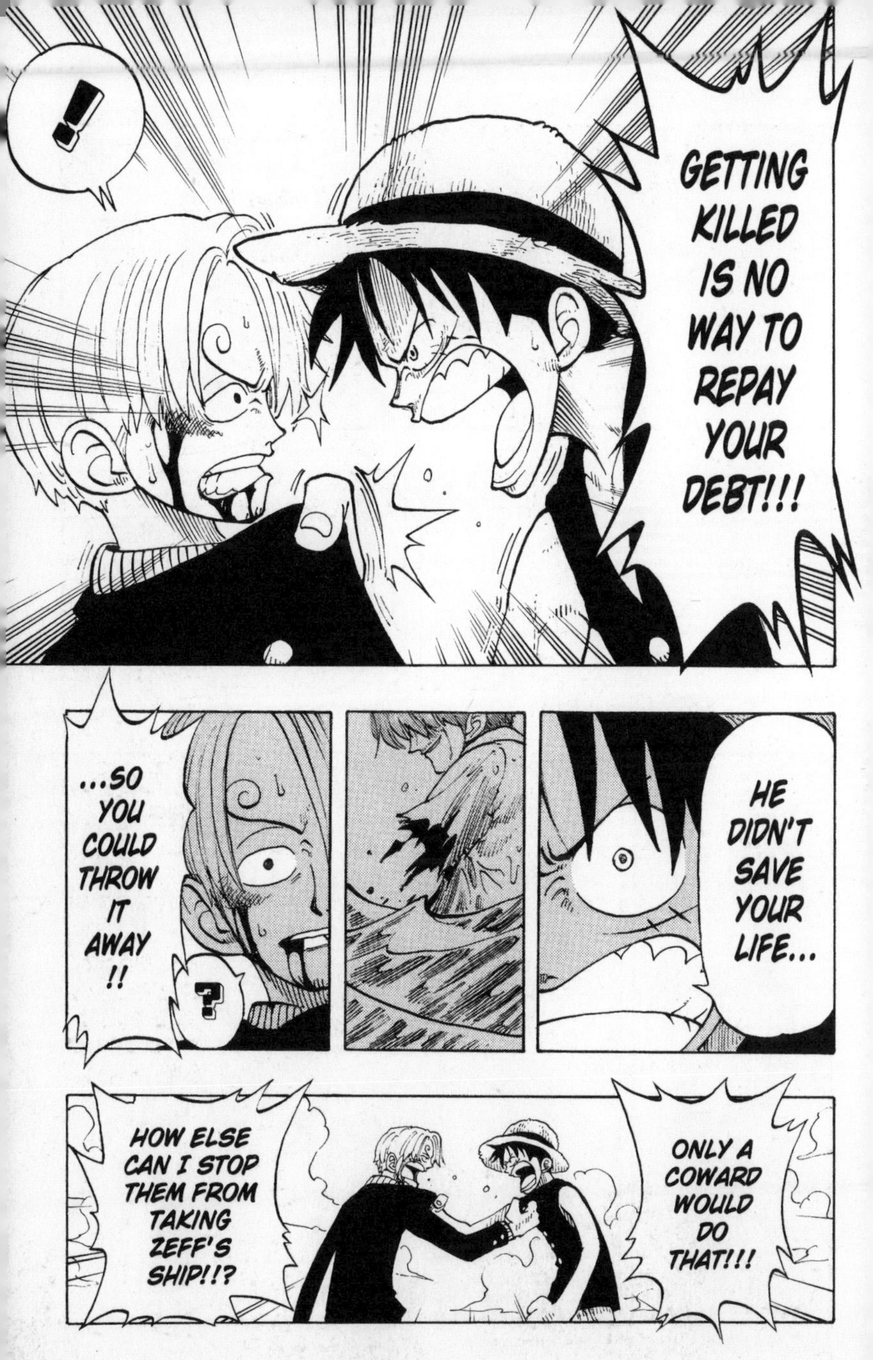
GETTING KILLED IS NO WAY TO REPAY YOUR DEBT!!!
!
HE DIDN'T SAVE YOUR LIFE...
...SO YOU COULD THROW IT AWAY !!
?
ONLY A COWARD WOULD DO THAT!!!
HOW ELSE CAN I STOP THEM FROM TAKING ZEFF'S SHIP!!?

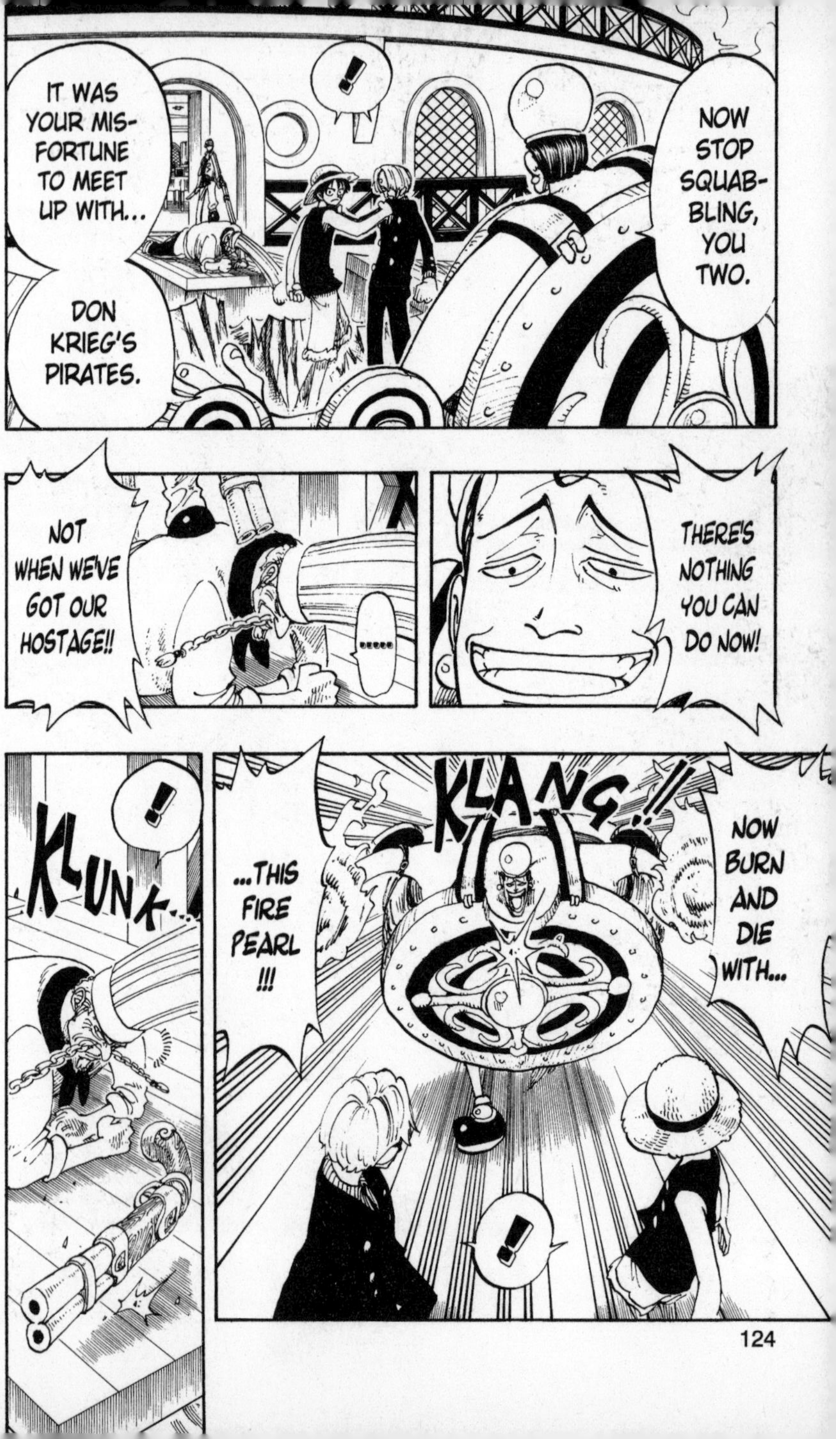
NOW STOP SQUAB-BLING, YOU TWO.
!
IT WAS YOUR MIS-FORTUNE TO MEET UP WITH...
DON KRIEG'S PIRATES.
THERE'S NOTHING YOU CAN DO NOW!
NOT WHEN WE'VE GOT OUR HOSTAGE!!
.....
NOW BURN AND DIE WITH...
KLANG!!
...THIS FIRE PEARL!!!
!
!
KLUNK...

WHOA!!

...!!

WHA--!!?

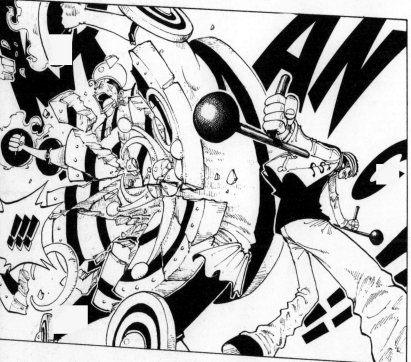

GIN!!!?

125

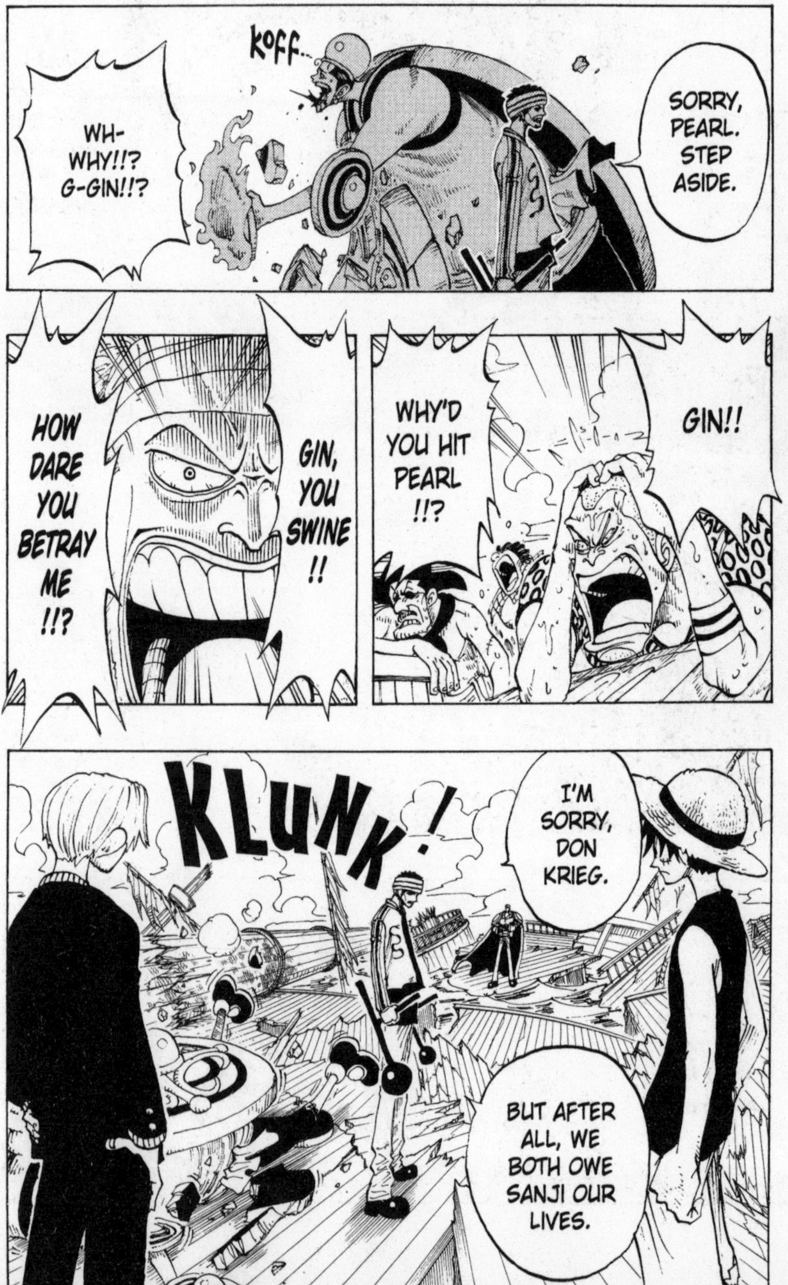
SORRY, PEARL. STEP ASIDE.
KOFF...
WH- WHY!!? G-GIN!!?
GIN!!
WHY'D YOU HIT PEARL !!?
GIN, YOU SWINE !!
HOW DARE YOU BETRAY ME !!?
I'M SORRY, DON KRIEG.
KLUNK!
BUT AFTER ALL, WE BOTH OWE SANJI OUR LIVES.

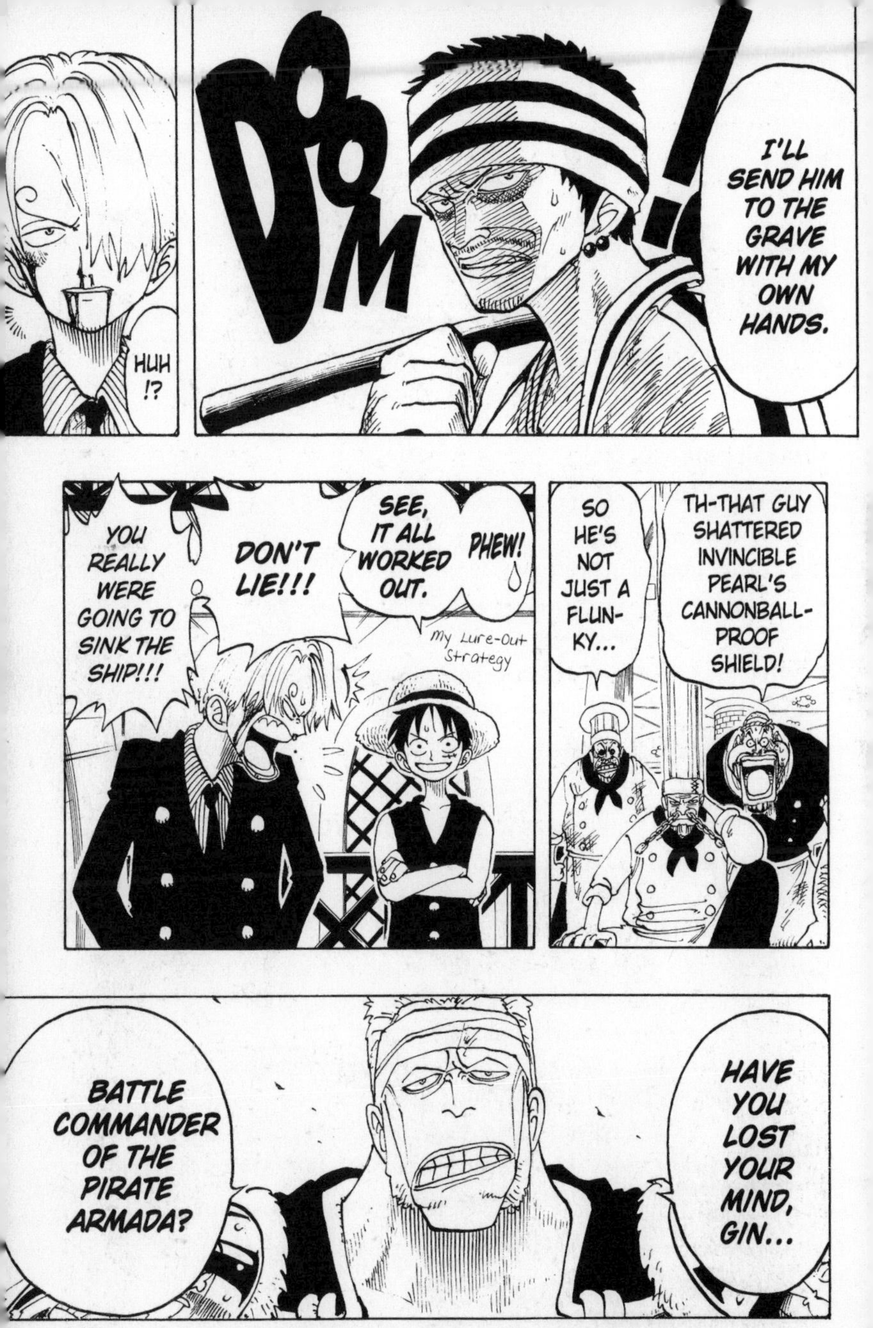
DOOM
I'LL SEND HIM TO THE GRAVE WITH MY OWN HANDS.
HUH !?
TH-THAT GUY SHATTERED INVINCIBLE PEARL'S CANNONBALL-PROOF SHIELD!
SO HE'S NOT JUST A FLUN-KY...
PHEW!
SEE, IT ALL WORKED OUT.
My Lure-Out Strategy
DON'T LIE!!!
YOU REALLY WERE GOING TO SINK THE SHIP!!!
HAVE YOU LOST YOUR MIND, GIN...
BATTLE COMMANDER OF THE PIRATE ARMADA?

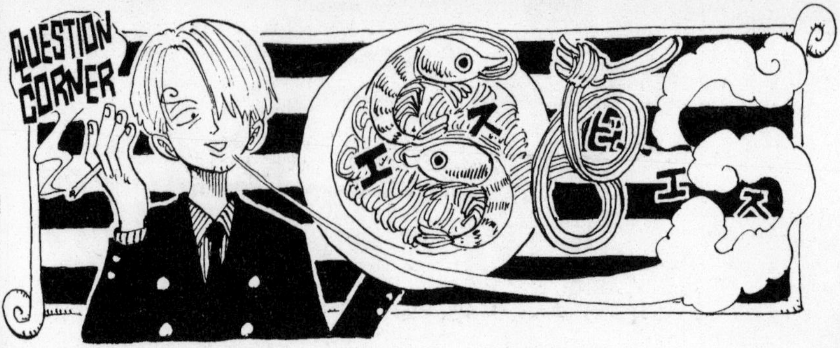
QUESTION CORNER

Q: Did you know that Koby's father is the world champion of jumping rope?

A: Really? I didn't know that. Koby's dad is very impressive...

Q: Is it true that Klahadore has a pet mammoth?

A: Really? I didn't know that either. Was there one at the mansion?

Q: What are your selection criteria for Usopp's Pirate Gallery?

A: Naturally, I consider skill, how interesting it is, style...But the most important thing is the spirit you convey in the postcard. Yeah.

Q: The other day while I was working at the fruit stand, this smart-aleck kid said, "You don't have Gum-Gum Fruit? What a dork." If a kid like that comes again, what should I say? Please tell me. (I'm serious.)

A: In a case like that, each character would probably respond as follows:

Makino: "You're right, I'm sorry we don't stock it." (Be an adult and let it pass.)

Shanks: "Ha ha ha ha ha!! You're ten years too young for a Devil Fruit!!" (Taunt him.)

Luffy: "I'll send you flying, right now." (No mercy.)

Try whichever approach you like--but don't hold me responsible.

Q: Please do a character popularity poll!!

A: Well, I won't be doing it in the comic book, but I did it in *Weekly Shonen Jump* and the results are in, so I'll present them on page 148.

(I think this poll was taken two or three weeks after *Chapter 49: Storm* came out.)

Chapter 60: RESOLUTION

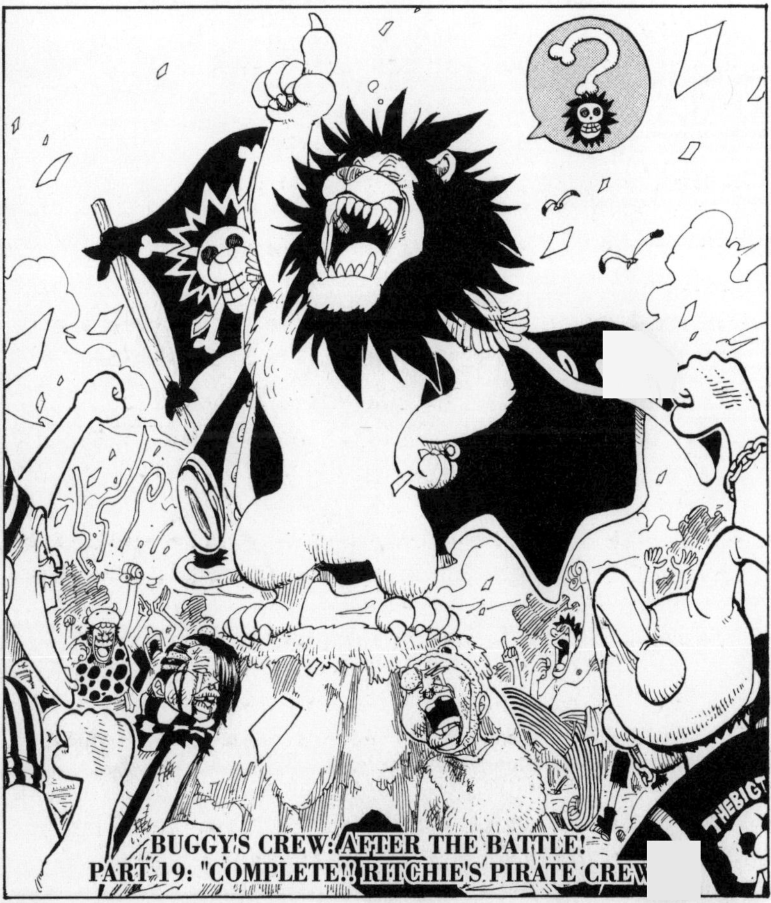
BUGGY'S CREW: AFTER THE BATTLE!
PART 19: "COMPLETE!! RITCHIE'S PIRATE CREW

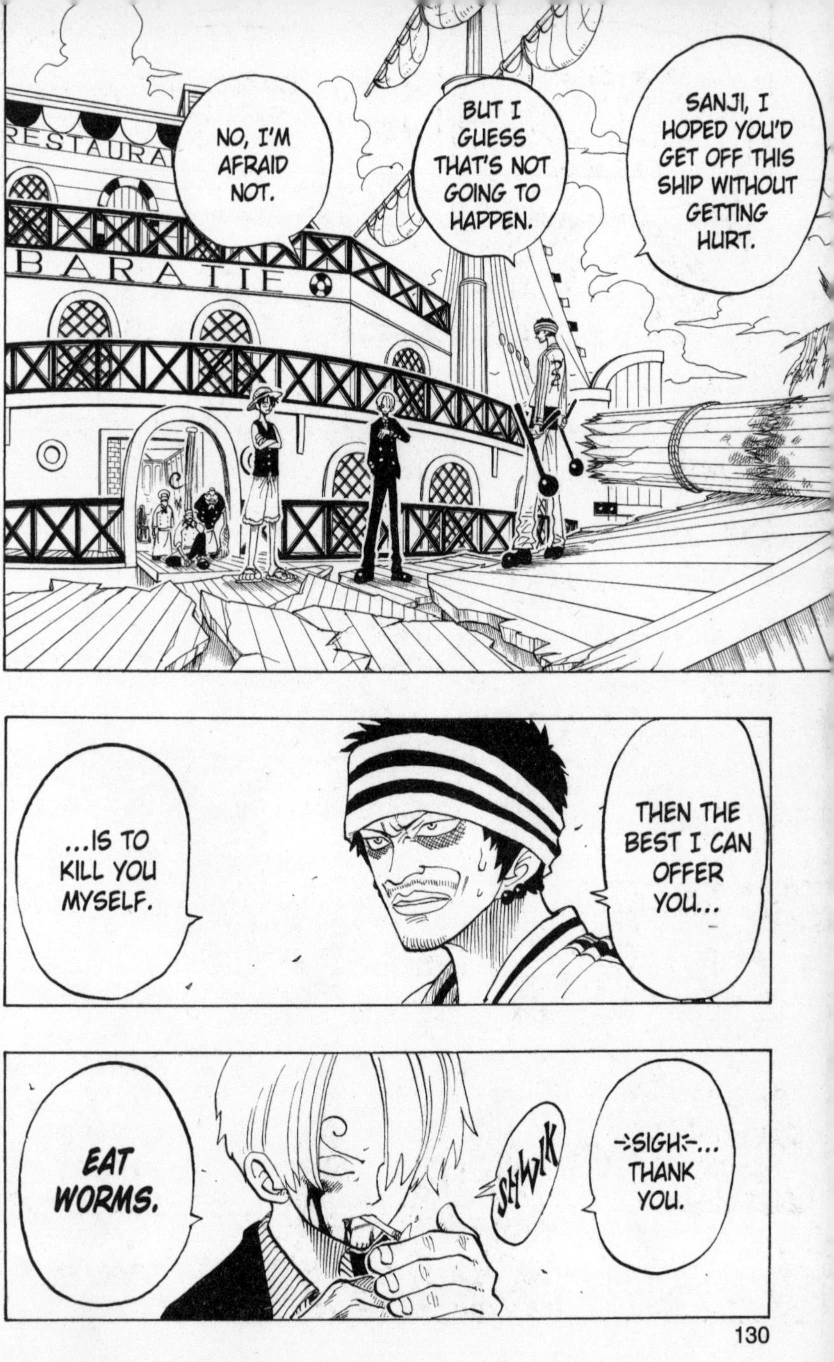
SANJI, I HOPED YOU'D GET OFF THIS SHIP WITHOUT GETTING HURT.
BUT I GUESS THAT'S NOT GOING TO HAPPEN.
NO, I'M AFRAID NOT.
RESTAURA
BARATIE
THEN THE BEST I CAN OFFER YOU...
...IS TO KILL YOU MYSELF.
-SIGH-... THANK YOU.
SHWIK
EAT WORMS.

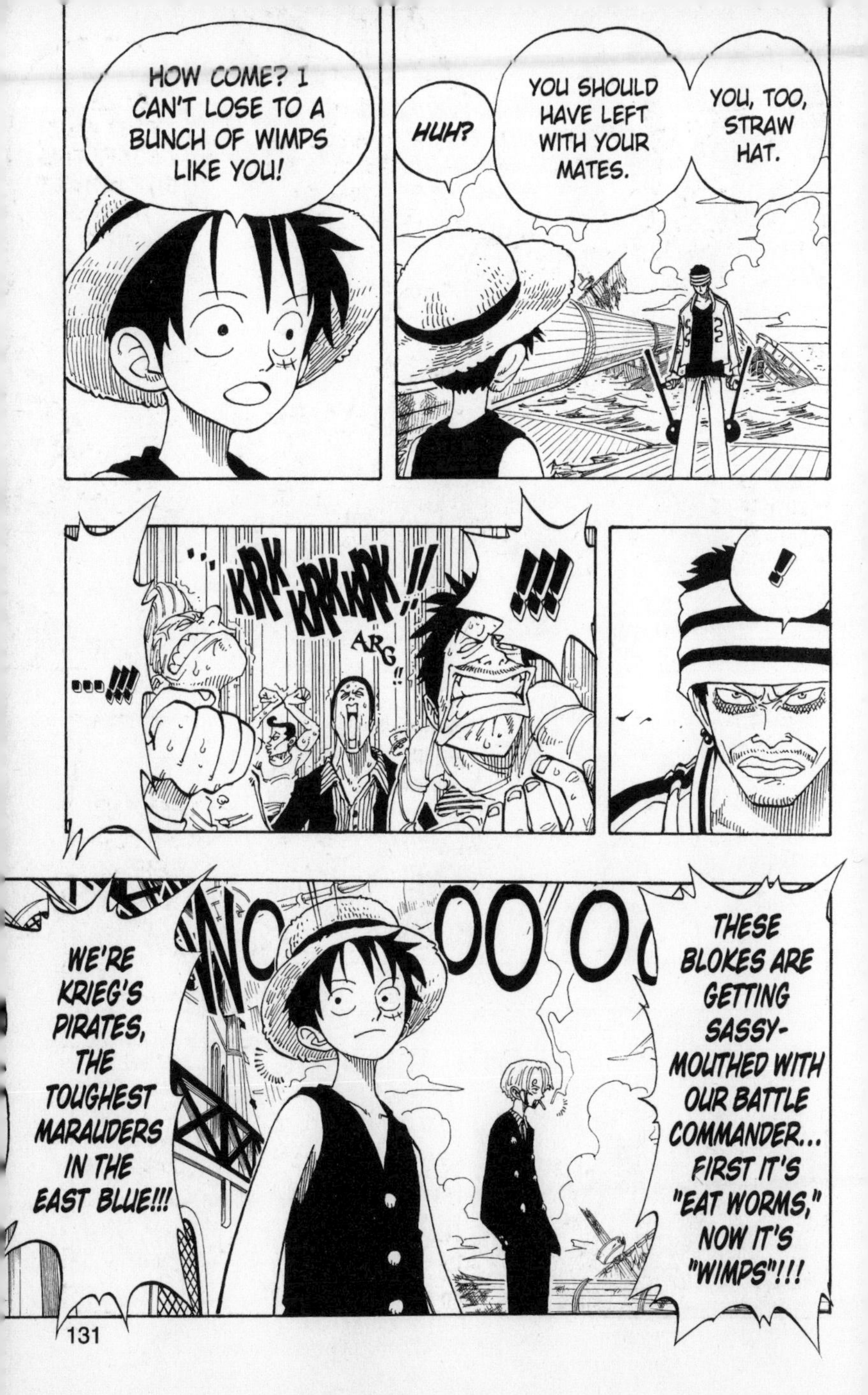
YOU, TOO, STRAW HAT.
YOU SHOULD HAVE LEFT WITH YOUR MATES.
HUH?
HOW COME? I CAN'T LOSE TO A BUNCH OF WIMPS LIKE YOU!
!
!!!!
KRK KRKKRK!!
ARG!!
...!!!
THESE BLOKES ARE GETTING SASSY-MOUTHED WITH OUR BATTLE COMMANDER... FIRST IT'S "EAT WORMS," NOW IT'S "WIMPS"!!!
WE'RE KRIEG'S PIRATES, THE TOUGHEST MARAUDERS IN THE EAST BLUE!!!

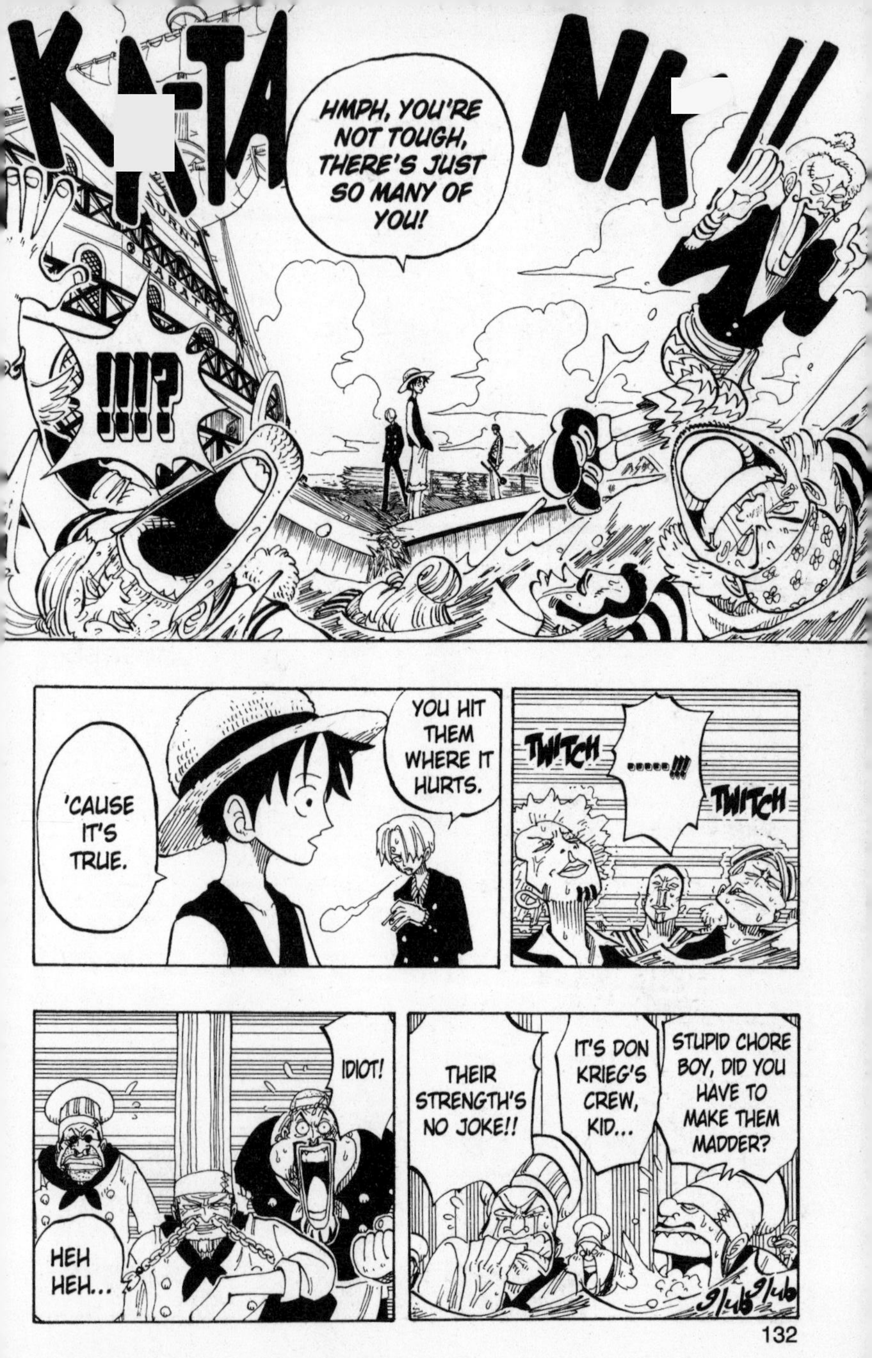
HMPH, YOU'RE NOT TOUGH, THERE'S JUST SO MANY OF YOU!
!!!?
TWITCH
.....!!!
TWITCH
YOU HIT THEM WHERE IT HURTS.
'CAUSE IT'S TRUE.
STUPID CHORE BOY, DID YOU HAVE TO MAKE THEM MADDER?
IT'S DON KRIEG'S CREW, KID...
THEIR STRENGTH'S NO JOKE!!
IDIOT!
HEH HEH...

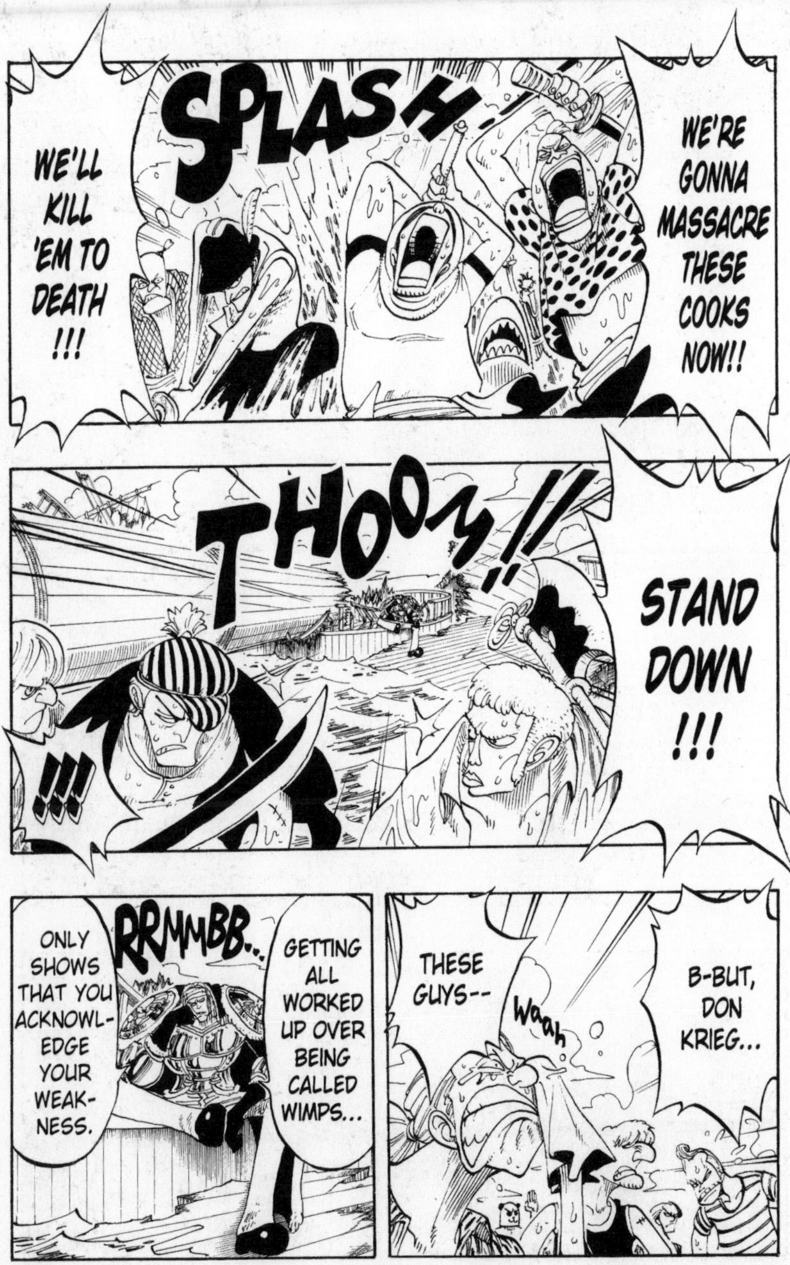
WE'RE GONNA MASSACRE THESE COOKS NOW!!
SPLASH
WE'LL KILL 'EM TO DEATH !!!
STAND DOWN !!!
THOOM!!
!!!
B-BUT, DON KRIEG...
Waah
THESE GUYS--
GETTING ALL WORKED UP OVER BEING CALLED WIMPS...
RRMMBB...
ONLY SHOWS THAT YOU ACKNOWL-EDGE YOUR WEAK-NESS.

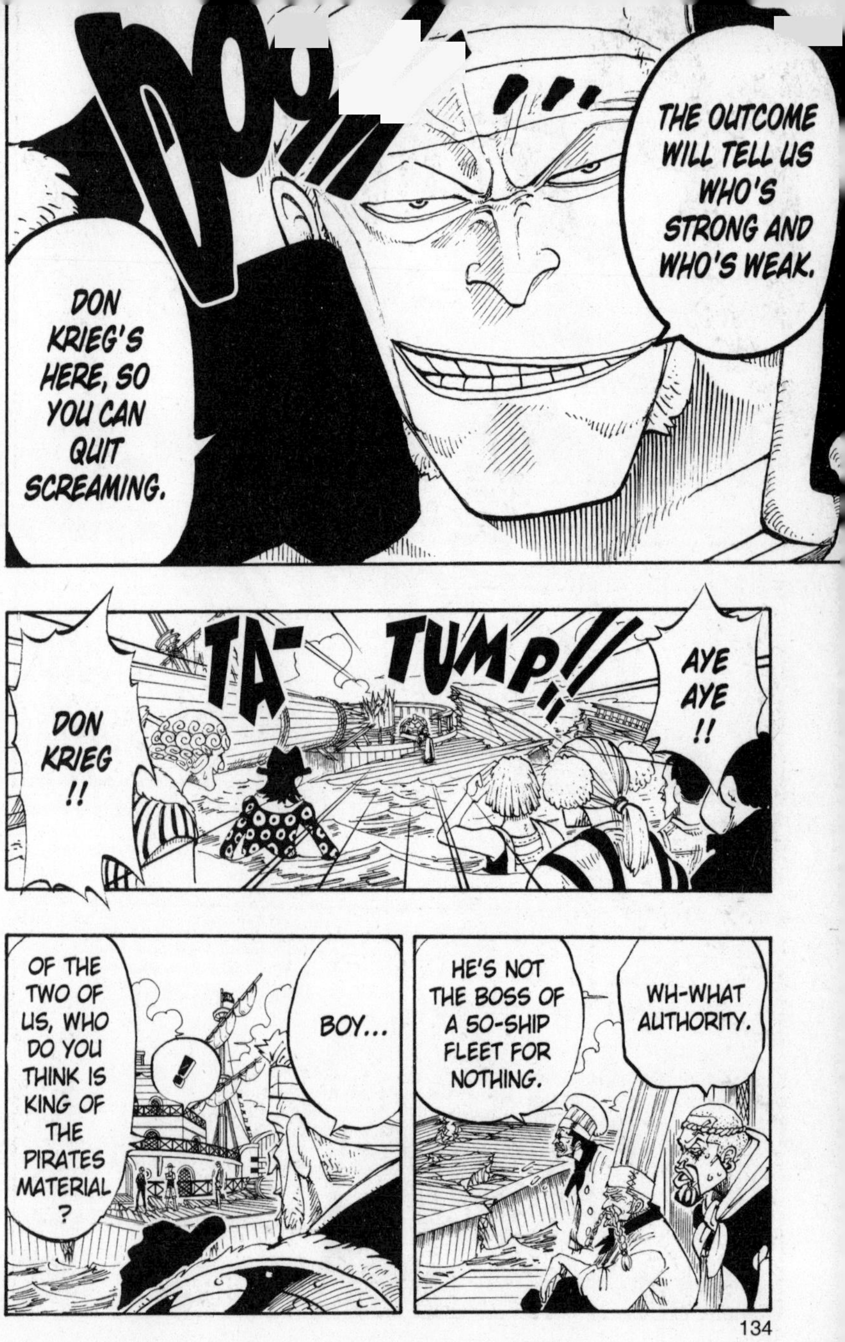

THE OUTCOME WILL TELL US WHO'S STRONG AND WHO'S WEAK.
DOO
...
DON KRIEG'S HERE, SO YOU CAN QUIT SCREAMING.
AYE AYE !!
TA- TUMP!!
DON KRIEG !!
WH-WHAT AUTHORITY.
HE'S NOT THE BOSS OF A 50-SHIP FLEET FOR NOTHING.
BOY...
!
OF THE TWO OF US, WHO DO YOU THINK IS KING OF THE PIRATES MATERIAL ?

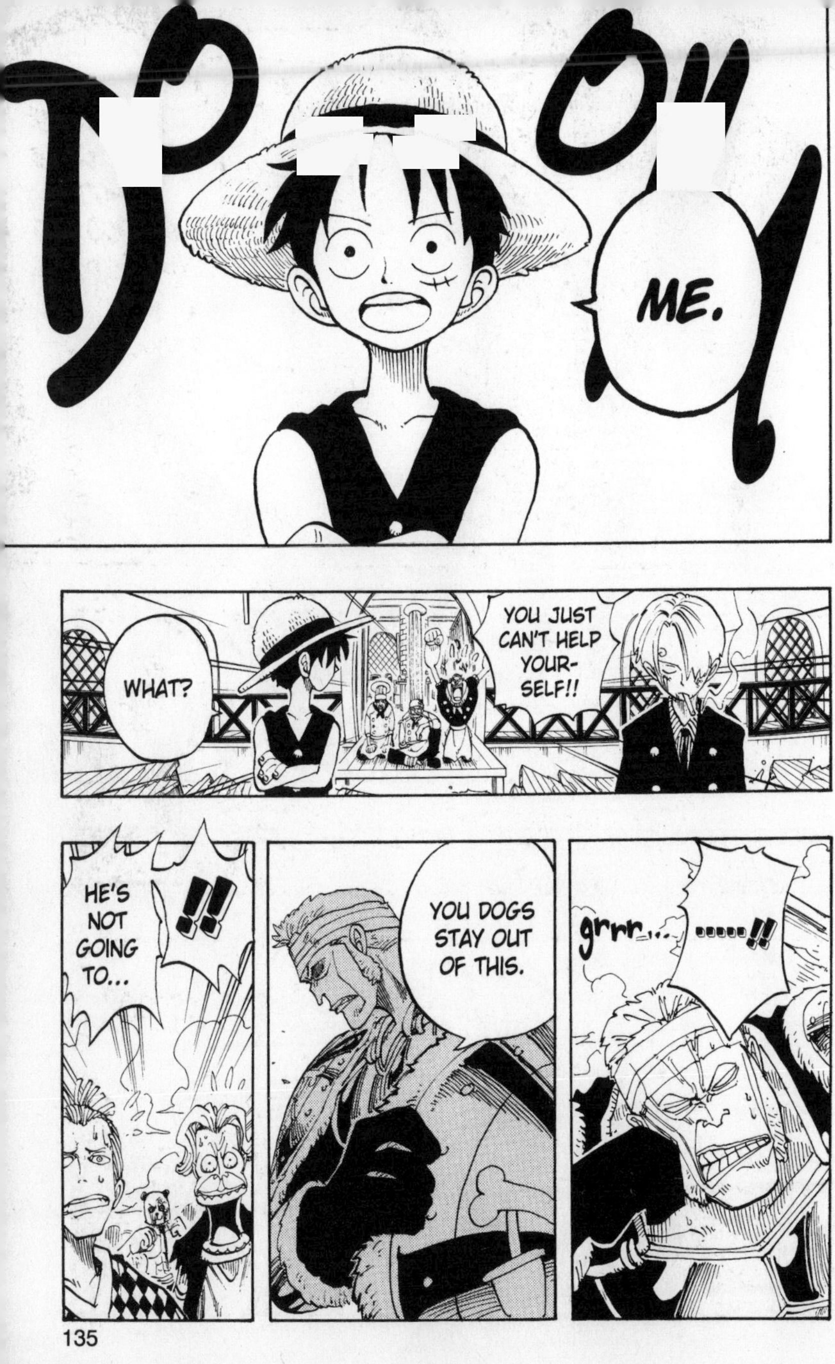
ME.
YOU JUST CAN'T HELP YOURSELF!!
WHAT?
grrr......
......!!
YOU DOGS STAY OUT OF THIS.
HE'S NOT GOING TO...
!!

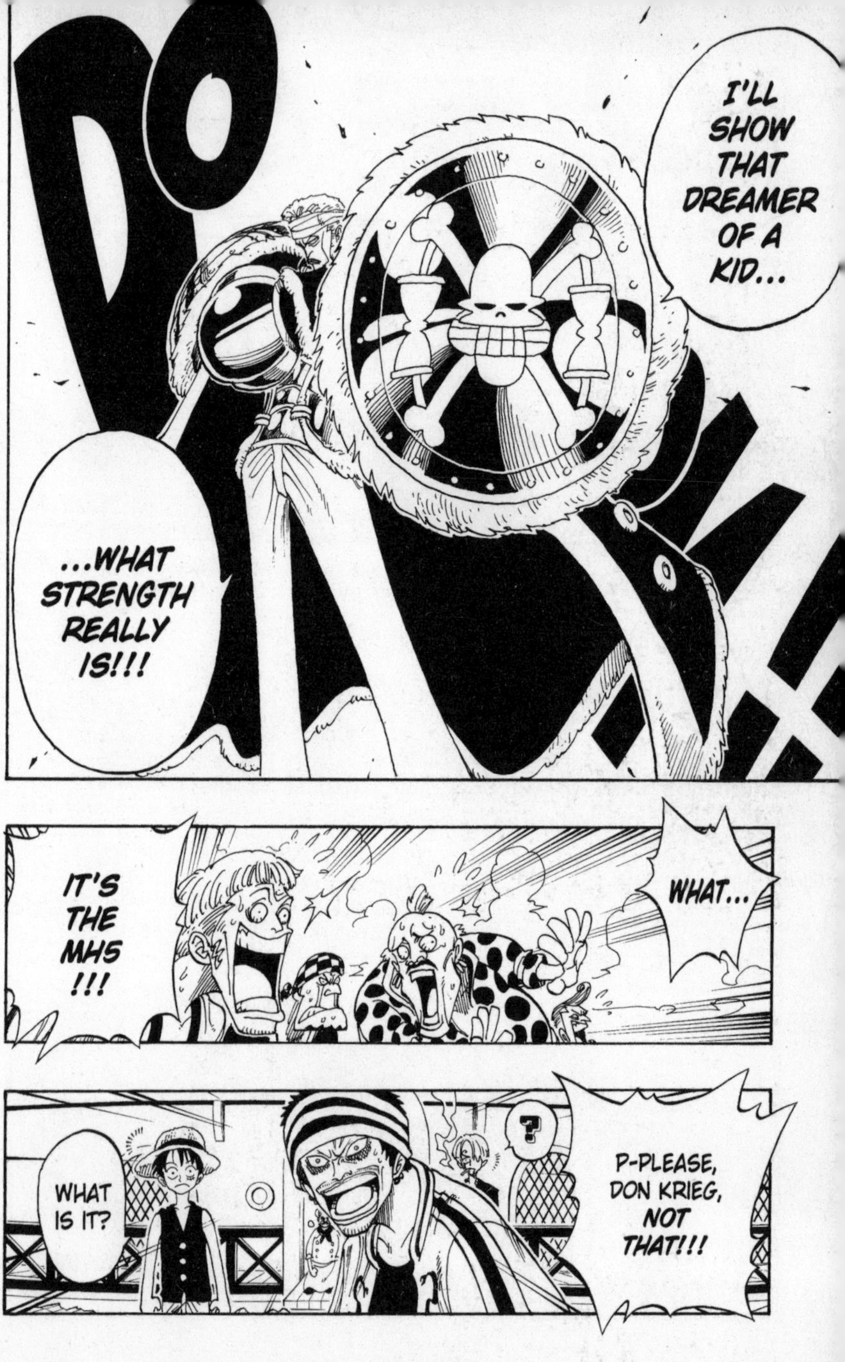
I'LL SHOW THAT DREAMER OF A KID...
DO
...WHAT STRENGTH REALLY IS!!!
WHAT...
IT'S THE MHS!!!
P-PLEASE, DON KRIEG, NOT THAT!!!
?
WHAT IS IT?

READ THIS WAY

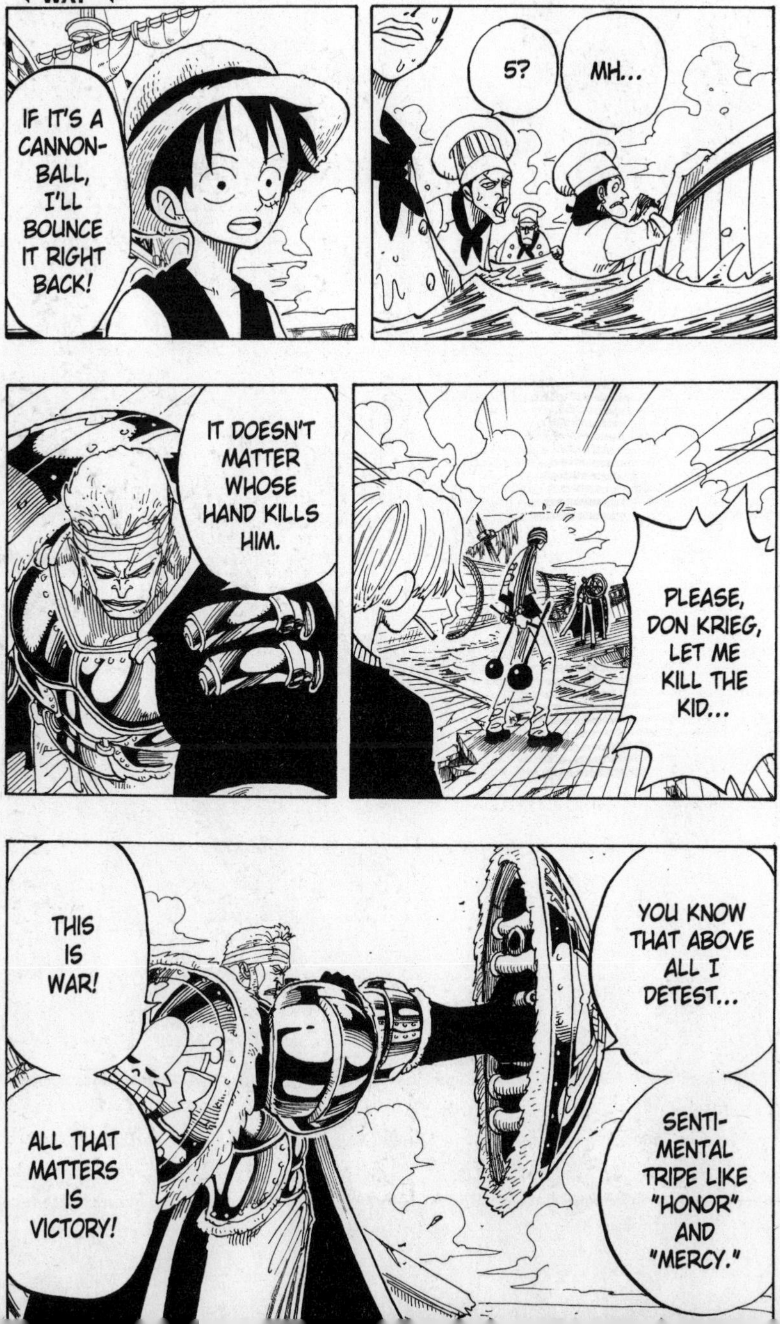
MH...
5?
IF IT'S A CANNONBALL, I'LL BOUNCE IT RIGHT BACK!
PLEASE, DON KRIEG, LET ME KILL THE KID...
IT DOESN'T MATTER WHOSE HAND KILLS HIM.
YOU KNOW THAT ABOVE ALL I DETEST...
SENTIMENTAL TRIPE LIKE "HONOR" AND "MERCY."
THIS IS WAR!
ALL THAT MATTERS IS VICTORY!

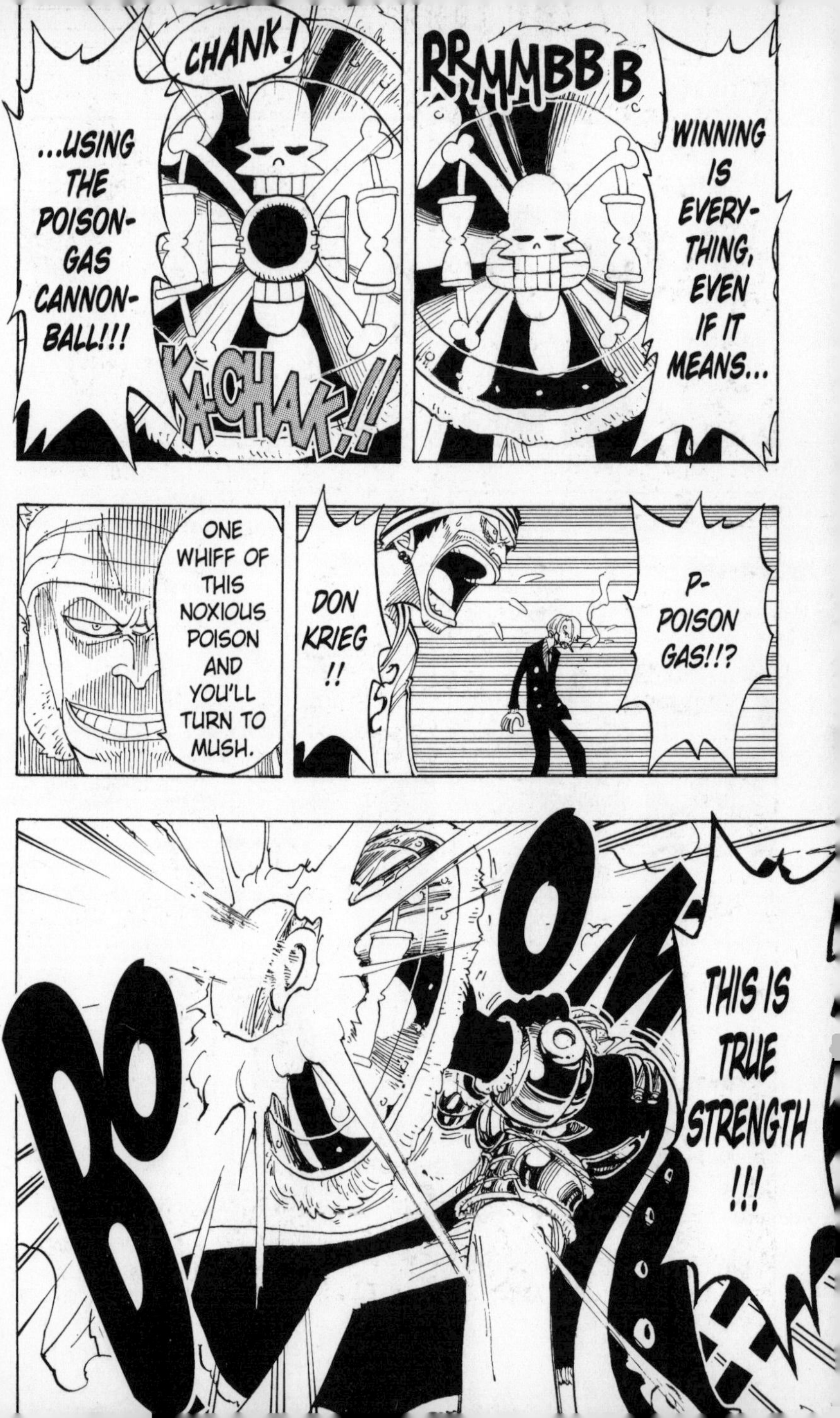
RRMMBB B
WINNING IS EVERYTHING, EVEN IF IT MEANS...
CHANK!
...USING THE POISON-GAS CANNONBALL!!!
KA-CHAK!!
P-POISON GAS!!?
DON KRIEG!!
ONE WHIFF OF THIS NOXIOUS POISON AND YOU'LL TURN TO MUSH.
THIS IS TRUE STRENGTH!!!
BOOM

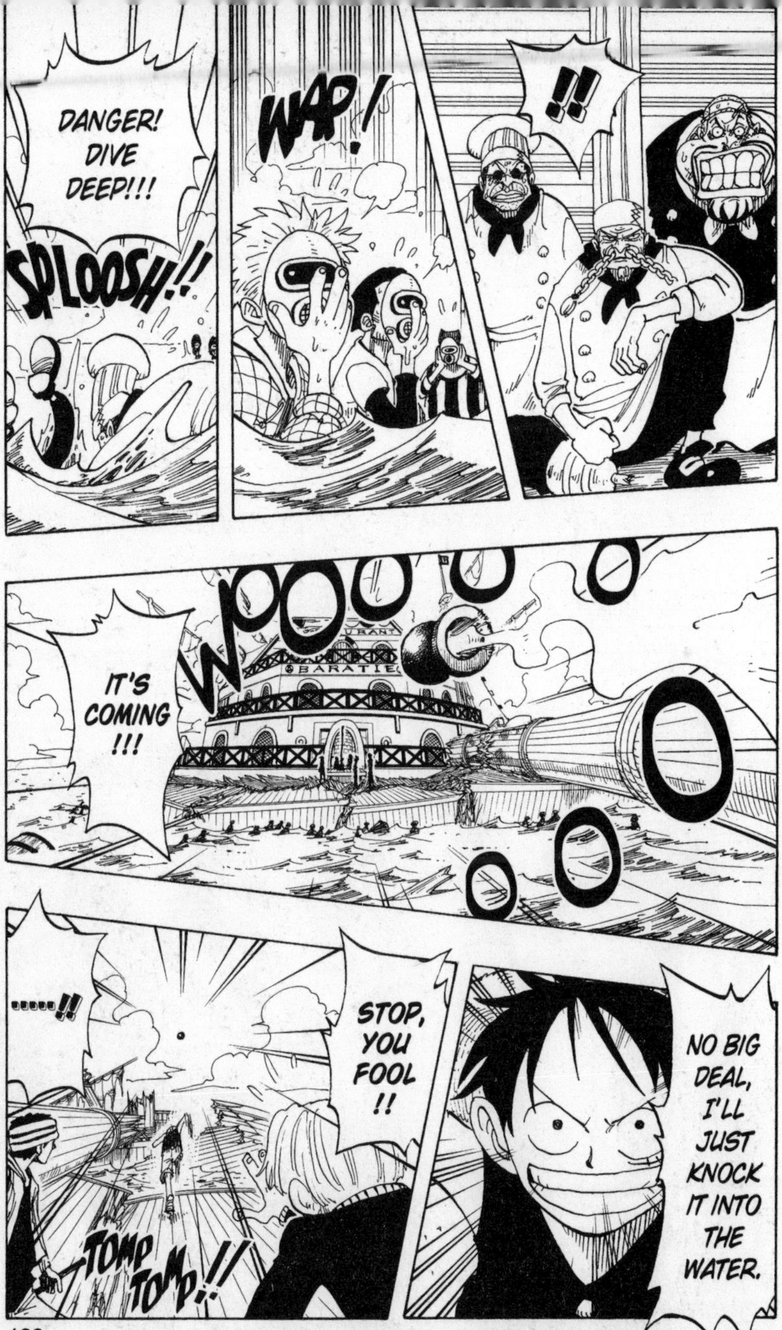
!!
WAP!
DANGER! DIVE DEEP!!!
SPLOOSH!!!
WPOOOOOOO
BARATIE
IT'S COMING!!!
NO BIG DEAL, I'LL JUST KNOCK IT INTO THE WATER.
STOP, YOU FOOL!!
......!!
TOMP TOMP!!

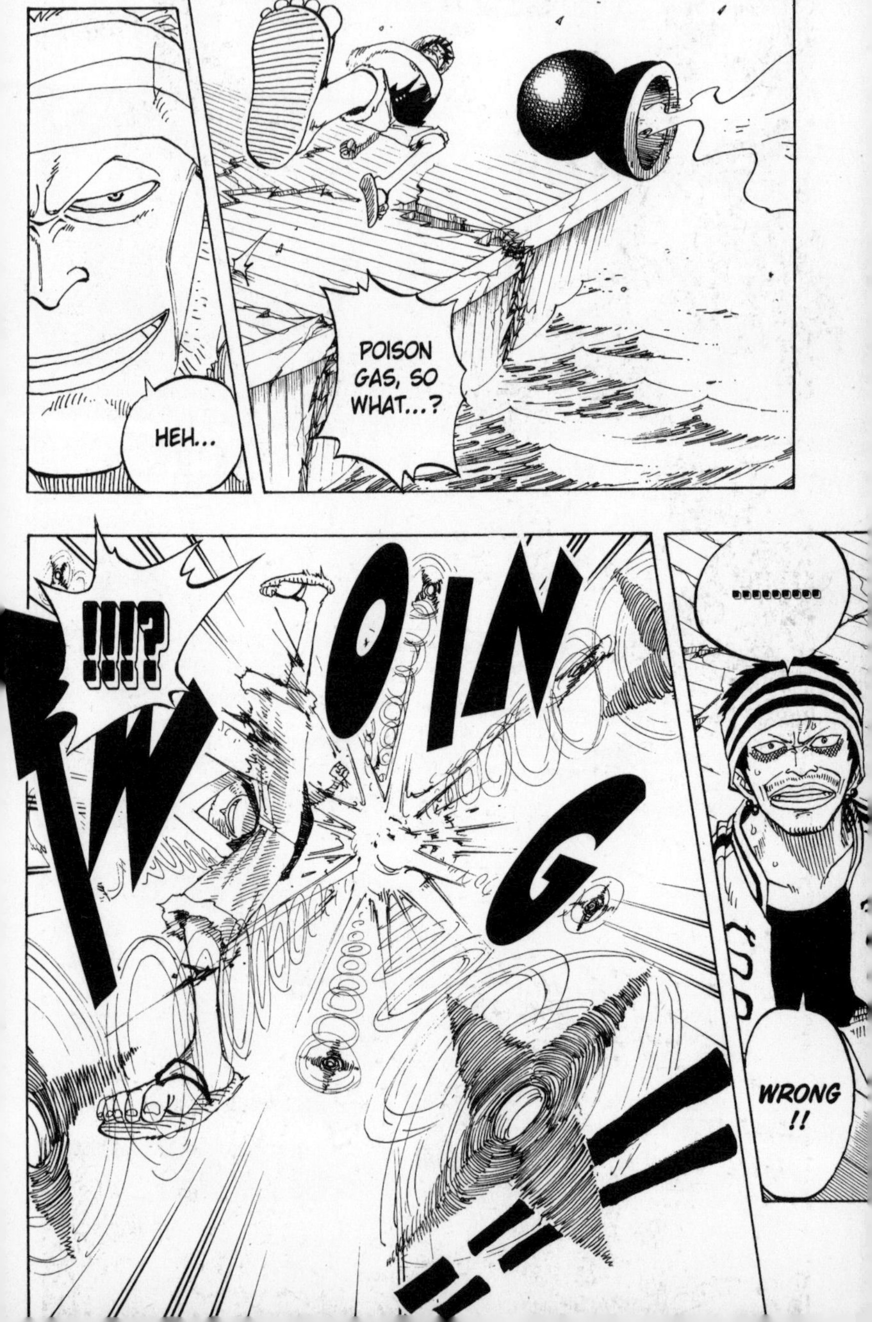
POISON GAS, SO WHAT...?
HEH...
....
WRONG!!
!!!?

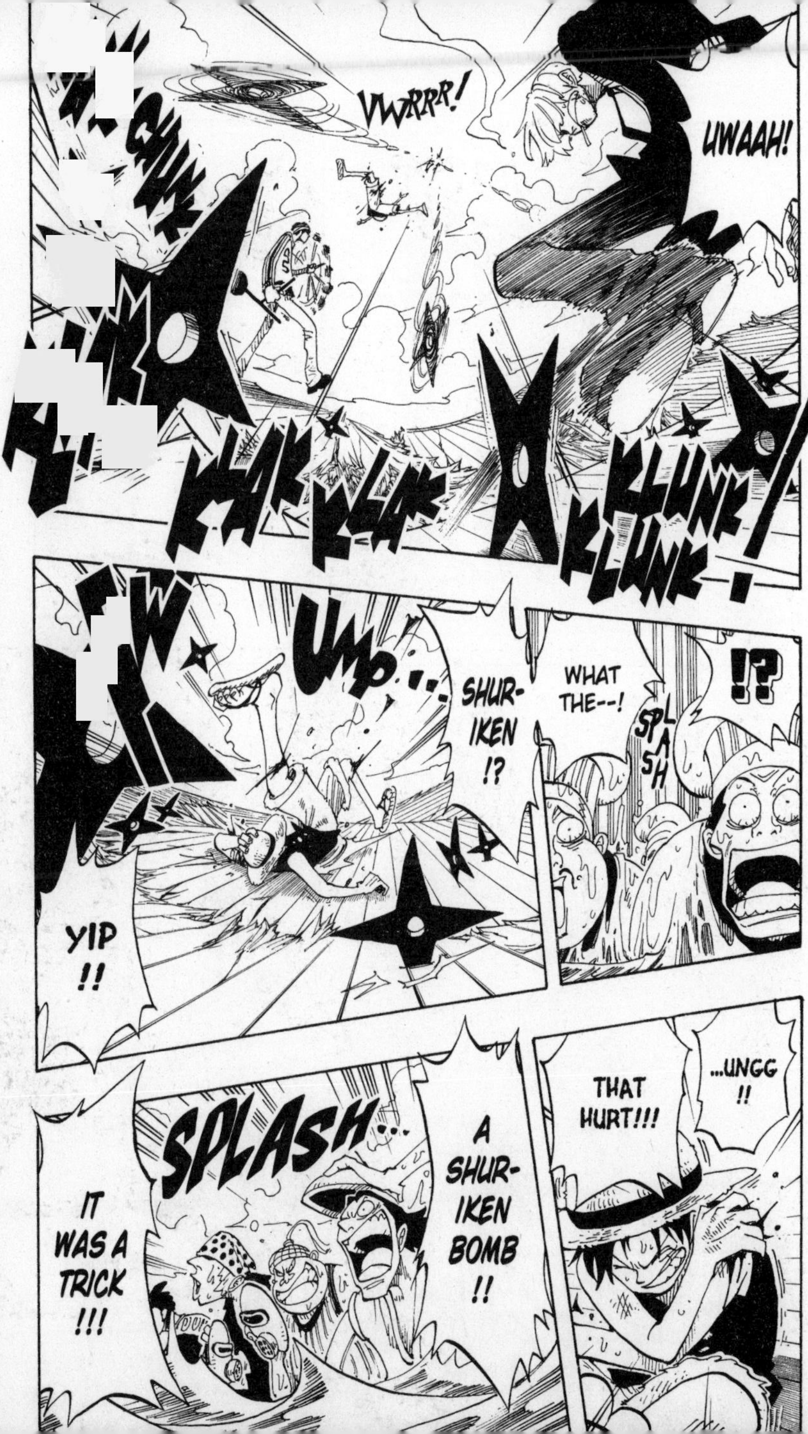
UWAAH!
VWRRRR!
CHUNK
KLUNK KLUNK!
KLAK KLAK
!?
WHAT THE--!
SPLASH
SHUR-IKEN !?
UMP...
YIP !!
...UNGG !!
THAT HURT!!!
A SHUR-IKEN BOMB !!
SPLASH...
IT WAS A TRICK !!!

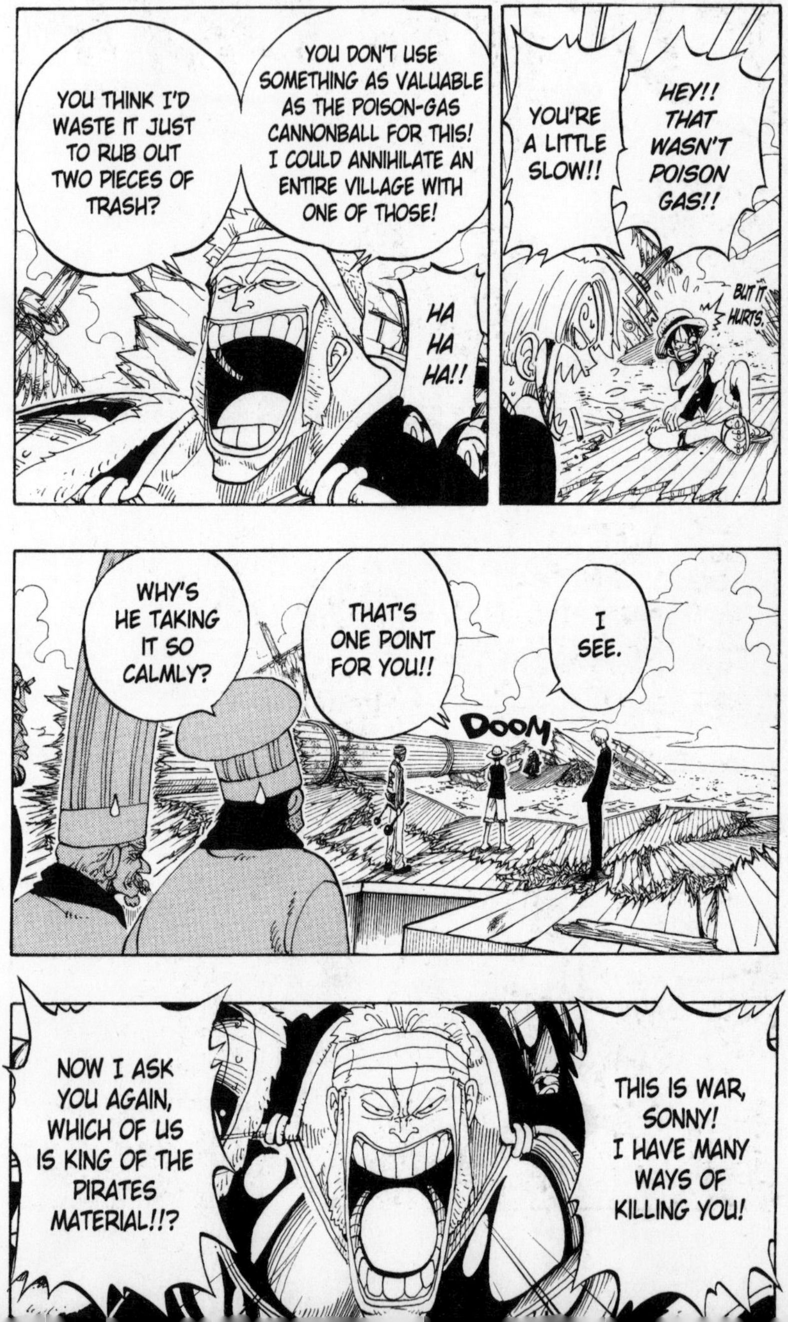
HEY!! THAT WASN'T POISON GAS!!
YOU'RE A LITTLE SLOW!!
BUT IT HURTS.
YOU DON'T USE SOMETHING AS VALUABLE AS THE POISON-GAS CANNONBALL FOR THIS! I COULD ANNIHILATE AN ENTIRE VILLAGE WITH ONE OF THOSE!
YOU THINK I'D WASTE IT JUST TO RUB OUT TWO PIECES OF TRASH?
HA HA HA!!
I SEE.
THAT'S ONE POINT FOR YOU!!
DOOM
WHY'S HE TAKING IT SO CALMLY?
THIS IS WAR, SONNY! I HAVE MANY WAYS OF KILLING YOU!
NOW I ASK YOU AGAIN, WHICH OF US IS KING OF THE PIRATES MATERIAL!!?

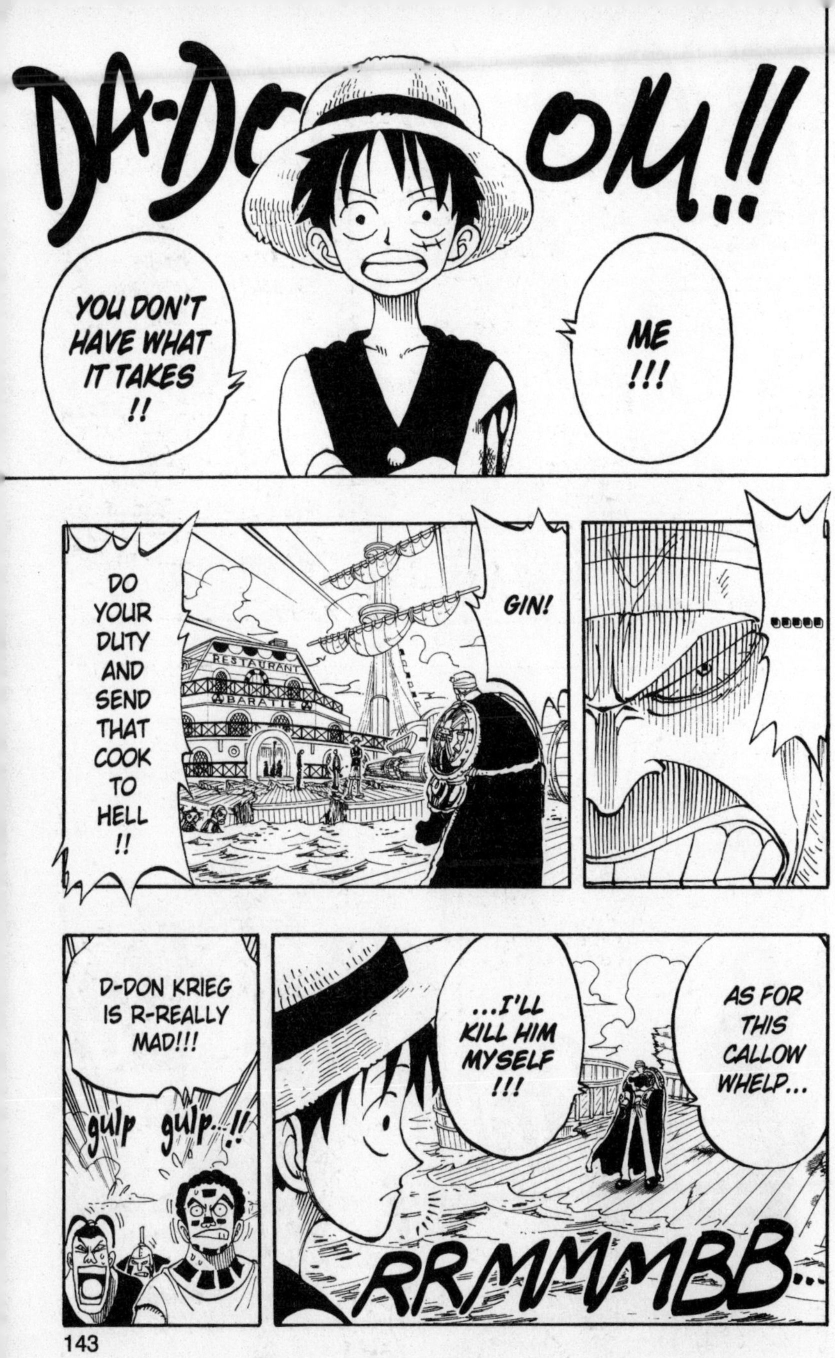

DA-DO OM!!
ME !!!
YOU DON'T HAVE WHAT IT TAKES !!
.....
GIN!
DO YOUR DUTY AND SEND THAT COOK TO HELL !!
AS FOR THIS CALLOW WHELP...
...I'LL KILL HIM MYSELF !!!
RRMMMMBB...
D-DON KRIEG IS R-REALLY MAD!!!
gulp gulp..!!

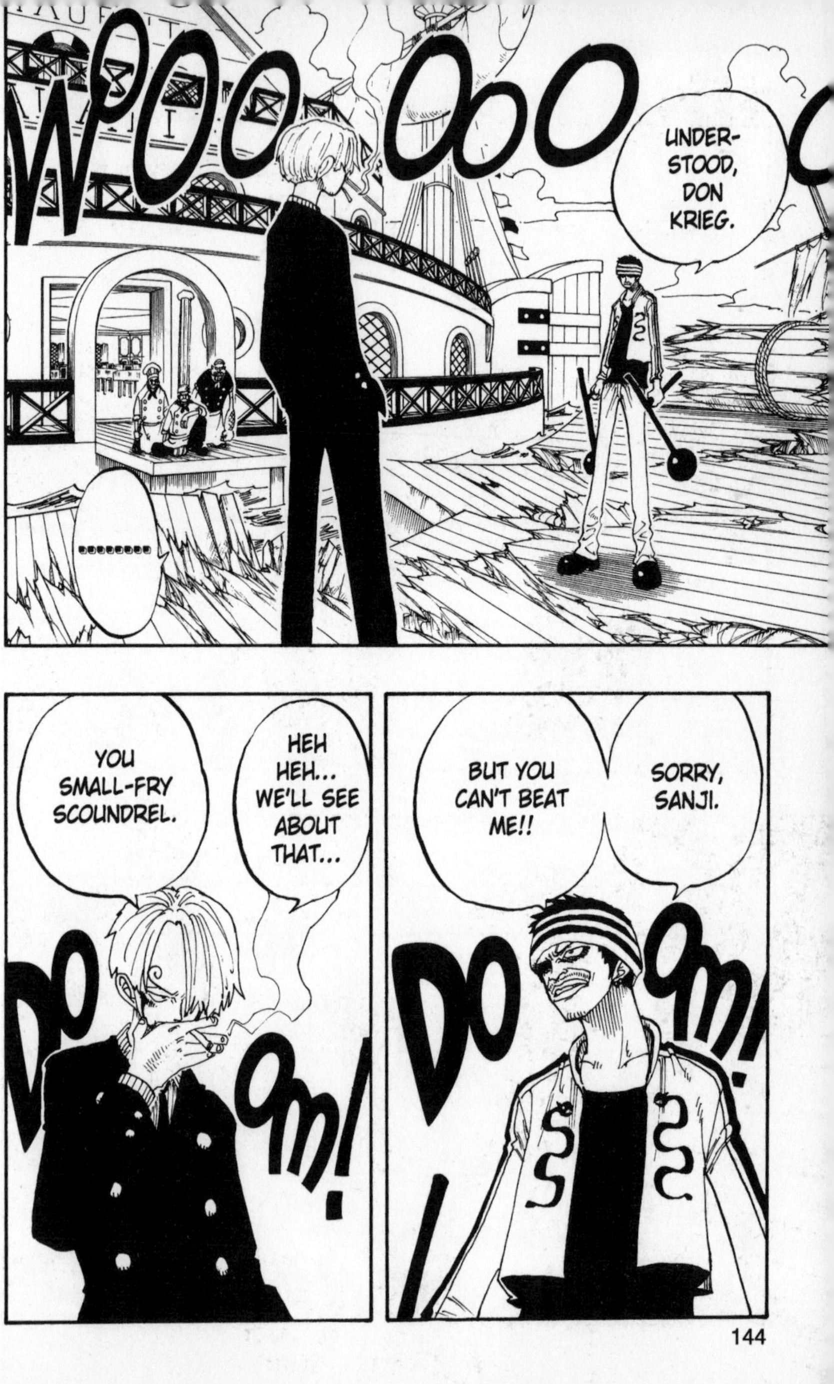
WOOOOOOO
UNDER-STOOD, DON KRIEG.
....
SORRY, SANJI.
BUT YOU CAN'T BEAT ME!!
DOOM!
HEH HEH... WE'LL SEE ABOUT THAT...
YOU SMALL-FRY SCOUNDREL.
DOOM!

READ THIS WAY

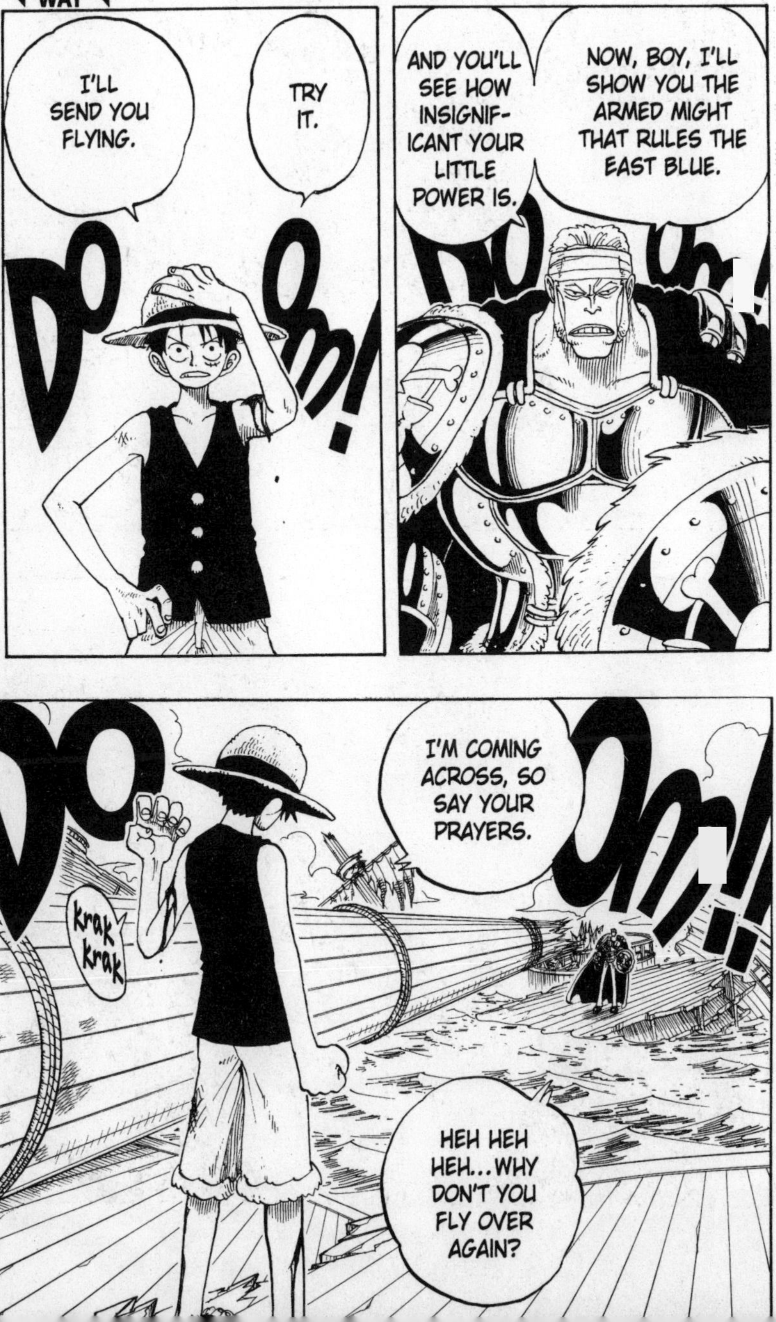
NOW, BOY, I'LL SHOW YOU THE ARMED MIGHT THAT RULES THE EAST BLUE.
AND YOU'LL SEE HOW INSIGNIF-ICANT YOUR LITTLE POWER IS.
TRY IT.
I'LL SEND YOU FLYING.
DOOM!
DOOM!!
I'M COMING ACROSS, SO SAY YOUR PRAYERS.
krak krak
HEH HEH HEH...WHY DON'T YOU FLY OVER AGAIN?

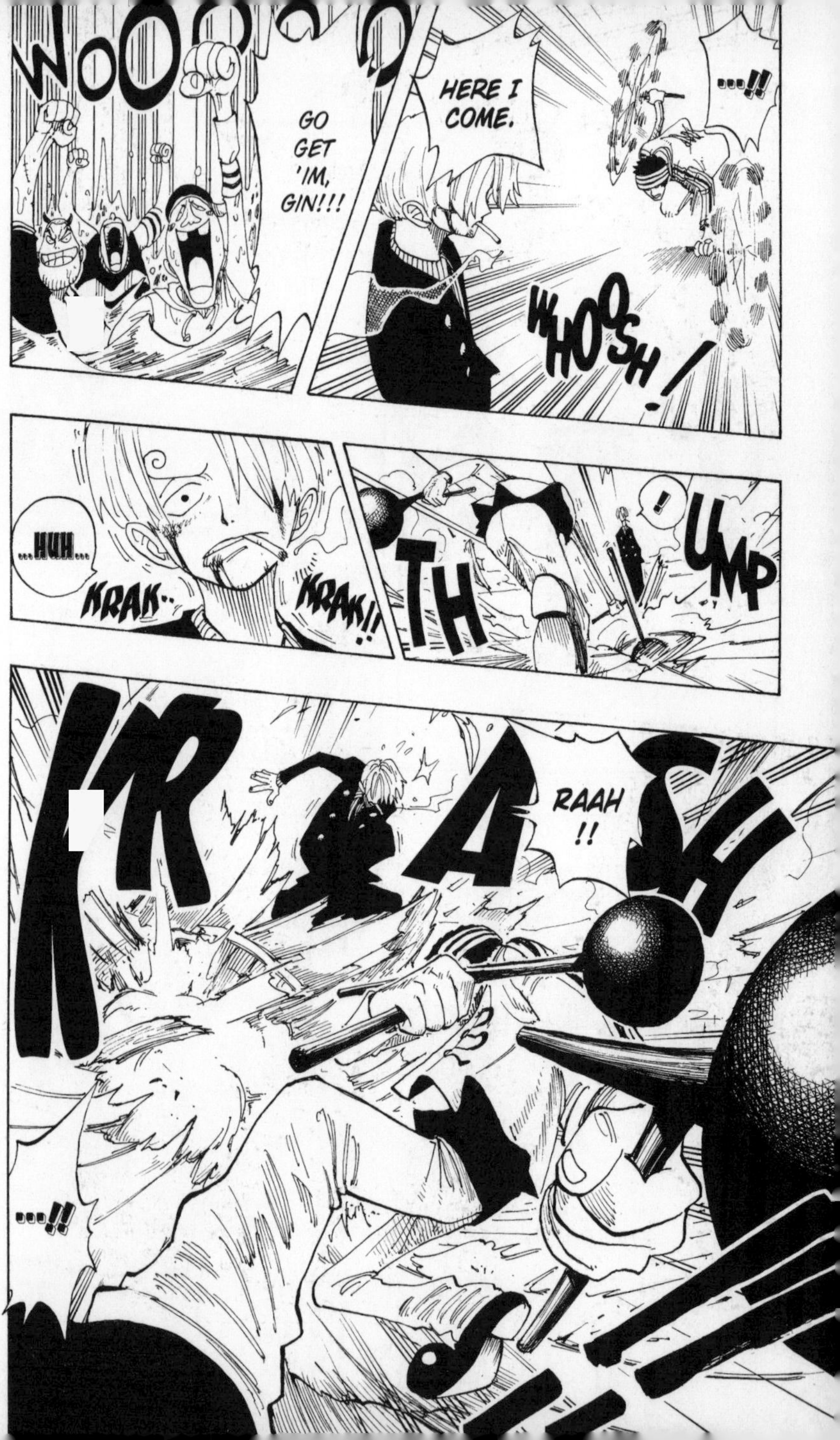
...!!
HERE I COME.
WHOOSH!
WOOOOO
GO GET 'IM, GIN!!!
!
THUMP
...HUH...
KRAK..
KRAK!!
KRASH
RAAH !!
...!!

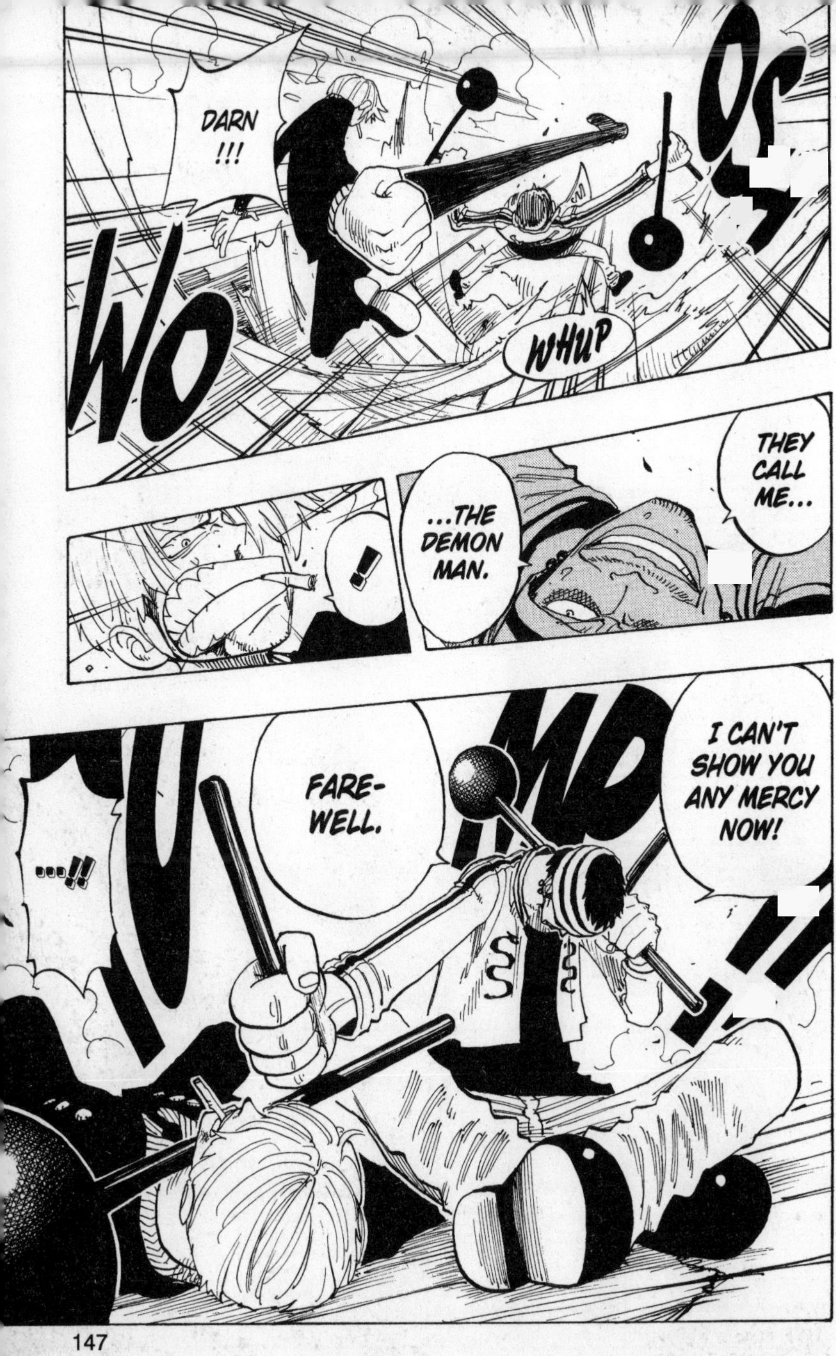
DARN !!!
WHUP
THEY CALL ME...
...THE DEMON MAN.
!
I CAN'T SHOW YOU ANY MERCY NOW!
FARE-WELL.
...!!

RESULTS OF THE 1st ONE PIECE CHARACTER POPULARITY POLL*

Total number of submissions: 36,000!!

1 Monkey D. Luffy — 8,055 votes

2 Roronoa Zolo — 7,260 votes

3 "Red-Haired" Shanks — 5,883 votes

8 Usopp — 781 votes

7 Buggy the Clown — 868 votes

6 Benn Beckman — 1,518 votes

4 Sanji — 4,300 votes

5 Nami — 4,213 votes

10 Kuina — 421 votes

9 Captain Kuro — 625 votes

33rd place	Rabbit-snake	26th place	Yasopp	19th place	Django	11th place	Gin
33rd place	Pig-lion	27th place	Patty	20th place	Meowban	12th place	Makino
35th place	Ganzak	28th place	Yosaku		brothers	13th place	Gold Roger
35th place	Rika	29th place	Pepper	21st place	Merry	14th place	Mihawk
35th place	Captain of the	30th place	Mayor Boodle	22nd place	Zeff	15th place	Gaimon
	Naval base	31st place	Master of the	23rd place	Mohji	16th place	Krieg
			Near Sea	24th place	Johnny	17th place	Kaya
Many votes for others, too.		32nd place	Panda	25th place	Cabaji	18th place	Koby

*Hey American **One Piece** fans! This popularity contest surveyed Japanese readers.
Who is your favorite **One Piece** character? Let us know at:
One Piece c/o SHONEN JUMP, P.O. Box 77010, San Francisco, CA 94107

Chapter 61: THE DEMON

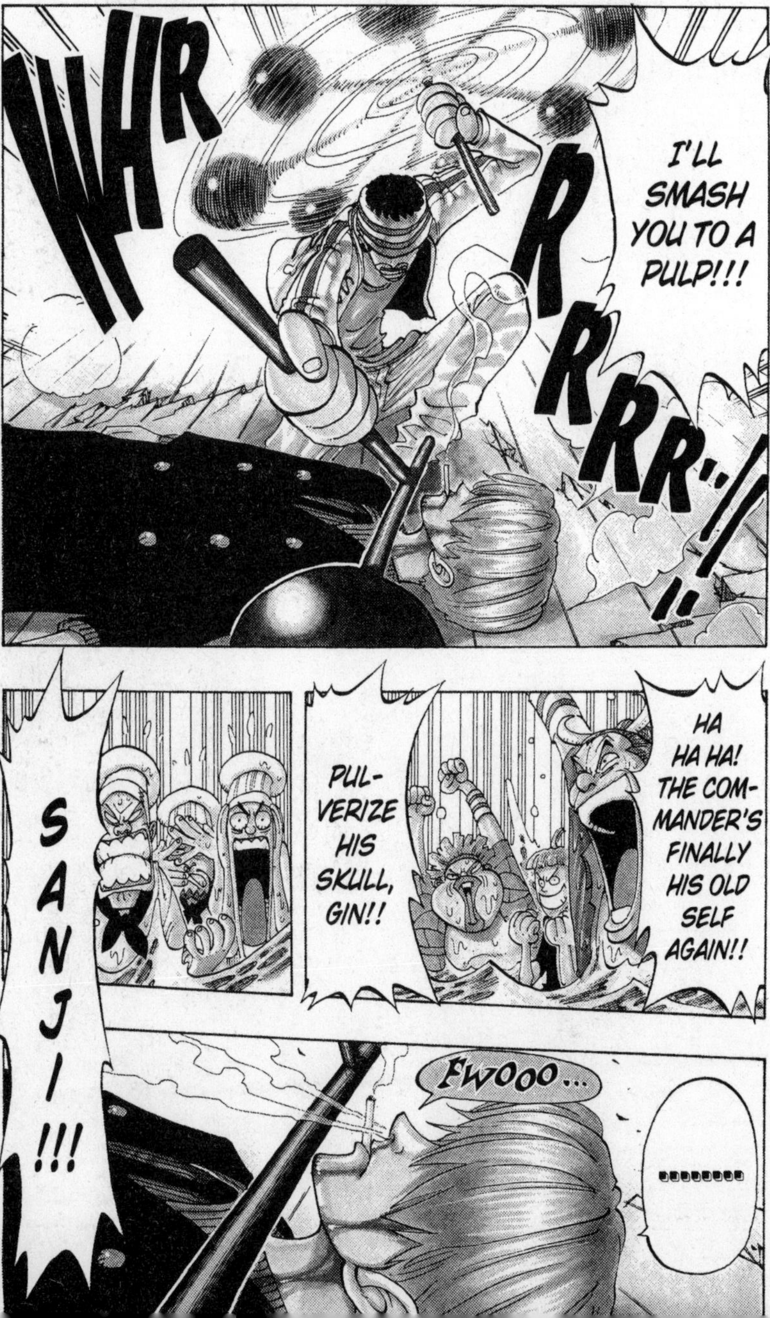
I'LL SMASH YOU TO A PULP!!!
WHRRRRR..!!
HA HA HA! THE COMMANDER'S FINALLY HIS OLD SELF AGAIN!!
PULVERIZE HIS SKULL, GIN!!
SANJI!!!
FWOOO...
....

Chapter 61: THE DEMON

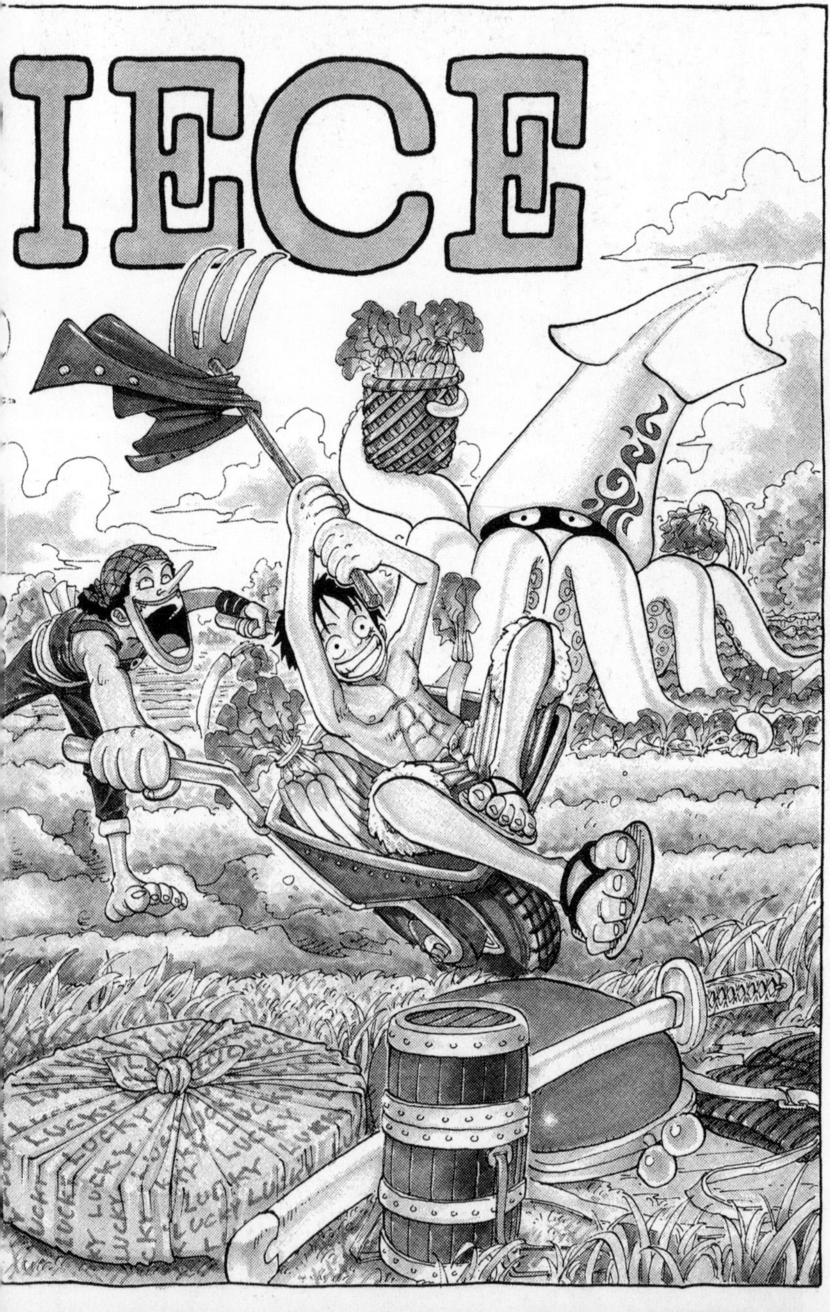
IECE
LUCKY

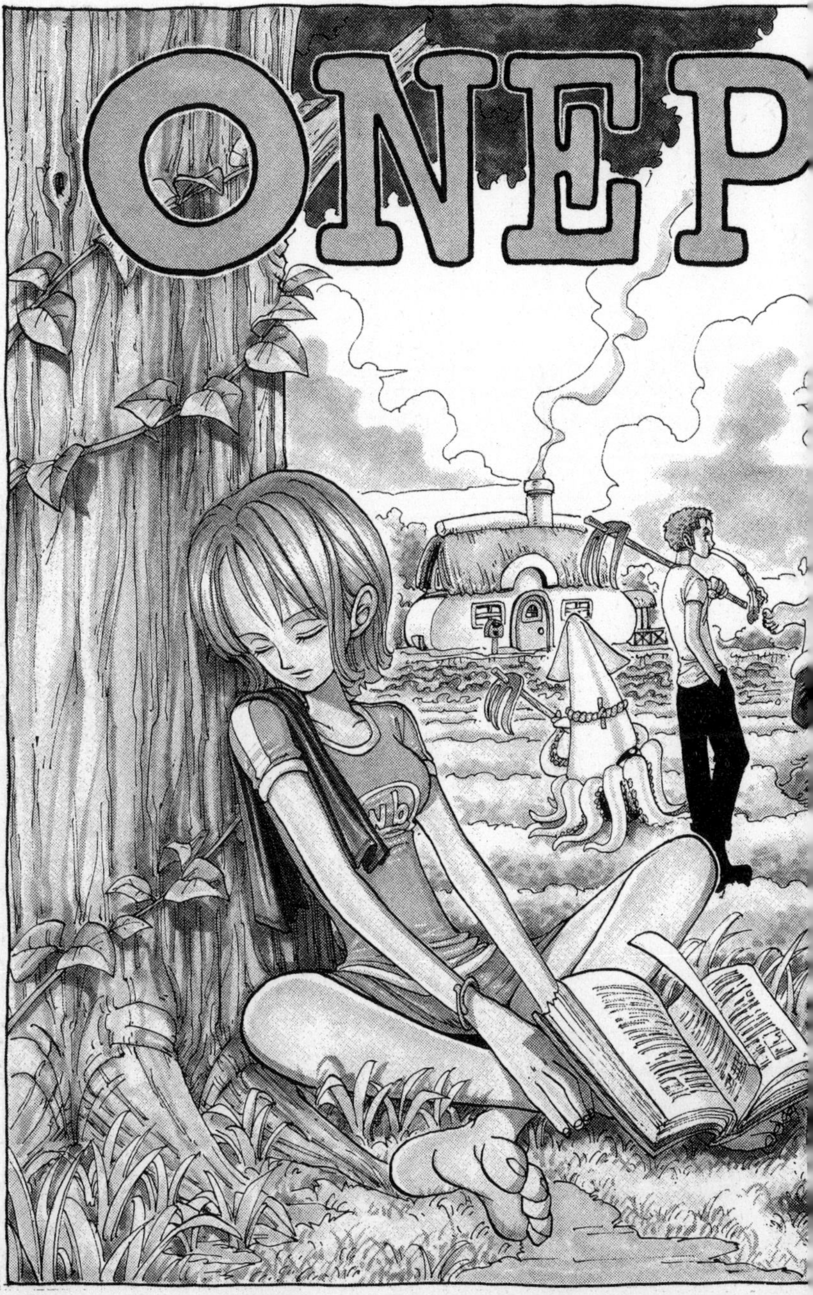
ONE P

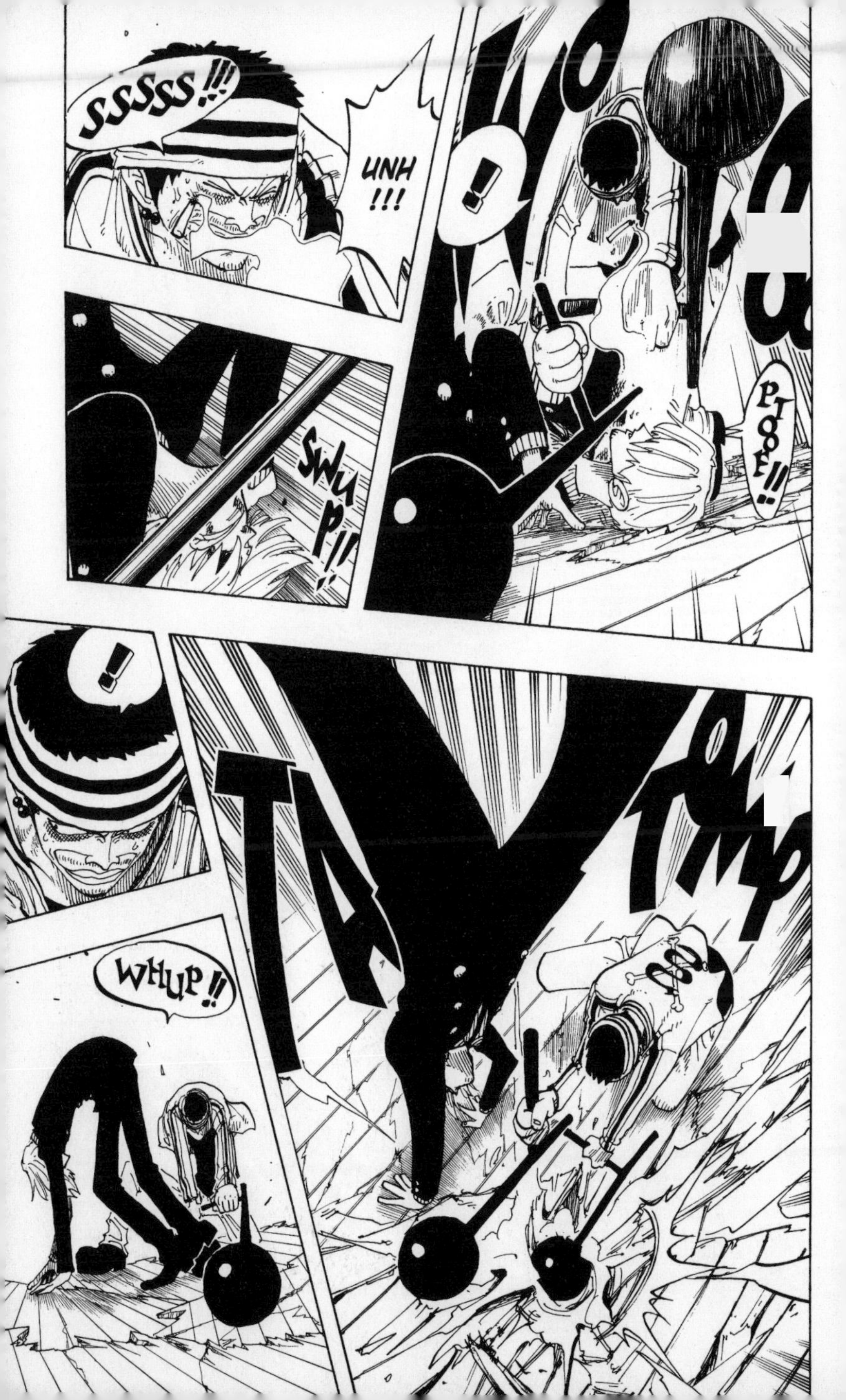
!
PTOOE!!
SSSSS!!!
UNH!!!
SWUP!!
!
WHUP!!

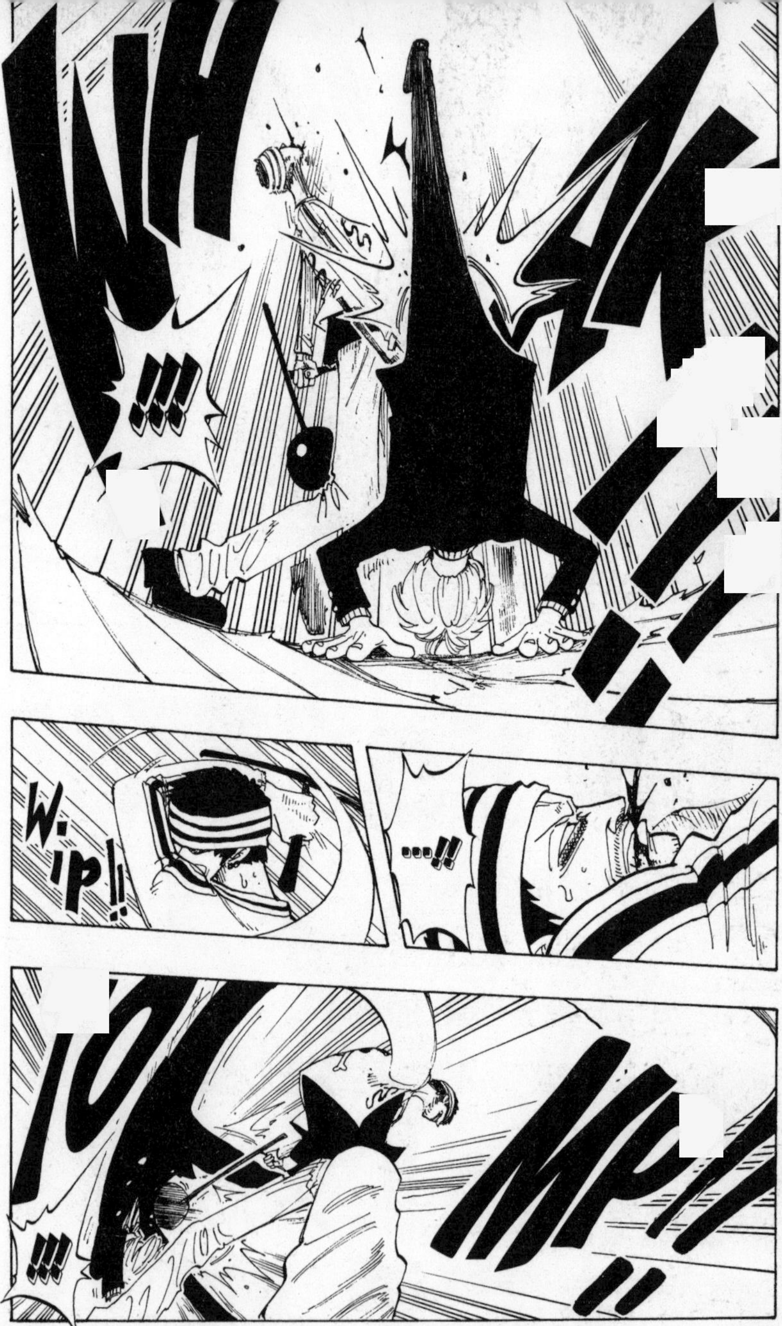
!!!!
...!!
Wip!!
!!!

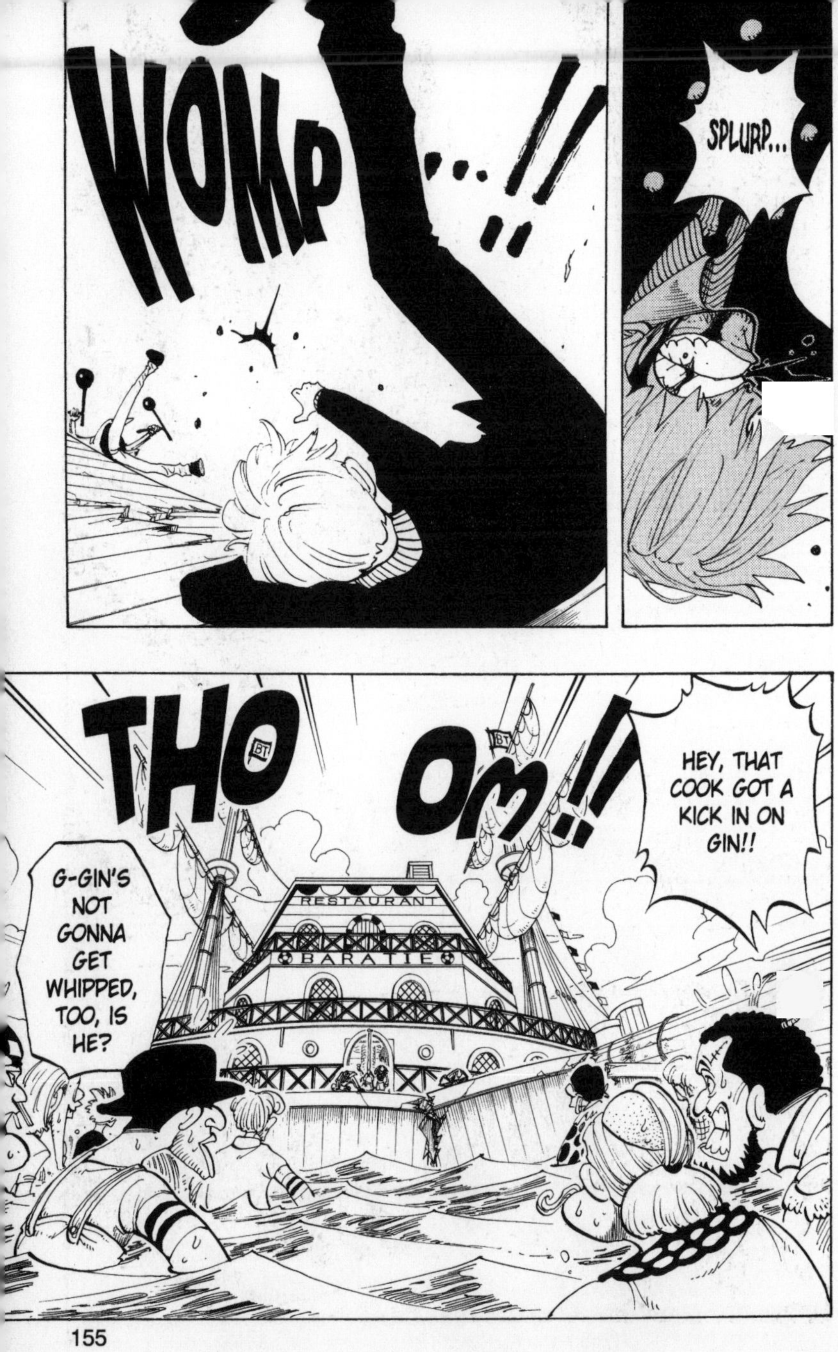
SPLURP...
WOMP...!!
THOOM!!
HEY, THAT COOK GOT A KICK IN ON GIN!!
G-GIN'S NOT GONNA GET WHIPPED, TOO, IS HE?

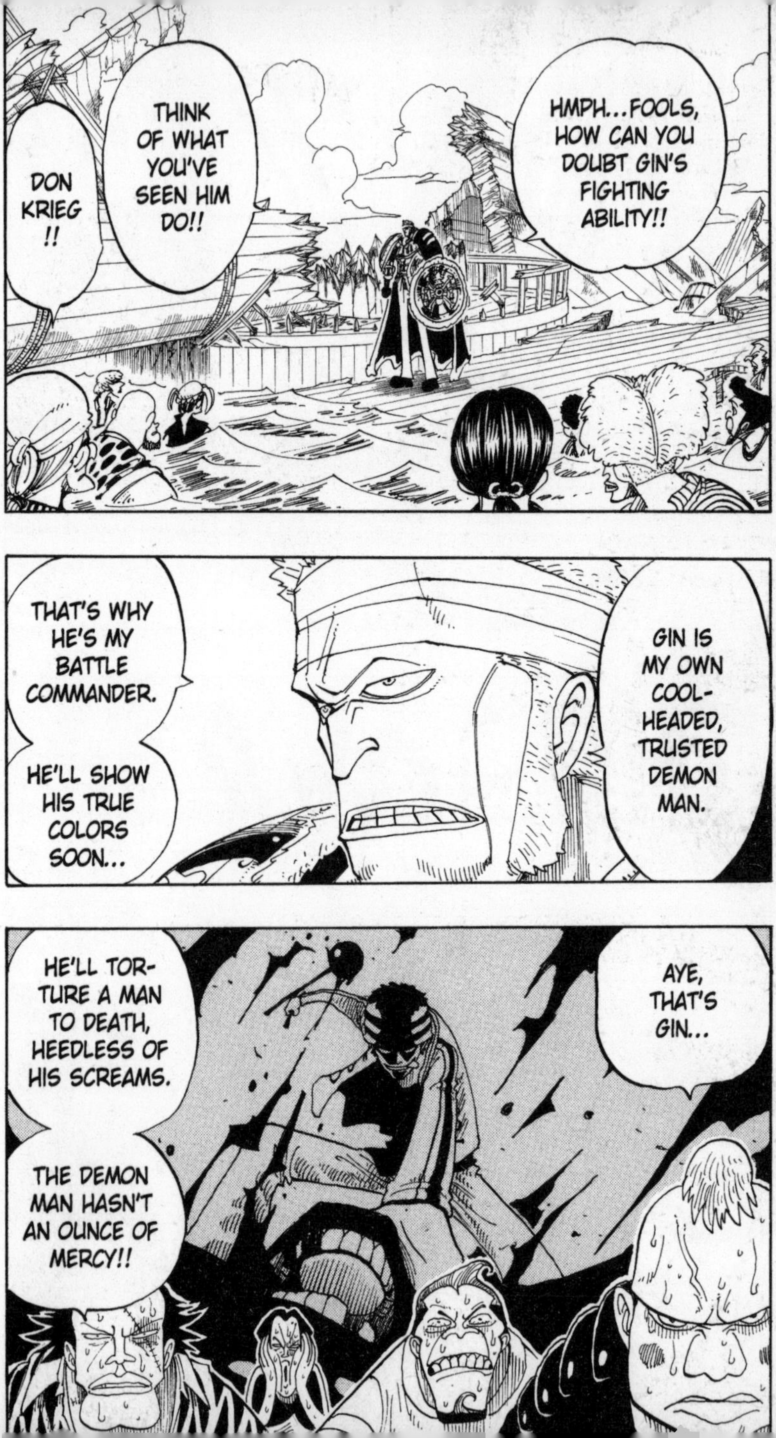
HMPH...FOOLS, HOW CAN YOU DOUBT GIN'S FIGHTING ABILITY!!
THINK OF WHAT YOU'VE SEEN HIM DO!!
DON KRIEG!!
GIN IS MY OWN COOL-HEADED, TRUSTED DEMON MAN.
THAT'S WHY HE'S MY BATTLE COMMANDER.
HE'LL SHOW HIS TRUE COLORS SOON...
AYE, THAT'S GIN...
HE'LL TORTURE A MAN TO DEATH, HEEDLESS OF HIS SCREAMS.
THE DEMON MAN HASN'T AN OUNCE OF MERCY!!

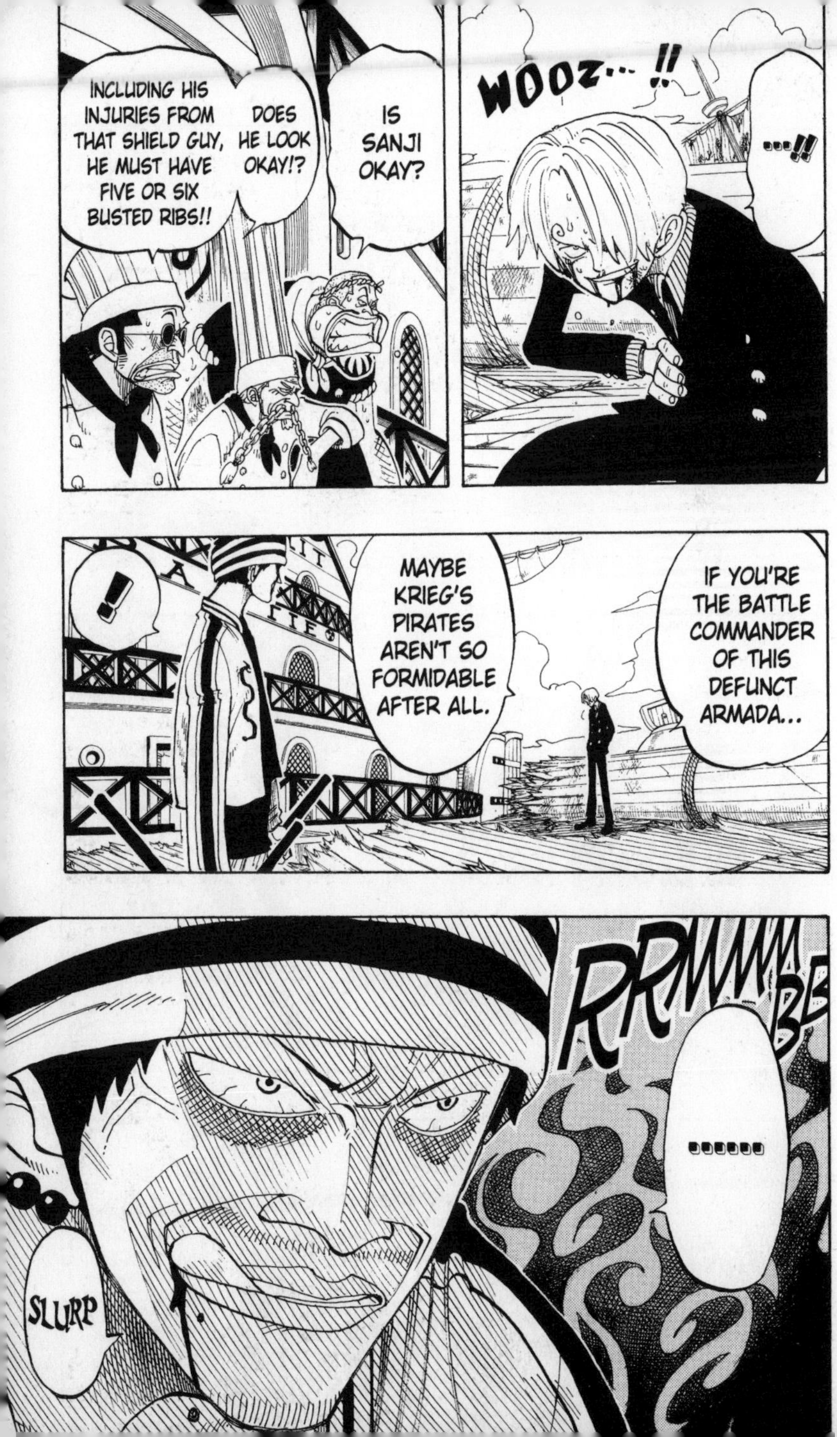
WOOZ... !!
...!!
IS SANJI OKAY?
DOES HE LOOK OKAY!?
INCLUDING HIS INJURIES FROM THAT SHIELD GUY, HE MUST HAVE FIVE OR SIX BUSTED RIBS!!
IF YOU'RE THE BATTLE COMMANDER OF THIS DEFUNCT ARMADA...
MAYBE KRIEG'S PIRATES AREN'T SO FORMIDABLE AFTER ALL.
!
RRMMMBB
......
SLURP

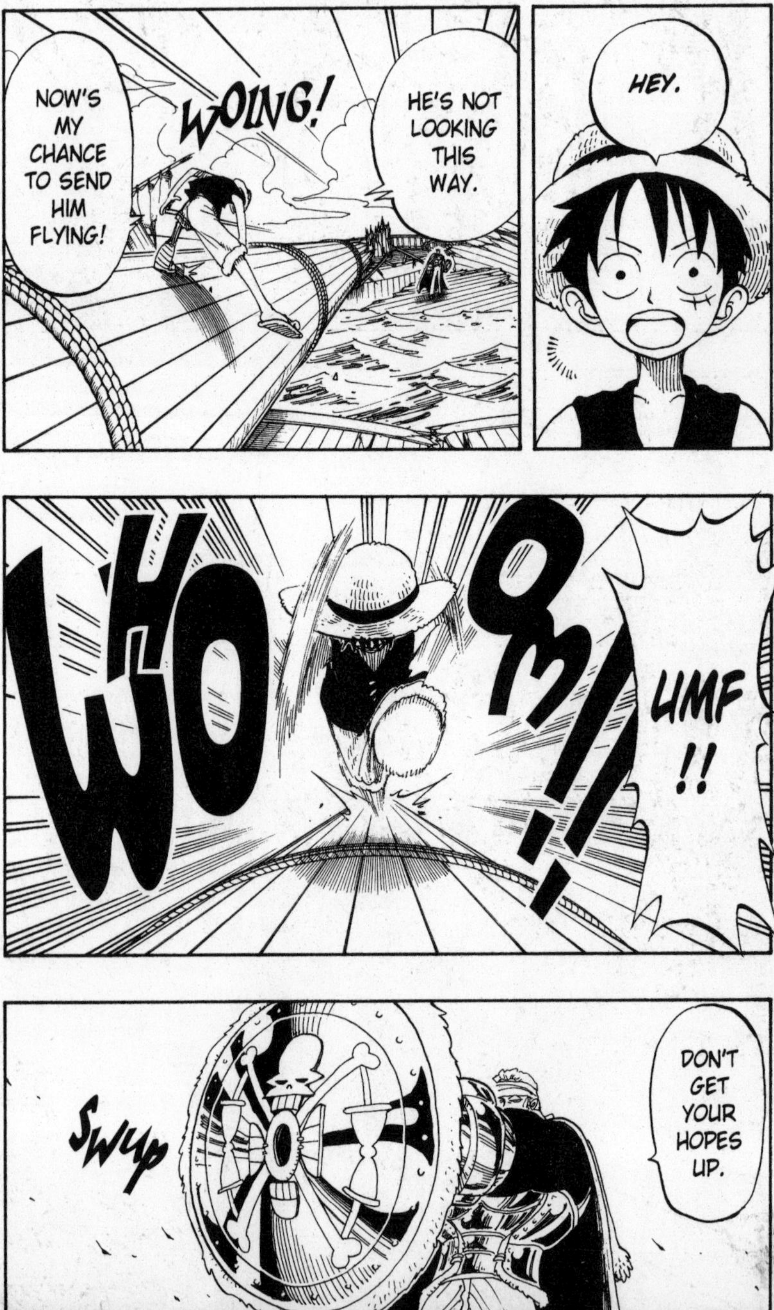
HEY.
HE'S NOT LOOKING THIS WAY.
WOING!
NOW'S MY CHANCE TO SEND HIM FLYING!
UMF !!
WOOM!!!
DON'T GET YOUR HOPES UP.
SWUP

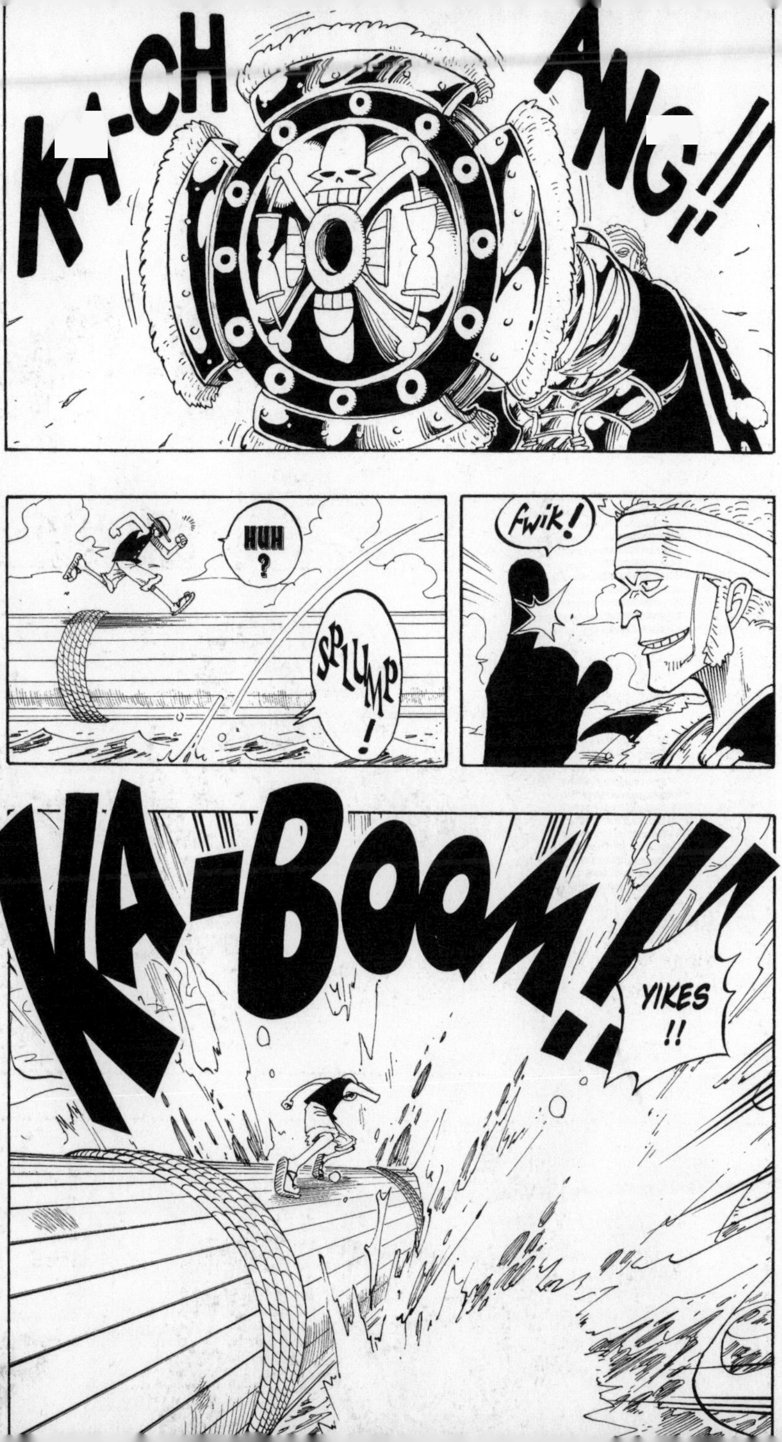
KA-CH
ANG!!
fwik!
HUH?
SPLUMP!
KA-BOOM!!
YIKES!!

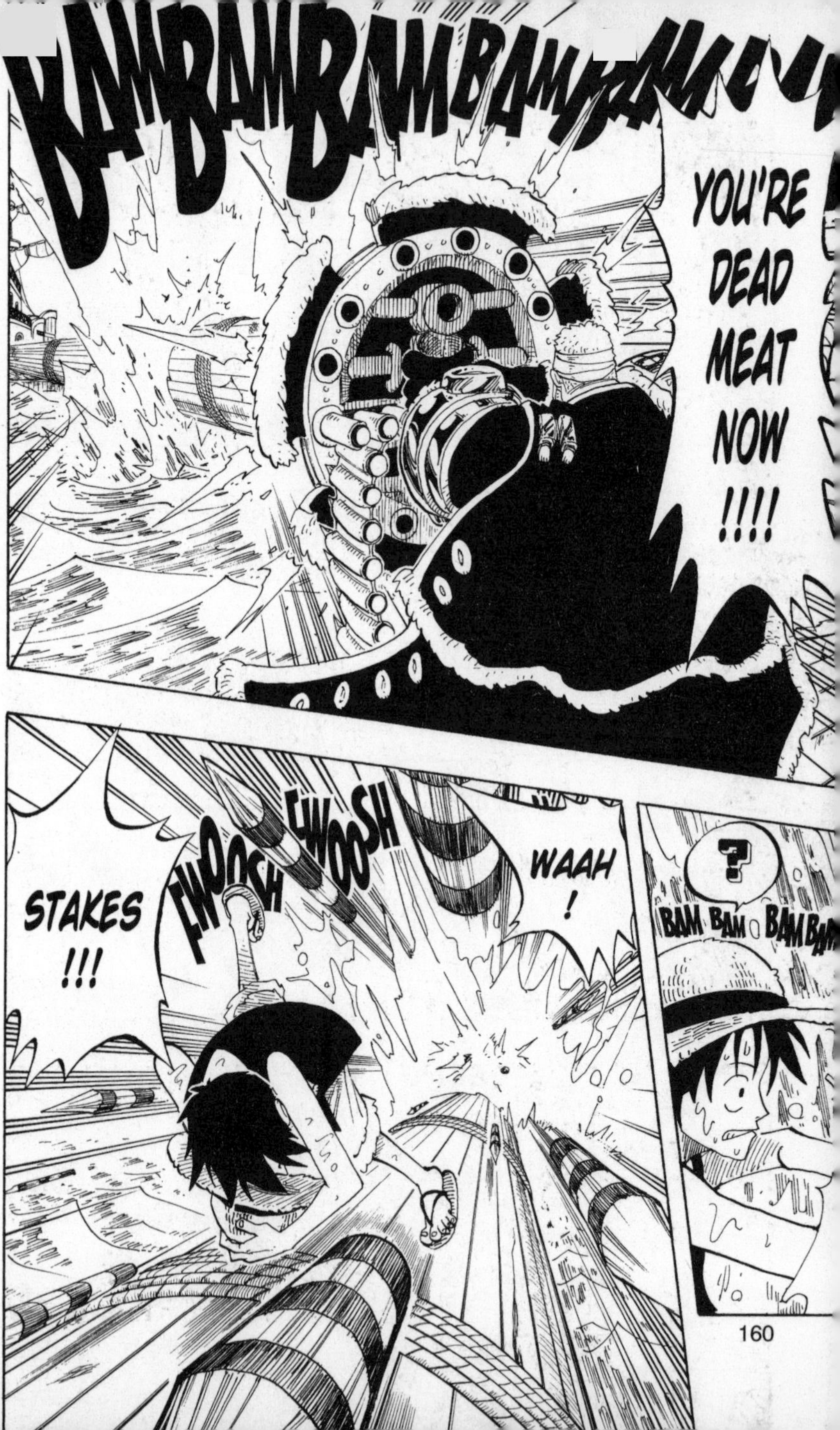
BAMBAMBAMBAMBAM
YOU'RE DEAD MEAT NOW!!!!
?
BAM BAM BAMBAM
WAAH!
FWOOSH
FWOOSH
STAKES!!!

READ THIS WAY

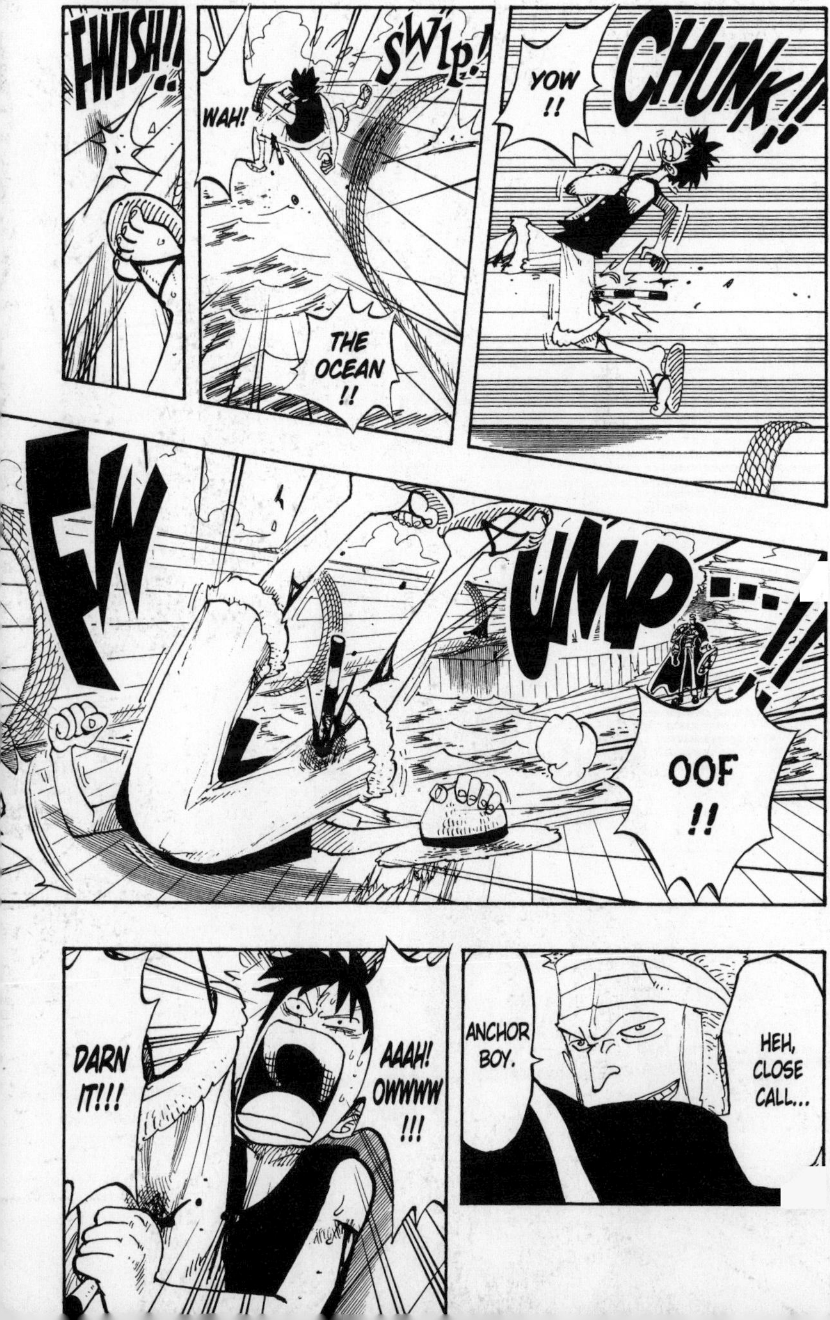
CHUNK!!
YOW!!
SWIP!
WAH!
THE OCEAN!!
FWISH!!
FWUMP...!!
OOF!!
HEH, CLOSE CALL...
ANCHOR BOY.
AAAH! OWWWW!!!
DARN IT!!!

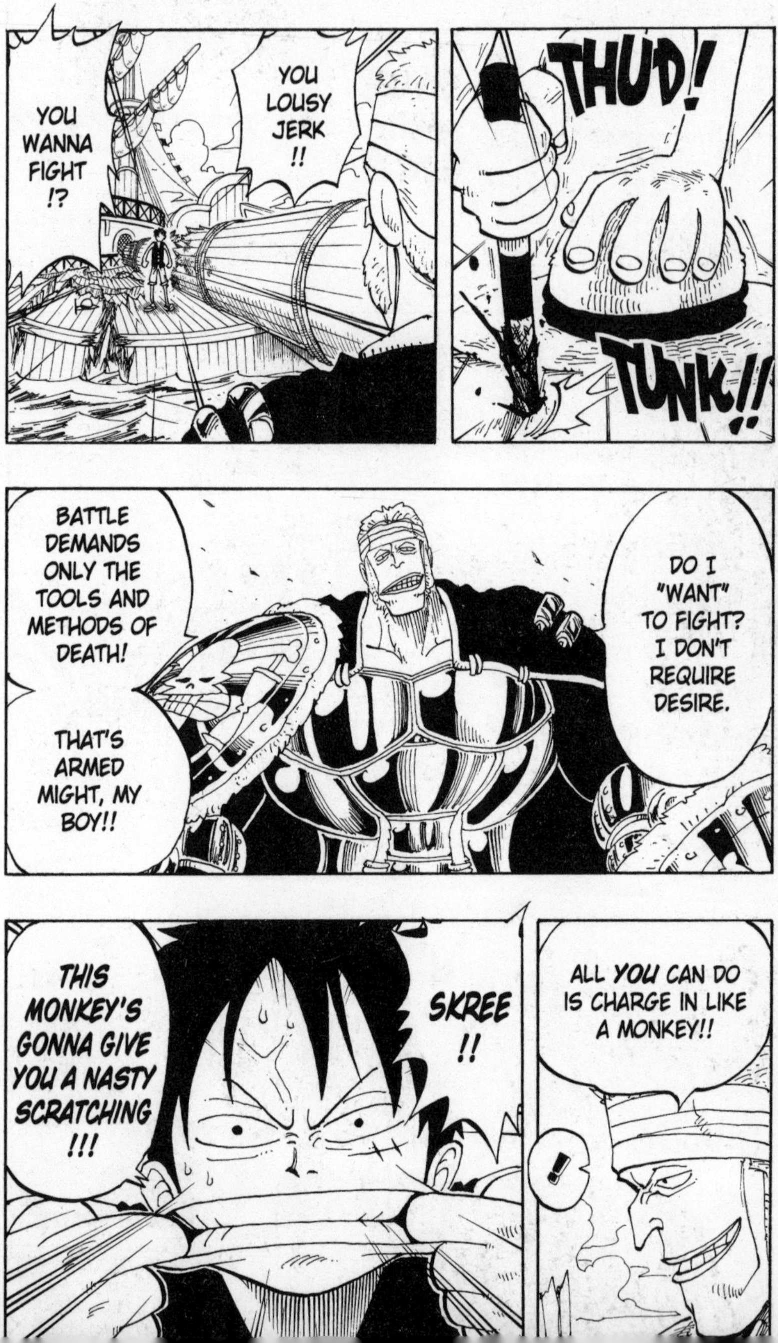
THUD!
TUNK!!
YOU LOUSY JERK!!
YOU WANNA FIGHT!?
DO I "WANT" TO FIGHT? I DON'T REQUIRE DESIRE.
BATTLE DEMANDS ONLY THE TOOLS AND METHODS OF DEATH!
THAT'S ARMED MIGHT, MY BOY!!
ALL YOU CAN DO IS CHARGE IN LIKE A MONKEY!!
!
SKREE!!
THIS MONKEY'S GONNA GIVE YOU A NASTY SCRATCHING!!!

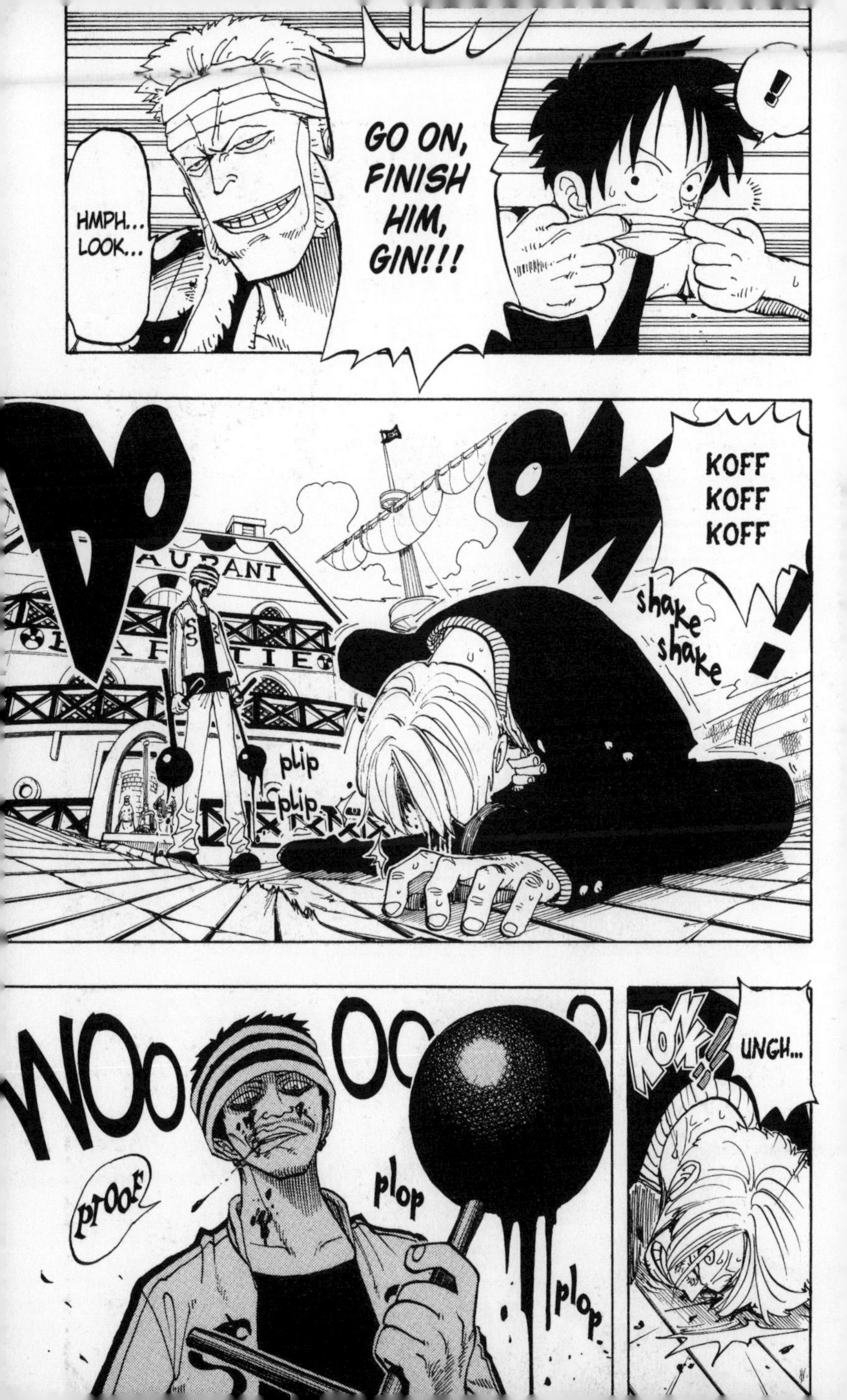
!
GO ON, FINISH HIM, GIN!!!
HMPH... LOOK...
KOFF KOFF KOFF
DOOM
shake shake
plip plip
KOK!!
UNGH...
WOOOOO
ptooF
plop
plop...

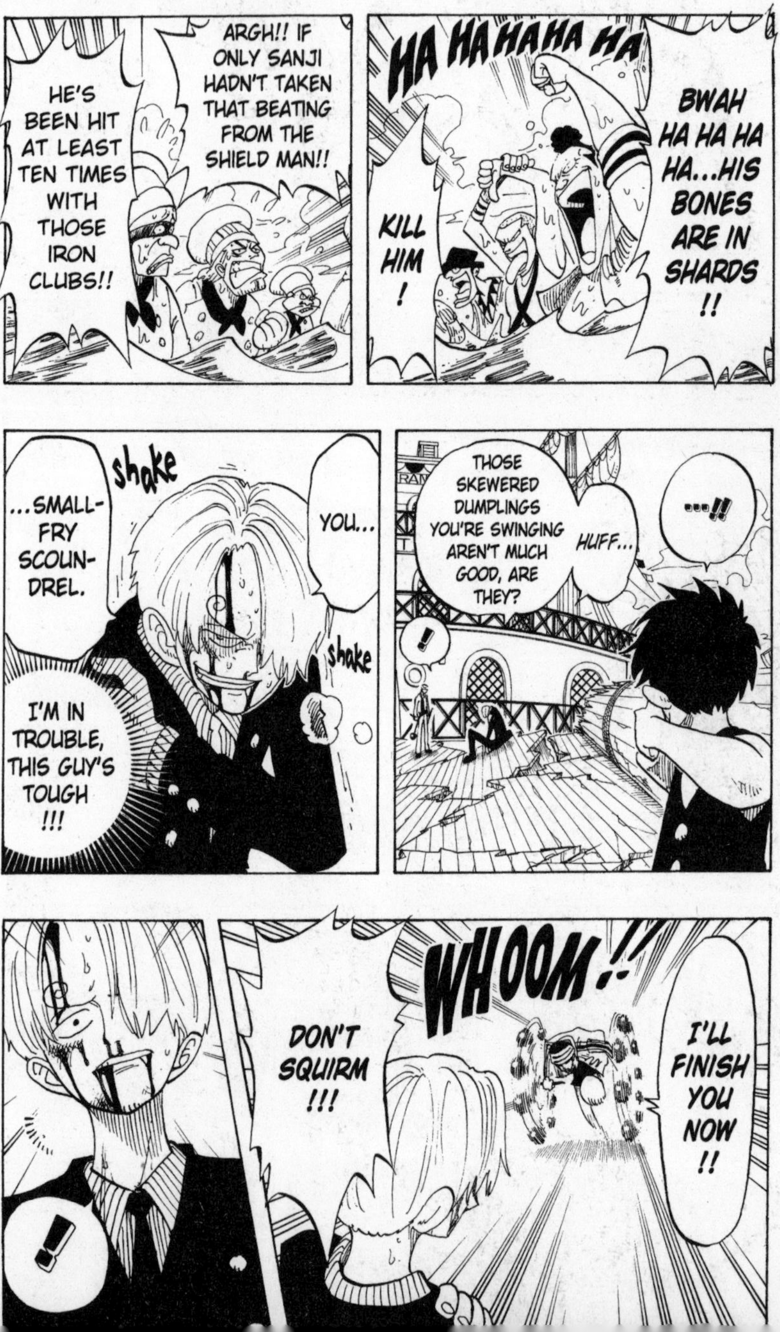
HA HA HA HA HA HA
BWAH HA HA HA HA...HIS BONES ARE IN SHARDS !!
KILL HIM !
ARGH!! IF ONLY SANJI HADN'T TAKEN THAT BEATING FROM THE SHIELD MAN!!
HE'S BEEN HIT AT LEAST TEN TIMES WITH THOSE IRON CLUBS!!
...!!
HUFF...
THOSE SKEWERED DUMPLINGS YOU'RE SWINGING AREN'T MUCH GOOD, ARE THEY?
!
YOU...
shake
...SMALL-FRY SCOUN-DREL.
shake
I'M IN TROUBLE, THIS GUY'S TOUGH !!!
I'LL FINISH YOU NOW !!
WHOOM!!
DON'T SQUIRM !!!
!

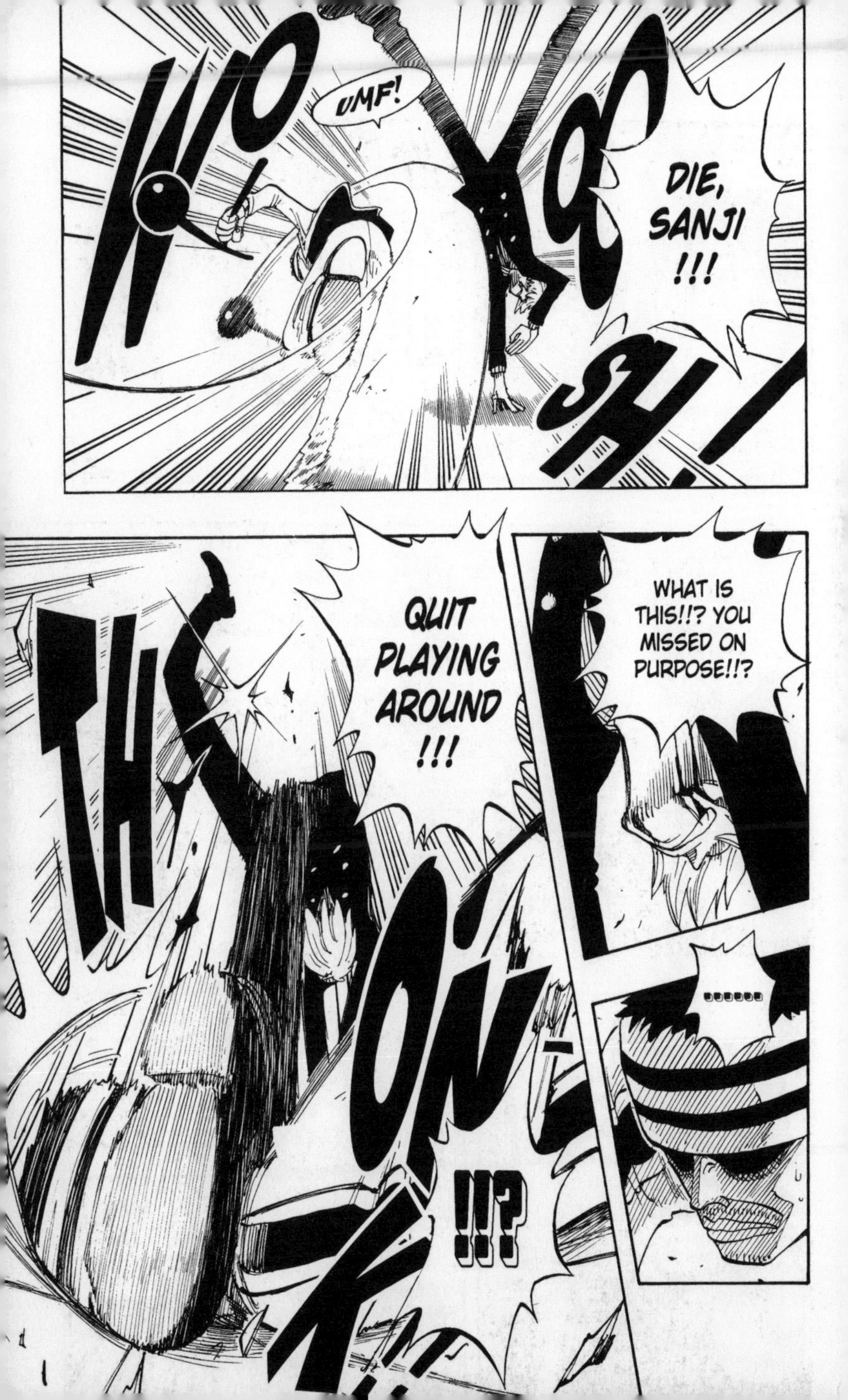
DIE, SANJI!!!
UMF!
WHAT IS THIS!!? YOU MISSED ON PURPOSE!!?
......
QUIT PLAYING AROUND!!!
!!?

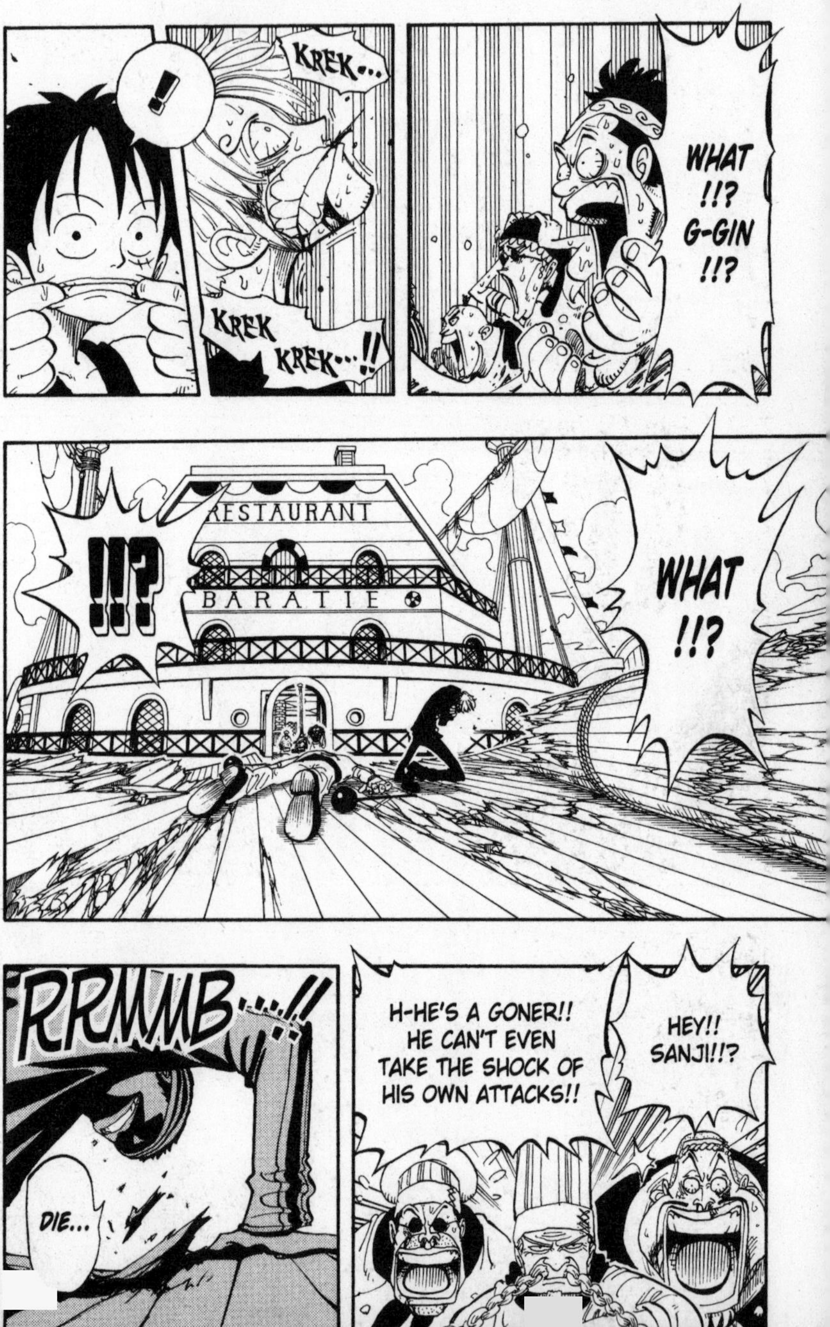
WHAT!!? G-GIN!!?
KREK...
KREK KREK...!!
!
WHAT!!?
RESTAURANT
BARATIE
!!?
HEY!! SANJI!!?
H-HE'S A GONER!! HE CAN'T EVEN TAKE THE SHOCK OF HIS OWN ATTACKS!!
RRMMB...!!
DIE...

READ THIS WAY

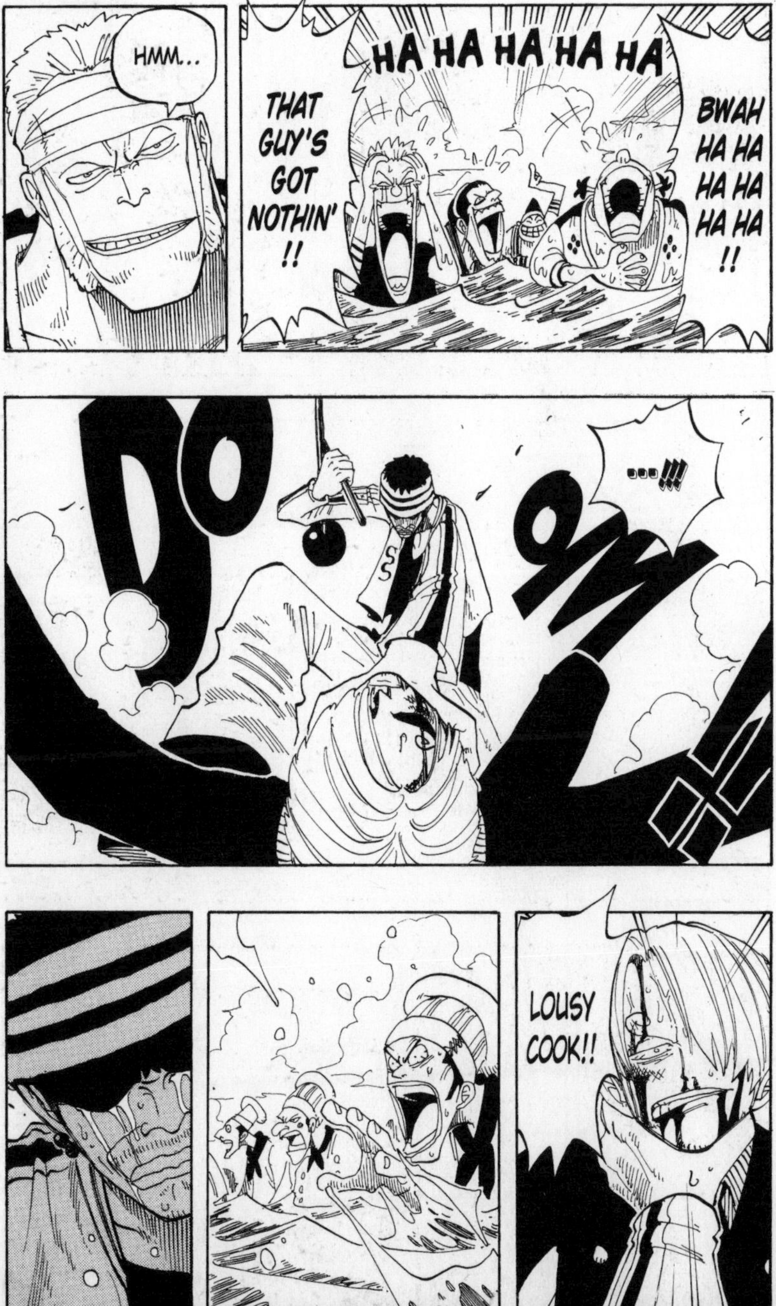

HA HA HA HA HA
BWAH HA HA HA HA HA HA !!
THAT GUY'S GOT NOTHIN' !!
HMM...
...!!!
DOOM!!
LOUSY COOK!!

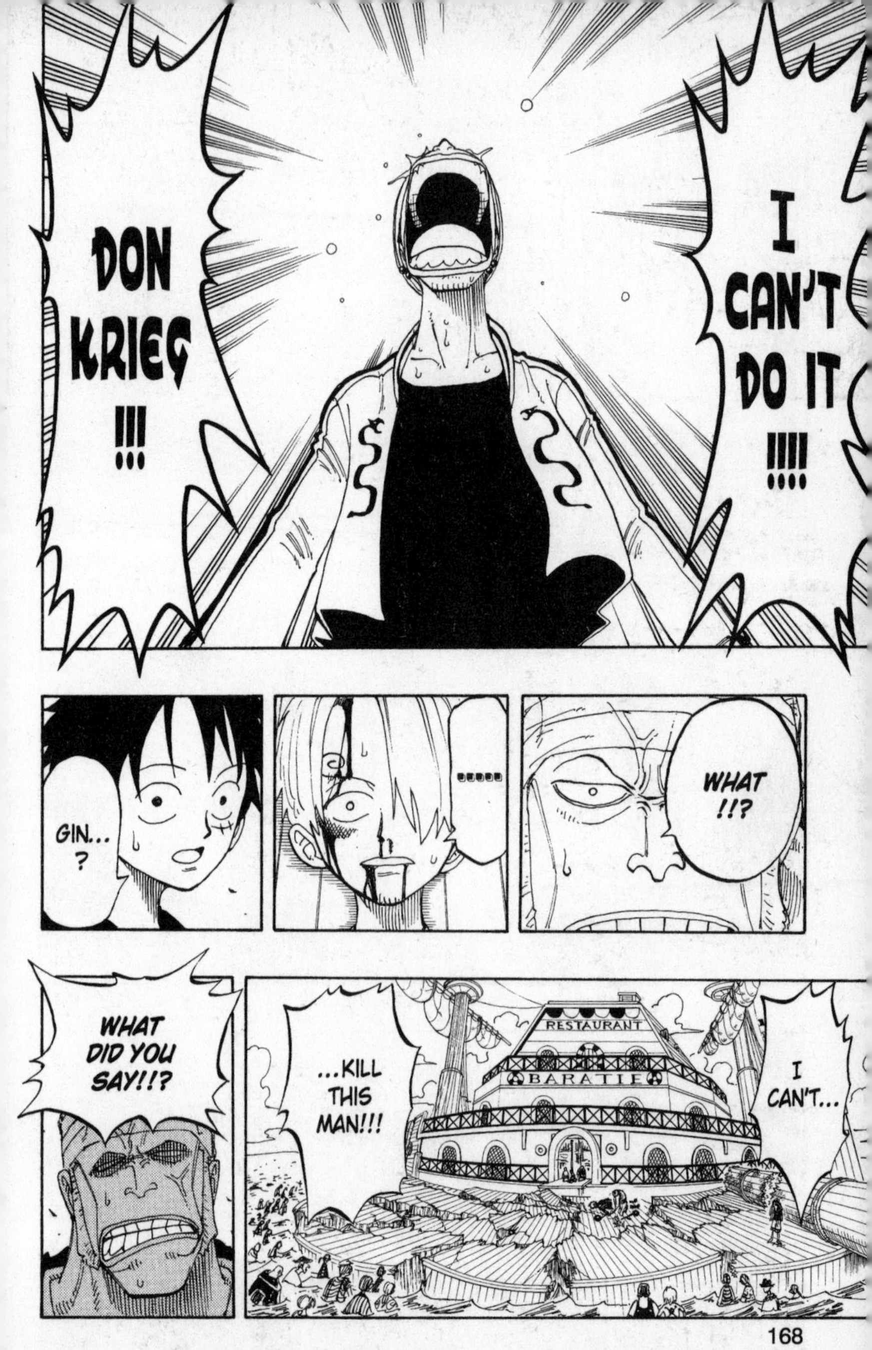
I CAN'T DO IT!!!!
DON KRIEG!!!
WHAT!!?
.....
GIN...?
I CAN'T...
...KILL THIS MAN!!!
RESTAURANT
BARATIE
WHAT DID YOU SAY!!?

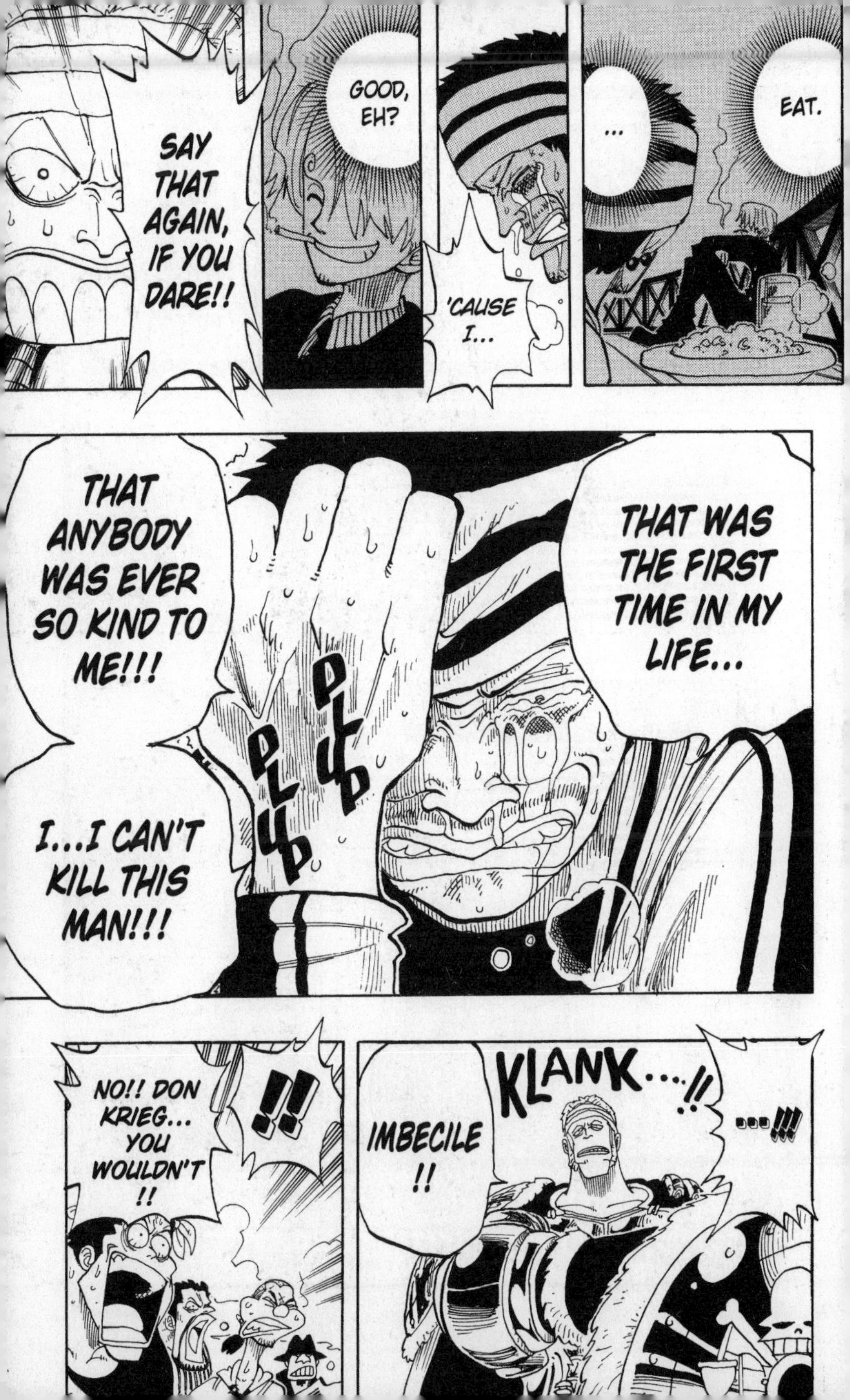

EAT.
...
GOOD, EH?
'CAUSE I...
SAY THAT AGAIN, IF YOU DARE!!
THAT WAS THE FIRST TIME IN MY LIFE...
THAT ANYBODY WAS EVER SO KIND TO ME!!!
PLUP
PLUP
I...I CAN'T KILL THIS MAN!!!
...!!!
KLANK....!!
IMBECILE !!
!!
NO!! DON KRIEG... YOU WOULDN'T !!

ONE PIECE

USOPP'S PIRATE GALLERY!

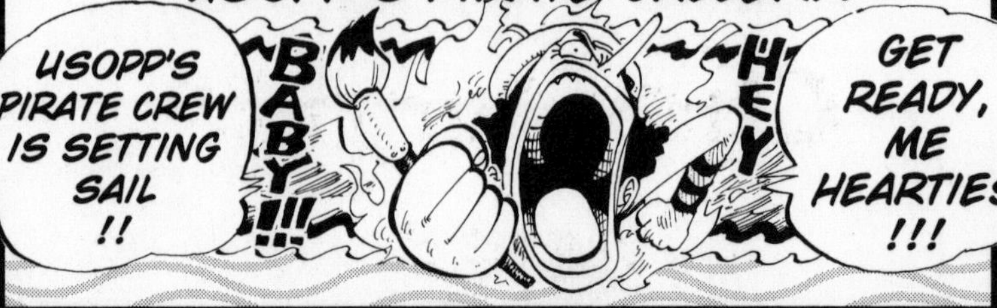
GET READY, ME HEARTIES !!!
HEY
BABY!!!
USOPP'S PIRATE CREW IS SETTING SAIL !!

A PORTRAIT OF VALOR.

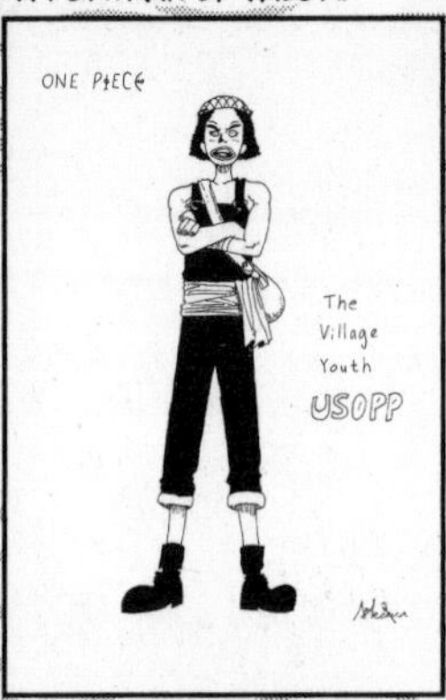
ONE PIECE
The Village Youth
USOPP

SAKEENA, 17

HEY! SOMEONE'S MISSING!

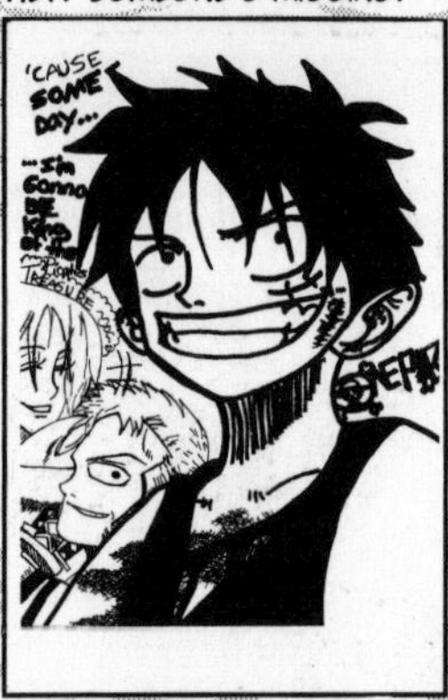
'CAUSE SOME DAY...

SARAH, 14

A SIGHT FOR SORE EYES...

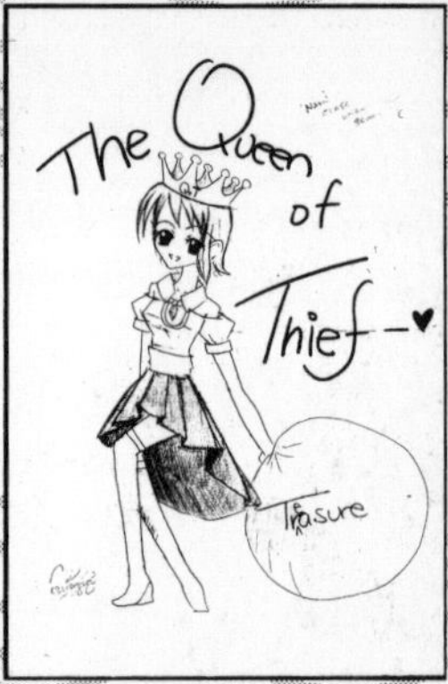
The Queen of Thief -♥
Treasure

VIVIANA, 15

...UM...NICE HAT...

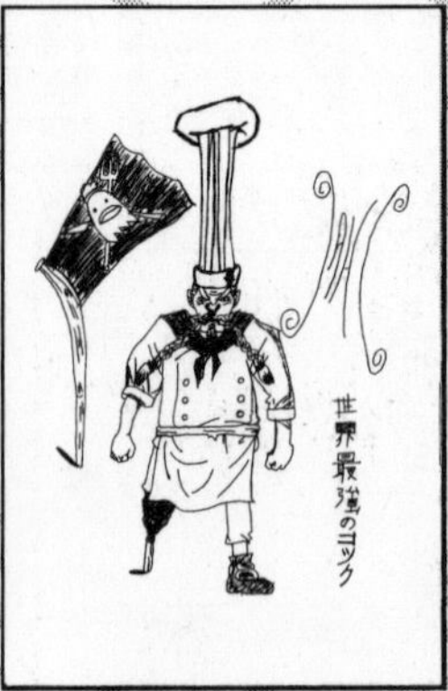
世界最強のコック

ANDREW, 13

THE GANG'S ALL HERE.

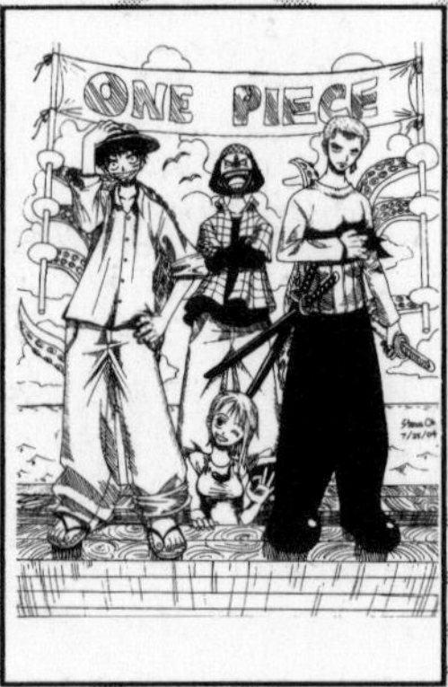
ONE PIECE

STEVE, 17

ZOLO'S...SO CUTE!

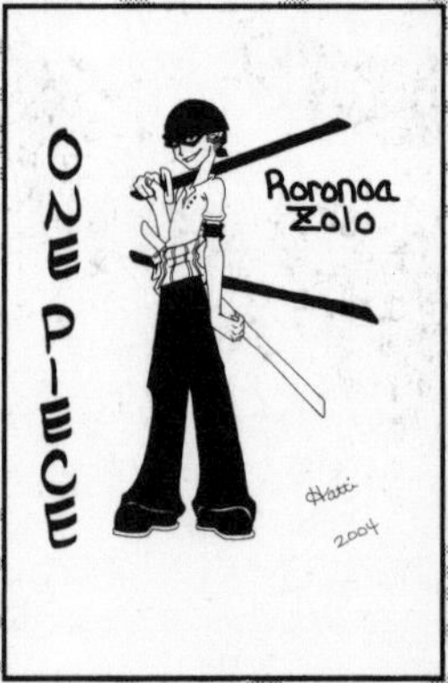
ONE PIECE
Roronoa Zolo
2004

HATTI, 19

SUBMIT YOUR FAN ART TO:
SHONEN JUMP C/O VIZ, LLC P.O. BOX 77010, SAN FRANCISCO, CA, 94107
REMEMBER TO INCLUDE YOUR NAME AND AGE!!

USOPP'S COMMENTS WERE TRANSMITTED THROUGH THE U.S. SHONEN JUMP TEAM—*EDITOR*

Chapter 62:
MH5

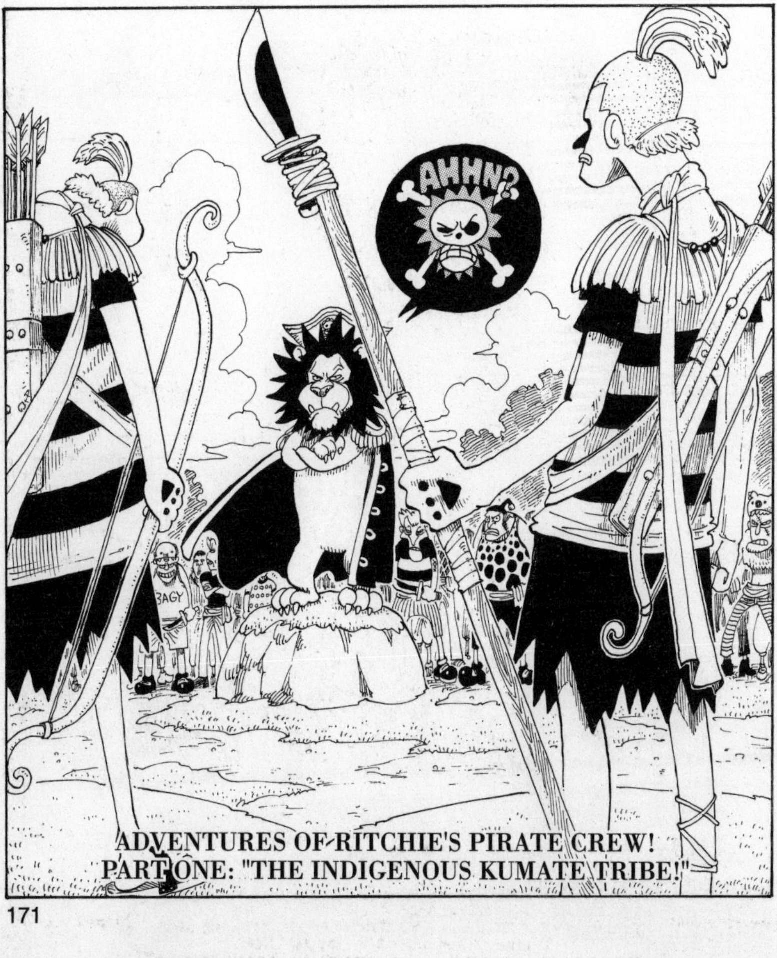
AHHN?
ADVENTURES OF RITCHIE'S PIRATE CREW!
PART ONE: "THE INDIGENOUS KUMATE TRIBE!"

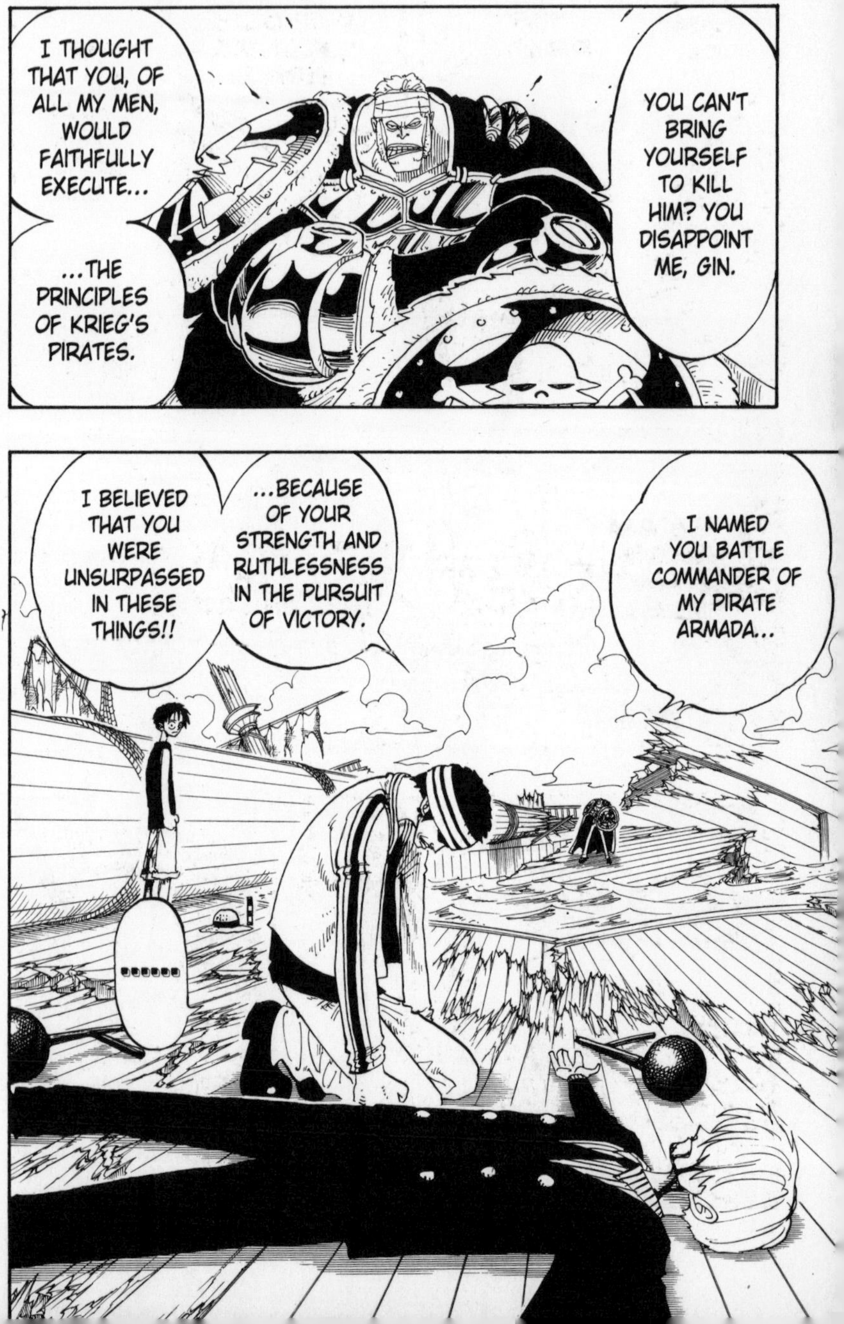
YOU CAN'T BRING YOURSELF TO KILL HIM? YOU DISAPPOINT ME, GIN.
I THOUGHT THAT YOU, OF ALL MY MEN, WOULD FAITHFULLY EXECUTE...
...THE PRINCIPLES OF KRIEG'S PIRATES.
I NAMED YOU BATTLE COMMANDER OF MY PIRATE ARMADA...
...BECAUSE OF YOUR STRENGTH AND RUTHLESSNESS IN THE PURSUIT OF VICTORY.
I BELIEVED THAT YOU WERE UNSURPASSED IN THESE THINGS!!
......

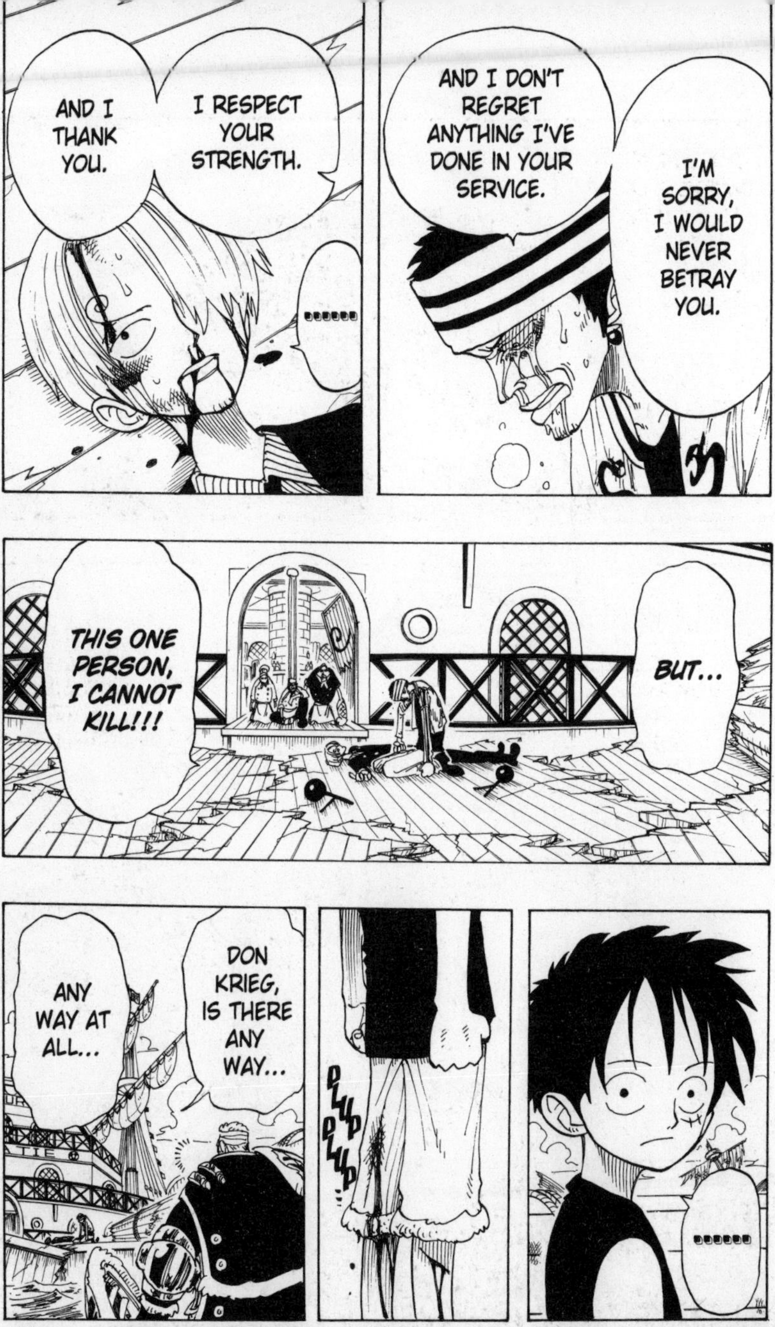
I'M SORRY, I WOULD NEVER BETRAY YOU.
AND I DON'T REGRET ANYTHING I'VE DONE IN YOUR SERVICE.
I RESPECT YOUR STRENGTH.
AND I THANK YOU.
......
BUT...
THIS ONE PERSON, I CANNOT KILL!!!
......
PLUP
PLUP
DON KRIEG, IS THERE ANY WAY...
ANY WAY AT ALL...

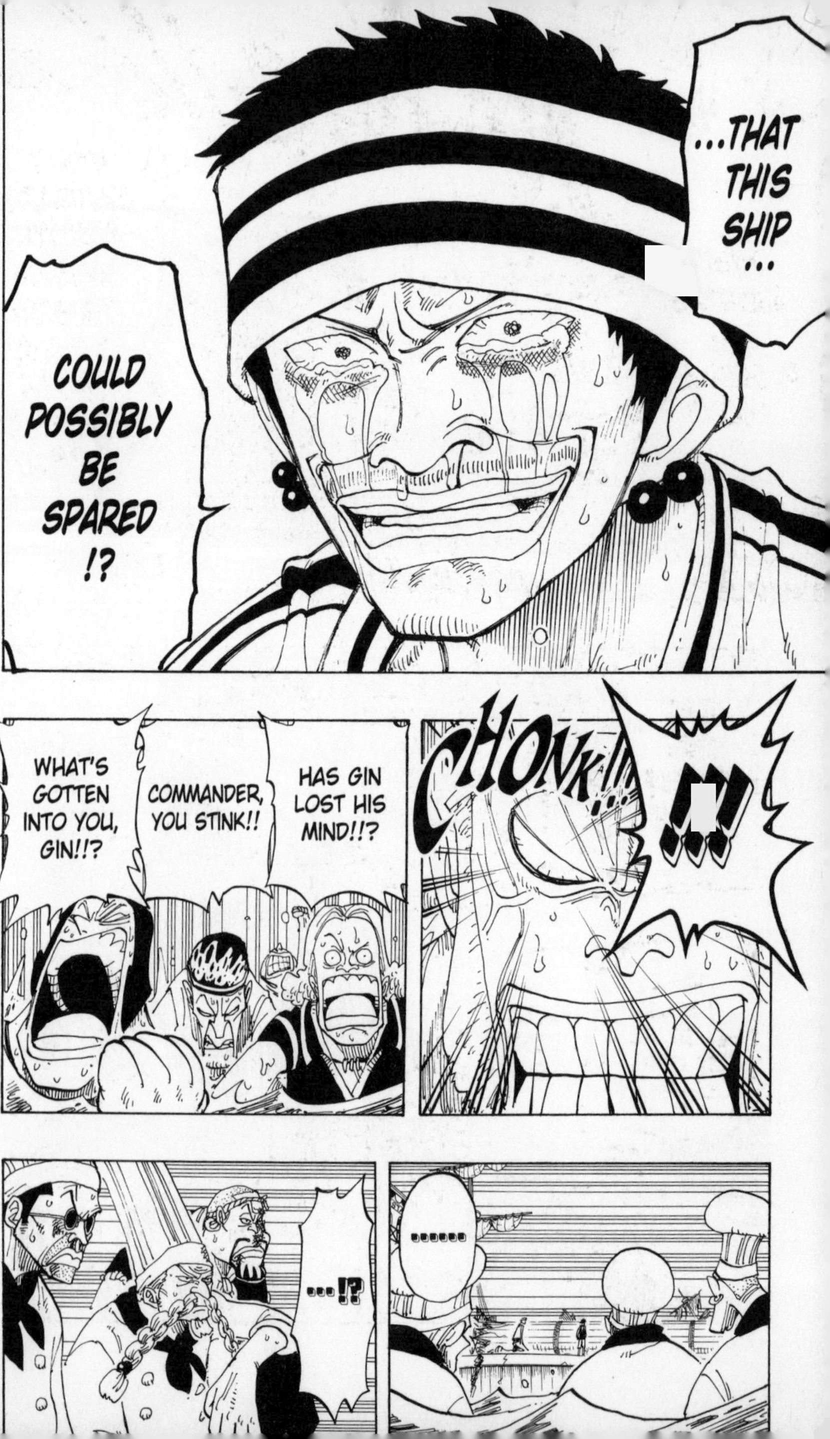
...THAT THIS SHIP...
COULD POSSIBLY BE SPARED!?
CHONK!!
!!
HAS GIN LOST HIS MIND!!?
COMMANDER, YOU STINK!!
WHAT'S GOTTEN INTO YOU, GIN!!?
......
...!?

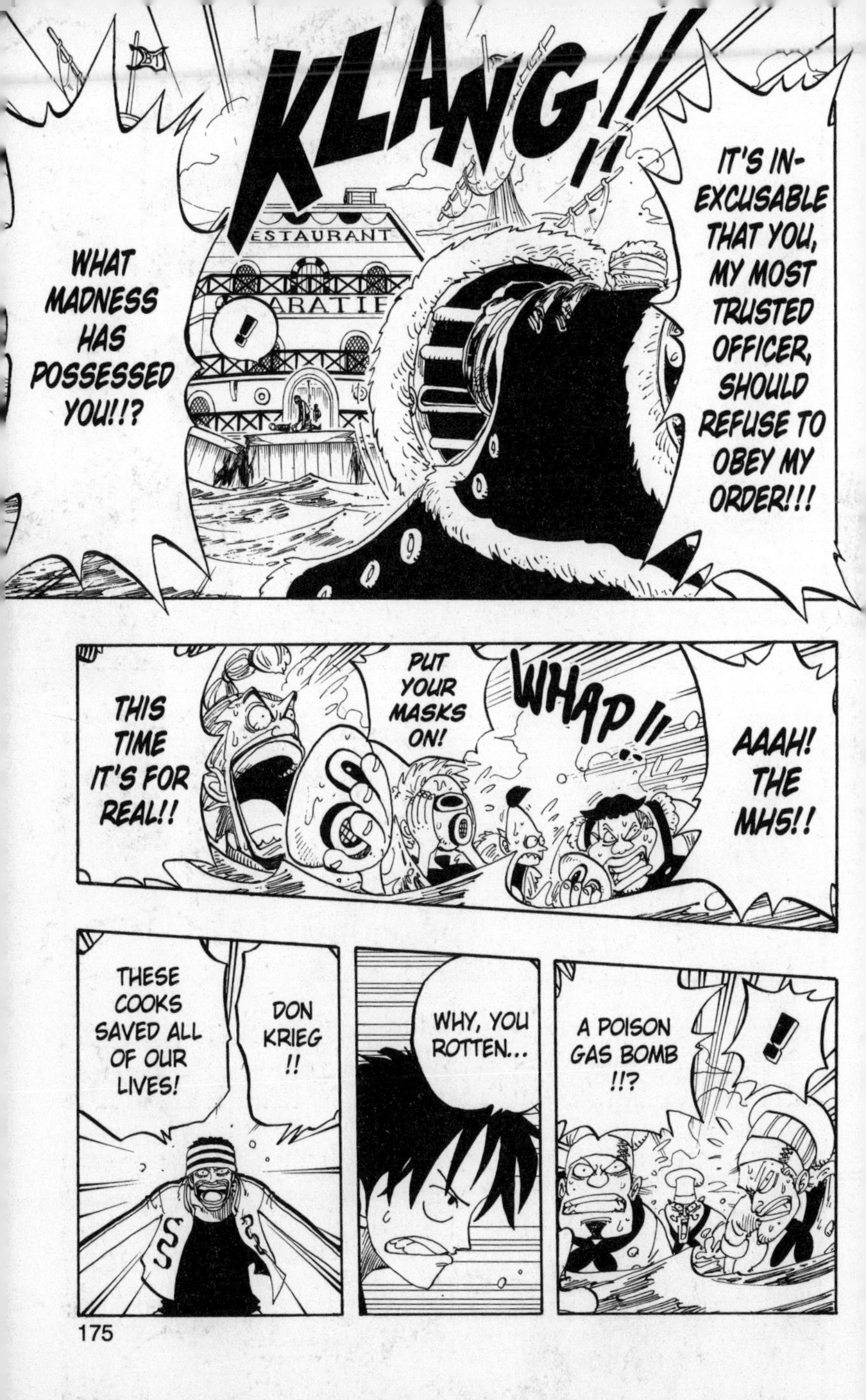
KLANG!!
IT'S IN-EXCUSABLE THAT YOU, MY MOST TRUSTED OFFICER, SHOULD REFUSE TO OBEY MY ORDER!!!
WHAT MADNESS HAS POSSESSED YOU!!?
AAAH! THE MH5!!
WHAP!!
PUT YOUR MASKS ON!
THIS TIME IT'S FOR REAL!!
A POISON GAS BOMB!!?
WHY, YOU ROTTEN...
DON KRIEG!!
THESE COOKS SAVED ALL OF OUR LIVES!

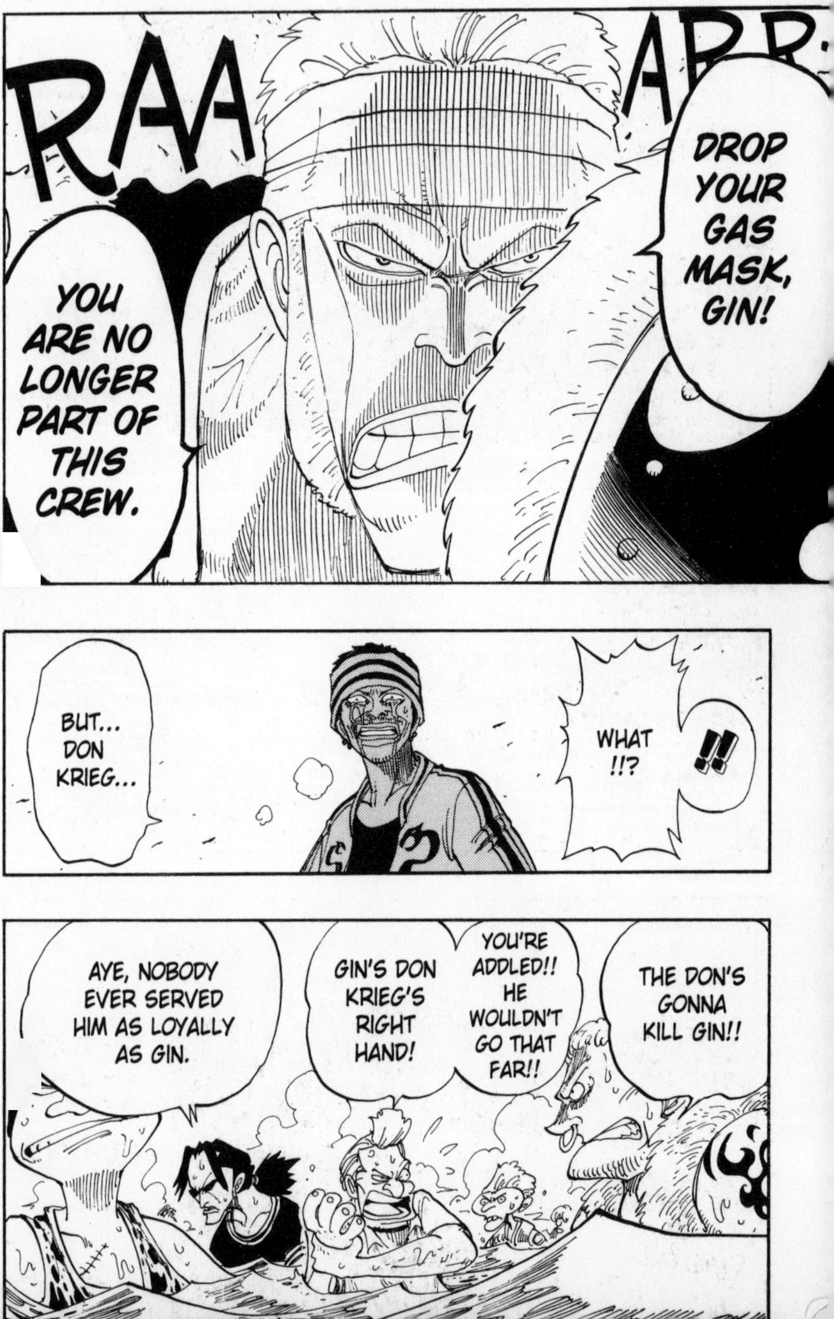
RAA ARR
DROP YOUR GAS MASK, GIN!
YOU ARE NO LONGER PART OF THIS CREW.
WHAT !!?
!!
BUT... DON KRIEG...
THE DON'S GONNA KILL GIN!!
YOU'RE ADDLED!! HE WOULDN'T GO THAT FAR!!
GIN'S DON KRIEG'S RIGHT HAND!
AYE, NOBODY EVER SERVED HIM AS LOYALLY AS GIN.

READ THIS WAY

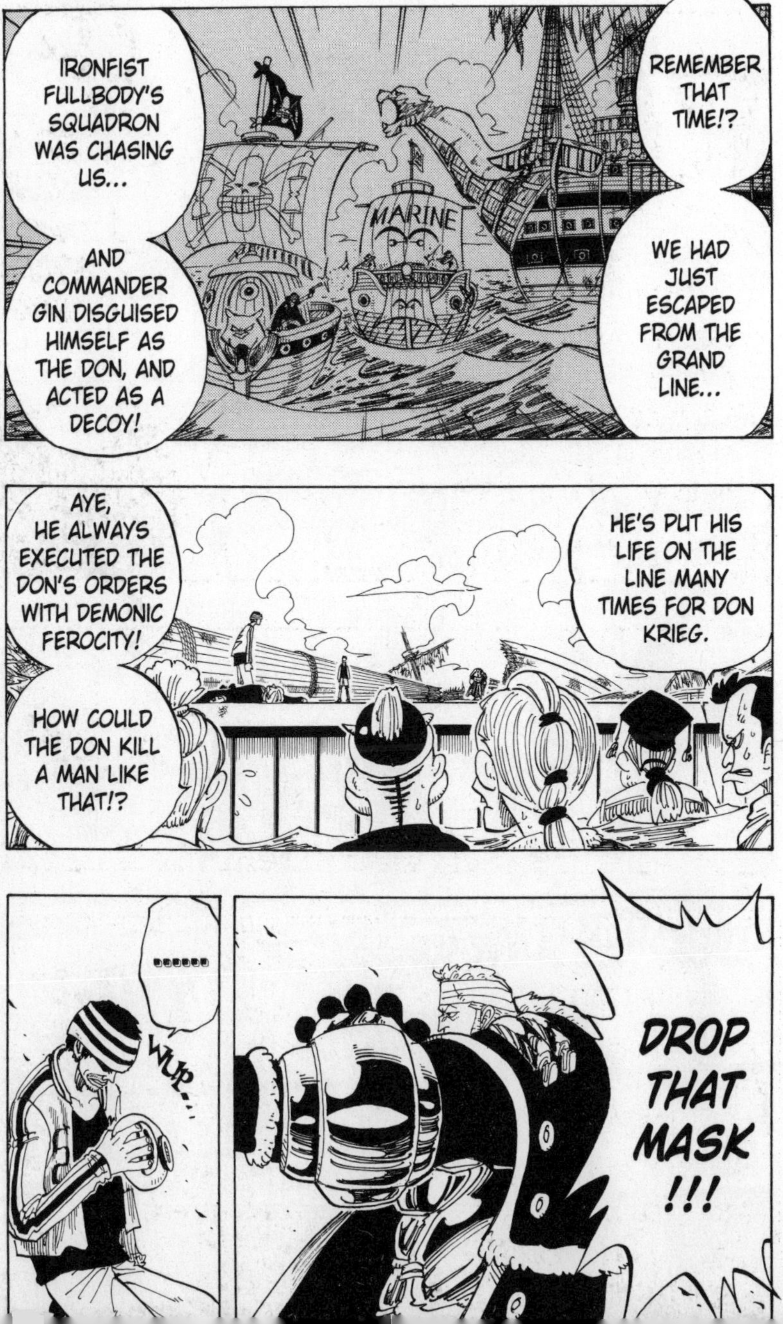
REMEMBER THAT TIME!?
WE HAD JUST ESCAPED FROM THE GRAND LINE...
IRONFIST FULLBODY'S SQUADRON WAS CHASING US...
AND COMMANDER GIN DISGUISED HIMSELF AS THE DON, AND ACTED AS A DECOY!
MARINE
HE'S PUT HIS LIFE ON THE LINE MANY TIMES FOR DON KRIEG.
AYE, HE ALWAYS EXECUTED THE DON'S ORDERS WITH DEMONIC FEROCITY!
HOW COULD THE DON KILL A MAN LIKE THAT!?
DROP THAT MASK!!!
......
WUP...

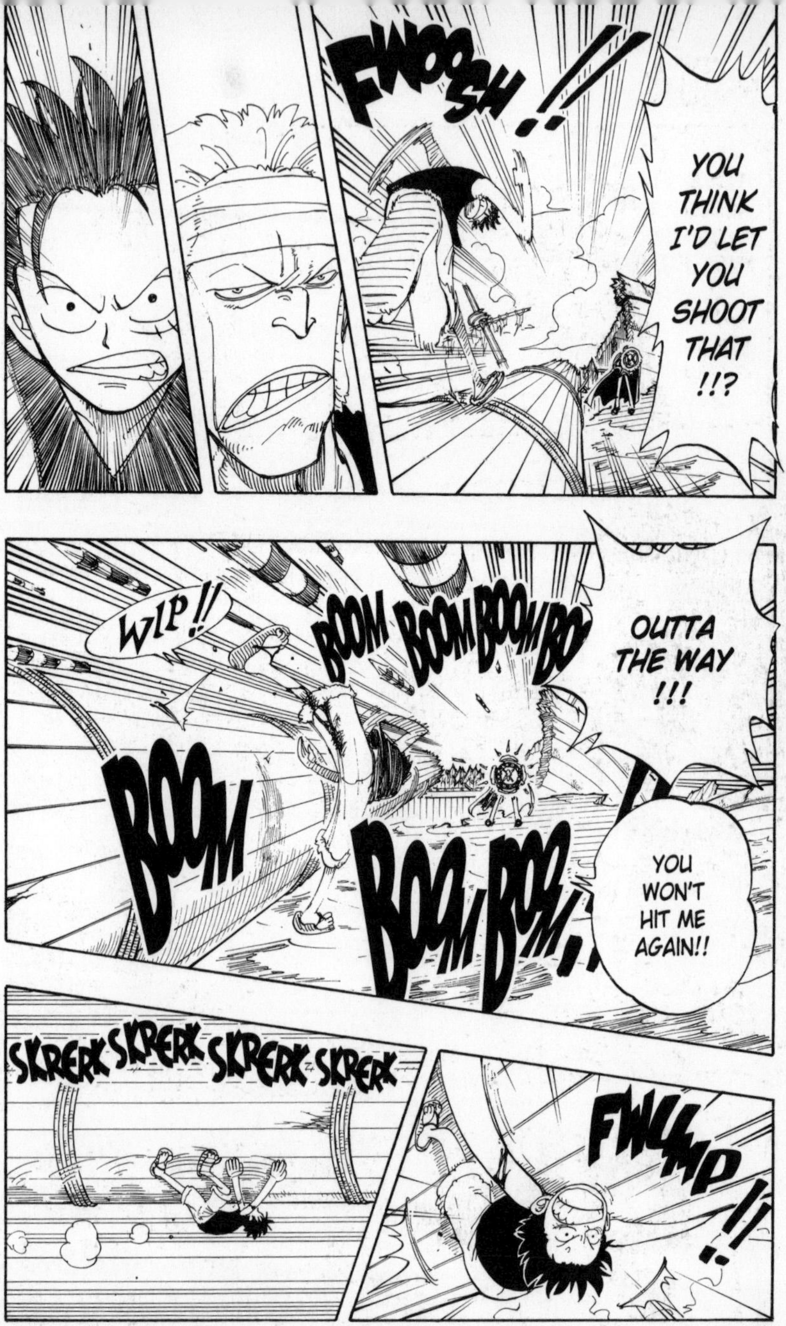
FWOOSH!!
YOU THINK I'D LET YOU SHOOT THAT!!?
OUTTA THE WAY!!!
BOOM BOOM BOOM BO
WIP!!
YOU WON'T HIT ME AGAIN!!
BOOM
BOOM BOOM!!
FWUMP!!
SKRERK SKRERK SKRERK SKRERK

READ THIS WAY

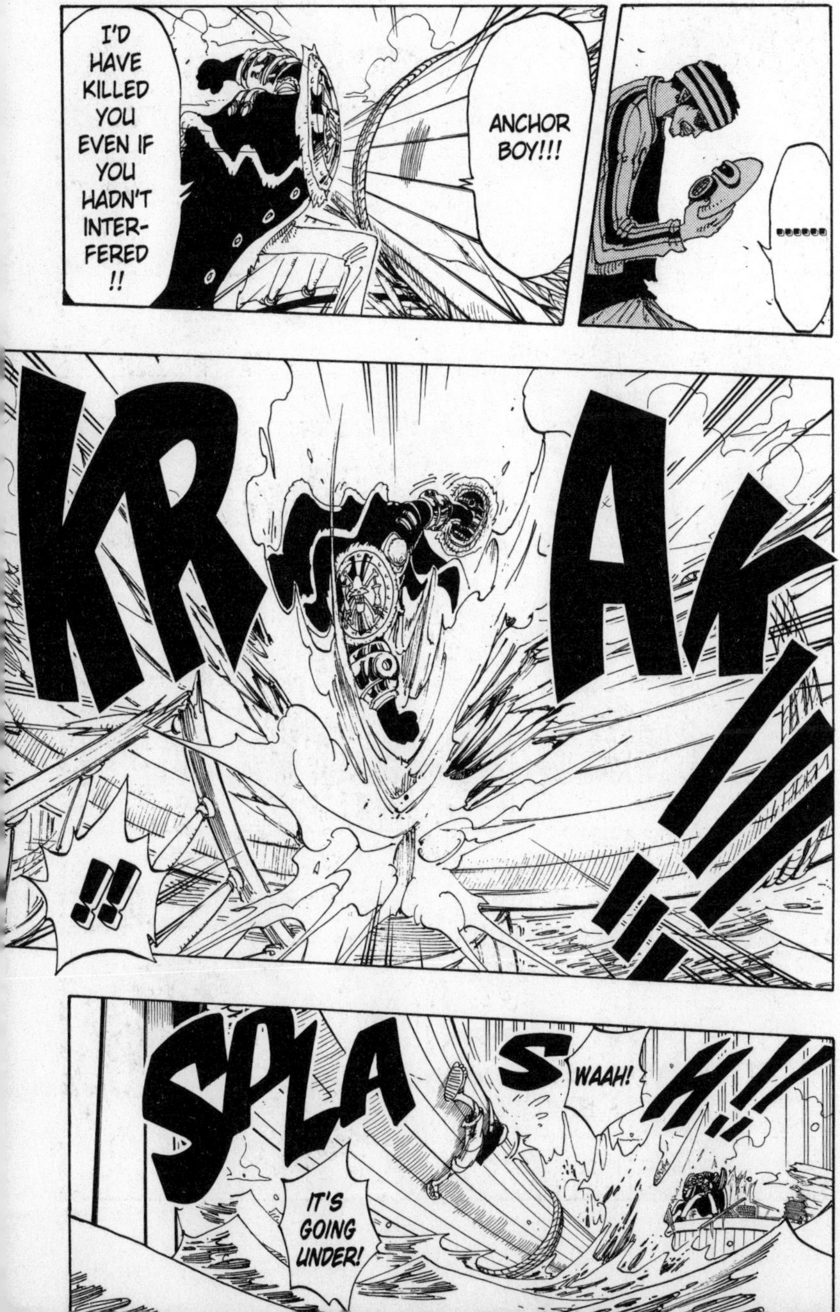
......
ANCHOR BOY!!!
I'D HAVE KILLED YOU EVEN IF YOU HADN'T INTER-FERED !!
KRAK!!!!
!!
SPLASH!!
WAAH!
IT'S GOING UNDER!

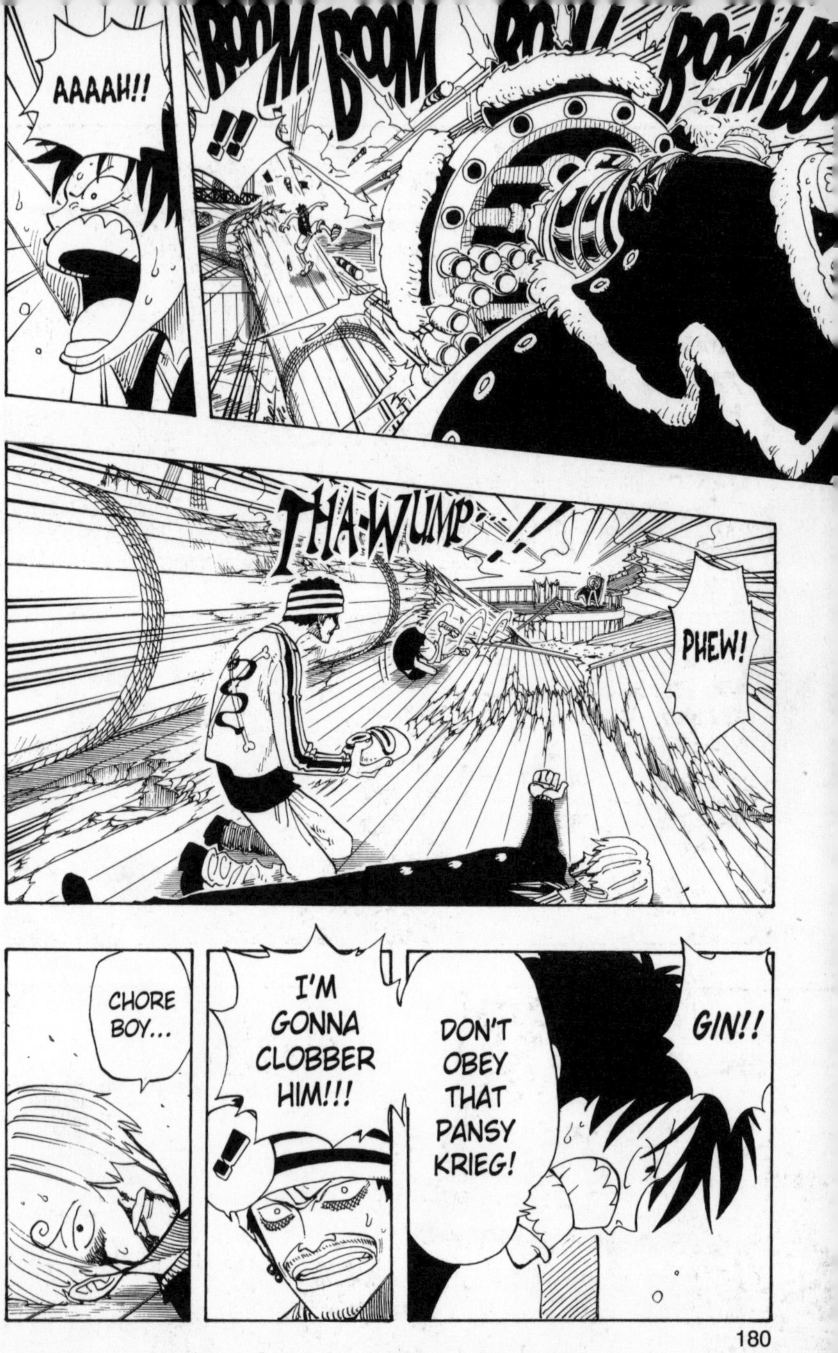
BOOM BOOM
!!
AAAAH!!
THA-WUMP..!!
PHEW!
GIN!!
DON'T OBEY THAT PANSY KRIEG!
I'M GONNA CLOBBER HIM!!!
!
CHORE BOY...

READ THIS WAY

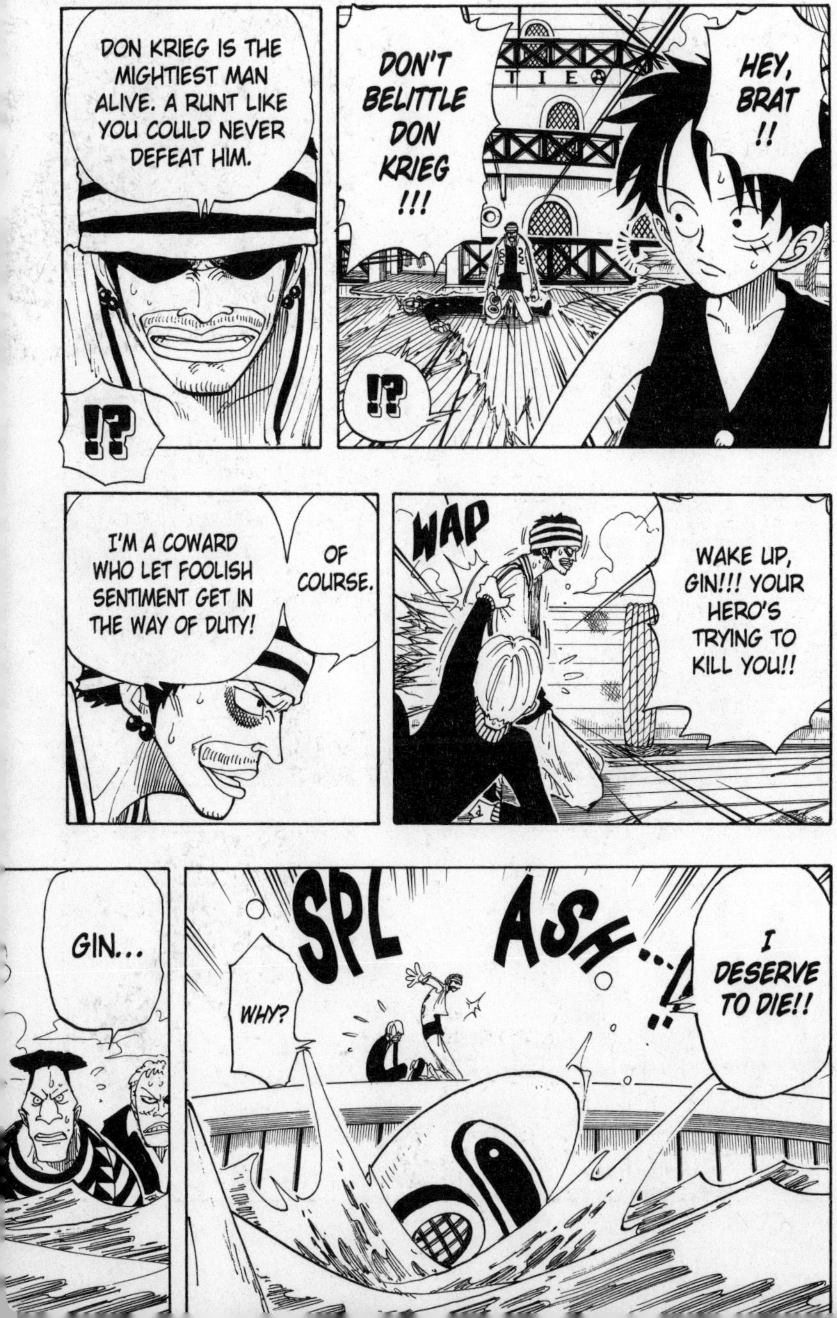

HEY, BRAT!!
DON'T BELITTLE DON KRIEG!!!
!?
DON KRIEG IS THE MIGHTIEST MAN ALIVE. A RUNT LIKE YOU COULD NEVER DEFEAT HIM.
!?
WAP
WAKE UP, GIN!!! YOUR HERO'S TRYING TO KILL YOU!!
OF COURSE.
I'M A COWARD WHO LET FOOLISH SENTIMENT GET IN THE WAY OF DUTY!
I DESERVE TO DIE!!
SPLASH...!!
WHY?
GIN...

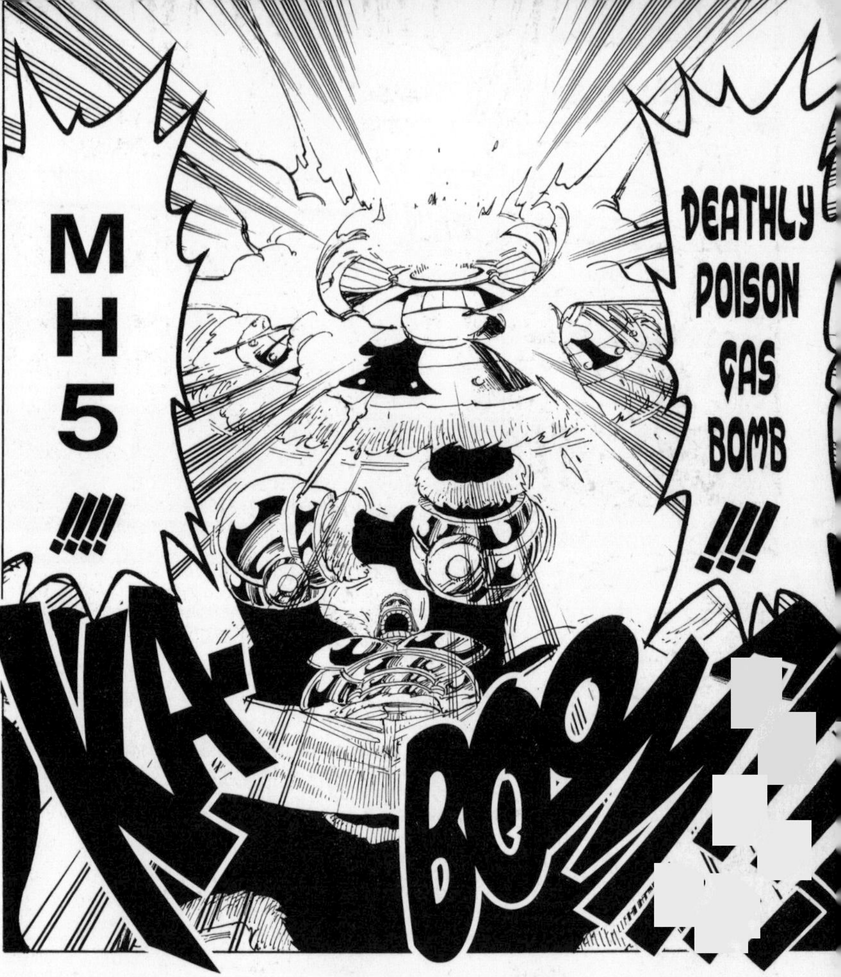
DEATHLY POISON GAS BOMB!!!
MH5!!!!
KA-BOOM

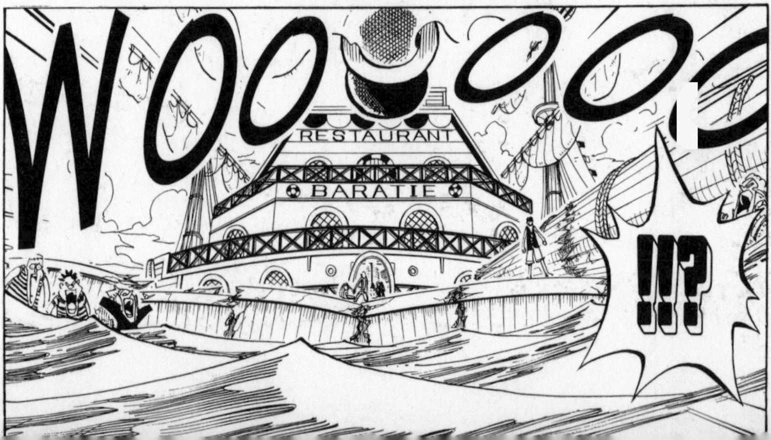
WOOOOOO
RESTAURANT
BARATIE
!!?

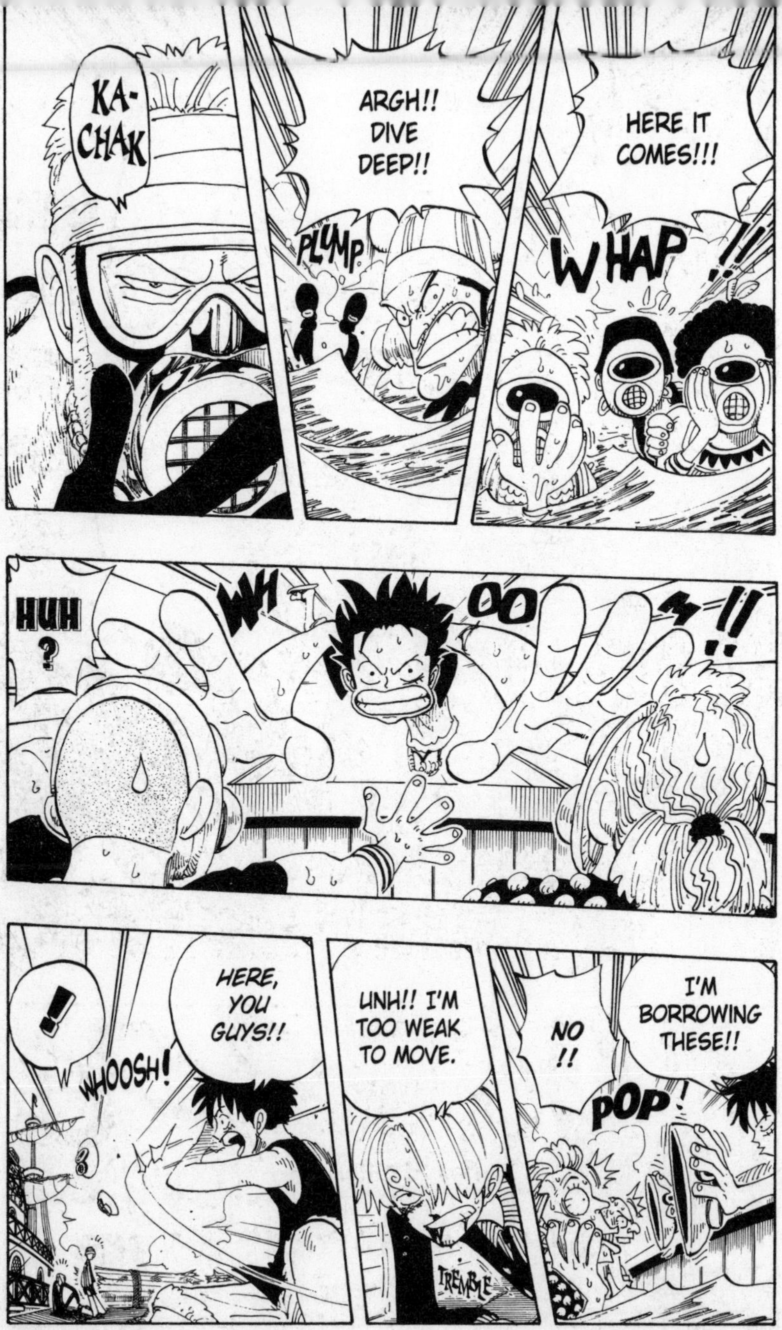
HERE IT COMES!!!
WHAP!!
ARGH!! DIVE DEEP!!
PLUMP
KA-CHAK
WHOOSH!!
HUH ?
I'M BORROWING THESE!!
POP!
NO !!
UNH!! I'M TOO WEAK TO MOVE.
TREMBLE
HERE, YOU GUYS!!
WHOOSH!
!

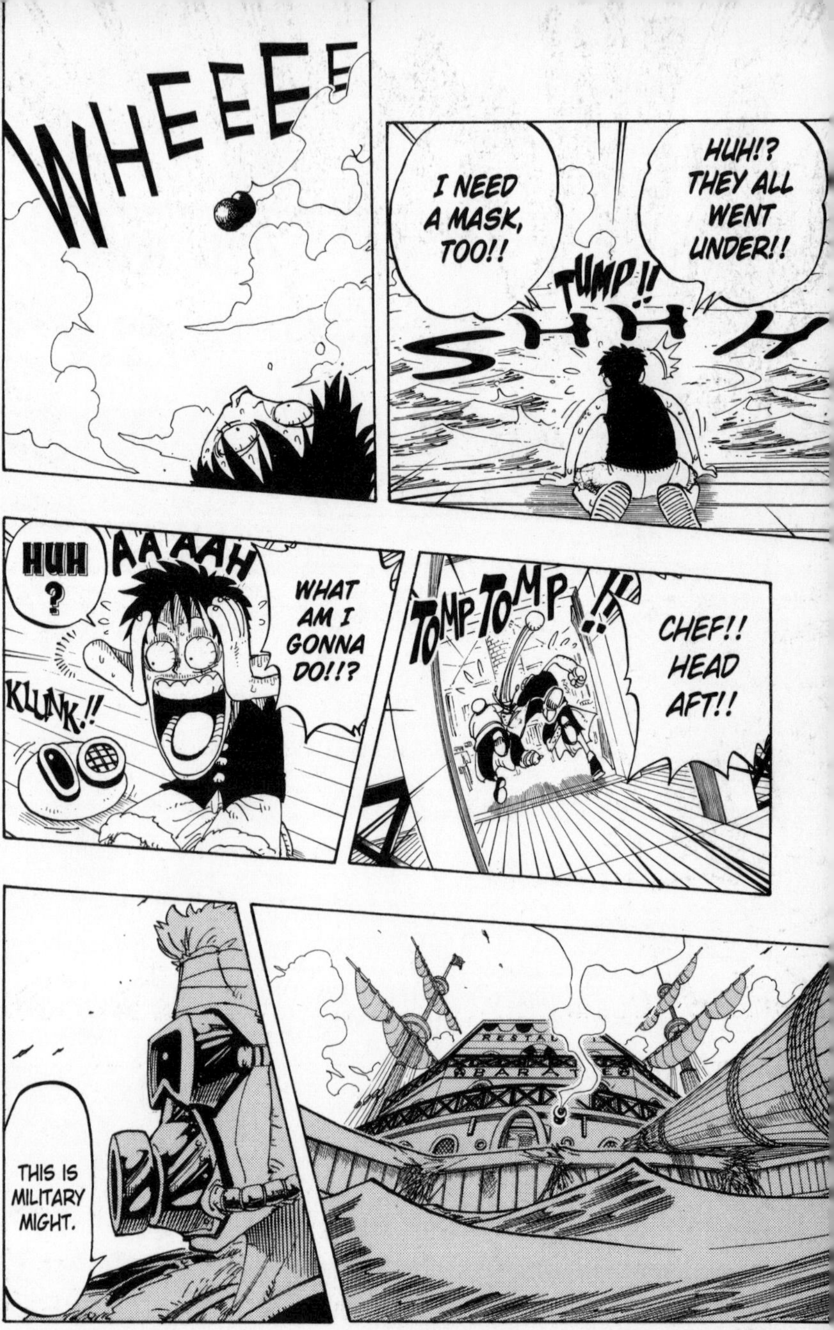
HUH!? THEY ALL WENT UNDER!!
I NEED A MASK, TOO!!
TUMP!!
SHHH
WHEEEE
TOMP TOMP!!
CHEF!! HEAD AFT!!
WHAT AM I GONNA DO!!?
AAAAH
HUH?
KLUNK!!
THIS IS MILITARY MIGHT.

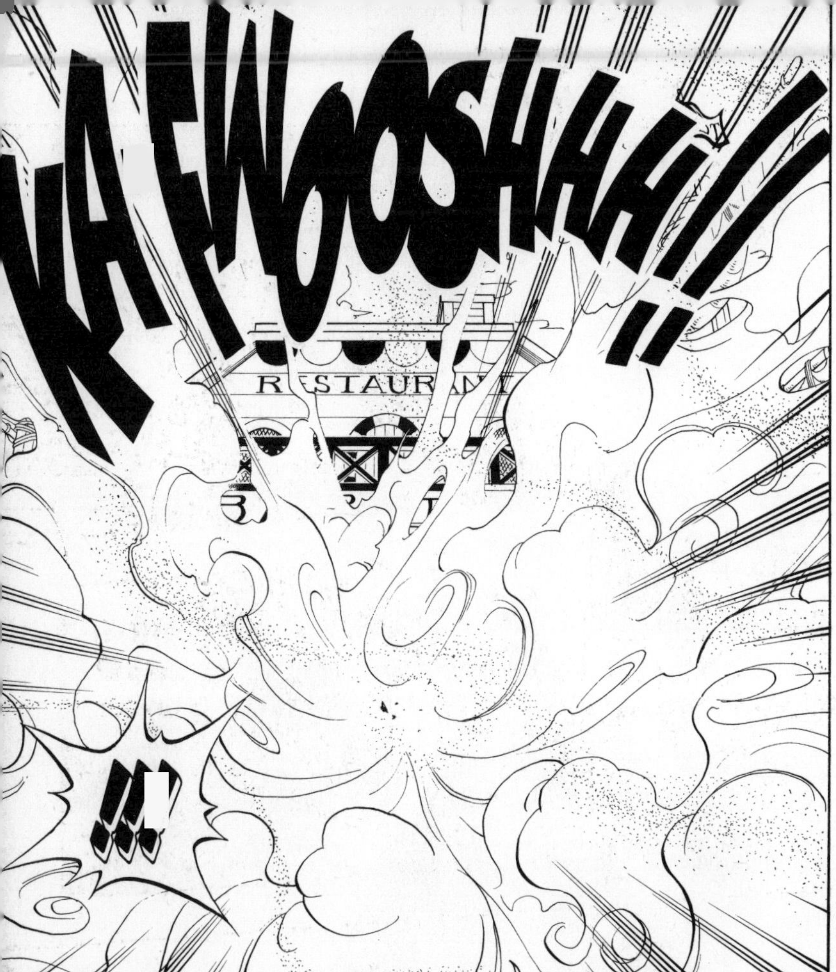
KAFWOOSHHH!!!
!!!

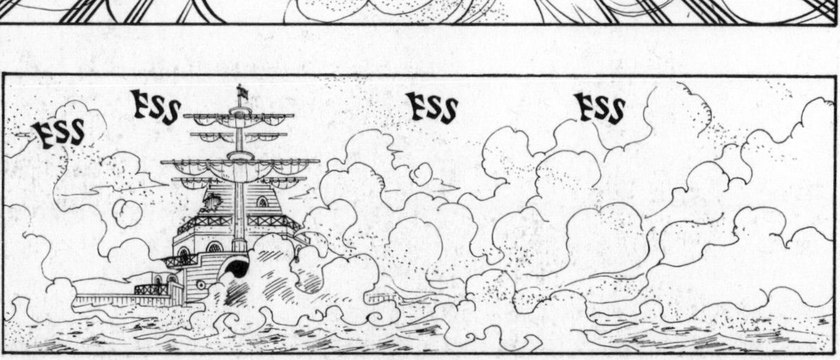
FSS
FSS
FSS
FSS

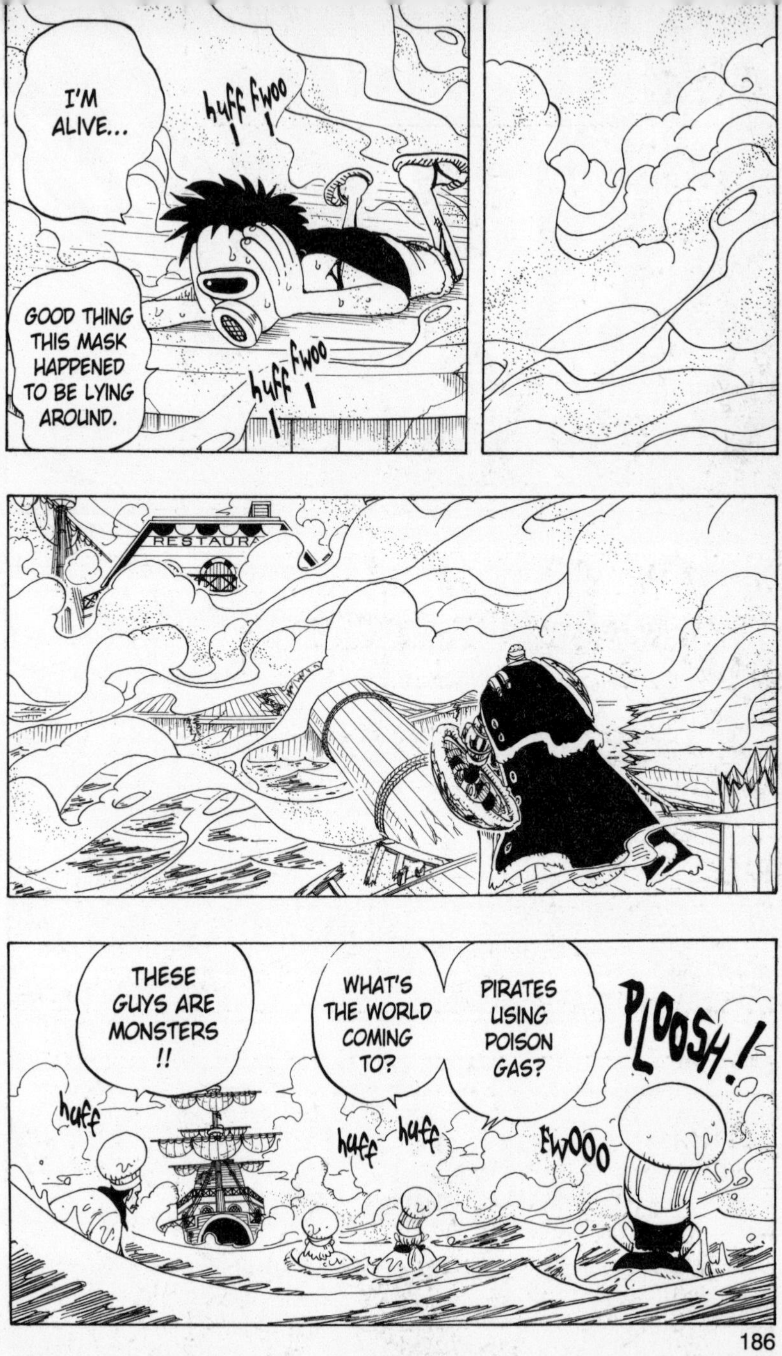
huff fwoo
I'M ALIVE...
huff fwoo
GOOD THING THIS MASK HAPPENED TO BE LYING AROUND.
PLOOSH!
FWOOO
PIRATES USING POISON GAS?
WHAT'S THE WORLD COMING TO?
huff
huff
THESE GUYS ARE MONSTERS!!
huff

READ THIS WAY

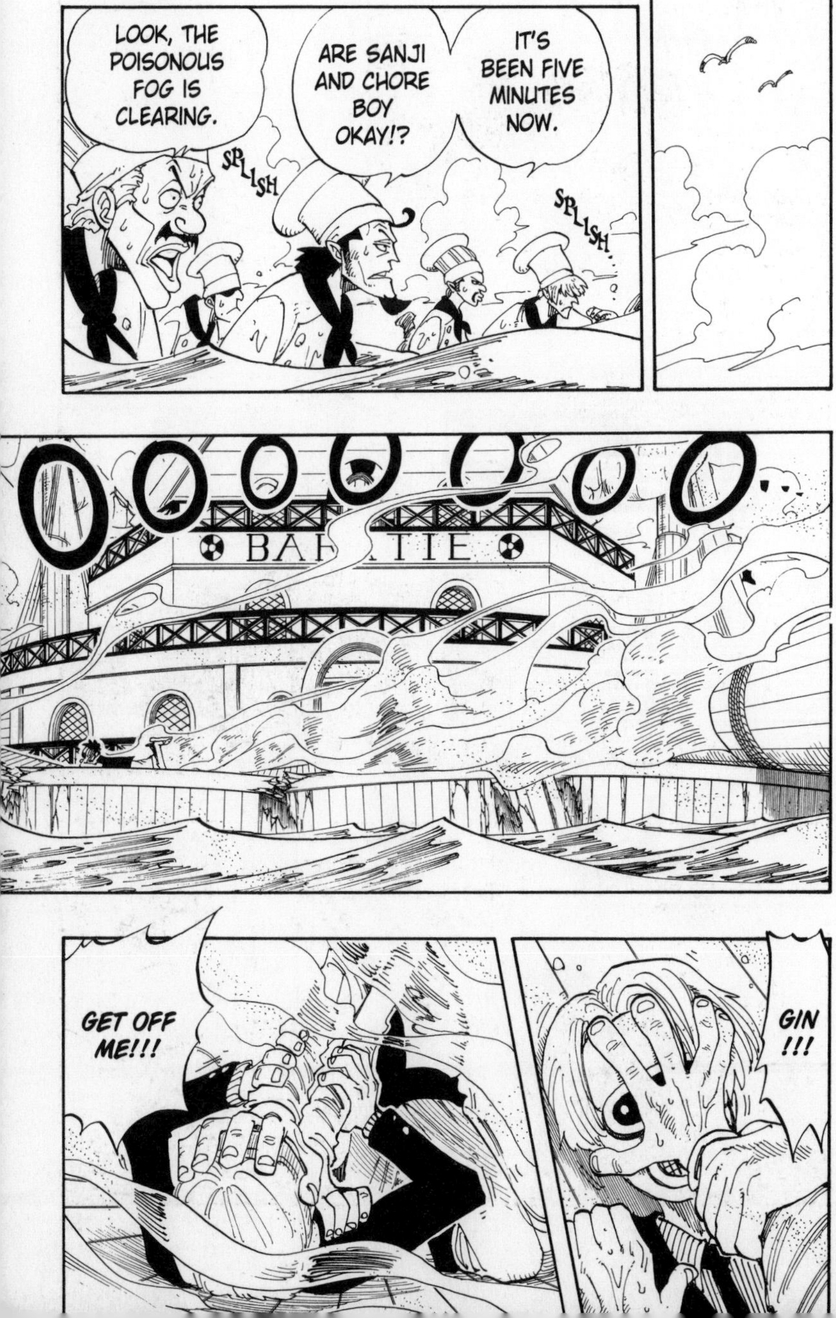
IT'S BEEN FIVE MINUTES NOW.
ARE SANJI AND CHORE BOY OKAY!?
SPLISH
LOOK, THE POISONOUS FOG IS CLEARING.
SPLISH
GIN!!!
GET OFF ME!!!

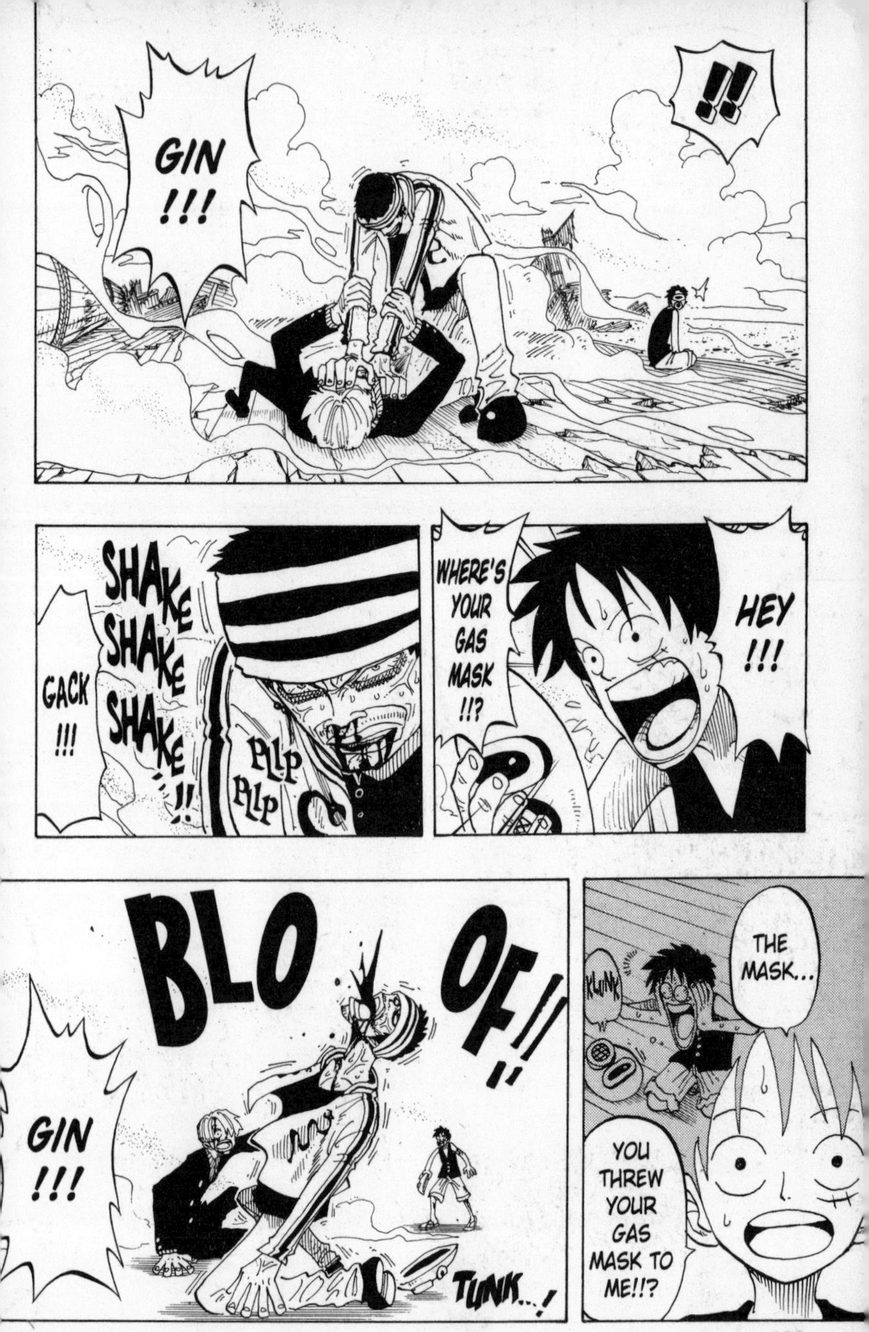
!!
GIN !!!
HEY !!!
WHERE'S YOUR GAS MASK !!?
SHAKE SHAKE SHAKE...!!
PLIP PLIP
GACK !!!
THE MASK...
KLUNK
YOU THREW YOUR GAS MASK TO ME!!?
BLO OF!!
GIN !!!
TUNK...!

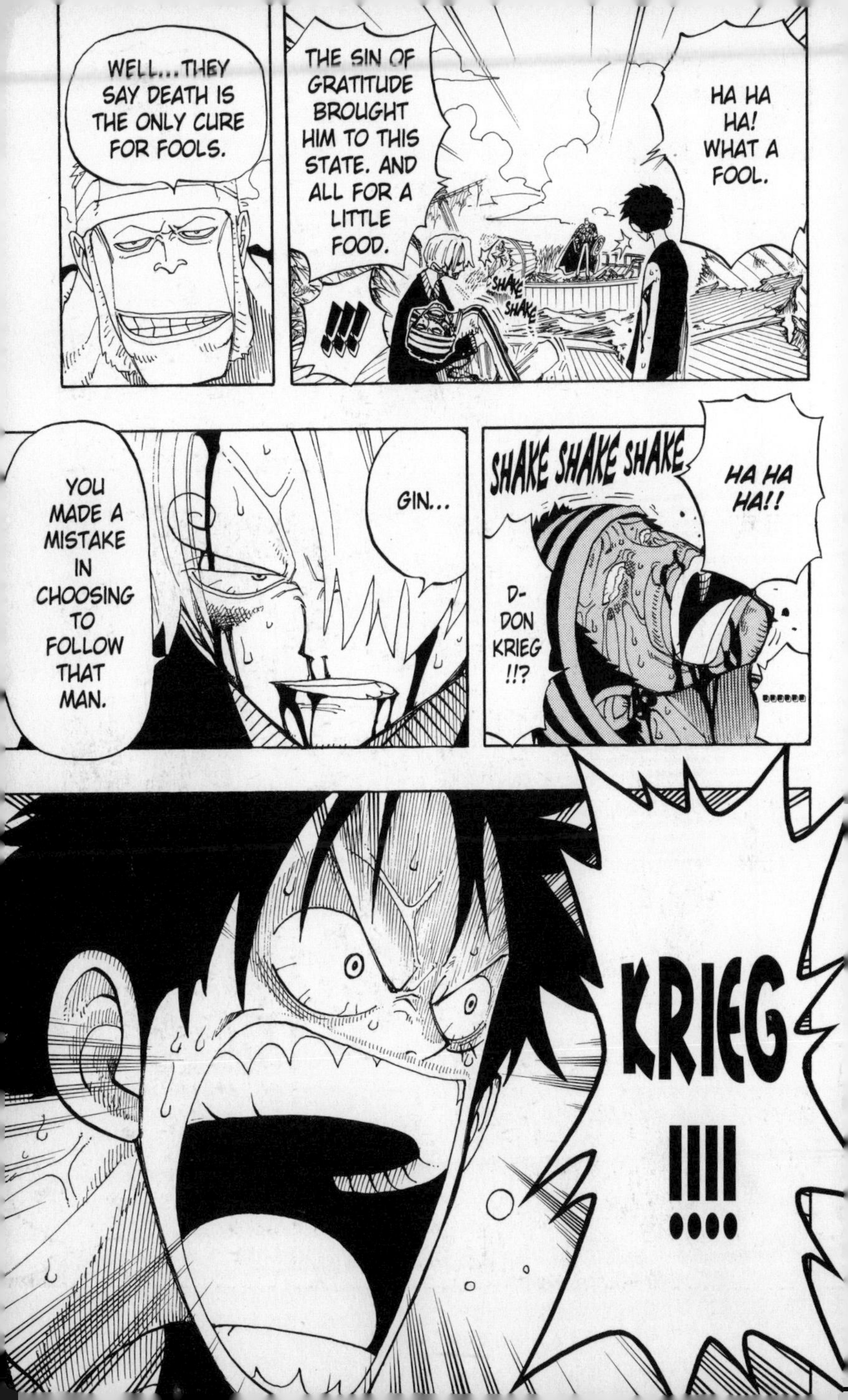
HA HA HA! WHAT A FOOL.
THE SIN OF GRATITUDE BROUGHT HIM TO THIS STATE. AND ALL FOR A LITTLE FOOD.
SHAKE SHAKE
!!!
WELL...THEY SAY DEATH IS THE ONLY CURE FOR FOOLS.
SHAKE SHAKE SHAKE
HA HA HA!!
D-DON KRIEG !!?
......
GIN...
YOU MADE A MISTAKE IN CHOOSING TO FOLLOW THAT MAN.
KRIEG !!!!....

COMING NEXT VOLUME:

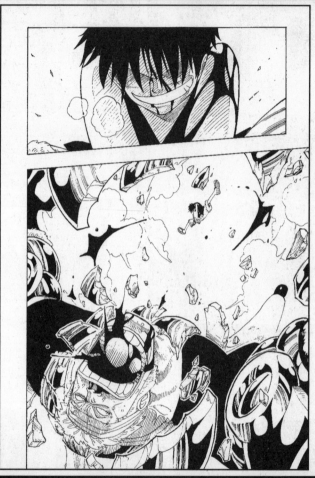

Johnny and Yosaku think they know where Nami's headed: Arlong Park, the stronghold of the treacherous Fish-Man pirates! It turns out there's more to Nami than meets the eye…

Meanwhile, Krieg continues his assault with a litany of weapons and sheer determination that rivals even Luffy's legendary pigheadedness. Will Sanji ever leave the Baratie? Will Luffy have to stay a chore-boy for one more year? It all boils down to a battle of wills.

ON SALE NOW!

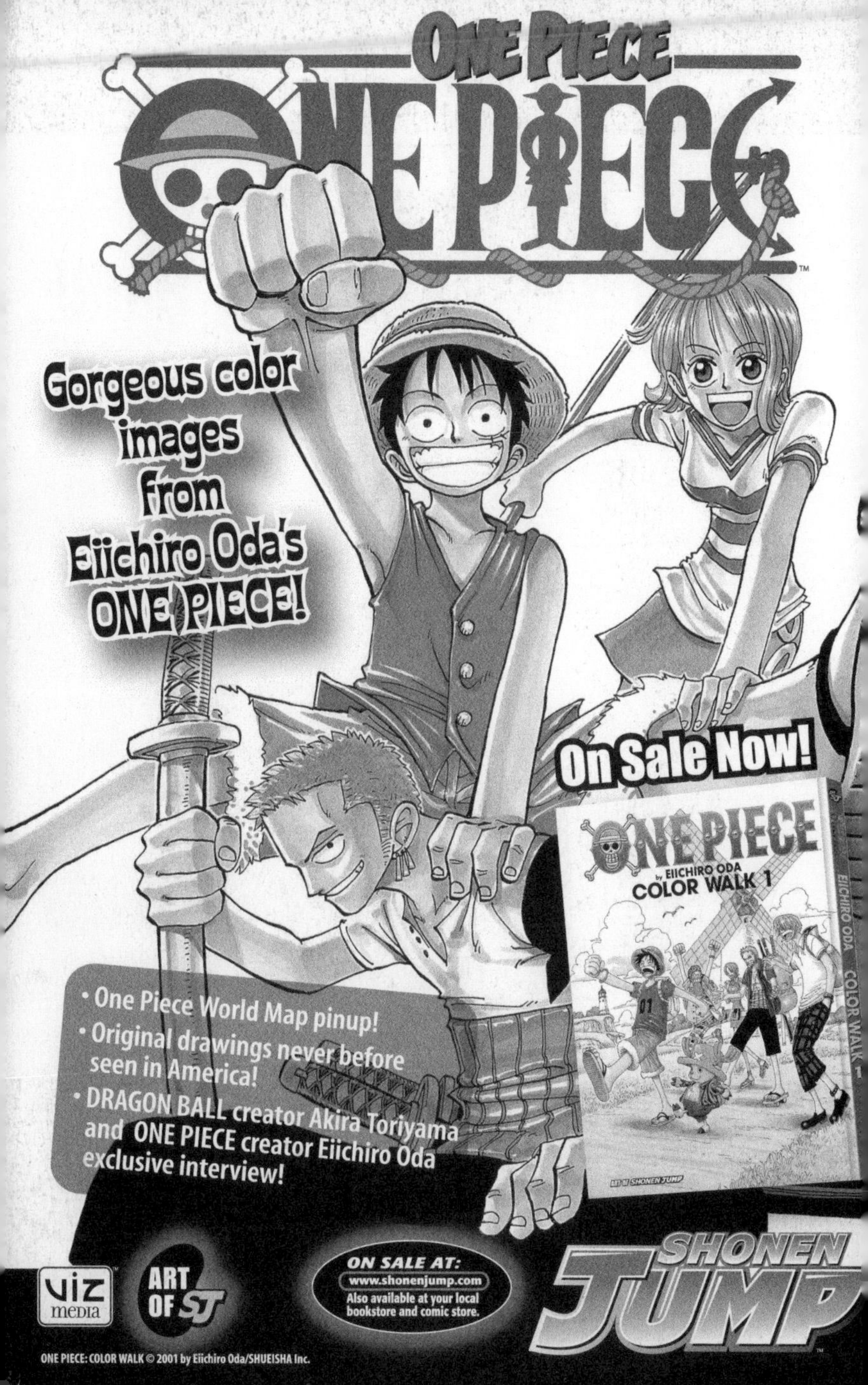

ONE PIECE
ONE PIECE
Gorgeous color images from Eiichiro Oda's ONE PIECE!
On Sale Now!
ONE PIECE
by EIICHIRO ODA
COLOR WALK 1
EIICHIRO ODA COLOR WALK 1
ART OF SHONEN JUMP
• One Piece World Map pinup!
• Original drawings never before seen in America!
• DRAGON BALL creator Akira Toriyama and ONE PIECE creator Eiichiro Oda exclusive interview!
viz media
ART OF SJ
ON SALE AT:
www.shonenjump.com
Also available at your local bookstore and comic store.
SHONEN JUMP
ONE PIECE: COLOR WALK © 2001 by Eiichiro Oda/SHUEISHA Inc.

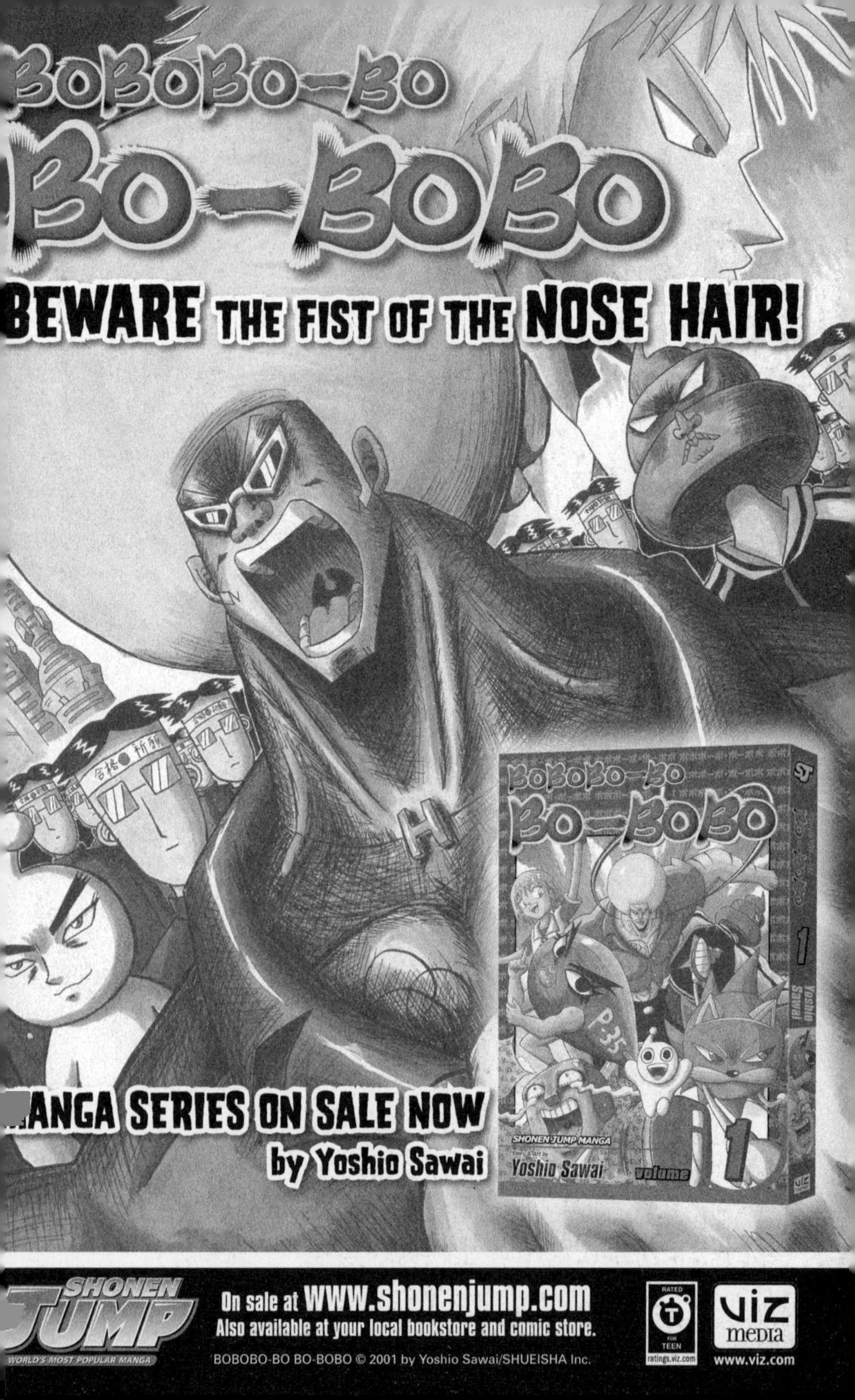
BOBOBO-BO BO-BOBO
BEWARE THE FIST OF THE NOSE HAIR!
ANGA SERIES ON SALE NOW
by Yoshio Sawai
BOBOBO-BO BO-BOBO
SHONEN JUMP MANGA
Story & Art by Yoshio Sawai
volume 1
SHONEN JUMP
WORLD'S MOST POPULAR MANGA
On sale at www.shonenjump.com
Also available at your local bookstore and comic store.
BOBOBO-BO BO-BOBO © 2001 by Yoshio Sawai/SHUEISHA Inc.
RATED T FOR TEEN
ratings.viz.com
viz media
www.viz.com

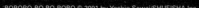

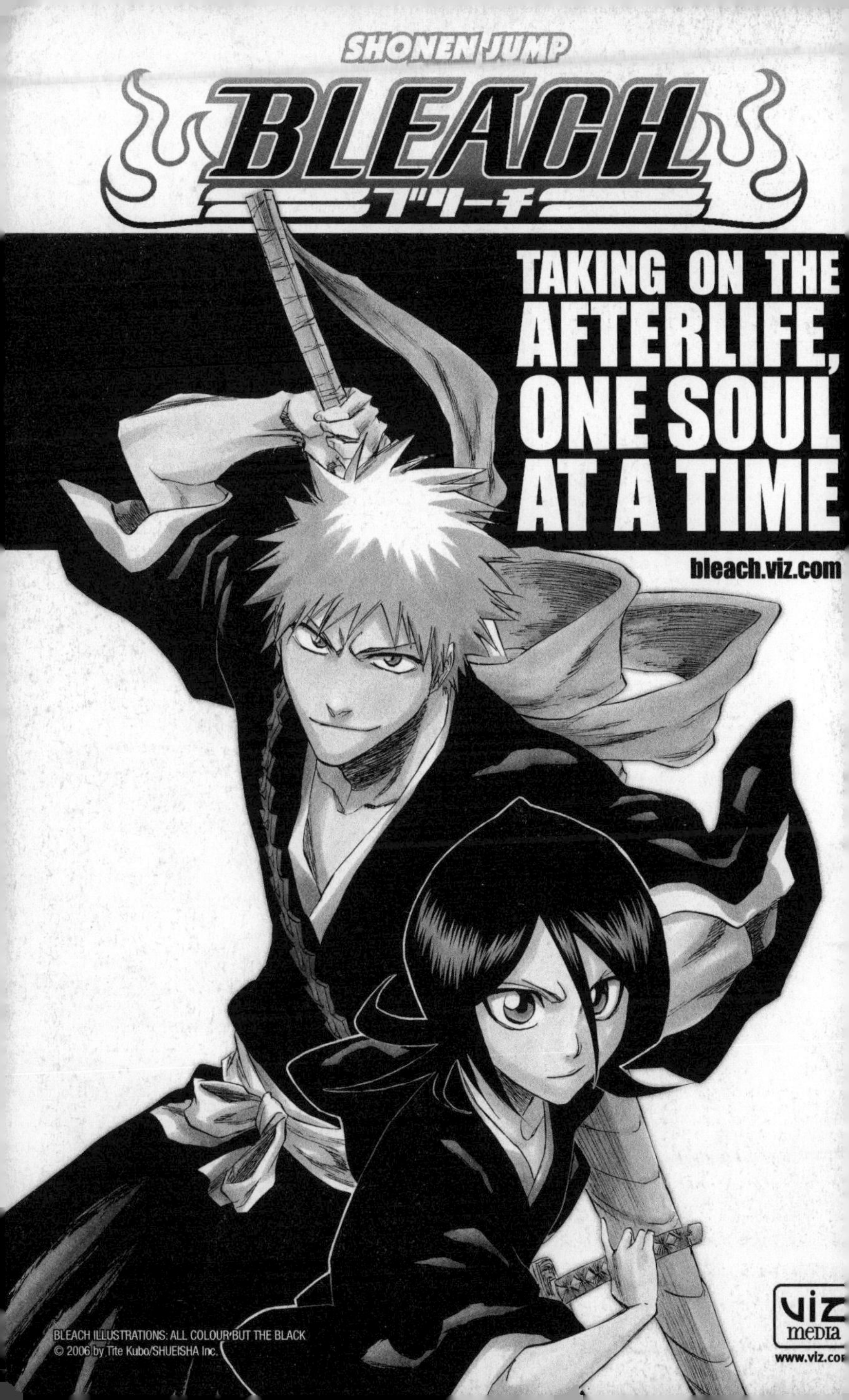
SHONEN JUMP
BLEACH
ブリーチ
TAKING ON THE AFTERLIFE, ONE SOUL AT A TIME
bleach.viz.com
BLEACH ILLUSTRATIONS: ALL COLOUR BUT THE BLACK
© 2006 by Tite Kubo/SHUEISHA Inc.
VIZ media
www.viz.co

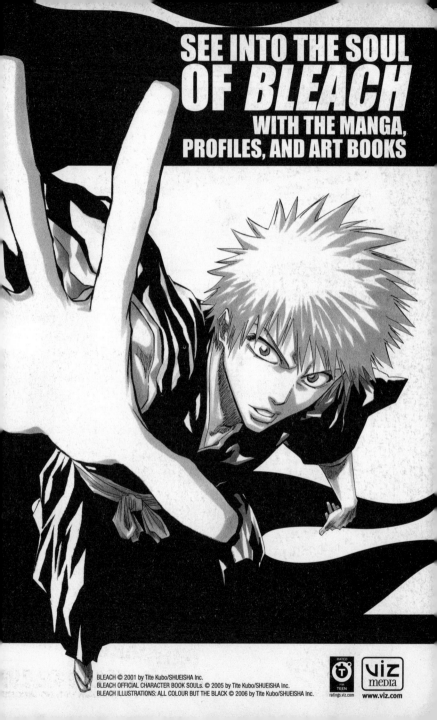

SEE INTO THE SOUL
OF *BLEACH*
WITH THE MANGA,
PROFILES, AND ART BOOKS

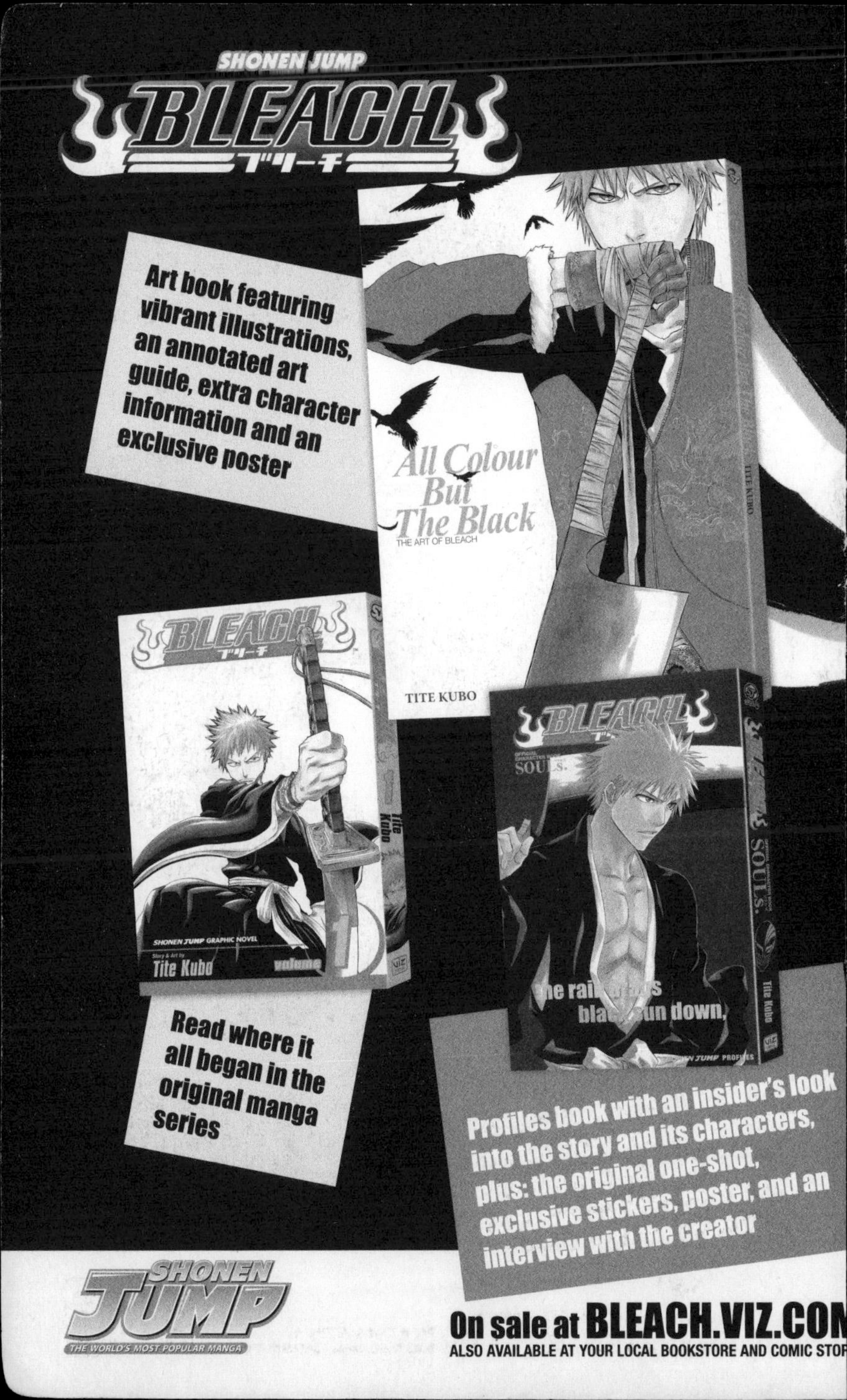
SHONEN JUMP
BLEACH
ブリーチ
Art book featuring vibrant illustrations, an annotated art guide, extra character information and an exclusive poster
All Colour But The Black
THE ART OF BLEACH
TITE KUBO
BLEACH
ブリーチ
SHONEN JUMP GRAPHIC NOVEL
Story & Art by
Tite Kubo
Read where it all began in the original manga series
BLEACH
SOULS.
Profiles book with an insider's look into the story and its characters, plus: the original one-shot, exclusive stickers, poster, and an interview with the creator
SHONEN JUMP
THE WORLD'S MOST POPULAR MANGA
On sale at BLEACH.VIZ.COM
ALSO AVAILABLE AT YOUR LOCAL BOOKSTORE AND COMIC STOR

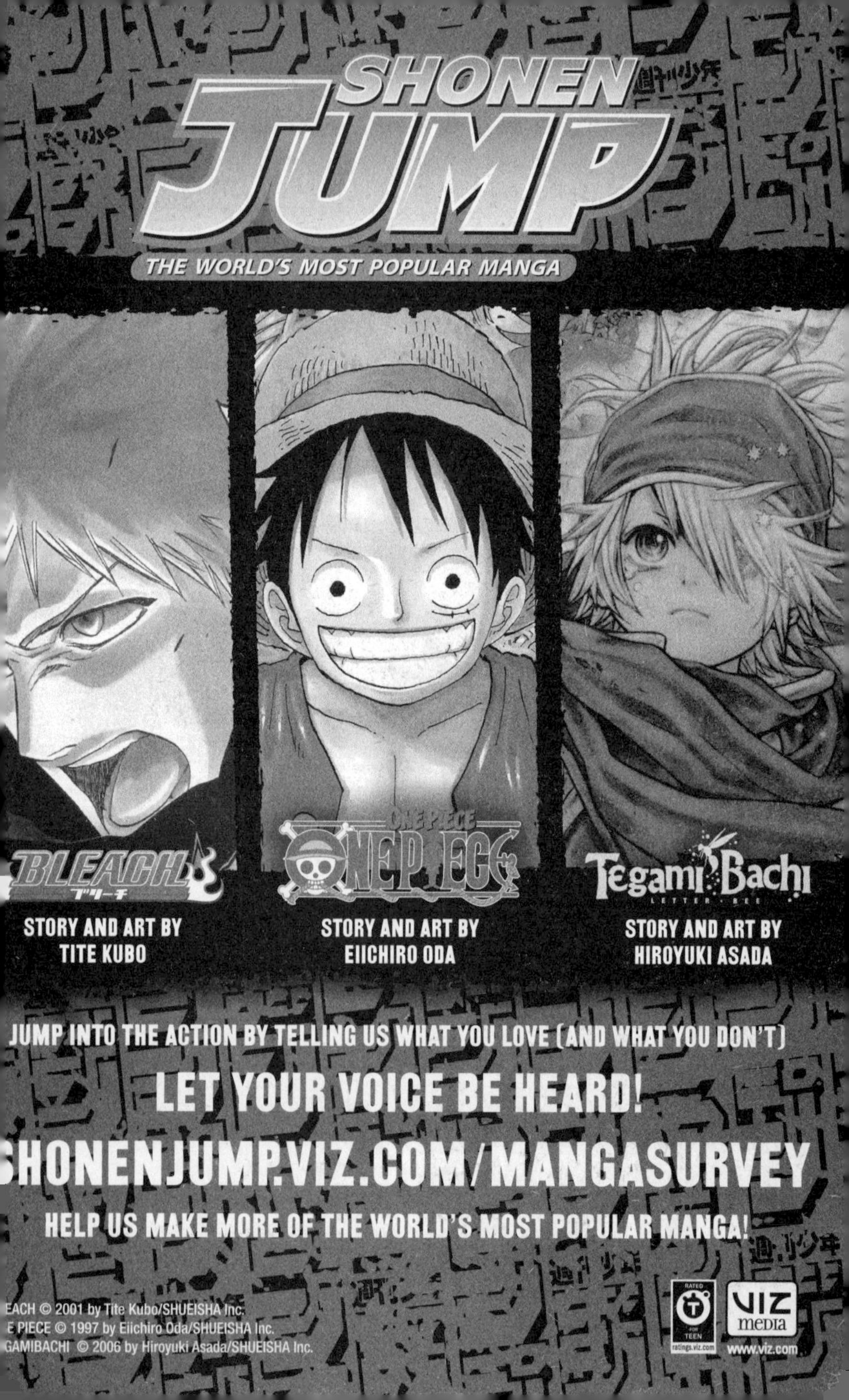
SHONEN JUMP
THE WORLD'S MOST POPULAR MANGA
BLEACH
ブリーチ
STORY AND ART BY
TITE KUBO
ONE PIECE
STORY AND ART BY
EIICHIRO ODA
Tegami Bachi
LETTER BEE
STORY AND ART BY
HIROYUKI ASADA
JUMP INTO THE ACTION BY TELLING US WHAT YOU LOVE (AND WHAT YOU DON'T)
LET YOUR VOICE BE HEARD!
HONENJUMP.VIZ.COM/MANGASURVEY
HELP US MAKE MORE OF THE WORLD'S MOST POPULAR MANGA!
EACH © 2001 by Tite Kubo/SHUEISHA Inc.
E PIECE © 1997 by Eiichiro Oda/SHUEISHA Inc.
GAMIBACHI © 2006 by Hiroyuki Asada/SHUEISHA Inc.
RATED T FOR TEEN
ratings.viz.com
VIZ media
www.viz.com